# ➤ HANGING CHADS ◄

# THE INSIDE STORY OF THE 2000 PRESIDENTIAL RECOUNT IN FLORIDA

JULIAN M. PLEASANTS

HANGING CHADS
© Julian Pleasants 2004

First published 2004 by
PALGRAVE MACMILLAN™
175 Fifth Avenue, New York, N.Y. 10010 and
Houndmills, Basingstoke, Hampshire, England RG21 6XS
Companies and representatives throughout the world

PALGRAVE MACMILLAN is the global academic imprint of the Palgrave Macmillan division of St. Martin's Press, LLC and of Palgrave Macmillan Ltd. Macmillan® is a registered trademark in the United States, United Kingdom and other countries. Palgrave is a registered trademark in the European Union and other countries.

ISBN 1–4039–6693–1 hardback

Library of Congress Cataloging-in-Publication Data
Pleasants, Julian M.
    Hanging chads : the inside story of the 2000 presidential recount in Florida / Julian M. Pleasants.
        p. cm.
    Includes bibliographical references and index
    ISBN 1–4039–6693–1
        1. Presidents—United States—Election–2000.  2. Bush, George W. (George Walker), 1946–  3. Gore, Albert, 1948–  4. Political campaigns—United States.  5. Contested elections—United States.
    6. Contested elections—Florida.  I. Title.

JK5262000.P58 2004
324.973'0929—dc22                                                                                          2004041587

A catalogue record for this book is available from the British Library.

Design by Newgen Imaging Systems (P) Ltd., Chennai, India.

First edition: September 2004
10  9  8  7  6  5  4  3  2  1

Printed in the United States of America.

For Nick and Beth

*We have been friends for many years and have shared wonderful experiences all over the world. My life has been enriched by your friendship and I owe you a debt I can never repay. Perhaps this dedication will, in some small way, express my gratitude.*

# ➤➤ Contents ◄◄

# ➤ INTRODUCTION ◄

Seemingly small occurrences have triggered some of the biggest turning points in our nation's history. If Frank Wills, the night watchman at the Watergate, had not discovered the break-in, the ensuing scandal might not have erupted and Nixon might not have had to resign. If Theresa LePore had not chosen the butterfly ballot, Al Gore might be president.

On November 7, 2000, Election Day, some residents of Palm Beach County, Florida were struggling with what later became known as the infamous butterfly ballot. LePore, the Supervisor of Elections for Palm Beach County and a dedicated public servant, had, with all good intentions, created a ballot with larger type to assist the area's generally elderly population. By Florida law, the ballot had to list all ten presidential candidates, and in order to include all the names with the larger type, LePore chose to use what is called a facing-page ballot (or butterfly ballot),[1] a decision with ramifications that she could have never imagined.

In this fold-out, two page configuration, the punch-holes for the candidates appeared in the center. George W. Bush, whose name occupied the first position on the left, had his punch hole on the right. The next name, typed on the facing page, was Pat Buchanan of the Reform Party. His punch hole was to the left of his name and immediately below that of Bush. The third hole belonged to Al Gore, whose name was right below Bush's on the left side, the punch-hole for Buchanan between them. The ballot included little arrows to direct voters to the proper hole, but many experienced voters became confused. Randi Rhodes, a pro-Gore talk show host with a large Jewish following, expressed the fears of many when she said on the air: "I got scared I voted for Pat Buchanan. I almost said, I think I voted for a Nazi."[2] Buchanan received 3,407 votes in a county heavily populated by a constituency least likely to support him, elderly Jews.[3] The butterfly ballot was proof positive that poor design can change the course of history.

By mid-morning of November 7, numerous complaints about the confusing ballots had been delivered to LePore, who initially dismissed them as isolated incidents. Two Democrats, Congressman Robert Wexler and Lois Frankel, a state representative, came into LePore's office demanding that something be done. LePore wrote up a statement urging voters to find the name of the person they wanted to vote for, and then follow the corresponding arrow to the punch hole. Copies of this statement were distributed to all 531 polling places.[4] This warning, however, did not appease Democrats, and by the end of the day, they had discovered 19,120 "overvotes" (ballots on which the voter punched a hole for two or more candidates) as well as thousands of "undervotes" (ballots that had no punched vote for president). The percentage of overvotes, 4.1 percent, was six times the number of overvotes in Palm Beach County than in the presidential election of 1996.[5] More than 4 percent of 462,000 votes cast were overvotes, though this figure does indicate that 96 percent of the voters voted correctly.

Such an innocuous scenario marked the beginning of the most tumultuous, litigious, highly contested, and closest presidential election in American history. Few Americans in their wildest dreams could have imagined that the 2000 election would come down to the narrow margin of 537 votes in the state of Florida, where the disputed election returns would be fought over and argued about for 36 days. The *Palm Beach Post* warned of the coming conflict with two banner headlines: on November 8, "It's not Over" and on November 9, "Ballot Bedlam."[6]

On November 7, when millions of Americans went to the polls to determine a new president, only 51 percent of the voting age population actually voted. The race was close and the outcome uncertain from the outset. Even the television networks were confused. Relying on flawed exit polls and some unreliable data from the Voter News Service, NBC, CBS, and ABC television newscasts called the key state of Florida for Gore by 8 P.M. They later determined that Bush had won Florida, but eventually backed off that prediction and stated that Florida was too close to call. At this point, it was clear that whoever won Florida would have the necessary 270 electoral votes to win the election.[7] Americans were experiencing what Jon Stewart, of Comedy Central's *The Daily Show*, called "Indecision 2000."

Many Americans, while understanding the serious nature of the disputed votes, were confused and angry at the networks. Dave Barry, the humor columnist, recalled staying up all night "watching the major networks, with their million-dollar anchor studs and their expert commentators and their research staffs and their exit polls and their computers. At some point, a thought occurred to you: *you would have been just as well informed about the outcome of this election if you had spent the entire night watching your toaster.*" Barry concluded that the networks were apparently getting their news from the same source: the Psychic Friends Network.[8]

Florida had voted for a Democratic presidential candidate only three times in the past forty years (Bill Clinton won the state in 1996) and the Republicans had: (1) a stranglehold on the state legislature and (2), George W. Bush's brother, Jeb, in the governor's office. Nonetheless, Florida was in play and up for grabs from the beginning. Gore spent 14 days in the state and there was a huge turnout from Florida's African American community. The Republicans probably underestimated the Democratic push[9] and now feared that all might be lost if Florida fell to Gore.

At 9 P.M. on November 7, after the networks switched their calls and awarded Florida to Bush, Al Gore phoned Bush and conceded the election. Gore then drove to Nashville's War Memorial Plaza to make his concession statement. Gore's advisors, primarily Michael Whouley, after learning that the vote in Florida had narrowed, tried to call Gore's motorcade on their cell phone but could not get through. Bill Daley finally contacted Gore when he was only one block from the War Memorial and urged him not to make a concession speech. Gore agreed, and, in a bizarre twist, called Bush to retract his concession. At this juncture, Bush unofficially lead Gore in Florida by 1,784 votes: 2,909,661 to 2,907,877. In the Electoral College count, however, Gore held a 267-246 advantage and was ahead of Bush in the national popular vote by over 218,000 votes. Since the vote margin was less than one-half of 1 percent, by Florida law, there was an automatic state-wide recount.[10]

Once the Bush and Gore camps recognized the closeness of the vote and the importance of Florida, they immediately rushed into battle a team of advisors, lawyers, and politicos who would carry the fight to win the recount. Bush dispatched James A. Baker II, former Secretary of State, along with Ben Ginsberg, a shrewd Republican lawyer from D.C., to head his Florida legal team. Baker had earned the sobriquet the "velvet hammer" for his sophisticated and deft handing of people and events. Gore countered with Warren Christopher, also a former Secretary of State, and William M. Daley, Secretary of Commerce under Clinton, to speak for him.[11] Attorney Ron Klain supervised and coordinated the activities of Gore's legal team. Almost all of the participants interviewed for this book agreed that from the outset the Republicans responded to the crisis more expeditiously and with better resources and organization than did the Democrats. At the time, this quick reaction did not seem significant, but the Bush forces were hell-bent on preserving his margin of victory, both by conveying an air of inevitability and by preventing recounts wherever possible.

The first critical issue to attract national attention was the butterfly ballot in Palm Beach County. Democratic officials and lawyers protested the ballot design, arguing that it was confusing, illegal, and had caused voters to inadvertently cast their ballots for Buchanan instead of Gore. These arguments were made despite the fact that the Democratic Party had already signed off on the ballot design before it was printed, published, and distributed. LePore had mailed out 655,000 sample ballots and had not received one complaint. Nonetheless, three Democratic voters filed lawsuits, consolidated under *Fladell v. Palm Beach County Canvassing Board*, claiming that the ballot design violated state law and asking for a re-vote as the legal remedy.

Gore, unwilling to depend on the Fladell suit and other litigation, decided to ask for hand recounts in four counties—Volusia, Palm Beach, Broward, and Miami-Dade—, all Democratic strongholds. According to the protest section of Florida election law, the candidate or a political committee or a political party may protest the results of an election. The protest can be on either of two grounds: erroneous returns or fraudulent returns. If there were errors in the vote tabulation, then the canvassing board could choose to manually recount all of the ballots.[12] Gore, pressed for time (the protest had to be filed within five days of the date of the election), chose to concentrate on the undervotes (no discernible vote cast or a vote not counted by the machine) in the four Democratic counties as his best chance for success.

On November 9, Secretary of State Katherine Harris, a Republican and one of eight co-chairs of the 2000 Bush campaign in Florida, announced that, according to Florida law, all canvassing boards had to report election results no later than one week after the election, November 14. By November 10, the automatic recount had been completed and Bush's lead had been reduced to 229 votes. In the automatic recount, 18 counties, with some 1.58 million votes, had not actually recounted the votes but had merely retallied the machine count. Prior to the election, on June 22, 2000, the secretary of state's office had issued a formal declaration: "Checking the totals is not enough. In order to do a recount, you should run every ballot through the machines again. The secretary of state's office believes that this is the only correct way to conduct an automatic recount."[13] If a proper recount had been done, how would those new figures impact the race? The results might have been dramatic. In Lake County the *Orlando Sentinel* found 376 uncounted ballots clearly intended for Gore and 246 uncounted ballots intended for Bush.

The Democrats, especially Jesse Jackson, Sr., were also upset about what they perceived as racial discrimination in voting. In Broward and Miami-Dade counties, the NAACP complained that many African

Americans and other minorities had been denied the right to vote due to confusing ballots, inferior voting machines, and a highway patrol traffic stop near a polling precinct in Leon County. The U.S. Commission on Civil Rights later investigated these complaints and, in their initial evaluation, the Status Report on Probe of Election Practices in Florida during the 2000 Presidential Election, concluded that the Voting Rights Act of 1965 had been violated and minorities had been discriminated against due to inferior equipment, moving of polling places without notice, nonfelons having been removed from the voting rolls (it is illegal for convicted felons to vote in Florida) and applications for the Motor-Voter Law not having been processed in a timely fashion. Although most of the evidence was hearsay and anecdotal, the commission decided that there was racial discrimination: in order to make this conclusion they did not have to prove an intent to discriminate, merely that the system "has the effect of diminishing minority voting opportunities."[14]

On November 11, Bush became the first candidate to file a lawsuit, despite his camp's earlier position that election issues should not be decided in court. The Bush advocates, fearful of the possibility that the hand recount in heavily Democratic counties could erase Bush's small lead, now concluded that the courts had a legitimate role to play after all. The Bush brief, in *Siegel v. LePore*, argued by Ted Olson before an overflow crowd in the federal courtroom in Miami, asked for an emergency stay of all four manual recounts, complaining of the subjective and unfair nature of hand-counting as opposed to machine counting. Olson observed that Florida law gave no standards governing a recount and thus the state was violating the equal protection clause of the Fourteenth Amendment of the U.S. Constitution. In other words, identical ballots in different counties would be counted differently. This would cause "irreparable harm" (the standard of law that had to be met to get an injunction) to Bush. Larry Tribe, speaking for the Democrats, insisted that this case was fundamentally a state issue that should remain out of federal courts. Recounts, continued Tribe, using the "intent of the voter standard," had been a traditional and widely used part of Florida election law for decades without any complaints.[15]

In his decision in *Siegel v. LePore*, Judge Donald Middlebrooks rejected the Bush argument by describing Florida election laws as "reasonable and non-discriminatory," as the system favored neither party, and these issues were unavoidable due to the inherent decentralization of different ballots and machines in 67 counties. Unless every county in Florida and the United States used the exact same tabulating machines, there would always be discrepancies. Middlebrooks recognized that the state legislature had broad powers in establishing electoral procedures and warned that federal courts should tread cautiously in intervening in state issues. The judge concluded that granting of the injunction might mean that the federal courts would be thrust into virtually every aspect of state elections. The Bush team, while not happy with the decision, had done what they set out to do—get the issues before the federal courts, where they thought they stood a better chance of winning than in the state courts of Florida. They appealed Middlebrooks' decision to the Eleventh Circuit Court of Appeals in Atlanta.[16]

L. Clayton Roberts, the director of Florida's Division of Elections, under the jurisdiction of the secretary of state's office, issued an advisory opinion requested by the Palm Beach County Canvassing Board to clarify their confusion about starting a recount. On November 13 he indicated that the canvassing boards' authority to do recounts "to correct errors in voting tabulation" would apply only when there was a machine malfunction. The failure of the machine to read an improperly punched or marked ballot was not an "error in vote tabulation" that the county had to correct. Thus, there should be no manual recounting. Secretary Harris followed up this pronouncement with a forceful public statement that, according to Florida law, she had no choice but to ignore any results received after 5 P.M. on November 14, seven days after the vote, unless the lateness was caused by a hurricane or some other natural disaster.[17]

Judge Charles Burton, chairman of the Palm Beach County Canvassing Board, requested an explanation and advisory opinion from both Secretary Harris and Attorney General Bob Butterworth. The issue in question was the wording of two statutes. Statute 102.111 stated that after 5 P.M. of the seventh day after the election "all returns *shall* [editor's emphasis] be ignored." Statute 102.112 indicated that late results "*may* [editor's emphasis] be ignored." The Gore advisors suggested that the late returns did not have to be ignored and that Harris's decision was unreasonable and arbitrary. The Bush lawyers saw her decision as objective and based on Florida law.

Legally the secretary of state's opinion was binding and the attorney general's instruction was only advisory. Bob Butterworth explained that the only exception was "that if the Division of Elections issues an opinion which the AG's office believes is contrary to the law of the state of Florida. As chief legal officer, I am obliged to put out what we believe to be the correct interpretation of the law." Roberts had argued that an error in vote tabulation occurred when the machine failed to count "properly marked ballots." Butterworth, in his opinion AGO 2065, said that a correctable error might result from the machine being unable to discern the choice of the voter as revealed in the ballot. If the ballot were marked so as to plainly indicate the voter's intent, it should be counted.[18] In other words, if a voter had circled Bush and written in Bush, instead of blackening the oval or pushing out the chad, anyone examining that ballot could determine that the voter intended to cast his or her ballot for Bush. The vote should be counted despite the voter's failure to follow proper procedure.

Katherine Harris, in her book, *Center of the Storm*, defended her office's opinion. She emphasized that, under the protest statute, an error in vote tabulation occurred only when a machine failed to count a "properly marked ballot." Harris explained that ballots marked incorrectly were the result of voter error, not tabulation error, and that they were invalid votes and should not be counted. Harris agreed with U.S. Court of Appeals Judge Richard Posner's view of the matter. The judge believed that the Democrats had confused voter tabulation with voter error and that Harris was right to conclude that the desire to recover votes from ballots spoiled by the voter was not a proper reason for the extension of the statutory deadline.[19] Eventually, however, the Florida Supreme Court sided with Butterworth's opinion, primarily because the Florida constitution emphasized the intent of the voter and the right to vote.

The canvassing boards in Palm Beach and Miami-Dade were in a quandary as to how to proceed with the recount. While Reverend Jesse Jackson, Sr. led rallies protesting voting irregularities and called for a recount, Palm Beach endured protracted arguments and confusion over the two different interpretations of state law. The canvassing board decided to request an opinion from the Florida Supreme Court on the two conflicting opinions. Since their attorneys had advised them to await the verdict from the high court, they did not begin their manual recount until November 16. Dade County officials decided against a recount while those in Broward, who had initially opted against a recount, changed their minds after the Butterworth opinion and began a full manual recount.

Volusia County officials, in the meantime, continued their recount, but were fearful that they could not finish by the 5 P.M. deadline set by Florida statute. The Volusia County Canvassing Board had agreed to perform hand recounts as requested by Gore's legal team. After Harris's statement about her strict enforcement of the seven-day Florida certification law, Judge Michael McDermott, the Republican chairman of the canvassing board, filed a lawsuit. The case, known as *McDermott v. Harris*, asked the judge for a temporary injunction to prevent Harris from enforcing the seven-day deadline and ignoring any late returns not received by the deadline, if the canvassing board were still engaged in the manual recounting of the votes. The case was assigned to Judge Terry Lewis, a Democrat. In the hearing, Lewis thought it was strange that state law gave a county the right to do a hand recount, but would not allow them the time and thus the opportunity to finish. Also, since there was a fine in state law for late returns, Lewis reasoned that there must be an option to turn the ballots in late or the statute would be meaningless.

In essence, Judge Lewis had to decide if Harris could be forced to accept vote counts after the deadline. The law, according to Lewis, was explicit. The courts should not decide the issue, since Harris was the administrative officer responsible for elections. He did not want to "come in and tell her what to do, . . . it's her job to make that decision, not mine." Judge Lewis ruled on November 14 that Harris may ignore late returns, but must not do so arbitrarily. She had to look at the reasons for the late returns and "use her discretion" before she made a decision. Lewis thought Harris could have easily waited until the absentee ballots were in on November 17, since she could not make a final certification of the election until that time. Without being overly specific, Judge Lewis implied to Gore's lawyers that if they disagreed with his decision the proper remedy, if legal votes had not been counted, would be to go directly to the contest. In other words, once the vote was officially certified, Gore could challenge the results of the election. He had to prove a "reasonable probability" that the results of the election would have been changed except for certain acts that occurred. The contest would be adjudicated by a Circuit Court judge in Leon County.[20]

Katherine Harris's advisors, Joe Klock and Mac Stipanovich, conferred about how to respond to Lewis' request that she use her discretion. Harris proposed asking the canvassing boards to cite the reasons for a delay. The Division of Elections sent a letter to the four boards in question, asking them to explain why they should be granted a reprieve from the November 14 deadline. The four counties replied, but their reasons did not match the criteria set up by Harris, that is, malfunctioning of the machines. She ruled that it was not enough for them to say, in effect, this is a big county and it's hard to count all the votes in four days. Harris thus denied the requests to include any late returns.

Mac Stipanovich, in advising Secretary Harris, explained that there was no discrepancy in the Florida statutes over the meaning of "shall" and "may." Secretary Harris could ignore late returns because they "shall" be ignored or she could choose to ignore them under the "may" provision. It was up to her. Judge Lewis had given her the right to use her discretion, and she had done so.[21]

The counties involved in the recount asked Lewis to find Harris in contempt of his order and compel her to accept late returns, but on November 17, in Lewis's second decision, known as *Lewis II*, he ruled that she had not abused her discretion. This decision was a critical victory for Bush. Jim Baker declared that "the rule of law has prevailed,"[22] a view he would not repeat after subsequent adverse rulings from the Florida Supreme Court. Many observers praised Lewis, a Democrat, for having the courage to go against his political views and rule on the law. Lewis was offended by the assumption, particularly from Republicans, that judges were partisan and that they would make decisions based on their politics. "I know that most of the judges that I work with . . . [are] always going to try to find in good faith what they think the law would require them to do."[23]

The Democrats immediately appealed Lewis's decision. The seven-person Florida Supreme Court accepted Palm Beach County's appeal for clarification of the disputed rulings between Secretary of State Harris and Attorney General Butterworth. This case was *Palm Beach County Canvassing Board v. Harris*. Aware that Harris was prepared to certify the election with Bush's lead at 930 votes, increased from a boost by military absentee ballots, the Florida Supreme Court enjoined her not to certify the election until further order from the court. In the midst of all the legal wrangling, Broward County, on November 15, began a manual recount of all their ballots and Palm Beach did the same on November 16.

Gore, worried that Harris would certify Bush as the winner, made a nationally televised address on November 15 and offered to end all further legal challenges if Bush would accept the manual recounts in Broward, Palm Beach, and Dade or agree to a state-wide recount. Bush brushed off Gore's offer by objecting to the unreliable and chaotic manual recounts. Since Bush was ahead and about to be certified as the winner, it made no sense for him to risk a state-wide recount. At this juncture, the Republican strategy was to prevent the counting of votes, while the Gore mantra was to "count all the votes."

Al Gore's fortunes took a turn for the better due to three events: the Florida Supreme Court blocked certification by Harris, the conservative Eleventh Circuit Court of Appeals denied Bush's request for an emergency injunction to halt the recounts, and Miami-Dade changed its mind and joined Broward and Palm Beach in recounting. In Broward, the Democrats persuaded the canvassing board to adopt a broader standard for determining votes: to count dimpled or one corner chads instead of chads with two or more corners punched through. Broward County, however, faced numerous difficulties in hand-counting 588,000 ballots. They found some 105 ballots where voters had taped presidential chads back into place and then punched out another chad. As a result, Gore got 88 votes, Bush 7 and Nader 1. The rest were rejected. One absentee ballot included a hand-written note from the voter. "I punched for George Bush by accident. I meant to vote for Al Gore." The board denied the vote. The amazed chairman observed: "Do they really think that the computer's going to read their letter?" This haphazard process led to an extraordinary situation where a few obscure election officials could decide the president of the United States by how they viewed hanging, taped, pregnant, and dimpled chads.[24] The Republicans protested, but in reality, the different standards applied by Broward and Palm Beach would help the Bush cause and would eventually be the legal basis for the penultimate U.S. Supreme Court decision.[25]

As the recount drama unfolded day after day, the American people were mesmerized by the frenetic television coverage of events. Sometimes perplexed, often anxious, adherents on both sides experienced ecstatic highs and depressing lows. Some days it appeared that it was all over for Al Gore and then a favorable court decision gave Democrats hope that he might win after all. No one seemed to know how it would turn out or how long it would take.

Although Gore and the Democrats advocated counting all the ballots, they began to question the counting of some military absentee ballots in Florida. The Republicans recognized that one of the best ways of ensuring victory for Bush was to "count the maximum number of ballots in counties won by Bush," particularly those with a high concentration of military voters, who predominately vote Republican. Lawyers Jason Unger, Fred Bartlitt, and other Republicans apparently managed to persuade 14 counties to go back and recount the overseas military ballots. They sent out a 52-page memo of detailed instructions on the legal intricacies of overseas ballots. Unger argued that those ballots should be accepted—even if they lacked the proper postmarks—since the troops were "overseas fighting for their country." These absentee ballots were recounted in several counties after the election had ended.

Judge Anne Kaylor, chairwoman of the Polk County Canvassing Board, noted that Republican pressure to give the fighting men and women the right to vote led to the counting of votes that probably would have been illegal in past years. According to Florida statute 101.67, all absentee ballots had to be received by the date of the election. The overseas military ballots had to be postmarked or signed and dated by the date of the election, November 7, had to be cast on Election Day, and had to be mailed from outside the United States. The absentee ballots had to be completed by the voter, signed, and dated with a signature and an address of a witness. Due to an administrative agreement with the federal government, Florida's military ballots could be received ten days after the election.

The *New York Times*, in a six-month investigation into the recounting of overseas military ballots, found 680 questionable votes, although it could not be determined for whom the ballots had been cast. The flawed votes included 344 ballots without postmarks or postmarked after the election, 96 ballots without witness signatures, 183 ballots mailed from cities within the United States, 169 ballots from voters who had not registered or who had not requested a ballot, 5 ballots received after the November 17 deadline, and 19 ballots from voters who had voted twice. The *Times* concluded that "all these ballots would have been disqualified had the state's election laws been strictly enforced." There was no evidence of vote fraud, but if these ballots were judged by markedly different standards, as they were, this was prima facie evidence of a violation of the Fourteenth Amendment. For example, in Alachua County, Jeff Livingston, an Air Force sergeant stationed in Holland, admitted that he voted for Bush after the election. His ballot was denied in Alachua County but would have counted in Okaloosa County.

The Democrats took an unpopular and untenable position in questioning the validity of the military ballots. The Republicans quickly accused the Democrats of being unpatriotic. Retired General Norman H. Schwartzkopf weighed in and announced that it was a sad day when military personnel were facing danger abroad and were denied the right to vote because of a technicality. The Republicans discovered a five-page memo from Gore lawyer Mark Herron, which merely outlined the state law on overseas ballots, but they cleverly presented it as a calculated plot to stop the military from voting. Now Gore, who had argued for counting all the votes and had denounced Secretary Harris as "hypertechnical," was bombarded by an effective Republican public relations offensive. Joe Lieberman, stung by the criticism, went on national television to suggest that military ballots be given every benefit of the doubt and the Democrats hurriedly backed off their challenge.

It is difficult to say what would have happened if Gore had proceeded with his challenge. Under Florida law, if the number of improper absentee ballots exceeded the margin of victory, a judge could, under some circumstances, disqualify all absentee ballots arriving after the election. Under this hypothetical scenario, the *Times* argued that Gore would have won by 202 votes. One of Gore's close advisors noted that he refused to mount a legal challenge to the military votes because if he won under these conditions, he did not believe he could govern.[26]

By November 16, when Palm Beach County began its recount, the world media and every politician who felt the need to bask in klieg lights had descended on the county. Governor Marc Racicot of Montana, Bob Dole, Governor George Pataki of New York, Jesse Jackson, Sr. and a veritable horde of attention seekers arrived to show support for Gore or Bush. There were television crews from around the world reporting on every activity and interviewing anyone who came within range of their camera. Along with the local and national media, Japanese, Germans, Chinese, French, British, and other crews offered full coverage of events. The national media, criticized for its over-the-top, excessive coverage of Monica Lewinsky and O.J. Simpson, now legitimately could provide 24-hour coverage of the tension-filled, history-making recount. Television's blanket coverage, despite repetitive, sometimes endless attention to trivial details, boosted news ratings and proved to be a boon for advertisers. A poll by the *Wall Street Journal* and NBC News indicated more than 80 percent of Americans were watching the recount closely, while 55 percent admitted to observing events "very closely." Internet use the day after the election was the heaviest in the history of the medium.[27]

Keenly aware of being the focus of world attention, the Palm Beach County Canvassing Board began their deliberations. The Republicans challenged virtually every ballot for Gore. Although the vote count was observed by representatives of both parties, as well as television cameras, the Republicans, especially Racicot, hinted at a conspiracy to deprive Bush of his victory. They claimed there were chads on the floor, that Democratic counters had taped chads to ballots and, in one case, had actually eaten some chads to hide the evidence. None of these accusations turned out to be accurate, but Republican supporters made it appear that the entire process of recounting by hand was chaotic, unreliable, and certainly no way to choose a president.[28] One never knows who was watching these scenes unfold, but it is likely that members of the Florida and the U.S. Supreme Court were aware of the turbulence and confusion.

One of the most dramatic moments in the recount came on November 20 when the Florida Supreme Court convened to hear briefs on *Palm Beach County Canvassing Board v. Harris.* Florida had, under the Sunshine Law, the most open rules in the country for public access to government. In the Supreme Court chamber, there were television cameras and a state-of-the-art sound system. In addition, Craig Waters, the Director of Public Information for the Court, set up a website that received up to 3,500,000 hits per day, and he posted the court's full decisions and documents for the press and public to read immediately after the decisions. Many people, for the first time, viewed the entire courtroom proceedings in a seminal case and were grateful that they could see the arguments without the information being filtered through the media.

Waters revealed that the court monitored some 15,000 e-mails per day, some praising the court, others posing distinct threats: "Run While You Still Can." Since the media and supporters from both sides mobbed the court building and there had been some threats against the justices, security forces escorted Waters and the justices when they left or entered the building. Waters, intrigued by the diverse group of protestors, described some of the "run-of-the-mill kooks" who showed up. "We had people dressed in tin foil with satellite dishes strapped to their backs that were trying to channel energy toward the court. One evening we had a prayer circle completely surrounding the court building. We had a gentleman who showed up here with one of the original Batmobiles, driving it around the building and honking his horn repeatedly. We had a woman who showed up with a pet skunk who could do backflips."[29]

David Boies and Dexter Douglass, the lead Florida attorney, appeared as primary counsel for Gore. They emphasized that Florida law allowed for use of manual recounts to insure the most accurate results. The key legal issue for Boies and Douglass was that the canvassing board had to examine each ballot in order to discover "the voter's intent," the basis of Florida election law. They accused Harris of delaying a lawful manual recount and called her actions "an abuse of discretion." The Bush attorneys, led by Michael A. Carvin and Florida lawyer Barry Richard, countered by insisting that Florida law allowed Harris to ignore late returns. The law was clear, declared the two attorneys, about the date that final vote totals, including recounts, were due in Tallahassee to be certified. If recounts were allowed to continue, they could go on indefinitely. Also, the court did not have the power to substitute a new deadline for the deadline created by the legislature. Finally, the Bush team noted that having no meaningful standards for determining a vote during the recount would be a violation of both the due process and equal protection clauses of the Fourteenth Amendment.

In its decision on Tuesday, November 21, the Florida Supreme Court unanimously ruled, 7-0, that Secretary Harris had abused her discretion by not accepting late returns from legally authorized recounts. They also ruled that the counties would have until 5 P.M. on Sunday, November 26, or until 9 A.M. Monday, November 27, if the secretary of state's office were not open, to turn in the results of the manual recounts. The court rejected the Bush argument of a firm deadline and said Harris had discretion to accept late votes. The court contended, as they did on a consistent basis, that the law must be liberally construed in favor of facilitating the citizen's right to vote, a pre-eminent right in the Florida Constitution. Technical statutory requirements should not be exalted over the right to vote. The court noted its reluctance to rewrite the Florida Election Code, leaving that to the legislature, but they had to "fashion a remedy" that would allow a fair and judicious resolution of the issues.[30] The Justices believed that Harris had given incorrect advice on Florida election law, so the court added five days to the certification date because that was how many days the canvassing boards had lost due to Harris' erroneous opinions.[31] Unfortunately, the justices did not immediately explain their reasoning for extending the certification date and it appeared to many that they were making law, not interpreting it.

Jim Baker was white-hot with rage. He called the ruling "unfair and unacceptable" and hinted darkly that the Florida legislature, controlled overwhelmingly by the Republican Party, might have to intervene. According to Baker, the Court had changed the election laws after the election, "in the middle of the game," and had overreached its authority. Bush's attorneys quickly appealed the decision to the U.S. Supreme Court, where Bush advisors wanted to end up.

On the surface, the 7-0 Florida Supreme Court vote seemed to be a complete victory for Gore. Many of his supporters now thought he would win Florida and become the next president. Gore's triumph was short-lived as he suffered a major and unanticipated set-back when the Miami-Dade Canvassing Board voted to halt their recount. This recount, led by David Leahy, the appointed Supervisor of Elections, began on November 20 and the canvassing board planned to count all 653,963 votes. Leahy, known for his integrity, realized they could not finish on time and the board decided to count only the 10,750 undervotes. The Republicans protested and a large group of shouting and shoving protestors, carrying signs such as "Sore-Loserman," a parody of Gore-Lieberman, assembled to observe the proceedings. Gore's opponents, who protested in both Miami-Dade and Broward, carried signs and wore t-shirts emblazoned with anti-Gore slogans. One sign featured Gore's head in a noose, "Gore, hanging by a chad," and a popular T-shirt explained: "How to steal an election: 1. Count all the votes 2. Re-count all the votes 3. Re-count some votes 4. Hand count some votes. 5. Change the Rules. 6. Exclude the military." Several protestors shouted epithets at the sparse crowd of Gore adherents.[32] The crowd, which included staffers of House Republicans who had been sent to help in the fight, were dismissed by the Democrats as a "Brooks Brothers mob".

When the Miami-Dade Canvassing Board decided to move up to the nineteenth floor, where the ballots were kept, the limited space reduced the crowd from several hundred to around fifty, although two observers from each party were allowed in. Due to the overcrowding and what was at stake, the situation became tense. The protestors began shouting, "they are stealing the election." When Joe Geller, chairman of the Dade Democratic Party, stopped by to pick up a sample ballot, the crowd yelled, "he is stealing a ballot" and surrounded Geller. Geller described the "mob" as angry and nasty and reported that he was shoved and jostled by the crowd, but eventually was rescued by police officers.

The canvassing board reconvened and decided that they simply did not have enough time to count the votes by the deadline and so unanimously ended the recount. Geller thought the board was intimidated by the mob, but Miguel DeGrandy, who represented Bush at the hearings, thought that the Republicans were right in protesting a violation of the Sunshine Law (everyone could not see the counting when the board moved to the nineteenth floor) and argued that the protestors did not force an end to the counting. De Grandy persuaded the board that, according to Florida statute, they had to count all 653,963 votes not just the undervotes. The board, noting that "the circumstances have dramatically changed," agreed that they did not have enough time to count all the votes.[33] All three of the board members insisted that they made their decision on the merits of the case and did not succumb to intimidation. Both the Miami-Dade Democratic Party and the Gore legal team sought a *writ of mandamus* to compel the canvassing board to continue the manual recount. The Democrats, upset because Gore had been denied the 168 votes he gained in the partial recount, thought there were many more Gore votes to be found. The Florida Supreme Court, in two brief decisions, denied the writs. The Supreme Court ruled that since the Miami-Dade Canvassing Board determined that they could not complete a full recount in the time remaining, then the court could not compel the performance of an act impossible to perform.[34] These two verdicts were examples of several occasions where the so-called liberal Democratic Supreme Court ruled against Gore.

In yet another extraordinary turn of events, the U.S. Supreme Court, on November 24, agreed to hear Bush's appeal of the 7-0 Florida Supreme Court decision, creating a new case, *Bush v. Palm Beach County Canvassing Board*. The Republican brief focused on the claim that the Florida Supreme Court had not followed Florida's election statutes. Bush's lawyers argued that Article II, Section 1 of the U.S. Constitution gave to state legislatures, not the courts, the sole authority to determine "the manner" in which presidential electors were appointed. They bolstered their argument by referring to Title 3 U.S. Code 5, which set up the so-called safe harbor provision, which prevented Congress from challenging the state's choice of presidential electors. According to Bush attorneys, the Florida Supreme Court had not only misinterpreted Florida statutes, but had also violated the federal constitution and federal law. Intriguingly, in this initial case, the U.S. Supreme Court did not comment on whether different standards in counting votes violated the Fourteenth Amendment.

Meanwhile, other recounts continued as the canvassing boards labored to meet the November 26 deadline. Miami-Dade, which had stopped its recount, sent certified numbers as of November 14. Broward met the deadline and the new total resulted in a net gain of 567 votes for Gore. Palm Beach, amid stalling tactics and numerous challenges by the Republicans, took Thanksgiving Day off and missed the deadline by only a couple of hours. Harris refused to accept the late, incomplete returns from Palm Beach, thus costing Gore either 176 or 215 votes (the correct number has never been verified).[35]

The new totals heightened anxieties on both sides as Bush's lead over Gore narrowed to 537 votes. There was much grousing by Democrats who cried partisanship when Harris opened her office at 5 P.M. on Sunday (which had never been done before) instead of waiting until 9 A.M. on Monday, when Palm Beach would have been finished with their recount. Harris announced on Wednesday, November 22, the morning after the Florida Supreme Court decision, that the office would be open on Sunday. She insisted that she had no idea that Palm Beach would take off Thanksgiving and not finish. Since the court's order was explicit that the deadline be met "in order to allow maximum time for contests," she was merely obeying the court's decision.[36] Nonetheless, not waiting until Monday made Harris' decision appear partisan. Harris advisor Mac Stipanovich agreed that for political purposes it would have been prudent to wait until Monday, but he correctly insisted that Secretary Harris had never violated the law in any of her decisions.[37]

At 7:30 P.M., on Sunday, November 26, the Florida Canvassing Board met and certified the election results. Harris then declared Bush the winner of Florida's 25 electoral votes. Gore refused to concede and decided to contest the certified vote totals in *Gore v. Harris*. In order to successfully challenge certified election results, one had to prove that the totals included a number of illegal votes or that a number of legal votes sufficient to change the result of the election had not been counted.

The hearings in the contest were held before Judge Sanders Sauls, in Leon County Circuit Court. Friends described Sauls, a registered Democrat appointed to the court by Republican Governor Bob Martinez, as a no-nonsense judge who ran a strict courtroom. However, he was from the "old school of civility" and would be tolerant of people as long as they were courteous. Tallahassee lawyers described Judge Sauls as philosophically conservative, more a Republican than a Democrat.[38]

Gore lawyers David Boies and Dexter Douglass asked the court to do several things: to continue the recounts, to add 215 votes to Gore's total from Palm Beach, and to have the Palm Beach Canvassing Board review 3,330 ballots determined to be illegal votes. In Miami-Dade County, they asked the court to include 168 votes from the partial recount, to count the 10,750 undervotes that Dade did not get to and to examine the 9,000 votes which registered as no-votes by the machine but had never been hand counted. Finally, they wanted Judge Sauls to require Nassau County to include the results of their manual recount. The county's resulting switch back to the original machine count, instead of the recount, cost Gore 51 votes.

On November 28, Judge Sauls denied Gore's request for an immediate recount of Miami-Dade's and Palm Beach's disputed ballots, but ordered all 1.1 million ballots delivered to Tallahassee, in case they needed to be counted. This decision created a memorable sight as Ryder trucks brought the ballots to Tallahassee under heavy guard. The trucks were followed by hordes of reporters and covered live by television news choppers, surely one of the most uneventful occurrences in the history of live news coverage.

The Florida Supreme Court, as legal experts expected, rejected Gore's argument that the Palm Beach County butterfly ballot was illegal and disenfranchised voters.[39] The battle now moved from the Florida Supreme Court into the hallowed halls of the U.S. Supreme Court where, on December 1, the court heard arguments in *Bush v. Palm Beach County Canvassing Board*. For the first time, perhaps in response to the favorable public reaction to the openness of Florida's courts, the U.S. Supreme Court released an audiotape of the proceedings immediately after their conclusion. Two experienced veterans, Ted Olson for Bush and Larry Tribe for Gore, made the initial presentations. Olson noted that, by changing the date of the election set by the legislature, the Florida Supreme Court was making law, not interpreting law. Tribe argued that there was no federal issue and the decision should be left to the state. Also, Tribe asserted that since the legislature had given the Florida Supreme Court the authority to review the statues, they were interpreting the statutes, not making law.

At 11:45 A.M., Monday, December 4, without prior notice, the U.S. Supreme Court announced its unanimous *per curiam* opinion. The court vacated the November 21 decision of the Florida Supreme Court to extend the deadlines for manual recounts. The U.S. Supreme Court remanded the case back to the Florida court asking them to clarify their decision as it related to federal law since there was "considerable uncertainty as to the precise grounds for the decision." The U.S. Supreme Court, and primarily Justice Antonin Scalia, wanted to know if the Florida court had decided exclusively on Florida statutes (interpreting the law) or whether they had relied on the state constitution. In the latter case, the state constitution would conflict with Article II of the U.S. Constitution and with federal law. This was a shot across the bow of the Florida court, in effect, asking them to explain or rehabilitate their decision and avoid future conflict with the U.S. Supreme Court.[40]

Amazingly, on the very same day in *Gore v. Harris*, Judge Sauls upstaged the U.S. Supreme Court by ruling against Gore in every particular, a total rejection of his claims. Mac Stipanovich, when asked about his reaction to Bush's victory in court, replied "when he [Sauls] rendered his decision, he just clubbed them like baby seals." Sauls concluded that the certification of Bush as the winner of Florida should stand, that the canvassing boards had not abused their discretion, and there was no credible evidence that would indicate a probability, not a possibility, that the election outcome would change as a result of the recounts. Gore quickly appealed Saul's decision to the Florida Supreme Court.[41]

On December 6, the conservative Eleventh Circuit Court of Appeals, in the cases *Siegel v. LePore* and *Touchston v. McDermott*, rejected Bush's request to declare manual recounts unconstitutional because they violated the due process and equal protection clauses of the Fourteenth Amendment. The bipartisan vote was 8-4 (5 Democratic appointees and 3 Republican appointees) that recounts would not irreparably harm Bush. The four dissenters vigorously expressed their displeasure with the opinion of the majority. This appeals court thus took a decidedly different view of the constitutional issues than did their brethren at the U.S. Supreme Court.

Two potentially significant court cases sneaked in under the media's radar. These were referred to as "sleeper cases," since everyone was concentrating on the butterfly ballot and the recounts. Observers and the press soon realized that if Gore won either case he could win the presidency. On November 17, a Democratic lawyer in Seminole County, Harry Jacobs, sued the Seminole County Canvassing Board to have all 15,215 absentee ballots disqualified because of the alteration of applications for absentee ballots. Sandra Goard, Supervisor of Elections, admitted that she allowed Michael Leach, an employee of the Republican Party, to come into the elections office, unsupervised, and put in voter identification numbers for Republican ballot requests that had been inadvertently left off by the vendor. Leach spent several weeks correcting 2,126 ballot applications that Goard had previously pronounced invalid. His efforts resulted in an additional 1,833 votes from registered Republicans that would otherwise not have been cast. Jacobs sued, because under Florida statute, the only person entitled to submit an absentee ballot request was the voter, his/her legal guardian, and a member of his or her family. Jacobs, who filed this suit on his own and not at the behest of the Democratic Party, asked that all absentee ballots be disqualified since there was no way to separate those amended applications from correct applications.[42]

Officials in heavily Republican Martin County reported a similar situation. Peggy Robbins, Supervisor of Elections, admitted that Republican election workers corrected as many as 500 absentee ballot applications and that she allowed them to remove the ballots from the elections office for several days. Democrats argued that Bush could have received an extra 2,000 votes from the corrected absentee ballots requests in both counties. There was no way of telling for whom these individuals cast their vote, but since they were all registered Republicans, one might assume the majority would be for Bush.

The Seminole and Martin County cases eventually came to the Leon County Circuit Court. Judge Nikki Clark, appointed by Governor Lawton Chiles and the first African American appointed to the circuit court, heard the Seminole County case, while Judge Terry Lewis presided over the Martin County case. Some Bush lawyers tried to recuse Judge Clark. They assumed, that since she was an African American female, because the black vote in Florida had been around 92 percent for Gore, and because she had been appointed by a Democratic governor that she would be biased in the case. The best argument the Republicans could muster for their racial and political stereotyping was that Governor Bush had turned her down for an appointment to the appeals court a few weeks earlier and they feared Clark might be vindictive.

Judge Clark dismissed the recusal motion as legally insufficient and responded by saying: "I was surprised that someone in such a major case would think I would be so childish and upset that I would not be able to do my job." Clark continued: "I think the most bothersome thing about it was that they were seeking to impugn my integrity. I value my integrity." She thought the media and the public had a flawed perception of the judiciary. Since everything in the court was open to the public and they could see the legal arguments and the evidence, then they would understand how the court system really works.[43]

Both cases were tried simultaneously in one courtroom. Court administrators had to coordinate the trial schedules since Barry Richard and other lawyers were participating in both cases. The plaintiffs had to demonstrate that the addition of voter registration numbers amounted to "substantial non-compliance" with election law and that the necessary remedy was the invalidation of all absentee ballots. Although they wrote their opinions separately, Lewis and Clark, as they were known to the media, released their decisions at the same time as a courtesy to the press. Both judges agreed that the two supervisors of elections, Robbins and Goard, had violated Florida law and chastised them for errors in judgment. But based on several legal precedents, including *Boardman v. Esteva*, they ruled that there was not substantial non-compliance. The technical violations that occurred did not affect the integrity of the absentee ballots since the additions were made only on the application for an absentee ballot, not on the actual ballots. To throw out all the absentee ballots because of irregularities in a few was a draconian remedy. To throw out legal votes would disenfranchise voters when the right to vote and the will of the people had to be viewed as paramount.[44] Both so-called Democratic judges had ruled on the law and against Gore. In Clark's case, her ruling on the facts of the case was a sharp rebuke to the cynical Republican attempt at recusal.

Judges Lewis and Clark were painfully aware of the extraordinary pressure they faced in deciding such crucial cases in such a short period of time. Clark recalled that the media attention was frenzied and unrelenting and, on one occasion, a Japanese television crew tried to follow her into the bathroom. Both judges got numerous threats and had to be protected by court bailiffs, deputy sheriffs, and the local SWAT team. One woman sent a hateful message to Judge Lewis, "I hope you burn in hell and have a long miserable life before that," and Judge Clark recalled getting "incredibly nasty," horrible phone calls and notes. Both, however, also received notes of praise for their integrity and courage.[45]

As the courtroom dramas unfolded, Republican leaders in the Florida legislature, outraged by the Florida Supreme Court's 7-0 decision, organized to resolve what they perceived to be a constitutional crisis. Tom Feeney, the designated Speaker of the House, feared that the delayed and chaotic recount process and Florida Supreme Court decisions would reverse the certified vote and send Al Gore to the White House. He stated that the Supreme Court, in its decision to extend the counting to November 26, had "changed the law after the election" and was not just "stretching the law, but ignoring very specific deadlines and statutes."

Feeney asserted that the court had taken authority that the legislature had invested in the secretary of state and had given precedence to the Florida Constitution's will-of-the-people provision over the explicit requirement of the statutes. Speaker Feeney believed that the legislature had a "constitutional responsibility" to act, lest Gore steal the election. He wanted to insure that if the legal issues were not decided by December 12, the date that he considered to be the safe harbor, Florida would not lose its electoral votes.

Feeney consulted several constitutional experts, including Charles Fried, former solicitor general of the United States, and they agreed that Article II of the U.S. Constitution invested state legislatures with the power to determine their electors, regardless of the popular vote. Such action, of course, would be an extraordinary decision that would preempt the franchise of millions of voters and would undermine the concept of judicial review. His legal advisors bolstered Feeney's case by determining that federal law, Title 3 U.S. Code, Section 2, also gave the legislature the authority to choose electors. The law read: "Whenever any State has held an election for the purpose of choosing electors, and has failed to make a choice on the day prescribed by law, the electors may be appointed on a subsequent day in such a manner as the legislature of such State may direct."

Once he was officially installed as speaker of the house (during the inaugural legislative session, scheduled by state law for two weeks after the election), Feeney appointed, along with President of the Senate John McKay, the Joint Legislative Oversight Committee on Electoral Certification Accuracy and Fairness. The purpose of the committee was to study the legal issues, determine how to resolve these issues in accordance with the legislature's constitutional duties, and determine the legislature's role in the recount. The Democrats accused the Republican-led legislature of taking orders from the Bush brothers. Lois Frankel, the Democratic leader in the House, commented: "Sadly, I have to say that I believe this is orchestrated, and the only thing missing was the postmark from Austin, Texas." Feeney denied the charge while admitting he had been advised by the Republican Party. He insisted that Governor Jeb Bush had urged caution and asked the legislature to wait until the court cases had been resolved or other possibilities had a chance to work.

On December 4, the Joint Committee recommended a special session of the Florida legislature and a proclamation was signed on December 6 to call the session for December 8. On Tuesday, December 12, while the U.S. Supreme Court was still considering *Bush v. Gore* but before they released their final decision, the Florida House of Representatives voted 79 (77 Republicans, 2 Democrats) to 41 (all Democrats), to approve a resolution to appoint the already certified 25 Bush electors. John McKay and the Florida Senate were reluctant to act, as it would be a difficult vote for members and they preferred to wait on the U.S. Supreme Court decision. Lois Frankel called the decision by the House to seat the Bush electors a partisan act that was unnecessary, unjust, and that would cast a dark stain on the integrity of the legislature. Some legal scholars agreed with Frankel and contended that the legislature had no appropriate constitutional role to play in appointing electors on their own. Feeney, however, had no regrets. He insisted that the legislature did the right thing and praised them for doing their constitutional duty.[46]

In the Gore camp, the court decisions by Judges Sauls, Lewis, and Clark were disheartening. In addition, according to polls, over half of the country was ready for Gore to concede. These results precipitated a deep gloom, bordering on despair, among the Gore attorneys. Although the conservative Eleventh Circuit Court of Appeals, on December 6, rejected Bush's claim that the manual recounts violated the equal protection and due process clauses of the Fourteenth Amendment, many Gore adherents believed that they had lost the presidency. Leon Panetta perhaps said it best: "We're entering the Hail Mary phase of this election." The *Tallahassee Democrat*'s headline for December 8 confirmed the bleak outlook: "Fourth Down and long for Gore."[47] Gore's only hope at this point was the Florida Supreme Court.

The oral arguments before the Florida Supreme Court in *Gore v. Harris* began on December 7. Very few legal experts expected that the court, under the exigencies of time and politics, would intervene to "revive Gore's fading hopes."[48] The Bush brief, presented by Barry Richard, reminded the court, based on the U.S. Supreme Court's remand, that they were treading on dangerous ground if they continued the current recount process. Richard also pointed out there was not enough time to complete a ballot count before December 12.[49]

The Florida Supreme Court, well aware of the U.S. Supreme Court's desire to have their earlier opinion clarified, did not immediately respond to the remand. Justice Major Harding explained why: "You know, we had a week of oral argument, we had these other cases, we had to prepare for the oral arguments in the last case, and it was just a question of being able to prioritize our time. I know Justice O'Connor in the audiotape of that case [*Bush v. Gore*] wondered why we had not responded. We just had a very full plate, and we could not get to it effectively until then [December 11]." The court, continued Harding, had to rule on some fifteen cases, including two death penalty cases, in a very short period of time. Usually the court had several weeks to hold hearings and rule, but, under these dramatic circumstances, the court had little time to contemplate. Harding recalled: "We had a lot of long days, early mornings and late nights." It was "very unusual for the court to get decisions out as quickly as we did, [but] we realized that the exigencies of these circumstances required that we do it. I thought that the opinions of the court, whether I agreed with them or disagreed with them, were thoughtful and well done and represented a lot of work in a short period of time." Despite all the pressure, continued Harding, "there was a certain peace, a certain sense of purpose that we had to resolve these issues."[50]

David Boies, representing Gore, asked for the recounts to continue since canvassing boards had already found 215 votes in Palm Beach and 168 in Miami-Dade. He was convinced that if undervotes were examined by hand, a neutral observer could determine the intent of the voter. Justices Fred Lewis and Barbara Pariente indicated in the hearing that the best remedy seemed to be a count of all the undervotes in the state, but Barry Richards kept arguing that the only standard for a recount was abuse of discretion by the canvassing board. There was no proof of such abuse nor was there any evidence of any uncounted legitimate votes.

At 4:01 p.m. on December 8, just a couple of hours after Judges Lewis and Clark had ruled in the Martin and Seminole County cases, the Florida Supreme Court spokesman, Craig Waters, walked to the podium outside the court building. David Cardwell, an attorney and CNN elections analyst, was an avid spectator in the CNN booth, where the network continued its "podium watch" from a perch high above the area known as "Chadville" (where all the television crews and reporters were staked out). Before throngs of television cameras and a world-wide audience anxiously waiting the verdict, Waters calmly announced that the court had voted 4-3 to reverse Judge Sauls. Pandemonium ensued. Cardwell and Bill Hemmer were stunned by the verdict and the court's pronouncement brought loud groans from the news media, who expected to be going home. Cardwell quoted Jeff Greenfield as saying "We have just left the gravitational pull of the sun, this is spinning out of control."[51]

In *Gore v. Harris*, a divided Florida Supreme Court ruled that only by examining the contested ballots could a final determination of the 2000 election be made. Justices Pariente, Lewis, Anstead, and Quince, writing for the majority, ordered the recount of all the undervotes in the remaining sixty-four counties that had not conducted manual recounts to begin forthwith. The court order required Harris to include in the certified total 168 votes in Miami-Dade and 215 (or 176, as previously noted) in Palm Beach, and asked for the counting of 9,000 votes in Miami-Dade that had not been manually examined. The majority opinion denied Gore 51 votes in Nassau County and refused to ask for the recount of 3,300 votes in Palm Beach County. The court was also unwilling to set a standard, since that might be construed as making law or changing the rules after Election Day. The standard remained "the clear indication of the intent of the voter."

Justices Harding, Wells, and Shaw dissented, and Chief Justice Wells fashioned a stinging rebuke for his colleagues. He was clearly upset with the decision and concluded that there was a real and present likelihood that this constitutional crisis would do substantial damage to the country, the state, and the court as an institution. Wells declared that the decision would not withstand the scrutiny of the U.S. Supreme Court, deplored the failure to set a standard, and feared that this decision would run the risk of having every election result subject to judicial testing.

Since Gore had increased his vote total by 383 votes and Bush's lead had narrowed to 154 votes, Democrats were jubilant. Republicans, understandably, were angry and outraged over the court's pronouncement. While Bush lawyers rushed to appeal the decision to the U.S. Supreme Court,

Jim Baker called the verdict "sad for the nation [and] sad for democracy." Tom DeLay, the House Majority Whip, was less reserved: "This judicial aggression will not stand." On the other hand, Bill Daley called the decision "a victory for fairness and accountability and our democracy itself." Barry Richard decided that the Florida Supreme Court "rendered a populist decision." Although he disagreed with their decision, "they had earlier case law in which they had said that ensuring that people get to make a choice takes precedence over a super technical interpretation of the statutes."[52]

The Florida Supreme Court ordered Leon County Circuit Court Judge Sauls, who had just been overturned, to begin the manual recount. Since he had been rebuked by the court, Sauls refused to take the case and organizing the recount was left in the hands of Judge Terry Lewis. Lewis quickly held a hearing and set the procedures for the state-wide recount. Acutely aware of the time pressure, Lewis ordered the count to begin at 8 A.M. on Saturday, December 9 and to conclude by 2 P.M. on Sunday, December 10. Party observers could monitor the process, but could not object. The observers could point out a disputed ballot and Lewis would later make the final adjudication. All counties had to fax Lewis an outline of their plans of action by late Saturday morning and he advised the counties to use judges wherever possible, although the method of the count would still be determined by the canvassing boards. Judge Lewis refused to set a standard since the Florida Supreme Court had twice declined to do so. The intent of the voter would be used as the standard, but Lewis cautioned the counters to use common sense. If the intent of the voter was not clear, don't count it. The judge came up with a great "Johnny Cochran sound bite" which he decided not to use: "If in doubt, toss it out."

Judges in Leon County began counting the Miami-Dade ballots. They were counting nearly a thousand ballots an hour, a pace that would permit them to finish well before the Sunday deadline. Several counties with few undervotes finished quickly, while other counties faced difficulties in extracting the undervotes from the regular ballots. For example, Duval County had to locate some 4,967 undervotes from a total of 291,000 ballots, a difficult and time-consuming process since they lacked the proper computer hardware. Republicans argued that, once again, there were inconsistent and varying standards across the state.[53]

Judge Lewis was certain that the recount would have been completed on time, but at 2:45 P.M. on Saturday, December 9 yet another bombshell rocked the body politic. The U.S. Supreme Court, to the astonishment of the Democrats, intervened and halted the recount still in progress. The Court granted Bush's request for a stay until arguments could be heard. The 5-4 vote on the stay reflected a court split down an ideological fault-line with the 5 more conservative justices (Rehnquist, Scalia, Thomas, O'Connor, and Kennedy) opposed by their more moderate brethren (Breyer, Ginsburg, Souter, and Stevens). The dissenters believed the court had violated judicial restraint and their avowed principles of federalism.

They did not agree with Scalia's view of "irreparable harm" (the legal basis for a stay) to Bush when he was still ahead in the count. Stevens wondered how counting every legal vote could amount to "irreparable harm." Scalia argued that to count first and rule legality afterward was not a recipe for producing election results that would gain public acceptance.[54]

The penultimate hearing of the 2000 election began on Monday, December 11, with David Boies arguing for Gore, Ted Olson for Bush, and Joe Klock representing Katherine Harris. The arguments on both sides were similar to previous presentations. On December 12, after the Florida Supreme Court upheld the decisions by Lewis and Clark in the Seminole and Martin County cases and after the Florida House of Representatives had voted 79 to 41 to seat the Bush electors, the U.S. Supreme Court handed down its momentous decision in *Bush v. Gore.*

At precisely 10 P.M. on Tuesday, December 12, the court ruled 5-4 that the Florida Supreme Court's authorization of the manual recounts and the absence of uniform rules to determine the intent of the voter violated the equal protection clause of the Fourteenth Amendment. In addition, since December 12 was the safe harbor day, insufficient time remained for a recount. The court then remanded the case back to the Florida Supreme Court yet again. The justices noted that this verdict was "limited to the present circumstances" and thus should not be used for precedent.

Some experts looked at the decision as 7-2 since Justices Souter and Breyer agreed the Florida system for manual recounts was unconstitutional under the Fourteenth Amendment. Souter and Breyer, however, while agreeing that there was an equal protection problem, believed that the problem could be corrected. Most constitutional mavens proclaimed that it was a 5-4 vote to stop the recounting, since four justices thought the recount should continue. Justices Scalia, Thomas, and Rehnquist, in a separate concurring opinion, supported the equal protection part of the decision, but also argued that the Florida Supreme Court had rewritten the law, thus violating Article II of the federal constitution.

Justice Breyer, in his dissent, urged that the court send the case back to Florida, ask the court to establish one standard, and then recount all the undervotes. There was time to finish, wrote Breyer, as the meeting of the Electoral College was not until December 18. Breyer did not like the prospect of an unelected court deciding the election. Justice Ginsburg thought that the court never should have taken the case, since the federal courts generally defer to state courts. Also, she concurred with Breyer's views that December 12 was not the final date and asserted that Florida had not violated the Fourteenth Amendment. Justice Stevens had the strongest dissent. He argued that the decision was "wholly without merit" and the intent of the voter standard was the same as the "reasonable man" standard used by juries all over the country. Stevens also noted: "Although we may never know with complete certainty the identity of the winner of this year's presidential election, the identity of the loser is perfectly clear. It is the nation's confidence in the judge as an impartial guardian of the rule of law."[55]

The reaction of the participants, the media, and both political parties was as expected. Most Americans, regardless of party affiliation, were relieved that the 36-day conflict was finally over. As Dave Barry put it: "The American public had pretty much lost interest in the election and had gone back to the mall. In the end, if the Supreme Court could have declared that the forty-third president of the United States was Richard Simmons, and the overwhelming public reaction would have been: Thank God they finally picked somebody."[56] The public wanted to get on with Christmas preparations and could now cease the endless hours watching the give-and-take of the legal battles on CNN.

Some of the more liberal newspapers, including *The New York Times* and the *Los Angeles Times*, were sharply critical of the decision. Other papers viewed this verdict as a blow to the credibility of the High Court. Republican partisans were ecstatic. Jim Baker issued a statement expressing his pleasure "that seven justices of the United States Supreme Court agreed that there were constitutional problems with the Florida recount ordered by the Florida Supreme Court." David Boies said the Gore attorneys were caught in a Catch-22. If the Florida Supreme Court had set a standard, they would have been making law. Since they did not set a standard, they violated the Fourteenth Amendment. Gore was going to lose either way.[57]

Vice-President Gore still hoped for a miracle. He contacted attorney Dexter Douglass late at night after the *Bush v. Gore* decision and asked Douglass if anything could be done by the Florida Supreme Court. "He really, I could tell, wanted to keep going," but Douglass told him that the highest court in the land had spoken and that the game was over. On December 13, Al Gore gave the concession speech that Bush had been waiting for since November 8. In a very gracious speech, perhaps his best of the campaign, Gore told the public that he had called Bush and congratulated him on being the forty-third President of the United States. And with a whimsical sense of humor missing from his campaign, Gore added: "and I promised him that I would not call him back this time." Gore also repeated his strong belief in the rule of law. "I've tried to make it my guide throughout the contest. Now the U.S. Supreme Court has spoken. Let there be no doubt, while I strongly disagree with the court's decision, I accept it." Governor Bush claimed victory and called for reconciliation.[58]

On December 18, the Electoral College met and Bush received 271 votes to Gore's 266. A joint session of Congress, presided over by Vice-President Gore, officially counted the Electoral College votes on January 6 and Gore announced that Bush had received a majority of the votes. Governor George W. Bush of Texas took the oath of office as President of the United States on January 20, 2001, a final culmination to many days of angst and uncertainty. The American people, by and large, celebrated the legal and constitutional inauguration of a new president. The nation had selected a new president without a revolution or tanks in the street. The rule of law had prevailed.

The momentous decision in *Bush v. Gore* case has been discussed and debated *ad infinitum* over the past four years and law students will continue to study this case for years to come. The court decided the president of the United States by one vote after the most contentious, lengthy legal fight in American electoral history. Never before in American history had a presidential election been decided by the Supreme Court.

A small sample of reactions by legal scholars to the significance of *Bush v. Gore* is instructive. Some comments were excessive and unfair in their denunciation of the U.S. Supreme Court. Alan Dershowitz, in his book, *Supreme Injustice*, called the court's ruling an egregious error and "the single most corrupt decision in Supreme Court history because it is the only one I know of where the majority justices decided as they did because of the personal identity and political affiliation of the litigants." Dershowitz accused the Rehnquist court of being an activist, right-wing Republican court.[59] Vincent Bugliosi, author of *Betrayal of America*, called the five majority justices criminals, with the crime being the theft of the presidency.[60]

Other constitutional experts supported the High Court's determination. John C. Yoo was upset with attacks on the court's legitimacy for using the Fourteenth Amendment and unhappy with critics of the decision. Yoo noted that 585 law professors had taken out a full-page ad in *The New York Times*, protesting *Bush v. Gore* and accusing the Supreme Court justices of acting as political partisans and propagandists rather than judges in a court of law. The court, according to Yoo, had a right to intervene and had issued a narrow decision on procedures to govern presidential election counts in a one-of-a kind case. Yoo contended that it did not act hypocritically, but appropriately. "The court's decision to bring the Florida election dispute to a timely and final end not only restored stability to the political system but was also consistent with the institutional role the court has shaped for itself over the last decade."[61]

Other experts were less partisan. Judge Richard A. Posner, in *Breaking the Deadlock*, wrote that the judgment of the U.S. Supreme Court was a pragmatic one, but not very persuasive legally. He thought that the equal protection rationale was not compelling as ballots have always been counted differently in different precincts and had not previously been thought to deny equal protection to voters. Nonetheless, he thought that the court acted properly to stop the recount since it could not have been completed on time and might have led to a constitutional and political crisis.[62]

## Conclusion

Although the *Bush v. Gore* verdict effectively ended the "Great Florida Recount of 2000," there are lessons to be learned from these traumatic 36 days, which evoked intense and sometime bewildering political and legal maneuvers as well as fierce passions on both sides.

After interviewing 42 key participants of the Florida recount: reading court cases and newspaper and magazine articles, and surveying some of the vast secondary literature on this election, I have come away from this research with several observations.

First of all, we will never know the winner of the Florida vote, and thus the 2000 presidential election. Several newspapers, including the *Miami Herald* and *USA Today*, formed teams of observers to review all of the undervotes. They used different standards and came up with different results. The above papers found that Bush would have won in three out of four scenarios. Under the most inclusive standard advocated by Gore, Bush would have won by 1,665 votes. If the standard were the one applied in Palm Beach, Bush would have won by 884. If two corners had to be detached, Bush won by 363. Using the more rigorous standard advocated by Bush, Gore would have won by 3 votes, a statistically insignificant number. All of these results are irrelevant, since there was no uniform standard used. Some of the punch-cards had been recounted and there was a tendency for chads to dislodge after much handling. Some ballots were discovered missing and in one precinct in Collier County, there were 21 more votes than signatures. All over the state, there were thousands of votes cast that should not have counted. These illegal ballots were cast by felons, individuals who had been purged from the voter rolls, underage voters, those who had never registered, and in one case, two people who voted four times.[63] Finally, the newspapers' recount did not include the counties that had completed their ballots prior to the Supreme Court stay, nor did the recount include any of the 110,000 overvotes. How then, could an accurate determination be made? It simply would not have been possible.

Observers noted that if the intent of the voter was used in a manual recount, the canvassing board, as happened in Broward, Palm Beach, and Miami-Dade, could often easily determine the vote. If, on optical scan ballots, the voter had circled Bush and had written Bush on the page, then they intended to vote for Bush. The crux of the problem for the canvassing boards was when the voter did not black out the oval and the machine could not read the vote. Technically, failure to black out the oval is an invalid vote and should not be counted. Republicans argued that if people were too dumb to cast their ballot properly, it should not count. In essence, they argued that the Democrats, in advocating a recount, confused tabulation error with voter error. The Florida Supreme Court, using the intent of the voter standard, thought votes could and should be determined by a manual recount. Intent of the voter standard had been a viable standard in Florida for many years. It was no different from the "reasonable-man standard," used in courts for years. A jury can send the accused to the electric chair on standards no more specific than the intent of the voter standard. Both of these standards varied from county to county and state to state. Thus, according to standards in place for years, the intent of the voter could be considered an accurate method of determining votes. The problem in recounting votes manually was that human beings were subjective and partisan, often tired and easily distracted by the constant legal challenges and glare of the spotlight.

Two observations seem certain. One, and this view was affirmed by Judge Richard Posner, Mac Stipanovich, and other Republicans, as well as the Democrats, that more people went to the polls intending to vote for Al Gore than for George Bush. Second, the only chance Gore had to win the recount was either through limiting the recount to the four strongly Democratic counties or asking for a state-wide recount that included undervotes and overvotes. The broader the base for a recount, the better chance Gore had. This latter option also had the advantage of being more fair than just counting four counties. Gore, for many reasons, never got around to formally requesting a state-wide recount other than finally contesting the certified vote.

From a historian's perspective, Al Gore lost a presidential campaign he should have won. With a Democrat in the White House, a sound economy, and good name recognition, Gore began with a clear advantage, yet numerous factors intervened: his poor performance in the debates, several gaffes on the campaign trail, his failure to win his home state of Tennessee as well as Clinton's home state of Arkansas, his unwillingness to use Bill Clinton on the campaign trail, the Clinton scandals, his constant personality "make-overs," and failure to attack Bush's record in Texas and to defend his administration's successes. Bush's huge election war chest did not help either. If any of these factors had been reversed, Florida's vote would not have mattered.

The election, however, did come down to Florida, and Gore's defeat could be attributed to any number of relatively small factors and events in the Sunshine State. Without the butterfly ballot Gore probably would have gained enough votes in Palm Beach to overcome Bush's lead. Gore's unwillingness to challenge the legitimacy of the military overseas ballots allowed the Republicans to profit by gaining an undetermined number of Bush votes. Gore was too concerned with public opinion and did not want to seem unpatriotic by challenging the military votes. His close advisors, including Mitch Berger, viewed Gore as a principled man who was concerned with the integrity of the law and American democratic institutions. Gore refused to allow his legal team to denigrate the courts or to recuse judges. Gore said that those institutions only work if they have the trust and the goodwill of the people, and he would not allow his candidacy to undermine those institutions.

If Gore could have obtained a verdict in either the Seminole or Martin county cases where election supervisors had allowed Republicans to put voter identification numbers on absentee ballot requests, Gore would have won Florida. It was just by happenstance that a Republican party operative discovered the lack of identification numbers and was granted the opportunity to provide them. The candidacy of Ralph Nader was another blow to Gore. Nader received 97,488 votes in Florida and 3,226 in Alachua County, home of the University of Florida. Surely more than 537 Nader supporters would have transferred their votes to Gore if Nader had not run. But, of course, he did run. Nader was vilified by the Democrats for running an ego-driven campaign, but Nader defended his quest for the presidency in his book, *Crashing the Party*. Nader argued that both the Democrats and Republicans were in thrall to the highest bidders at the expense of the democratic process and there would not be much difference in their policies if either Bush or Gore were elected.[64] On the other hand, Gore won New Mexico by a mere 366 votes (no recount) and if that count had been reversed, Florida would have been ignored.

Those interviewed for this book generally conceded that the Republicans were better organized, quicker to the attack, had more money to spend, and were more willing to fight vigorously for their candidate. Jim Baker was essential in organizing and effectively leading the Republicans in the recount struggle. The Democrats, after Warren Christopher and Bill Daley left, seemed more disorganized.

The two presidential contenders had totally different legal and political strategies in the Florida recount. George Bush stayed in Texas and allowed Jim Baker, Ben Ginsberg, and his legal team to make important decisions. Barry Richard said the Bush team permitted him to plan and carry out the legal strategy (with input from Baker and Ginsberg). He only talked with George Bush twice; both were congratulatory and informational phone calls. Bush did not offer legal advice. On the other hand, according to several sources, Al Gore was a hands-on candidate, making almost all of the final decisions. He frequently contacted his Florida attorneys, but did not always heed their advice. Dexter Douglass argued early and forcefully for a move to the contest (for *contest*, see Court Cases and Legal Terms) and a state-wide recount. Douglass noted that just about all the Democratic lawyers agreed with him and anyone who knew Florida election law would have agreed. Barry Richard,[65] Mac Stipanovich, and other supporters of Bush also agreed with Douglass's view. Douglass thought Gore had too many advisors, was too indecisive about legal choices, and was too concerned about what went on in the Washington Beltway. Douglass argued, in his own inimitable way, that the Republicans beat the Democrats in the public relations contest and in their willingness to fight for their cause. "It was kind of like you a boxing match and one side is really stronger, but he [Gore] fights by the Marquis of Queensbury rules. And the other side is not as strong, but he kicks you in the [groin], he hits you in the kidney, he does everything dirty, and wins. They were street-fighting, which used to be the Democratic strong[point]. The Democrats were acting like they all went to Harvard."[66]

Both sides were hypocritical and played loosely with facts. Republicans described chaos in the Palm Beach recount when there was none. Jim Baker originally praised the rule of law after Judge Lewis's pronouncement upholding the certification date, but thought it was a sad day for the law after the 4-3 *Gore v. Harris* decision. The Republicans demanded strict adherence to the law on the certification date, but asked for flexibility when recounting military ballots. The Democrats and Jesse Jackson cried racial discrimination in voting when there were only a few isolated incidents and anecdotal evidence at best. Al Gore insisted on counting every vote, but wavered on this position when considering challenging the military ballots and in the Martin and Seminole County cases.

Another point often missed in media and historical accounts of this election was the charge that the Florida Supreme Court was a Democratic, liberal court since all but one member had been appointed by a Democratic governor. The Florida Supreme Court ruled against Gore on at least four occasions (resuming the Miami-Dade recount, the appeal of Martin and Seminole county cases, the illegality of the butterfly ballot). In their most controversial verdict, *Gore v. Harris*, three members of the so-called Democratic court dissented. These three dissents, especially the one by Justice Wells, may well have helped the U.S. Supreme Court in justifying their final decision. Two liberal Democrats, Judges Lewis and Clark, ruled against Gore on every issue.

If one were to take the Supreme Court decision in *Bush v. Gore* to its logical (or illogical) conclusion, then every county in America would have to use the same machine and have the same standard. Clearly, if punch-card machines, used by counties all over America, were less accurate than optical scan machines, then that in and of itself would be a violation of the equal protection clause of the Fourteenth Amendment. The high court, however, intended its decision to be limited to the Florida recount and specifically indicated that this verdict was not to be used as precedent.

Although Florida was trashed by the media as the state that could not count, "Flori-duh," Florida was no worse than many other states. Under the glare of the world media, many states would have had their problems and inefficiencies exposed. Several states still used the punch-card machines and experienced problems similar to those in Palm Beach. Also, other states had more overvotes and undervotes than Florida. One could never be sure about the accuracy of votes in Illinois and Louisiana, but there was little or no fraud discovered in Florida.

Everyone's eyes are once again on Florida as the 2004 presidential election approaches. The state will be a pivotal battleground in 2004; Karl Rove has called it "ground zero." President Bush, anticipating another fierce struggle for Florida's electoral votes, has visited the state 19 times since he took office. No one, however, least of all Governor Jeb Bush, would like a repeat of 2000.

## Notes

1. Interview with Theresa LePore by Pam Iorio, February 23, 2001, 5, 41. Interview in possession of Iorio.
2. Jake Tapper, *Down and Dirty: the Plot to Steal the Presidency*. Boston: Little, Brown and Co., 2001, 17–21; Jeffrey Toobin, *Too Close To Call: The Thirty-Six Day Battle to Decide the 2000 Election*. New York: Random House, 2001, 13–15.
3. Martin Merzer et al, *The Miami Herald Report: Democracy Held Hostage*. New York: St. Martin's Press, 2001, 43.

4. LePore interview, 4–5.
5. Abner Greene, *Understanding the 2000 Election*. New York: New York University Press, 2001, 140–42.
6. *Palm Beach Post*, November 8, 9, 2000.
7. Diana Owen, "Media Mayhem: Performance of the Press in Election 2000," 140–48, in Larry J. Sabato, editor, *Overtime: The Election 2000 Thriller*. New York: Longman, 2002.
8. Dave Barry, *Dave Barry Hits Below the Beltway*. New York: Ballantine Books, 2001, 161–66.
9. Author's interview with Bob Butterworth, March 11, 2003, POHP, 7–10.
10. Howard Gillman, *The Votes That Counted*. Chicago: The University of Chicago Press, 2001, 17–20; Toobin, *Too Close To Call*, 16–29; Tapper, *Down and Dirty*, 27–38; Florida Statute #102.141 (3).
11. Tapper, *Down and Dirty*, 42–43, 50–51, 70–72.
12. David E. Cardwell, *Elections and Ethics: the Law in Florida*. Norcross, Georgia: the Harrison Company Publishers, 1980, 63.
13. Toobin, *Too Close To Call*, 64–66.
14. U.S. Commission on Civil Rights, Status Report on Probe of Election Practices in Florida during the 2000 Presidential Election, March 9, 2001, preface and ten chapters. Preface, 2; chapter one, 3–5.
15. *Siegel v. LePore*, Emergency Motion for a Temporary Restraining Order and Preliminary Injunction, United States District Court for the Southern District of Florida, November 11, 2000, Case No. 00–9009, 1–8; Toobin, *Too Close To Call*, 99–101; Gillman, *The Votes That Counted*, 34–36.
16. Greene, *Understanding the 2000 Election*, 74–75; Gillman, *The Votes That Counted*, 38–39; Robert M. Jarvis, Phyllis Coleman, Johnny C. Burris, *Bush v. Gore, The Fight for Florida's Vote*. New York: Kluwer Law International, 2001, 1–21; *Siegel V. LePore*, S. D. Florida, November 13, 2000, 1–16.
17. Florida Division of Elections, Opinion DE 00–11, Definitions of Errors in Vote Tabulation, November 13, 2000; Toobin, *Too Close To Call*, 101–02, Florida Statute, 102.112.
18. Author's interview with Butterworth, 47–56; Gillman, *The Votes That Counted*, 39–40; Florida Attorney General, Advisory Legal Opinion, AGO 2000–65, November 14, 2000; Florida Statute 102.111 and 102.112.
19. Katherine Harris, *Center of the Storm*. Nashville, Thomas Nelson, Inc. 2002, 65–70; Richard A. Posner, *Breaking the Deadlock: The 2000 Election, the Constitution and the Courts*. Princeton, New Jersey: Princeton University Press, 2001, 94–95.
20. Author's interview with Judge Terry Lewis, December 19, 2002, POHP, 4–11; Greene, *Understanding the 2000 Election*, 47–54; *McDermott v. Harris*, Case No. CV 00–2700, in the Circuit Court of the Second Judicial Circuit, in and for Leon County, November 14, 2000; Jarvis, Coleman, and Burris, *Bush v. Gore*, 17–21; Tapper, *Down and Dirty*, 133–34.
21. Author's interview with Mac Stipanovich, June 10, 2002, POHP, 13–16.
22. *Los Angeles Times*, November 18, 2000, A1; Gillman, *The Votes That Counted*, 46–47.
23. Author's interview with Terry Lewis, 7–8.
24. *St. Petersburg Times*, November 23, 2000.
25. Gillman, *The Votes That Counted*, 49–52; Toobin, *Too Close To Call*, 160–63; Arthur J Jacobsen and Michel Rosenfeld, eds., *The Longest Night: Polemics*

*and Perspectives on Election 2000*. Berkeley: University of California Press, 2002, 30–31.

26. *The New York Times*, July 15, 2001; The *Washington Post*, January 31, 2001; author's interview with Beverly Hill, Supervisor of Elections, Alachua County, May 17, 2001, POHP, 17; author's interview with Mark Herron, May 15, 2002, POHP, 14–27; author's interview with Mitchell Berger, March 5, 2002, POHP, 35–36; Gillman, *The Votes That Counted*, 52–53; Toobin, *Too Close To Call*, 130–32.

27. Roger Simon, *Divided We Stand: How Al Gore Beat George Bush and Lost the Presidency*. New York: Crown Publishers, 2001, 267–68; Diana Owen, "Media Mayhem," 146–47; Toobin, *Too Close To Call*, 152–53.

28. Author's interview with Judge Charles Burton, POHP, April 5, 2001, 14–15; author's interview with Carol Roberts, POHP, December 12, 2001, 18, 25–26; Tapper, *Down and Dirty*, 210–11, *The New York Times*, November 19, 2000; Toobin, *Too Close To Call*, 164–68.

29. Author's interview with Craig Waters, POHP, October 3, 2002, 4–11.

30. *Palm Beach County Canvassing Board v Harris*, in Jarvis, Coleman, Burris, *Bush v. Gore*, 49–73; Gillman, *The Votes That Counted*, 55–68; Toobin, *Too Close To Call*, 132–36; Greene, *Understanding the 2000 Election*, 50–55.

31. Author's interview with Justice Major Harding, August 20, 2003, POHP, 22–23.

32. Tapper, *Down and Dirty*, 289–90; Gillman, *The Votes That Counted*, 73–74.

33. Author's interview with Joe Geller, March 13, 2003, POHP, 29–60; author's interview with Miguel DeGrandy, August 21, 2002, POHP, 11–21; Toobin, *Too Close To Call*, 153–57.

34. Jarvis, Coleman, Burris, *Bush v. Gore*, 81–83.

35. Gillman, *The Votes That Counted*, 73–75; Greene, *Understanding the 2000 Election*, 58.

36. Harris, *Center of the Storm*, 121–23.

37. Author's interview with Mac Stipanovich, 17.

38. *St. Petersburg Times*, November 28, 2000.

39. Jarvis, Coleman and Burris, *Bush v. Gore*, 85–86; Gillman, *The Votes That Counted*, 73–83.

40. Gillman, *The Votes That Counted*, 81–96; Jacobs and Rosenfeld, *The Longest Night*, 37.

41. Author's interview with Mac Stipanovich, 28; Toobin, *Too Close To Call*, 228–99

42. Author's interview with Harry Jacobs, November 20, 2002, POHP, 2–12; Gillman, *The Votes That Counted*, 108–10.

43. Author's interview with Judge Nikki Clark, September 25, 2003, POHP, 6–11; author's interview with Barry Richard, October 10, 2002, 50–51; Gillman, *The Votes That Counted*, 138; Toobin, *Too Close To Call*, 208–10.

44. Author's interview with Terry Lewis, December 19, 2002, POHP, 17–27; author's interview with Nikki Clark, 11–15; Greene, *Understanding the 2000 Election*, 151–59.

45. Author's interview with Nikki Clark, 17–20; author's interview with Terry Lewis, 23.

46. Author's interview with Tom Feeney, November 21, 2002, POHP, 3–55; author's interview with John McKay, October 3, 2002, POHP, 2–21; Greene *Understanding the 2000 Election*, 163–67.

47. *Tallahassee Democrat*, December 8, 2000, A1; *Los Angeles Times, December 7, 2000;* A1, A42.

48. *Los Angeles Times*, December 7, 2000, A1, A 42.

49. Toobin, *Too Close To Call*, 230–32; author's interview with Barry Richard, October 10, 2002, POHP, 64–68

50. Author's interview with Justice Major Harding, August 20, 2003, POHP, 6–9, 30.

51. Author's interview with David Cardwell, October 16, 2001, POHP, 92–93.

52. Jarvis, Coleman and Burris, *Bush v. Gore, Gore v. Harris*, 240–58; Toobin, *Too Close to Call*, 230–37; Gillman, *The Votes That Counted*, 111–18; author's interview with Barry Richard, 39.

53. Author's interview with Terry Lewis, 27–31; Toobin, *Too Close To Call*, 248–53; Gillman, *The Votes That Counted*, 119–22.

54. Author's interview with Terry Lewis, 27–31; Toobin, *Too Close to Call*, 248–53; Gillman, *The Votes That Counted*, 119–28.

55. Jarvis, Coleman and Burris, *Bush v. Gore*, 121 Supreme Court 525 (U.S. December 12, 2000), 331–70; Toobin, *Too Close To Call*, 258–67; Gillman, *The Votes That Counted*, 137–51; Tapper, *Down and Dirty*, 451–56.

56. Dave Barry, *Hits Below the Beltway*, 173.

57. "Florida Election 2000: Insiders at the Intersection of Law, Politics, and the Media," forum held at the University of Florida, February 26, 2001, 20–22; Gillman, *The Votes That Counted*, 151.

58. Toobin, *Too Close to Call*, 267–70; Gillman, *The Votes That Counted*, 151–60; author's interview with Dexter Douglass, 57–58.

59. Alan Dershowitz, *Supreme Injustice: How the High Court Hijacked Election 2000*. New York: Oxford University Press, 2001, 174.

60. Vincent Bugliosi, "None Dare Call it Treason," *Nation*, February 5, 2001, 11–19; Vincent Bugliosi, *The Betrayal of America: How the Supreme Court Undermined the Constitution and Chose our President*. New York: Nation Books, 2001, 15–29.

61. John C. Yoo, "In Defense of the Court's Legitimacy," in Cass R. Sunstein and Richard A. Epstein, eds., *The Vote: Bush, Gore and the Supreme Court*. Chicago: University of Chicago Press, 2001, 223–40; *The New York Times*, December 13, 2000.

62. Richard A. Posner, *Breaking the Deadlock*, ix–x; Gillman, *The Votes That Counted*, 155–57.

63. *St. Petersburg Times*, December 14, 2000.

64. Ralph Nader, *Crashing the Party*. New York: Thomas Dunne Books, 2002, 304.

65. Author's interview with Barry Richard, 4–5.

66. Author's interview with Dexter Douglass, 59; author's interview with Bob Butterworth, 91–92.

# ➤ COUNTY-BY-COUNTY VOTES IN FLORIDA ⬅

### Vote for President and Vice President by County
### November 7, 2000

| County | Republican Bush/Cheney | Democrat Gore/Lieberman | Green Nader/LaDuke | Reform Buchanan/Foster |
|--------|------------------------|-------------------------|--------------------|------------------------|
| Alachua | 34,124 | 47,365 | 3,226 | 263 |
| Baker | 5,610 | 2,392 | 53 | 73 |
| Bay | 38,637 | 18,850 | 828 | 248 |
| Bradford | 5,414 | 3,075 | 84 | 65 |
| Brevard | 115,185 | 97,318 | 4,470 | 570 |
| Broward | 177,902 | 387,703 | 7,104 | 795 |
| Calhoun | 2,873 | 2,155 | 39 | 90 |
| Charlotte | 35,426 | 29,645 | 1,462 | 182 |
| Citrus | 29,767 | 25,525 | 1,379 | 270 |
| Clay | 41,736 | 14,632 | 562 | 186 |
| Collier | 60,450 | 29,921 | 1,400 | 122 |
| Columbia | 10,964 | 7,047 | 258 | 89 |
| Desoto | 4,256 | 3,320 | 157 | 36 |
| Dixie | 2,697 | 1,826 | 75 | 29 |
| Duval | 152,098 | 107,864 | 2,757 | 652 |
| Escambia | 73,017 | 40,943 | 1,727 | 502 |
| Flagler | 12,613 | 13,897 | 435 | 83 |
| Franklin | 2,454 | 2,046 | 85 | 33 |
| Gadsden | 4,767 | 9,735 | 139 | 38 |
| Gilchrist | 3,300 | 1,910 | 97 | 29 |
| Glades | 1,841 | 1,442 | 56 | 9 |
| Gulf | 3,550 | 2,397 | 86 | 71 |
| Hamilton | 2,146 | 1,722 | 37 | 23 |
| Hardee | 3,765 | 2,339 | 75 | 30 |
| Hendry | 4,747 | 3,240 | 104 | 22 |
| Hernando | 30,646 | 32,644 | 1,501 | 242 |
| Highlands | 20,206 | 14,167 | 545 | 127 |
| Hillsborough | 180,760 | 169,557 | 7,490 | 847 |
| Holmes | 5,011 | 2,177 | 94 | 76 |
| Indian River | 28,635 | 19,768 | 950 | 105 |
| Jackson | 9,138 | 6,868 | 138 | 102 |
| Jefferson | 2,478 | 3,041 | 76 | 29 |

*Continued*

| County | Republican Bush/Cheney | Democrat Gore/Lieberman | Green Nader/LaDuke | Reform Buchanan/Foster |
|---|---|---|---|---|
| Lafayette | 1,670 | 789 | 26 | 10 |
| Lake | 50,010 | 36,571 | 1,460 | 289 |
| Lee | 106,141 | 73,560 | 3,587 | 305 |
| Leon | 39,062 | 61,427 | 1,932 | 282 |
| Levy | 6,858 | 5,398 | 284 | 67 |
| Liberty | 1,317 | 1,017 | 19 | 39 |
| Madison | 3,038 | 3,014 | 54 | 29 |
| Manatee | 57,952 | 49,177 | 2,491 | 271 |
| Marion | 55,141 | 44,665 | 1,809 | 563 |
| Martin | 33,970 | 26,620 | 1,118 | 112 |
| Miami-Dade | 289,533 | 328,808 | 5,352 | 560 |
| Monroe | 16,059 | 16,483 | 1,090 | 47 |
| Nassau | 16,404 | 6,952 | 253 | 90 |
| Okaloosa | 52,093 | 16,948 | 985 | 267 |
| Okeechobee | 5,057 | 4,588 | 131 | 43 |
| Orange | 134,517 | 140,220 | 3,879 | 446 |
| Osceola | 26,212 | 28,181 | 732 | 145 |
| Palm Beach | 152,951 | 269,732 | 5,565 | 3,411 |
| Pasco | 68,582 | 69,564 | 3,393 | 570 |
| Pinellas | 184,825 | 200,630 | 10,022 | 1,013 |
| Polk | 90,295 | 75,200 | 2,059 | 533 |
| Putnam | 13,447 | 12,102 | 377 | 148 |
| Santa Rosa | 36,274 | 12,802 | 724 | 311 |
| Sarasota | 83,100 | 72,853 | 4,069 | 305 |
| Seminole | 75,677 | 59,174 | 1,946 | 194 |
| St. John | 39,546 | 19,502 | 1,217 | 229 |
| St. Lucie | 34,705 | 41,559 | 1,368 | 124 |
| Sumter | 12,127 | 9,637 | 306 | 114 |
| Suwannee | 8,006 | 4,075 | 180 | 108 |
| Taylor | 4,056 | 2,649 | 59 | 27 |
| Union | 2,332 | 1,407 | 33 | 37 |
| Volusia | 82,357 | 97,304 | 2,910 | 498 |
| Wakulla | 4,512 | 3,838 | 149 | 46 |
| Walton | 12,182 | 5,642 | 265 | 120 |
| Washington | 4,994 | 2,798 | 93 | 88 |
| Sub Total | 2,911,215 | 2,911,417 | 97,426 | 17,479 |
| Fed Absentee | 1,575 | 836 | 62 | 5 |
| Total | 2,912,790 | 2,912,253 | 97,488 | 17,484 |
| Percentage | 48.8% | 48.8% | 1.6% | 0.3% |

# PART I

# ➤ CAST OF CHARACTERS ◄

John Ahmann—Owner of small election supply company in California; expert-witness in 2000 election lawsuit, Gore v. Harris (before Judge Sanders Sauls) about chad–build-up in punch-card machines.

Roger Ailes—Chairman and CEO of Fox News, 1996–present; president of CNBC, 1993–1996; media advisor for campaigns of Richard Nixon in 1968, Ronald Reagan in 1984, and George Bush in 1988.

Joe Allbaugh—Political advisor and campaign manager for George W. Bush in 2000.

Harry Lee Anstead—Justice, Florida Supreme Court, 1994–2002.

James Baker—George W. Bush's spokesman during the recount crisis; longtime career politician and statesmen as a Republican, including stints as U.S. Secretary of State, 1989–1992; campaign manager for President George Bush, 1988; and White House chief of staff under President Reagan, 1981–1985.

Nick Baldick—Political consultant and national deputy finance director, 2000 Al Gore presidential campaign.

Martha Barnett—President, American Bar Association, 2000–2001; partner, Holland & Knight LLP law firm.

David Barstow—Journalist for the *New York Times;* wrote story after the 2000 election regarding military absentee-ballots.

Fred Bartlit—Corporate litigator and attorney for George W. Bush in 2000 election working on the military-ballot issue in *Fox v. Harris* and *Harrell v. Harris*.

Jeremy Bash—Legal advisor for Al Gore in 2000 election.

Phil Beck—Attorney for George W. Bush in 2000 election.

Mitchell Berger—Close friend of and attorney for Al Gore in 2000 election.

Mary Francis Berry—Member, U.S. Civil Rights Commission, 1980–present and chairperson, 1993–present; former assistant secretary for education, U.S. Department of Health, Education and Welfare.

Jim Boczar—Florida State Senator; ran against Katherine Harris in 1994.

David Boies—Chief attorney for Al Gore in 2000 election. Pleaded the Democratic "contest" before Judge Sauls; appeared before the Florida Supreme court in *Gore v. Harris*, and made the major presentation before the U.S. Supreme Court in *Bush v. Gore*.

Bill Bradley—U.S. senator from New Jersey 1979–1997 and Democratic presidential candidate in 2000.

Stephen G. Breyer—Associate justice, U.S. Supreme Court, 1994–present.

Daryl Bristow—Attorney for George W. Bush.

Corrine Brown—U.S. representative, 1993–present; Florida state representative, 1983–1993.

Kurt Browning—Supervisor of elections, Pasco County, 1980–present.

Pat Buchanan—Unsuccessful presidential candidate, 1992, 1996, 2000; director of communications under Ronald Reagan, 1985–1987; special assistant to Richard Nixon, 1969–1974.

Charles Burson—Chief of staff to Vice-President Al Gore, 1999–2001; chief counsel to Vice-President Al Gore, 1997–1999; former attorney general for state of Tennessee; former president of the National Association of Attorneys General.

Charles Burton—Judge, County Court, Palm Beach County; chairman, Palm Beach County Canvassing Board.

George W. Bush—U.S. president, 2001–present; Texas governor, 1995–2001.

Jeb Bush—Florida governor, 1999–present and brother of George W. Bush; Florida Secretary of Commerce, 1987–1988.

Bob Butterworth—Attorney general of Florida, 1986–2002.

Johnny Byrd—Speaker, Florida House of Representatives, 2002–2003; state representative since 1996.

Al Cardenas—Chairman of the Florida Republican Party in 2000.

David Cardwell—Attorney and CNN elections analyst; author of *Election and Ethics: The Law in Florida*.

Kerey Carpenter—Assistant general counsel for the Florida Department of State, represented Katherine Harris in Palm Beach County dispute.

Jane Carroll—Supervisor of elections, Broward County; member, Broward County Canvassing Board who quit during recount.

Michael Carvin—Attorney for George W. Bush in 2000 election; appeared before Florida Supreme Court in *Palm Beach County Canvassing Board v. Harris*.

Frank Cerabino—Columnist, *Palm Beach Post*.

Richard "Dick" Cheney—U.S. vice-president, 2001–present; Secretary of defense under President George Bush, 1989–1993; U.S. representative from Wyoming, 1979–1989; White House chief of staff, 1975–1977.

Warren Christopher—Spokesman for Gore recount team; former U.S. secretary of state, 1993–1997.

Nikki Clark—Judge, Leon County Circuit Court; made ruling in *Jacobs v. Seminole County Canvassing Board*.

William Jefferson Clinton—U.S. president, 1993–2001; Arkansas governor, 1983–1993.

Sue Cobb—Attorney for George Bush in 2000 election on the legal team that contested recounts in Miami-Dade; former U.S. ambassador to Jamaica.

Kendall Coffey—Attorney for Al Gore regarding overall strategy in 2000 election; appeared before Miami-Dade Canvassing Board; former U.S. attorney in Miami.

Roger Cossack—CNN legal analyst.

Bob Crawford—Florida agricultural commissioner; replaced Jeb Bush on State Canvassing Board after Jeb Bush recused himself.

William Daley—Campaign manager for Al Gore in 2000 election; secretary of commerce, 1997–2000.

Larry Davis—Attorney representing Commissioner Sue Gunzburger in Broward County.

Miguel De Grandy—Represented George W. Bush before Miami-Dade Canvassing Board; Florida state representative, 1989–1994.

Alan Dershowitz—Lawyer; professor; author of *Supreme Injustice: How the High Court Hijacked Election 2000*.

Denise Dytrych—Republican county attorney for Palm Beach County.

Robert J. Dole—Unsuccessful Republican presidential candidate, 1996; U.S. senator from Kansas, 1969–1996.

Dexter Douglass—Lead Florida attorney for Al Gore in 2000 election; chairman, Florida constitutional revision commission.

Matt Drudge—Administrator of "The Drudge Report," a conservative Internet news/rumor website.

Einer Elhague—Harvard Law School professor, advisor to Florida Speaker of the House, Tom Feeney, on constitutional issues.

John Ellis—Fox News election analyst, head of decision desk during 2000 election; first cousin of George W. Bush.

Margarita Esquiroz—Judge, Miami-Dade County Circuit Court.

Tom Feeney—U.S. representative, 2002–present; Florida state representative, 1990–1994, 1996–2002; Speaker of Florida House of Representatives, 2000–2001; Republican nominee for lieutenant governor of Florida, 1994.

Tom Fiedler—Executive editor, *The Miami Herald*.

Harold Ford Jr.—U.S. congressman from Tennessee.

Lois Frankel—Florida House Democratic leader (2000–2002); state representative since 1986. Mayor of West Palm Beach, 2002–present.

Charles Fried—Attorney and Harvard Law School professor who advised the Republican-led Florida legislature in the 2000 election on constitutional matters. Served as former U.S. solicitor general and Massachusetts supreme court justice.

Joe Geller—Chairman, Miami-Dade County Democratic Party.

David Gergen—Advisor to U.S. presidents Richard Nixon, Gerald Ford, Ronald Reagan, and Bill Clinton; editor-at-large, *U.S. News and World Report*.

Ben Ginsberg—Attorney, coordinated legal strategy and personnel for George W. Bush in 2000 election.

Ruth Bader Ginsburg—Associate justice, U.S. Supreme Court, 1993–present.

Sandra Goard—Supervisor of elections, Seminole County; defendant in *Jacobs v. Seminole County*.

Elian Gonzalez—Cuban refugee boy who provoked political controversy after being rescued at sea on Thanksgiving Day, 1999; federal authorities broke into a relative's home to forcibly return him to his father in Cuba.

J. Dudley Goodlette—Florida state representative, 1998–present.

Adam Goodman—Political media consultant; media advisor to Florida Secretary of State Katherine Harris during her 1998 campaign.

Albert Arnold Gore, Jr.—Unsuccessful Democratic presidential candidate, 2000; U.S. Vice-President, 1993–2001; U.S. senator from Tennessee, 1985–1993.

Robert "Bob" Graham—U.S. senator from Florida, 1987–present; Florida governor, 1979–1987.

Murray Greenberg—Assistant county attorney, Miami-Dade County, 1980–present.

Jeff Greenfield—CNN news analyst and commentator, 1998–present; author of *Oh Waiter! One Order of Crow!*

Suzanne Gunzburger—Member, Broward County Canvassing Board.

*Hannity & Colmes*—Political talk-show on Fox News.

Paul Hancock—Attorney for Florida Attorney General Bob Butterworth.

Major Harding—Justice, Florida Supreme Court, 1991–2002.

Katherine Harris—U.S. representative, 2002–present; Florida secretary of state, 1998–2002; Florida state senator, 1994–1998.

Paul Hawks—Chief policy coordinator for Tom Feeney.

Bill Hemmer—News anchor for CNN.

Nicholas Hengartner—Yale University statistician who testified for the Democrats in the *Gore v. Harris* lawsuit.

Mark Herron—Florida attorney; sent memo to Democratic attorneys on Florida law regarding absentee and overseas ballots.

Tony Hill—Florida state representative, 1992–2000; coordinator of "Arrive With Five" campaign to increase African American voter participation in Florida during the 2000 election.

Jesse Jackson, Sr.—Activist; civil rights leader; unsuccessful candidate for Democratic presidential nomination in 1984 and 1988; founder of the Rainbow Coalition.

Harry Jacobs—Personal-injury lawyer from Longwood, Florida; plaintiff in Seminole County case.

Ed Jennings, Jr.—Florida state representative, 2000–present.

Frank Jiminez—Chief lawyer, deputy chief of staff for Governor Jeb Bush.

Deborah Kearney—General counsel, Florida Department of State.

Will Kendrick—Florida state representative, 2000–present.

Anthony M. Kennedy—Associate justice of the U.S. Supreme Court, 1988–present.

Bob Kerrey—U.S. senator from Nebraska, 1989–2001; former governor of Nebraska (1983–1987).

John Kerry—U.S. senator from Massachusetts, 1985–present.

Peter Knight—Close friend and fundraiser for Al Gore.

Lawrence King—Judge, Miami-Dade County; chair, Miami-Dade County Canvassing Board.

Larry King—Host of *Larry King Live* talk-show on CNN.

Deeno Kitchen—Attorney for Al Gore in 2000 election; appeared in *McDermott v. Harris* (otherwise known as *Lewis I*).

Ron Klain—Chief of staff to Vice-President Al Gore; head of legal operations for Al Gore in 2000 election.

Joseph P. Klock—Managing partner, Steel Hector Davis law firm; attorney representing Katherine Harris during 2000 election; appeared before U.S. Supreme Court in *Bush v. Gore*.

Carl Koch—Staffer for vice-president Al Gore.

Ben Kuehne—Expert on Florida election law, attorney and advisor for Al Gore in 2000 election.

Jorge LaBarga—Circuit judge, 15th Judicial Circuit in West Palm Beach, Florida; rendered opinion in *Fladell v. Elections Canvassing Commission* and in *Florida Democratic Party v. Palm Beach County Canvassing Board*.

Michael Lavelle—Chicago attorney consulted on Al Gore's behalf during 2000 election case; involved with affidavit controversy over the counting of dimples in the *Pullen v. Mulligan* case.

David Leahy—Supervisor of elections, Miami-Dade County; member, Miami-Dade County Canvassing Board.

Robert W. Lee—Judge, Broward County Circuit Court; member, Broward County Canvassing Board.

Myriam Lehr—Judge, Miami-Dade County; member, Miami-Dade County Canvassing Board.

Theresa LePore—Supervisor of elections, Palm Beach County; designer of the so-called butterfly-ballot.

R. Fred Lewis—Justice, Florida Supreme Court, 1998–present.

Terry Lewis—Judge, 2nd Judicial Circuit; made rulings in *McDermott v. Harris* (*Lewis I and II*) and in *Taylor v. Martin County Canvassing Board*.

Joseph I. Lieberman—U.S. senator from Connecticut, 1989–present; unsuccessful Democratic vice-presidential candidate, 2000; Attorney general of Connecticut, 1983, 1986–1988.

Rush Limbaugh—Conservative radio talk-show host.

Jim Magill—Director of Senate campaigns for Republican Party, 1994–1996.

Roger Magnuson—Dean of Oak Brook College of Law in Fresno, California; advisor to the Florida Senate on constitutional issues.

Gwen Margolis—Chairperson of the Dade County Commission.

Bobby Martinez—Attorney for George W. Bush in 2000 election; worked with Miguel DeGrandy before the Miami-Dade Canvassing Board.

Bill McBride—Democratic nominee for governor of Florida in 2002, lost to Jeb Bush.

Mary McCarty—Commissioner, Palm Beach County Commission, 1990–present, chairman, 1992–1994.

Michael McDermott—Judge and chair of Canvassing Board, Volusia County.

Ben McKay—Chief of staff for Florida Secretary of State Katherine Harris.

John McKay—Florida state senator, 1990–present; president of Florida Senate, 2000–2002.

Kendrick Meek—Florida state senator, 1998–present; Florida state representative, 1994–1998; U.S. Congressman, 2002–present.

Donald Middlebrooks—U.S. District Court judge, Southern District of Florida (Miami); Rendered decision in *Siegel v. LePore.*

Jon Mills—Former dean of University of Florida law school.

Mary Ellen Miller—Miami-Dade County Republican Party chairman.

Robert Montgomery—Palm Beach County attorney for Theresa LePore in 2000 election.

Lucy Morgan—Pulitzer Prize–winning investigative reporter and Tallahassee bureau chief for the *St. Petersburg Times.*

Sandy Mortham—Florida secretary of state, 1998–2002.

Rupert Murdoch—Media mogul and owner of Fox News.

Ralph Nader—Green Party presidential candidate, 2000; activist; author of *Crashing the Party*, an account of the 2000 presidential bid.

Bill Nelson—U.S. senator from Florida, 2000–present.

John Newton—Attorney for Al Gore in 2000 election.

Tim Nickens—Political reporter, *St. Petersburg Times.*

Sandra Day O'Connor—Associate justice, U.S. Supreme Court, 1981–present.

Ted Olson—Attorney for George W. Bush in 2000 election; argued *Bush v. Gore* in U.S. Supreme Court; currently U.S. solicitor general.

Barbara J. Pariente—Justice, Florida Supreme Court, 1997–present.

George Pataki—Republican governor of New York, 1995–present.

Paul Patton—Democratic governor of Kentucky, 1995–present.

Alex Penelas—Mayor, Miami-Dade County, 1996–present; county commissioner, Miami-Dade County, 1990–1996.

Bob Poe—Chairman, Florida Democratic Party, March 2000–January 2003.

Richard A. Posner—Judge, Seventh Circuit, U.S. Court of Appeals; author of *Breaking the Deadlock: The 2000 Election, the Constitution and the Courts.*

Peggy A. Quince—Justice, Florida Supreme Court, 1998–present.

Mark Racicot—Montana governor, 1993–2001; Chairman, Republican National Committee 2002–03.

William Rehnquist—Chief justice of the U.S. Supreme Court, 1986–present; Associate justice since 1972.

Barry Richard—Chief Florida attorney for George W. Bush in 2000 election.

Gerald Richman—West Palm Beach attorney for Harry Jacobs in his case against the Seminole County Canvassing Board.

Peggy Robbins—Supervisor of elections, Martin County.

Carol Roberts—Vice-chair, Palm Beach County Commission; member, Palm Beach County Canvassing Board.

Clay Roberts—Director, Florida Division of Elections.

Bruce Rogow—Attorney for Theresa LePore in 2000 election; argued for Gore in *Siegel v. LePore*.

Don Rubottom—Administrator of five committees in the Florida House of Representatives; advisor to Tom Feeney, speaker of the Florida House regarding constitutional significance of Amendment II of the U.S. Constitution.

Leon St. John—Palm Beach County attorney.

Joseph E. Sandler—General counsel for the Democratic National Committee; attorney for Al Gore in Florida recount.

N. Sanders Sauls—Circuit judge, Second Judicial Court, Tallahassee, Florida; rendered opinion in *Gore v. Harris*.

Chris Sauter—Attorney for Al Gore in 2000 election; co-author of "The Recount Primer," used to assist Democratic candidates facing recount challenges in 1994 campaigns.

Antonin Scalia—Associate justice, U.S. Supreme Court, 1986–present.

Bill Schneider—Senior political analyst, CNN, 1991–present.

Norman Schwarzkopf—Retired general, U.S. Army; Allied commander during the first Gulf War; Criticized the Democratic attempt to deny U.S. servicemen and servicewomen the right to vote.

Leander Shaw—Justice, Florida Supreme Court, 1983–present; Chief justice, 1990–1992.

Chesterfield Smith—Founder and chairman emeritus of powerful Holland & Knight LLP law firm; former president of American Bar Association (1973–1974).

David Hackett Souter—Associate justice, U.S. Supreme Court, 1990–present.

Dwight Stansel—Florida state representative who voted with the Republicans in trying to authorize a slate of Bush electors.

John Paul Stevens—Associate justice, U.S. Supreme Court, 1975–present.

Mac Stipanovich—Republican strategist and lobbyist; advised Katherine Harris during the 2000 recount; chief of staff for Governor Bob Martinez, 1987; campaign director, Bob Martinez, 1986.

Ken Sukhia—Attorney for George W. Bush in 2000 election; Tallahassee attorney; former U.S. Attorney.

Jake Tapper—Washington correspondent for Salon.com; author of *Down and Dirty: The Plot to Steal the Presidency*.

Irv Terrell—Member of Baker Botts law firm and key organizer for the Bush legal team; Worked on the Miami-Dade recount and on *Gore v. Harris*.

George Terwilliger—Attorney with the office of Baker, Botts, a legal advisor for George W. Bush in 2000 election; worked on *Gore v. Harris*.

Abigail Thernstrom—Commissioner, U.S. Civil Rights Commission; issued strong dissent to the report by the U.S. Commission on Civil Rights on the 2000 election in Florida.

Clarence Thomas—Associate justice, U.S. Supreme Court, 1991–present; Chairman, U.S. Equal Employment Opportunities Commission, 1982–1990.

John Thrasher—Florida state representative, 1993–2001; speaker of Florida House of Representatives, 1999–2000.

Gerald B. Tjoflat—Judge, U.S. Court of Appeals for the 11th Circuit (Atlanta, Georgia); dissented in *Siegel v. LePore* and *Touchston v. McDermott* rulings.

Jeffrey Toobin—Attorney and legal analyst for ABC News during the recount controversy (now with CNN); author of *Too Close to Call: The Thirty-Six Day Battle to Decide the 2000 Election*.

Laurence "Larry" Tribe—Harvard Law School legal scholar; author; attorney for Al Gore in 2000 election; helped write briefs, and argued constitutional issues before Judge Middlebrooks in *Siegel v. LePore*.

Lynn Utrecht—Legal counsel for Al Gore in 2000 campaign and election.

Don Van Natta—Journalist for the *New York Times*; wrote story after the 2000 election regarding military absentee ballots.

Greta Van Susteren—Legal analyst for CNN; Currently with Fox.

Mark Wallace—Attorney for George W. Bush in Palm Beach County recounts.

Craig Waters—Director of public information for Florida Supreme Court during 2000 election.

Charles T. Wells—Justice, Florida Supreme Court, 1994–present; served as chief justice from 2000–2002.

Robert Wexler—U.S. representative from Florida, 1997–present; Florida state senator, 1990–1996.

Byron "Whizzer" White—U.S. Supreme Court justice, 1962–1993.

John Yoo—Professor of law at the University of California at Berkeley School of Law; Advisor on constitutional law to Tom Feeney.

Jack Young—Recount specialist and attorney for Al Gore in 2000 election.

Steve Zack—Attorney for Al Gore in 2000 election; Active in *Gore v. Harris*.

Bob Zoellick—Chief of staff for James Baker during Florida recount.

Bob Zelnick—Professor of journalism, Boston University; author of *Gore: A Political Life;* former television reporter.

# Part II

## ➤ Court Cases and Legal Terms ◄

### 3 U.S. Sec. 5

U.S. Code, Title 3, Chapter 1, Section 5. Also known as the "safe harbor provision," regarding the determination of controversy as to appointment of electors. The statute reads: "If any State shall have provided, by laws enacted prior to the day fixed for the appointment of the electors, for its final determination of any controversy or contest concerning the appointment of all or any of the electors of such State, by judicial or other methods or procedures, and such determination shall have been made at least six days before the time fixed for the meeting of the electors, such determination made pursuant to such law so existing on said day, and made at least six days prior to said time of meeting of the electors, shall be conclusive, and shall govern in the counting of the electoral votes as provided in the Constitution, and as hereinafter regulated, so far as the ascertainment of the electors appointed by such State is concerned."

### Absentee Ballots

Florida laws governing the use of absentee ballots in elections includes:

- Florida Statute 101.62: requests for absentee ballots
  "The supervisor may accept a written or telephonic request for an absentee ballot from the elector, or, if directly instructed by the elector, a member of the elector's immediate family, or the elector's legal guardian. . . . The person making the request must disclose: the name of the elector for whom the ballot is requested; the elector's address; the last four digits of the elector's Social Security number; the registration number on the elector's registration identification card; the requester's name; the requester's address; the requester's Social Security number and, if available, the driver's license number; the requester's relationship to the elector; and the requester's signature (written requests only)."
- Florida Statute 104.047: absentee ballots and violations
  "Except as provided in s. 101.62 or s. 101.655, any person who requests an absentee ballot on behalf of an elector is guilty of a felony of the third degree. . . . "

- Florida Statue 102.68: rules for counting absentee ballots
  "After determining that all absentee ballots to be counted have been accounted for, the canvassing board proceeds to count each absentee ballot. The information on the back of the envelope and the signature is compared to determine if the vote is legal. If not, the envelope is not opened and the ballot is declared illegal. Any protests to the ballot must be adjudicated by the board. After the protests are rejected or upheld, all legal absentee ballots are counted and added to the machine totals."

## Protest Statute

Florida law governing the protest of an election is found in Florida Statutes 102.166: Any candidate for nomination or election, or any elector qualified to vote in the election complained of, may protest the return of that election. The protest may be on either of two grounds: (1) the returns are erroneous (2) the returns, or events affecting the election, were fraudulent. The protest on the basis of erroneous returns is filed with the county canvassing board. A protest alleging fraudulent returns is filed in circuit court and the venue lies in the county where the fraud occurred. In either case, the protest must be filed prior to the adjournment of the canvassing board or within five days of the date of the election, whichever occurs last. In other words, to prevail in an election protest, the complaining party must show that the outcome of the election would have been different but for the alleged error or fraud.

The protest phase allows the candidate to file an immediate complaint that the returns were either fraudulent or erroneous. That would lead to the county canvassing boards doing a check of the machines or a recount to determine the validity of the challenge. If there were no irregularities, then the vote would be officially certified by the Secretary of State. Gore protested the vote totals in four counties and asked for a manual recount in each of those counties.

## Contest Statute

Florida Statute 102.168 treats the contestation of elections:

An action may be brought in circuit court contesting the results of any election. It may be brought by any unsuccessful candidate in the case of an election for public office, or by any taxpayer in the case of a referendum. The complaint must be filed within 10 days after the adjournment of the canvassing board. The complaint must allege the grounds on which the contestant claims right to the office. The canvassing board is a party defendant. Venue for the contest is in the county where a candidate qualified or if the election was in more than one county, then in

Leon County [Tallahassee]. The complaint must allege that certain acts occurred sufficient to have affected the result. A showing of a "reasonable possibility" that the results of an election "could" have been changed by irregularities, is not sufficient to sustain voiding the election. There must be a showing of "reasonable probability" that the results would have been changed but for the complained of acts.

The contest phase of Florida election law allows the candidate to challenge the results of the certified vote. The candidate must prove a "reasonable probability", not possibility, that the results of the election would have been changed except for certain acts that occurred. In Gore's case, he argued that numerous under-votes in the state, which reflected the intent of the voter, had not been counted.

## Attorney General Opinion, 00–65 (November 14, 2000)

The Attorney General of Florida, Bob Butterworth, replied to a request by the Palm Beach County Canvassing Board by issuing an advisory opinion in regard to section 102.166 of the Florida statutes and the meaning of the statute's reference to an "error in voting tabulation which could affect the outcome" of an election. Butterworth determined that the Secretary of State's opinion, Division of Elections Opinion 00–11, was "clearly at variance with the existing Florida Statutes and case law." That opinion indicated that "error in the vote tabulation" referred only to a counting error in the vote tabulation system. If the voting system failed to read an improperly marked ballot, a recount would no longer be justified. Butterworth disagreed, saying the language of the statute clearly refers not to an error in the vote tabulation *system* [editor's emphasis], but to an error in vote tabulation. An error in vote tabulation might be due to a malfunction of the system, but might also be due to the failure of a properly functioning machine to discern the voter's choice. The key is voter intent and that can be determined by a manual examination of the ballot by the canvassing board. Butterworth also concluded that the Division of Elections exceeded the authority granted to the division by Florida law. *See also* Division of Elections Opinion 00–11.

## Certification

Florida law regarding election certification includes:

- Florida Statute 102.111 — (1) "The county canvassing board . . . shall file the county returns for the election of a federal or state officer with the Department of State immediately after certification of the election results. Returns must be filed by 5 P.M. on the 7th day following the first primary and general election. . . . If the county returns are not received by the Department of State by 5 P.M. of the seventh day following an election, all missing counties *shall* [editor's emphasis] be ignored and the results shown by the returns in file shall be certified." (2) The department shall fine each board member $200 for each day such returns are late, the fine to be paid only from the board member's personal funds . . . .

- Florida Statute 102.112—"If the returns are not received by the department [of State] by the time specified, such returns *may* [editor's emphasis] be ignored and the results on file at that time may be certified by the department."

## *Gus Beckstrom v. Volusia County Canvassing Board*, 707 So. 2d 720 (Fla., 1998)

1998 Florida Supreme Court ruling that established that, to contest an election, a plaintiff does not have to show fraud or intentional wrong-doing. An election could be voided even if there was no fraud, if there were substantial noncompliance with statutory election procedures and if there were reasonable doubt that the election expressed the will of the voters.

## *Boardman v. Esteva*, 323 So. 2d 259 (Fla., 1975)

In the October 3, 1972 election to a seat on the Second District Court of Appeals for Florida, Edward Boardman beat Henry Esteva by 249 votes. That majority came entirely from 3,389 absentee ballots. Esteva brought suit in the circuit court since he had received 404 more machine votes than Boardman. Esteva alleged 1,450 irregularities in the absentee ballot count, but a trial judge found only 88 irregularities and ruled for Boardman. The District Court of Appeals reversed the verdict and found for Esteva. The Florida Supreme Court overturned the DCA and ruled finally for Boardman.

The Florida Supreme Court's decision stated that the principal consideration in an election contest is whether the will of the people has been affected. The Court ruled that the foremost concern in determining validity of absentee ballots was whether they were cast by qualified, registered voters, who were entitled to vote absentee and did so in a proper manner. The court provided further guidance to the canvassing boards by listing the following factors to be considered:

(1) The presence or absence of fraud, gross negligence, or intentional wrongdoing,
(2) Whether there has been substantial compliance with the essential requirements of the absentee voting law, and,
(3) Whether the irregularities complained of adversely affect the sanctity of the ballot and the integrity of the election.

In this case, the Supreme Court ruled that strict compliance with the absentee voting law was not necessary and that merely technical violations of absentee ballot rules would not invalidate the absentee votes. In effect, in order to invalidate absentee ballots, the plaintiff had to prove more than a technical violation of the law, but need not prove anything as serious as fraud.

## *Bush v. Gore*, 531 U.S. 98 (2000)

The 5-4 *per curiam* decision by the U.S. Supreme Court at 10 P.M. on December 12 ended the recount controversy and awarded the presidency to George W. Bush. The Supreme Court stopped all recounting and did not remand the decision back to Florida for a resumption of the recount. The five justices in the majority were Rehnquist, Scalia, O'Connor, Thomas, and Kennedy. Dissenting were Stevens, Breyer, Ginsburg, and Souter. The high court accepted Bush's appeal of the Florida Supreme Court's 4-3 decision in *Gore v. Harris*, which mandated the counting of the undervotes in the state where there had not already been a recount and had awarded Gore votes in Miami-Dade and Palm Beach County. The U.S. Supreme Court ruled, by 7-2 vote, that the Florida system of manually recounting ballots violated the equal protection clause of the Fourteenth Amendment [*see Equal Protection Clause*]. On this issue, Justices Scalia, Thomas, Rehnquist, O'Connor, and Kennedy were joined by Souter and Breyer, while Stevens and Ginsburg dissented. Souter and Breyer, however, while agreeing that there was an equal protection problem, concluded that the problem could be corrected. The 5-member majority of the court decided that because different standards were used in different counties and, as such, with an absence of specific standards, the recount could not avoid arbitrary and disparate treatment of the members of the electorate. Justices Souter and Breyer argued that the state courts in Florida could decide on a fair system of hand-counting and allow for the hand-counting to resume. Justice Ginsburg thought the issue should have been resolved by state courts. Justice Stevens saw no constitutional violations. The court also ruled that the issues were moot. Because of the safe harbor provision, which took effect two hours after the court handed down its verdict, the state did not have time to complete the recount. Finally, the U.S. Supreme Court declared that the Florida Supreme Court, in changing certification from November 14 to November 26, had changed the law and thus had violated Article II of the U.S. Constitution. Justice Stevens noted in his dissent that in the 2000 election, "the identity of the loser is perfectly clear. It is the Nation's confidence in the judge as an impartial guardian of the rule of law."

## "Cert"

*See Writ of Certiorarl*

## Chads

The bits of paper from an IBM card or numbered tabs punched out with a stylus by the voter. [*See* Votomatic]. Classifications of chads include the following:

- Dimpled or pregnant chads: a visible impression, best seen from the back of the ballot, that has pushed the chad up, but did not detach it from the ballot.
- Pinprick: a mark in which the ballot has been punched through with a stylus and light can be seen through the hole, but the chad has not been dislodged.
- Detached chad: one, two or three corners. When the chad has been detached from the ballot by the number of corners indicated, but has not been completely punched through.
- Cleanly punched chad: A clear vote, although the machines might have missed these ballots or the chads might have fallen off after November 7.

## *Darby v. State*

Florida Supreme Court ruling in 1917 stating that when voters' intent can be discerned, the vote should count, even if a mistake is made on the ballot. Each ballot should be examined for evidence of the voter's intent based on the totality of the circumstances

## DCA

District Court of Appeals

## *Delahunt v. Johnson*, 423 Mass. 731 (1996)

1996 Massachusetts Superior Court case in which William Delahunt, under Massachusetts law, which required elections officials to gauge the "intent of the voter," won a Congressional primary when 956 dimpled ballots were counted as valid.

## *De Novo*

To begin anew.

## Division of Elections Opinion 00–11 (November 13, 2000)

Given in response to a request from the Palm Beach County Canvassing Board to clarify the meaning of Florida Statue 102.166, to wit, "error in voting tabulation which could affect the outcome of" an election. The Division's opinion, which was legally binding, concluded that the error in vote tabulation referred only to a counting error in the vote tabulation *system* [editor's emphasis]. The inability of a voting system to read an improperly marked ballot would not trigger a recount of all ballots.

## Election Canvassing Commission

Florida statute 102.111 establishes this commission which by law consisted of the governor and two members of the cabinet selected by the governor. In 2000, the commission included Governor Jeb Bush, the secretary of state (Katherine Harris), and the director of the Division of Elections (Clay Roberts). In the 2002 recount Governor Jeb Bush recused himself and was replaced by Bob Crawford, Secretary of Agriculture. The law states that the commission "shall, as soon as the official results are compiled from all counties, certify the results of the election and determine and declare who has been elected for each office."

## Electoral Count Act, 1877

Enacted to avoid future chaos after the disputed Rutherford B. Hayes-Samuel Tilden election of 1876. Part of this act was incorporated into U.S. Code as 3 U.S.C. section 15. The act provided a regulatory apparatus for the ascertainment and counting of lawful electoral votes in Congress. The act gave the states the leading role in resolving disputes involving electors and an incentive to have in place a method for resolving those controversies in a timely fashion. The law provided that if a state does not chose electors by the date set by law, the state legislature is authorized to choose electors. Subsequent sections of the act specified the procedures that Congress would follow if the state failed to meet the safe harbor or if two or more sets of electors are submitted from a state to Congress. The key issue arising from this act in *Bush v. Gore* was whether or not the "safe harbor" could be interpreted as a firm deadline beyond which recounts could not proceed. In *Bush v. Gore*, the U.S. Supreme Court ruled decisively in the affirmative. [*See Bush v. Gore*]

## Electoral Reform Act of 2001

Legislation passed by the Florida legislature to address some of the problems highlighted by the 2000 U.S. presidential recount. Provisions of the Act included:

- Punch-cards, paper ballots and lever machines were eliminated and all new systems had to employ precinct based tabulation, allowing the voter to correct a mistake. Funding was provided to purchase the new machines.

- Voters whose eligibility cannot be determined on Election Day may vote a provisional or conditional ballot. If the voter is determined to be eligible, then the ballot will be counted in the final tally.
- With regard to recounts:
  (1) To address the equal protection problems identified by the U.S. Supreme Court, the act requires the same manner of recount to be conducted in each affected jurisdiction. For state-wide elections, recounts will be conducted in every county in Florida and there would be no more partial recounts. The act does away with the canvassing boards' standardless and unfettered discretion to order recounts. An automatic manual recount of the overvotes and undervotes will be conducted if the margin of victory is one-quarter of one percent or less. If the margin of victory is between one-quarter and one-half of one percent, an affected candidate or party is entitled to a manual recount of the over-votes and under-votes if requested in writing no later than 5 P.M. on the second day after the election.
  (2) A vote will count only if there is a "clear indication on the ballot that the voter has made a definite choice." The Department of State was charged with describing precisely what "definite choice" meant.
- The second primary was eliminated for the 2002 election cycle.
- All registered voters may cast an absentee ballot without restrictions as the "for cause" requirement was deleted. In other words, anyone was entitled to request an absentee ballot and did not have to provide a reason (illness, out of town). The voter no longer needed to provide Social Security or voter identification numbers. The only requirements are the signature of the voter and the signature and address of a witness eighteen years or older.
- The act also provided for increased training for poll workers, better voter education, the posting of a Voter's Bill of Rights and Responsibilities at each polling place, and the creation of a state-wide Voter Registration Database.
- The act eliminated the previous provision which allowed a circuit judge unfettered discretion in fashioning orders, or in ordering investigations to correct any alleged wrong and providing direct relief.

## En Banc

In full court, with full judicial authority and with all the judges present.

## Electors (Presidential)

According to Article II of the U.S. Constitution: "Each state shall appoint in such manner as the legislature thereof may direct, a number of electors, equal to the whole number of Senators and Representatives to which the

State may be entitled in Congress. . . . The Congress may determine the time of choosing the electors and the day on which they shall give their votes, which day shall be the same throughout the United States."

## Equal Protection Clause

As part of the Fourteenth Amendment to the U.S. Constitution. Section 1: "All persons born or naturalized in the United States, and subject to the jurisdiction thereof, are citizens of the United States and of the state wherein they reside. No state shall make or enforce any law which shall abridge the privileges or immunities of citizens of the United States; nor shall any state deprive any person of life, liberty or property, without due process of law; *nor deny to any person within its jurisdiction the equal protection of its laws*" [editor's emphasis].

## Fourteenth Amendment

*See* Equal Protection Clause.

## *Andre Fladell v. Palm Beach County Canvassin Board*, 772 So. 2d 1240 (Fla., 2000)

Andre Fladell and two other voters in Palm Beach County brought the first lawsuit of the 2000 recount. The lawsuit challenged the legality of the Palm Beach butterfly ballot, argued it was confusing and caused voters to miscast their votes and asked for a new election. Judge LaBarga ruled that he had no authority to order a re-vote in a presidential election. The Florida Supreme Court upheld LaBarga in a unanimous *per curiam* opinion. The justices concluded that "a court should not void an election for ballot form defects unless such defects cause the ballot to be in substantial non-compliance with the statutory election requirements . . . [and that] such defects operate to prevent [a] free, fair and open choice."

## First Amendment

"Congress shall make no law respecting an establishment of religion, prohibiting the free exercise thereof; or abridging the freedom of speech, or of the press; or the right of the people peaceably to assemble, and to petition the government for a redress of grievances."

## *Force Majeure Provision*

An Act of God or an inevitable accident (such as a hurricane) or war that excuses the fulfillment of a contract.

## *Gore v. Harris*, 772 So. 2d 1243 (Fla., 2000)

On December 8, in a shocking and unexpected vote of 4-3 (with Justices Pariente, Anstead, Quince, and Lewis in the affirmative and Harding, Wells, and Shaw dissenting), the Florida Supreme Court overturned Judge Sanders Sauls's decision in which he denied Gore's contest of the election and his bid to have additional votes counted in Miami-Dade, Palm Beach, and Nassau counties. Sauls had ruled that Gore did not prove a probability that the election outcome would be changed (although Sauls counted no votes) and that the canvassing boards had not abused their discretion.

The Florida Supreme Court ordered a recount of all the undervotes in the state, awarded Gore 215 votes in Palm Beach County, 168 votes in Miami-Dade and demanded the counting of approximately 9,000 votes in Miami-Dade which had never been manually reviewed. They ordered the Circuit Court, under Judge Terry Lewis, after Judge Sauls recused himself, to begin all recounts forthwith. The basis of the court's ruling was that the contest statute in Florida required judges to correct any problems when a certified election failed to include a number of legal votes which might have changed the outcome of the election. The Court, in addition, accepted the view that a ballot was "legal," even if it was filled out improperly so that it could not be read by the machine, if the intent of the voter could be determined.

## Grandfather Clause

A statutory or constitutional device passed by seven southern states between 1895 and 1910 to prevent American blacks from voting. The laws provided that those who enjoyed the right to vote prior to 1866–67, or their lineal descendants, would be exempt from any educational, property, or tax requirements for voting. Since blacks had not been granted the franchise until 1870, this law eliminated the possibility of former slaves voting, but assured the vote for illiterate and poor whites. The U.S. Supreme Court invalidated the grandfather clause in 1915 on the grounds that it violated equal voting rights guaranteed by the Fifteenth Amendment.

## Greenberg-Traurig Law Firm

Law firm of Barry Richard, with headquarters in Tallahassee. This was the primary firm representing George W. Bush in numerous court cases.

## Hatch Act

Passed by the U.S. Congress in 1939 and amended in 1940, aimed at eliminating corrupt practices in federal elections. Sponsored by Senator Carl Hatch of New Mexico, the act forbade bribery or intimidation of voters and restricted political campaigning by federal employees. It also significantly limited contributions by individuals to political campaigns and spending by campaign committees.

## Hayes-Tilden Election (1876)

A close election between Rutherford B. Hayes and Samuel Tilden in which the election was decided by a special commission. The dispute began when Florida and three other states, plus one electoral vote in Oregon, submitted two slates of electors—a total of 20 electoral votes. Hayes had 165 electoral votes and Tilden had 184, with 185 needed for election. In Florida, the Republican state canvassing board submitted a slate of electors favoring Hayes while the Democratic legislature did the same for Tilden. To adjudicate the dispute, Congress appointed an Electoral Commission, made up of five congressmen, five senators and five members of the U.S. Supreme Court. On purely partisan grounds, the commission voted 8-7 to award all 20 disputed electoral votes to Hayes, thus making him President. To prevent this from happening again, Congress passed the Electoral Count Act of 1877. *See* Electoral Count Act (1877).

## *Harry Jacobs v. Seminole County Canvassing Board*, 773 So 2d 519 (Fla., 2000)

Referred to as "the Seminole County case." Harry Jacobs, a local Democratic lawyer not affiliated with the Gore campaign, brought suit to challenge the effort of Republican Party officials who were allowed to supply missing voter information on Republican absentee ballots. Jacobs charged that Sandra Goard, the Supervisor of Elections for Seminole County, allowed Republican party operatives to spend ten days in her office correcting 2,126 Republican absentee ballot applications so they would not be thrown out. The result was 1,833 additional votes from registered Republicans. The lawsuit argued that Florida law stated that third parties were prohibited from filling in information on forms already signed, that this action had not been allowed before and that Democrats were not provided the same opportunity as Republicans. Judge Terry Lewis ruled that while Goard demonstrated bad judgment, her actions were not egregious enough to warrant the extreme remedy of disqualifying all the absentee ballots in the county and thwarting the will of the people. There was no evidence of fraud or a substantial noncompliance with the election statutes. Despite irregularities in the request for absentee ballots, the results reflected the full and fair expression of the will of the voters. On December 12, 2000, the Florida Supreme Court unanimously affirmed Judge Lewis's ruling.

## Intent of the Voter Standard

Florida law governing the canvassing of election returns includes these excerpts of Florida Statute 101.5614:

- No vote shall be declared invalid or void *if there is a clear indication of the intent of the voter as determined by the canvassing board* . . . [editor's emphasis].
- If an elector marks more names than there are persons to be elected to an office [often called an overvote–editor] or if it is impossible to determine the elector's choice, the elector's ballot shall not be counted for that office, but the ballot shall not be invalidated as to those names which are properly marked. . . .
- The return printed by the automatic tabulating equipment, to which has been added the return of write-in, absentee and manually counted votes, shall constitute the official return of the election. . . .

## "*Lewis I*" and "*Lewis II*"

See *McDermott v. Harris*.

## *McDermott v. Harris*

Also known as *Lewis I*. The Volusia County Canvassing Board filed a complaint in the state circuit court asking the court to allow them to certify the results of the presidential recount "without regard to the deadline of 5 P.M. November 14, 2000" and to issue an injunction against the Secretary of State preventing her from ignoring results submitted after that deadline. Judge Terry Lewis initially ruled that Katherine Harris could not decide ahead of time what late returns would or would not be ignored but had to "properly exercise her discretion in making a decision on the returns. . . . " He ruled that he did not have the authority to enjoin the Secretary to make a certain decision and explained that the law was explicit in requiring the filing of returns by 5 P.M. on November 14. In *Lewis II*, the judge ruled that the Secretary had the legal discretion to refuse to accept late-filed returns in the certified results. She had exercised her discretion and had not acted arbitrarily.

## *Marbury v. Madison,* 5 U.S. 137 (1803)

The 1803 case that establishes judicial review, the idea that courts should determine whether statutes were unconstitutional.

## *McPherson v. Blacker,* 146 U.S. 1 (1892)

An 1892 case over the constitutionality of a Michigan statute that allowed the legislature to allocate electors on the basis of a congressional district rather than by the state as a whole. The U.S. Supreme Court ruled that since the federal constitution gives the power to the states to determine how electors are chosen and the duly elected and constitutionally mandated legislature acts, then Michigan may allot electors any way it chooses. Also the U.S. constitution allowed state legislatures under Article II the power to select electors and the state is limited in circumscribing that authority.

## Miami-Dade Democratic Party v. Miami-Dade Canvassing Board, 773, So. 2d 1179 (Fla., 2000)

The Miami-Dade Democratic Party sought an emergency *writ of mandamus* to compel the Canvassing Board to continue the manual recount of ballots. The board had voted on November 22 that it would have been impossible to meet the November 26 deadline set by the Florida Supreme Court and thus suspended the manual recount. The Florida Supreme Court denied the writ since it had been determined that the task was impossible. One of several decisions by the Florida Supreme Court that went against Gore.

## One Florida Initiative

On November 9, 1999, Governor Jeb Bush announced the creation of the One Florida Initiative. The goal was to increase opportunity and diversity in state universities without using discriminatory policies or quotas. Governor Bush indicated it was not to abandon affirmative action, but to redefine it. One key aspect was to guarantee students in the top twenty percent of their graduating class admission to one of the eleven state universities and to give them priority for the awarding of scholarship funds based on need.

## Optical-Scan Voting Machines

Forty-one counties in Florida used these machines: some were precinct-based, others were counted in a central location. Voters in these counties darken an oval or connect two parts of an arrow with a special pen or pencil provided. Some voters underlined, circled, or otherwise mismarked their ballots. The precinct-based machines would catch an overvote and notify the elector.

## Palm Beach County Canvassing Board v. Harris, 772 So. 2d 1220 (Fla., 2000)

The Palm Beach County Canvassing Board asked for a clarification of Florida law as to whether Secretary of State Harris could accept returns after 5 P.M. on the seventh day after the election (November 14). By a 7-0 vote, the Florida Supreme Court ordered the recounts to continue and ordered Harris to accept the results of these recounts until 5 P.M. on Sunday afternoon, November 26, if the office were open. If not, the amended certifications would be accepted until 9 A.M. on Monday, November 27. The Court stressed the importance of the will of the people and that the election laws must be liberally construed in favor of the citizen's right to vote. In effect, they chastised Harris for "summarily" disenfranchising innocent voters in order to punish canvassing boards for late returns. In fashioning this remedy, the court did not explain how it arrived at the November 26 date and this would became a critical issue when the U.S. Supreme Court, in *Bush v. Palm Beach Count Canvassing Board*, vacated the Florida Supreme Court's decision in the above case. The U.S. Supreme Court remanded the case back to the Florida Supreme Court for a clarification as to whether their decision was based exclusively on the Florida statutes or on a legal standard other than the Florida statutes, such as the Florida constitution or the court's own equitable powers.

## Per Curiam

A decision written by the court as a whole rather than authored by an individual justice.

## Prima Facie Case

A case in which the evidence presented is sufficient for a judgment unless the evidence is contested.

## Pullen v. Mulligan

A 1990 Illinois case in which the Illinois Supreme Court ruled that where the intent of the voter can be ascertained with reasonable certainty, those votes must be counted, even thought the ballot is not strictly in conformity with the law. A ballot should not be invalidated simply because the machine cannot read it.

## Punch-Card Machines

*See* Votomatic.

## "Safe Harbor Provision"

*See* 3 U.S. 5.

## "Seminole County Case"

See *Harry Jacobs v. Seminole County Canvassing Board*.

## *Siegel v. LePore and Touchston v. McDermott*

Suits brought by the Bush campaign to challenge the practice of conducting recounts in Florida as a violation of the Fourteenth Amendment (since votes were evaluated by a different standard in each county) and due process. They sought to enjoin four Florida counties from conducting manual recounts. The district court had denied their appeal for injunctive relief and, by a vote of 8-4, the 11th Circuit Court of Appeals, in an *en banc* decision, affirmed the lower court to deny the injunction. Chief Judge R. Lanier Anderson, writing for the majority, did not find that a recount would provide irreparable harm to Bush and that plaintiffs had failed to establish a reason for federal court intervention on either equal protection or due process grounds. However, the dissenters argued that the selective manual recounts violated the equal protection rights of voters in other counties not chosen for the recount by the Gore team.

## Steel Hector Law Firm

Prominent Miami law firm whose managing partner at the time, Joe Klock, represented Katherine Harris and used the expertise and resources of the firm to assist in the representation.

## Sunshine Law, Fla Statute ch. 286.011

Florida state law requiring public access to any governmental meeting, court proceeding, processes, records, etc.

## *Ronald Taylor v. Martin County Canvassing Board*

The Republican Party had disseminated preprinted absentee ballots forms (requesting an absentee ballot), but the voter identification numbers were left off the form. The Democrats also put out such forms, but their forms contained the voter identification number. Peggy Robbins, Supervisor of Elections, received a number of Republican request forms with missing or incorrect voter identification numbers on them. There was a policy in the supervisor's office of not issuing absentee ballots when the elector's voter registration number was missing or incorrect on the request form. There was also an office policy not to fill in any missing information or make any corrections or alterations to the request form without the express author-ity of the elector. Nonetheless, Robbins allowed Republican Party officials to take the forms, which would have been rejected, from the building and fill in the proper identification numbers. The corrected forms were processed and the absentee ballots were mailed to the voters.

Democratic voters in the county sued to invalidate all the absentee ballots. The suit alleged that Robbins had violated Florida election law and thus was guilty of "non-compliance" with the law. The remedy was to throw all the absentee ballots in the county or adjust the certified vote totals to eliminate the inappropriate benefit Bush derived from the altering of the requests. A statistician estimated that Bush received 558 extra votes.

Lewis, in his decision, presented jointly with Judge Nikki Clark's ruling in the Seminole County case, agreed that Martin had violated state statute, but since the documents in question were ballot requests, not the absentee ballots themselves, this technical violation did not affect the integrity of the ballots. It was decided that the elimination of all absentee ballots was too draconian a remedy and punished those who had properly applied for an absentee ballot. Also, Martin had not treated the Democrats unequally and the sanctity of the ballot and the integrity of the election were not affected. The Florida Supreme Court upheld Judge Lewis's ruling.

## Twelfth Amendment

This part of the U.S. Constitution stipulates that, after the chosen electors meet in their respective states and cast their ballots, the votes are then sent to the president of the Senate, who "shall, in the presence of the Senate and House of Representatives, open all the certificates and the votes shall then be counted."

## Votomatic

Also known as punch-card machines. Twenty-five Florida counties use this method, which was invented in 1962. There are several different brands of Votomatic machines.

Voters are directed to insert an IBM "punch-card" into the machine and then use a stylus or other sharp object to punch through tabs or "chads" corresponding to the candidate's name, leaving a hole to indicate a vote for that candidate. The Votomatics were considered very reliable machinery (and, in fact, had fewer rejected ballots than the optical-scan machines), but some experts argued that there could be a "chad build-up," which might lead to dimpled ballots through no fault of the voter.

## *Writ of Certiorari*

Often called "cert" by attorneys. A written order from a higher court to a lower court requesting a transcript of judicial proceedings of a case for review, a writ of certiorari can serve as a method of getting a case heard on appeal by the Supreme Court of the United States.

## *Writ of Mandamus*

A written order from a superior court ordering a public official, a lower court, or an individual body to perform a specified duty.

# PART III

# INTERVIEWS: PALM BEACH COUNTY CANVASSING BOARD

# ➤ JUDGE CHARLES BURTON ◄

Charles Burton, a County Court Judge, served as the chairman of the Palm Beach Canvassing Board during the 2000 recount controversy. He received his undergraduate degree from Suffolk University in 1980 and his Juris Doctorate from Nova University College of Law in 1984. After law school, he was a partner in the law firm Burton and Burton in Boca Raton from 1990 to 1995. Following that, he served as Assistant State Attorney in the Fifteenth Judicial Circuit. In May of 2000, Governor Jeb Bush appointed Burton to the Palm Beach County Court.

Judge Burton began his interview with a discussion of how he came to be a member of the Canvassing Board, his responsibilities on Election Day when he realized that it was going to be an extraordinary election, and how the board organized the manual recount. When asked about the accuracy of the Votomatic, Burton answered that "the key to voting in this country is not in the machinery," but in "voter education, and until we get people learning how to vote and in taking the act of voting seriously, you are never going to have accuracy." Burton then reflected on the partisanship of Katherine Harris and Attorney General Bob Butterworth, both of whom Burton felt were acting solely on behalf of their respective parties.

In response to the 7-0 Florida Supreme Court decision, Burton observed that the election laws are "horribly written . . . with so many inconsistencies." He pointed out that during the recount "it was not right to be going back changing [the] standards because one party was unhappy with the vote totals they were coming out with," and that "it was ridiculous the way [the standards] were being applied." He also noted that the 4-3 Florida Supreme Court decision on December 8 that ordered an immediate manual recount of all undervotes in the state was "clearly contrary to Florida law on a manual recount." Burton felt that the recount was "all strategy, political strategy" and that bothered him more than anything. He concluded his discussion of the recount with the observation that it was amazing "that we can elect a president by counting dings and nicks and spit-marks."

Burton elaborated on the difficulty in counting votes under extraordinary pressure, especially when it "became clear that the Republicans were there to slow down and hinder the process because they never wanted to see the count finished." When asked about the Palm Beach County Canvassing Board's request to extend its counting process beyond the November 26 deadline, Burton answered that he did not find Katherine Harris's decision to deny the request as persuasive and he "did not believe that she actually read any of those requests for the extension." He also stated that the "Gore team would have been much better off either (1) asking for a full state recount [or 2], just bypassing the recount and . . . [contesting] the election statewide." He concluded his interview with an assessment of the newspaper recounts conducted by the *New York Times*, the *Miami Herald*, and other papers. Since they all resulted in different numbers, the recount was inconclusive. Burton believed that "manually recounting the punch-cards is not a very accurate process . . . and [we] will never know who won this election."

Judge Charles Burton was interviewed by the author on April 5, 2001.

P: How did you come to be a member of the Palm Beach County canvassing board?

B: I was appointed to the bench in May of 2000 as county court judge. Sometime around August . . . of 2000, I was contacted by our chief judge's office. His judicial assistant called me and said that the chief judge would like me to serve on the canvassing board, to which my response was, that is fine, but what the hell is a canvassing board? And [I] was told that basically the function of a canvassing board was, you pretty much supervised the voting equipment, and because this was a presidential year, you may have to work a little late on that particular day. That is pretty much how I came to be there . . . [since] Florida statute states that the canvassing board shall consist of a county court judge who shall serve as chairman, a county commissioner, and a supervisor of elections.

P: What is your political affiliation?

B: I have been a registered Democrat my whole life. Of course, as a judge, you serve nonpartisan and that is . . . how I . . . viewed my role here.

P: And the other two members of the canvassing board were also Democrats?

B: Right, Carol Roberts, the county commissioner, is a Democrat, and Theresa LePore, who was the supervisor of elections, is also a registered Democrat.

P: Should the supervisor of elections be nonpartisan?

B: Absolutely. I think it is ridiculous to make the supervisor of elections, certainly outwardly, owe any allegiance to any party. [He or she] should certainly be in the same position a judge is in, to be nonpartisan.

P: What were your responsibilities on Election Day?

B: I went over to the elections office at 4:00 that afternoon, November 7, and met with Theresa LePore and Carol Roberts. About 4:00, we got together in a conference room and went through the remaining absentee ballots that needed to be looked at. We also do another testing of the machine counters. A preprogrammed set of ballots are run through all the machines to make sure they are counting accurately, and we go through those results and make sure there is no error.

P: When did you realize that this was going to be an extraordinary election?

B: I had voted myself [by] absentee [ballot] the Friday before, and so when I got there at 4:00, I do not remember if it was Theresa or Carol, one of them, brought over a ballot—it was the Votomatic—and said, vote for Gore. So I put in a ballot and I looked at it and punched out Gore and [said,] what is the problem? Well, people have been complaining they are confused by the ballot, and there is a big hoopla going on. As the night went on, we realized it was a close election, but quite honestly, Gore was way ahead in Palm Beach County. He had won Palm Beach County by over 100,000 votes, so I really was not thinking anything was going to be happening in Palm Beach. I probably got home about 3:30 that morning. I got a call from Theresa LePore about 10:00 the next morning saying we had to do a mandatory recount, and you need to come back in.

P: The difference in the voting was one-half of one percent and thus required an automatic recount?

B: The original recount we had to do was mandatory under statute, so that was simply running all the ballots through the machines. After we did the mandatory recount, the Democratic Party filed the request for a hand recount, the Republican Party filed the request that we do another machine recount, and we granted both of those. So the first manual recount is one percent. The precincts are chosen by the party requesting it, so they were chosen by the Democratic Party. What we did was pull out the three precincts they wanted to have looked at. Those came up a little bit less than one percent of the vote, so then Theresa LePore, the supervisor, just picked another precinct that would be closest to that number. So, at the same time we were doing the 1 percent hand recount, we were also in the process of running them all through the machine again.

P: How accurate is a hand recount?

B: One thing that I think has been demonstrated in manual recounting of punch-card ballots is [that] no two people get the same results. So I think [manual recounts] leave a lot to be desired [regarding accuracy], and I think that it is far too subjective a process to be able to have any certainty as to the results.

P: Why did Theresa LePore choose the "butterfly ballot," and did you have any input into that decision?

B: Florida law has a Division of Elections which is under the control of the Secretary of State, but each of the 67 counties has their own supervisor of elections. While the Division of Elections, through the secretary of state's office, tells the various supervisors the order the candidates must be in, that is all they tell them, and so ballot design is up to the individual supervisors. It is strictly up to the supervisor, so we did not have any input in the ballot design. But Theresa's main thing is she has been fairly active in dealing with the [Americans with] Disabilities Act and, knowing the population here in south Florida, quite a few elderly, she felt that if she had put the twenty names, the [presidential] candidates plus the ten vice-presidential candidates, on one page, the print was going to be very small and people were going to have difficulty reading it. She thought it would be a better idea to make the print bigger and split it over two pages. Needless to say, no good deed goes unpunished.

P:   How accurate is the Votomatic, the punch-card voting machine?

B:   I will tell you I certainly don't have any extraordinary expertise in this area other than having just been through this last election, but I really believe the key to voting in this country is not in the machinery. If people do not know how to vote, it really does not matter what system you use or how technologically advanced it is. The key, in my view, is voter education, and until we get people learning how to vote and taking the act of voting seriously, you are never going to have accuracy. I think the Votomatic is okay, but it is clear to me [that] people do not use it right. The other thing that really occurred to me in this whole process is that this stuff has been going on for years, politicians have known about it for years, it just never was an issue, because we never had an election this close.

P:   What was the reason for the large number of both undervotes and overvotes in Palm Beach County?

B:   Overvotes were interesting. Granted, in Palm Beach, we saw more combinations, for example, of Gore-Buchanan overvotes. Obviously, the ballot was a factor. [Y]ou know, if you vote for two people for the same race, your vote is not going to count. It struck me as odd that people . . . did not know that.

P:   If you had to judge an overvote.

B:   You cannot. It is impossible. That is what struck me about the manual recount of overvotes, because overvotes are where two or more are punched. If you have a Gore vote clearly punched and a Buchanan vote clearly punched, there is no way to determine what the intent of the voter is. Now, I have had people say to me, well, gee, obviously they intended to vote for Gore. Well, I don't think you can make that assumption, because then as a board you are not counting votes, you are casting votes.

The undervotes are a different problem. The undervotes have now become famous, the dimples and nicks and dings and impressions, and those are left when a person touches that part of the ballot and does not punch all the way through. [T]he Democratic Party wanted every impression, ding, nick, dimple, spit mark [to] count as a vote. The Republicans, of course, did not. But that was always my concern . . . does some little impression that you can hardly see really show the clear intent of the voter or not?

P:   I thought it was very interesting that 96 percent of the people who voted in Palm Beach County did it correctly. That indicates more of a voter error than a machine error, does it not?

B: It clearly indicates voter error. Those machine counters were tested a total of seven times, and every time, certainly on the preprogrammed ballots, they tested 100 percent accuracy. [I]f the voter does not do it right, do you just toss it or do you go through this process of manual recounting to try and determine voter intent?

P: What is your reaction to the charge that, if their vote was invalid as an undervote or overvote, the problem was due to the machine or a confusing ballot and thus, voters have been disenfranchised?

B: I have never liked the term "voter disenfranchisement" as it pertained to this election. Were there votes that did not get counted? Absolutely, there were a lot of them. But while people focus, for example, on Palm Beach County, . . . if you really want to know who won this election, let us go across the country, because there were 1.2 million undervotes, and let us go count all of those. I have come to realize voting is something that we need to, as citizens, pay more attention [to]. I just think it is incumbent on the voter to do it right.

P: When the canvassing board decided to do a manual recount of all the ballots, what was behind your thinking?

B: We had been doing the one-percent manual recount and the total machine recount again . . . and our county commissioner [Carol Roberts] at that time made a motion for a full manual recount. We had found in the one-percent recount that Gore had gained 19 votes, and her opinion was that, gee, that is one percent, so if we multiply that out, there could be a difference of 1,900 votes and that would be enough to affect the election, and we ought to move forward with a manual recount. I was concerned about even the legality of a recount, because the Florida statute talked about if there is an error in the vote tabulation system. So, number one, you need an error in the vote tabulation system, and we felt our vote tabulation system had checked out 100 percent.

There was a lawyer from the Division of Elections [Kerey Carpenter] here that evening who was basically telling me she did not think the manual recount was lawful. I just simply felt we ought to look into it before rushing into a decision. Quite honestly, I was upset by the entire tenor because, rather than a motion to have a manual recount, it appeared to me to be more of a Gore-Lieberman pep rally.

P: And you did request an opinion about the recount from the Florida Secretary of State?

B: Not the Secretary of State, [but] the Florida Division of Elections. For some reason, I was criticized . . . for calling or asking the state Division of Elections, who was in charge of all this. Of course, now I know the reason I was criticized was because the Democrats realized the opinion we were going to get and then, therefore, why would you go ask? I always found that interesting that, as a judge, I am sitting here trying to follow the law and obey the law, and they are basically . . . [saying,] you are better off ignoring the law, because you are not going to like the answer you get. So, two days later when we met, we basically agreed to ask the Division of Elections [and the Florida] Attorney General [to] give us some help and give us some guidance.

P: Let me ask you about the opinion from Clay Roberts. He seemed pretty clear that you would only be justified in a manual recount if there had been a machine error.

B: Right.

P: Then Bob Butterworth presented a totally different opinion. Butterworth said Roberts had misinterpreted the law and the canvassing board had the authority to conduct a manual recount. So now you have two conflicting legal opinions. What did you do at that point?

B: As I said, being a new judge, I am trying to be as nonpartisan as humanly possible, and ultimately what we wound up realizing is that everybody up the chain was acting very partisan. We had the Secretary of State who controls the Division of Elections, who is a Bush campaign supporter, giving us one view. We have the [Florida] Attorney General, who is a Gore campaign supporter, giving us another view. What was actually interesting to me is, if you go to the Attorney General's website, he specifically states on the website, which we did not know beforehand, if you have an elections opinion, you need to go to the Division of Elections because we do not do those, but yet he did [give an opinion] in that instance. What I did not realize ahead of time, but did learn subsequently, is that the opinion of the Division of Elections is binding on the party who asked for it. We asked for it as a board, and I felt we were bound by it. My attitude and our legal counsel's attitude was that we ought to just go to a court and say, tell us what to do; we have got two opinions.

P: If you were just looking at those two opinions from a judge's point of view, would you have been persuaded by either one?

B: Well, the Attorney General's opinion dealt with the issue of the legislative intent that all votes should be counted, and that clearly is our history. We certainly want to try and count all votes. I think the Division of Elections opinion was more accurate, based on statutory construction. We had error in getting the votes counted, but we felt that was really as a result of voter error, not the machine error.

P: Expand on your reaction to what you clearly feel were "political" decisions by Bob Butterworth and Katherine Harris.

B: I think it was clear that Secretary of State Katherine Harris would have certified this election on November 6 if she could have, but I think it is equally clear that the Attorney General was doing what he could for his party to keep the recounts going. That is the thing that, when I look back on this whole experience, was one of the most frustrating things. I honestly believe that the judiciary was acting in a nonpartisan way, trying to do what they did because they think it is right under the law.

P: Katherine Harris decided that she was going to hold to her standard: the legal deadline of seven days, November 14. Did you think that was a partisan decision?

B: Do I think she was motivated by partisanship? Absolutely. On the other hand, I will tell you, do I think she had the legal footing under the law to do what she did? Absolutely, and that was the real dilemma because our election law, as it was written, allowed for her to do these things.

P: The law is a little bit confusing, because in one section the law says that ballots missing the deadline "*shall*" be ignored and then later it says "*may*" be ignored.

B: I wrote to the Division of Elections to get an opinion on that very issue: we have one statute that says "*shall*," one statute that says "*may*." Of course, they come back with the opinion that we interpret the "may" to be only in natural disasters, hurricanes, tornados, whatever, so we are going to hold you to that, and if Palm Beach County's votes are not in [by November 14], none of Palm Beach County's votes are going to get counted. Of course, that was one of my concerns, you talk about disenfranchising, that we are going to wind up disenfranchising 460,000 people in the process.

P: She could have delayed certification three days until November 17 when the overseas absentee-ballots were counted, could she not?

B: It is interesting, Florida law provides for manual recount, yet under the law as it is written, counties like Dade, Broward, Palm Beach, big counties, would never be able to do it in [this] time frame. I think if she had come out initially and said, you know, we have got until November 17, we have got overseas absentee ballots coming in, we are going to let the canvassing boards do what they want to do, and as long as they get the results in by November 17, we are going to accept them, I don't think there is a court that would have touched that decision. Yet it just seemed to me her zeal to certify this election flew in the face of what ultimately people are trying to do, and that is . . . to get all votes counted.

P: Why didn't you begin your recount on Tuesday, November 14?

B: What happened was Judge [Jorge] LaBarga rendered his opinion [allowing the recount to begin]. At this point, the Florida Supreme Court had accepted our case. Although we had decided to resume the recount, we again met on that Tuesday and decided we were going to wait. So, we met on Wednesday morning [November 15], and Bruce Rogow had said that, you know, the Florida Supreme Court has accepted this case, you have asked them what to do, I think . . . you really ought to wait. So, we did, and, of course, the opinion actually came out on [November] 16. They said, you may count, and that is when we actually started off the recount, on November 16.

P: Did you agree with the 7-0 Florida Supreme Court decision in *Palm Beach County Canvassing Board v. Harris*, which mandated that the recounts must be included in the certification and set November 26 as the new deadline for certification?

B:    I don't know. [Y]ou read Florida election law, and it is clearly the legislative intent that all votes should get counted. Horribly written law, and so many inconsistencies built into it. So, on the one hand, while I understand the Florida Supreme Court's decision to . . . count all votes, you ought to do that. I started realizing [that] this [was] going to be a problem when the dates started changing and the rules started changing and, for example, when they came up with November 26 . . . where did this come from? Because they were clearly changing what the law was.

I also was unhappy with the opinion in that it never addressed the standards the canvassing boards are going to look at. That was my main concern from the beginning. We are looking at ballots a certain way, Broward is looking at them a certain way, Dade is looking at them, everybody is looking at them differently. This is no way to elect a president. So I was frustrated. We tried to get an opinion from Judge LaBarga, you know, Judge, you tell us how to do it and we will do it that way—he would not touch it. We were hoping the Florida Supreme Court would, and they did not.

P:    Do you think the Gore legal team made a mistake in not requesting a statewide recount?

B:    I have talked to some of the lawyers, and they said it was actually the trial lawyers' view that they should be doing a statewide recount. Here is the problem. In Palm Beach County in the September primary, we had a state House candidate that lost by 14 votes [and] asked for a manual recount. Unanimously, the board denied it. Now you have a candidate [Gore] who wins Palm Beach County by 120,000 votes, and he gets a manual recount. You go explain to the candidate who lost by fourteen votes: you do not get one but this candidate does. I just think that reeks of partisanship. If we are talking about a national or statewide race, then either every county ought to get counted or none of the counties ought to get counted.

P:    So you think the Florida Supreme Court was partisan in this case?

B:    Look, I don't want to say that the [Florida] Supreme Court justices are partisan. I think it was an opinion to clearly try and give effect to legislative intent. Legally, though, you could not justify it. When I got to go to the first U.S. Supreme Court argument, that was one of the first questions, where is November 26 written in the law? The rules kept changing as the process went, and . . . I . . . felt, the more the rules keep changing, the less likely this is ever going to pass constitutional scrutiny.

P:    When you started the manual recount, how did you, as a canvassing board, decide on the standard?

B:    [B]ack in 1990, [the Palm Beach County Canvassing Board] came up with a written standard that said if one corner of the chad is removed, they would count that as a vote, but the dimples or indentations do not count as votes, because even they recognized that people can touch and then . . . put down . . . the stylus and decide they made a mistake and go vote for someone else. It was actually the standard that was in effect on November 7, or at least the only written policy this county had. I had said to our county attorney, Denise Dytrych, you know, we ought to call Broward [County] and see what they are doing, because we ought to be doing the same thing; that will be one less issue. So, we called and talked to their county attorney down there, who said they were actually applying two corners, if two corners of the chad were punched out, it would be counted as a vote, and they were not counting individual dimples or anything like that. We decided we would count them [the dimples] if there was a consistent pattern and it showed that is how the voter voted, but basically, if there were one or two votes by dimples, we were not going to count them. That is how we came up with it, really, just more or less to be consistent with Broward.

Of course, four days go by and Broward decides, well, we are going to go back and count some of these dimples. That was their decision. I just kind of felt that, once we started, we needed to be consistent, and it was not right to be going back changing your standards because one party was unhappy with the vote totals they were coming out with. [Also] somebody mentioned, what about a sunshine standard? And, what is that? Well, if you can see light through it, okay. So I said, fine, whatever. We went back and we started looking at ballots. Now, we started holding up a ballot that, in the presidential call, maybe there are three candidates with dings [and] you see a little pinhole of light through one of them, and they are counting these as votes. Really nothing distinguishing between the three dings on the three different candidates other than one as a little pinhole of light. I was concerned. It was ridiculous the way it was being applied. We were just about finished with one precinct, and I brought it up. I said, this is crazy, . . . we are finding votes that . . . there is nothing distinguishing, the paper is hardly pierced and yet there is a little nick-hole of light. We talked about it and agreed that we were just going to go back to the one-corner rule, if you will, the 1990 standard, so what we did was go back and redid that precinct.

P: How did the canvassing board get along at this point? Obviously, there are some disagreements about how you count the votes.

B: Personally, we were doing fine. I was a little unhappy with our county commissioner member [Carol Roberts]. I felt she was acting a little too partisan. My attitude was that whatever we are doing here, we ought to be open and we ought to be public and we ought to be consistent, because at least that way hopefully people will have confidence in the outcome. So I did not think it [Roberts' behavior] was appropriate. I think as time went on, we certainly were fairly on the same page.

P: How difficult was it counting votes under this extraordinary pressure with lawyers protesting and outside agitators?

B: It was hard. You just kind of get numb after a while. It is not the most exciting duty in the world. I give these people so much credit. I don't care if they were getting paid or were volunteers, . . . just to sit there, holding up a ballot, showing it to the other counter, putting it down, just over and over again.

Now, the problem [is] you got these observers from each party, so you got a Democratic observer and a Republican observer. It became clear that the Republicans were there to slow down and hinder the process because they never wanted to see the count finished. The Democrats wanted every little spit-mark to be counted as a vote. So, instead of . . . the canvassing board probably looking at some 6,000 ballots ultimately to decide, we wound up with over 16,000 ballots, which was ridiculous, because we wound up looking at ballots that clearly had Gore punches or clearly had Bush punches, but the observers were objecting and getting in fights with the counters.

P: And then the Republicans were charging that people were eating chads and that there were chads all over the floor. How did you react to those kind of charges?

B: It is funny, I would go outside for a cigarette and the media would come. Tucker Askew was the Republican spin guy, and he would just be saying all this stuff and I was laughing. I mean, it was ridiculous because we had the media able to have cameras in there. We allowed reporters of print and, I think, radio. We had a still photographer . . . in there. I used to say to the reporters, you know, you are reporting this stuff, but yet you have been in there and you know what is going on; why are you even reporting this nonsense? That was ridiculous. I did not see anybody eating any chads. I don't think they tasted good.

P: How did you react when the Republicans sent people like Bob Dole and the Democrats sent Jesse Jackson to plead their case?

B: [W]e were not too happy with the initial stuff going on. I look back now and I think the stuff that [Robert] Wexler and Jesse Jackson did really hurt their cause more than it helped, because it created a very antagonistic atmosphere. And what ultimately happened with that count? We did not get it done in time. I thought it was interesting that they were there to see the process. To me, to see Governor Pataki and some of these Republicans, . . . inside sitting there with us, knowing exactly what we were doing and then walking out and to say it is chaos, that just irritated me because that was totally not true.

P: Gore and Bush, of course, eventually fought this out in the U.S. Supreme Court, when Bush appealed the Florida Supreme Court 4-3 decision. Should the U.S. Supreme Court have taken that case?

B: I had the opportunity to go up to Washington for that one. I know I am jumping ahead of the question, but people have been very critical of the U.S. Supreme Court, and people have been critical of judges in general on this matter. I think it is the real partisan people . . . [who] feel that the judiciary acted politically. I never quite saw it that way. It just struck me as odd that this is an awful way to be electing a president. Here we have a country of voters, close elections in so many states, and yet we are leaving it up to three counties in the state of Florida to decide this thing; . . . coupled with the lack of standards in reviewing these.

I have never been what I would consider a constitutional scholar, but I think certainly once these things started hitting the courts, it was pretty clear that the U.S. Supreme Court was going to decide it one way or the other. [A]s I sat there [in the U.S. Supreme Court] and Justice O'Conner, one of her first questions is, where did this November 26 date come from? That is a problem. All these things that were in place on November 7 were now being changed as you go, the standards of the canvassing boards were changing. From county to county, within a county, they were changing. Time limits, deadlines, everything was changing. So, we knew it was a problem.

P: In trying to get your votes counted by November 26, you realized that it was a slow process, so you asked Secretary of State Harris for an extension. She turned that down. Did you find her reasoning persuasive?

B: No. I don't believe she actually read any of those requests for an extension. I think she just simply decided. I just think the way the secretary handled herself left her open to a great deal of criticism, and I think she had her mind made up that we were not going to give extensions.

P: In retrospect, do you wish you had not taken Thanksgiving off?

B: Of course. There are a lot of things, certainly if I ever had to go through this again, I would do. We had been at this since, really, Election Day, nonstop, and people needed a break. Do I wish the canvassing board themselves, Carol, Theresa [and I] had come in for four or five hours? Sure. But hindsight is a wonderful thing. They never once said to us, Judge, if you take it, you will never finish, there are X amount of ballots left. Nobody ever said that to us, because if they had, that certainly might have affected our decision.

P: The Florida Supreme Court gave the Secretary of State the option of accepting the ballots either 9:00 A.M. Monday or 5:00 P.M. Sunday.

B: The Florida Supreme Court says the certified results, if the Secretary of State's office is open on Sunday at 5:00 P.M. to receive them, if not, 9:00 A.M. Monday. Well, they could have said 2:00 A.M. Sunday, and she would have been open to get them. We knew that, which is why we worked through the night that Friday. Saturday, we went straight through the night into Sunday. We knew in any event she was going to be there at 5:00 to get them. As time got a little closer, we realized we were not going to make it. I basically sent a letter off saying, give us [an extension] until Monday morning, which I kind of realized we were not going to get it. But when it came down to where I saw [in] another hour or two hours, we would be done, I called Clay Roberts, and [said] we have not yet gotten a response from our request for

Monday morning, and he says, well, we are just getting ready to fax you something. I said, what does it say? He says, "no." I said, look, you know, we got people working twenty hours a day, they have been breaking their butts, another two hours we will be done, and give us the two hours. He says, let me get back to you. Then ten minutes later, we get a letter saying no.

P:  When you testified before Judge Sanders Sauls, in the contest hearing, you stated that you had exercised due diligence in counting votes, that you and the canvassing board had worked very hard and that there had not been any tampering or malfeasance. Your testimony, in effect, turned out to be a contribution to the Republican side.

B:  Right. What happened was . . . I get a call [and was told] you are being subpoenaed up in Tallahassee, you are going to need to testify there. I didn't even know who subpoenaed me. I later found out it was actually a subpoena from Joe Klock, who was Harris's lawyer. When I got there, one of the Republican lawyers said, we may be calling you as a witness. I really thought it was, more or less, describe how you went through ballots and describe the standards you used, and that is basically what I did.

P:  Judge Sauls ruled that Gore had failed to prove a reasonable probability, not a possibility, that the outcome would be different after a recount or that the canvassing board had abused their discretion. Was that a correct ruling?

B:  I believe so. I think where Judge Sauls's opinion got into problems is when he talked about the canvassing boards not abusing their discretion and an abuse of discretion standard, which really did not exist. I guess the Democratic Party felt, even in dealing with the standards, that he should be looking at these ballots or appointing masters or somebody else to look at these ballots. But . . . on the one hand, the law gives these canvassing boards all this discretion, on the other hand, the Democrats are arguing, well, you need to look at them twice. That is why I always felt if that was [the Gore attorneys'] contention, they should have just done away with the recounts and just gone right to a contest phase, state-wide.

P:  One of the arguments made by the Bush attorneys was that if you are going to have the court counting the votes, you might just do away with the canvassing boards.

B:  Absolutely, which is why go through this manual recount? The fact is, it was all strategy, political strategy, and that bothered me more than anything.

P:  Your reaction to the December 8 Florida Supreme Court 4-3 vote in *Gore v. Harris* to do a manual recount of all the undervotes in the state?

B:  Clearly contrary to Florida law on a manual recount. I would have liked to have just done the undervotes, but what the statute says is you must manually recount all the votes. So here we are, wasting our time going through 460,000 ballots when many of them, 430,000 were clean votes, but yet we got to go through them all anyway. Now, they are saying, well, just go back and count all the undervotes. We certainly would have finished our process a lot sooner if we could have just pulled out the undervotes and looked at those. Again, changing Florida law.

P: The U.S. Supreme Court ruled 5-4 to stop the recount. The main part of that decision was that all the different standards in the recount violated the Fourteenth Amendment equal-protection clause. This ruling was very interesting in two ways, because the Rehnquist Supreme Court had generally respected states' rights and, second, they had infrequently decided cases under the Fourteenth Amendment. What was your reaction to that 5-4 decision?

B: I actually had a bigger reaction from Justice Scalia putting a stop to the counts, talking about irreparable harm. I thought that was a reach. I certainly did not see any irreparable harm, but it certainly convinced me how they are going to rule. If they had five votes to just stop everything, it was pretty clear which way they were going. You know, the fact that Broward [County], I thought, had, four days into the recount, relaxed their standard, and they went from 170-odd votes to 570 votes like nothing. So I do not necessarily disagree with what the U.S. Supreme Court was saying. You should have a procedure for manual recounts . . . [and] you got to have a standard.

P: Justice John Paul Stevens had a stinging dissent and said the court had acted unwisely. Justice Ruth Bader Ginsberg felt they should never have taken the case.

B: Well, the interesting thing to me is seven of the nine justices found problems with Florida law. I think that is significant. Now, they disagreed on the remedy. Four of them felt we ought to be letting them continue, and five of them said we ought to put a stop to it. I know Justice Stevens felt that this was going to do a lot of damage to the judiciary, . . . that people are going to feel that judges are acting politically. I am a judge, I am supposed to be nonpartisan, and yet to put a judge in the middle of this most partisan process is difficult. The reality is we ought to be able to make decisions because we think this is what the law demands, not because of the winds of popular opinion, not because a judge fears he is not going to get re-elected. We ought to be able to decide because we think this is what the law demands us to do and for no other reason.

P: David Boies said it would not have mattered what the Florida Supreme Court did. If they had set standards, the U.S. Supreme Court would have said, well, they are legislating, not interpreting; if they didn't set standards, they were going to lose based on the Fourteenth Amendment. It was a Catch-22.

B: Well, I disagree, because I think had the Florida Supreme Court come out and said, we interpret the intent of the voter to mean any indication on a punch-card is evidence that a vote should be counted, or on the other hand, we interpret that to mean unless the voter clearly followed the instructions, votes do not get counted. I think they could have gotten away with that. I think had they set a standard, quite honestly, I'm not even convinced the U.S. Supreme Court would have halted the state-wide recount, had there been a uniform standard. They went up to Tallahassee to count all the undervotes still with no standard, and I think that is what really got the U.S. Supreme Court to say enough already.

P: What do you think the outcome would have been had there been a state-wide count? We see by the *Miami Herald* and *New York Times* recount that Bush would have won under all but one scenario.

B: It is funny, we have seen recounts now from the *Miami Herald*, more recently the *Ft. Lauderdale Sun-Sentinel* did a recount, *Palm Beach Post* did a recount. Every one is different. Their numbers are different, the number of votes are different, how many they found for Gore are different, which leads me to believe that manually recounting the punch-card ballots is not a very accurate process, not a very reliable process. I am convinced, quite honestly, that no matter how much America wants to know who won this election, I don't think we will ever know who won. I look at it and I am amazed, because what are the odds you are going to have such a close election, not only close across the country but particularly in Florida. I think had any county in any state across the country been put under the same microscope, they would have found just as many problems, particularly with punch-cards.

P: In the Florida Supreme Court, the vote was 4-3, not 7-0, and this vote, plus other decisions the court made against Gore, perhaps does not indicate a partisan, liberal Democratic court, as charged by Jim Baker.

B: I don't believe the Florida Supreme Court ever acted partisan. That was never my impression. I think what is clear is that the Florida Supreme Court was trying to give effect to the law that obviously had been intended. Number one is to allow a manual recount of votes, and number two is to make sure all votes get counted. I think if you go through the election law, it is clearly the intent of the legislature.

P: The number of invalid votes in Florida is a sad commentary on the literacy and the ability of our voters.

B: Absolutely. What was frustrating for me was to watch Congressmen Wexler and all the senators up there talking about the disenfranchisement. This is nothing new, apparently, to elections. We had more undervotes, I think, in the 1996 presidential election than we had in 2000 in Palm Beach County. There were God knows how many undervotes and overvotes up in Duval County this past election. Had any supervisor of elections gone to their county commission four years ago and said, by the way, I want $10,000,000 to buy new voting equipment, they would have been laughed out, and the same public would have been in an uproar that they were going to spend this money. Nobody would spend money on voting. Well, unfortunately, we have had to now pay the price for that, and now all of sudden people don't mind spending the money.

P: Also, I noticed that the state spends 70 million a year advertising the lottery but only 7 million on voter education. Maybe we need to change our priorities.

B: If you teach people and explain to people what is going on, you can educate the public a lot less expensively than having to pay all this money for all this equipment.

P: How has this election changed Palm Beach County?

B: Other than being the butt of all the jokes across the country? I think Palm Beach County has clearly, whether the legislature does away with punch-cards or not, placed themselves in a position where they have to [do away with the punch-card machines], and if it means the county commission finding the money, they are going to do that.

P: How has this experience changed your life?

B: Well, other than now I go walking down the street and everybody recognizes me . . . , it has been interesting. People have been very nice. I will tell you that I probably got about 500 letters from across the country and 800 e-mails [from] people just saying very nice things, people who had just seen me on TV.

P: How do you think it has impacted Theresa LePore?

B: I think Theresa has had a rough time with it. Anybody who knows Theresa will tell you she is the nicest woman you would ever meet. You know, she designed the ballot obviously without any evil intent; it was only to assist people. I personally did not find it that confusing. I think if you take a second to look at what you are doing, you can figure it out. Both parties had the sample ballots. Maybe it was not an exact duplicate, but it was enough to tell people you got to be careful, that you got names on both sides. She has gotten some horrible hate mail. She clearly made a mistake, it is something she will never do again, but I just think she has been unfairly demonized over this.

P: Do you think that decision on the butterfly ballot cost Al Gore the election?

B: I think a lot of decisions probably cost Al Gore the election. We had a great economy. Gore should have cleaned up on this election. Maybe that says more about Al Gore than it says about Theresa LePore. I certainly would not say Theresa LePore cost him the election.

P: Frank Cerabino of the *Palm Beach Post* wrote, I thought, a good column about the election, and he said at the end that the county's legacy was that Bush got a fair shake from a Democratic canvassing board in a Democratic county.

B: I think he did get a fair shake, and I think people assumed that you have got a three Democrat canvassing board, . . . they are out to steal the election. I thought we conducted ourselves as fairly and openly as possible.

# ➤ THERESA LePORE ◄

In 1971, Theresa LePore began her career as a file-clerk in the Supervisor of Elections office at the age of 16. Twenty-five years later, she was elected to head the office. She has been active in a number of professional organizations, including serving as secretary, vice-president and president-elect for the Florida State Association of Supervisors of Elections.

Perhaps the most denigrated and criticized of the election recount participants, Theresa LePore chose the infamous "butterfly-ballot" as an act of good will. She thought this design would provide bigger print for the many elderly voters in the county. The ensuing confusion over recounts in Palm Beach County held the entire country in suspense for 36 days.

In her interview LePore described the typical frustrations of election day, how she responded to the complaints about the "butterfly ballot," and how she came up with the ballot design. She explained how local events increasingly had national implications and recalled the pressure of performing her duties without sleep and under intense world-wide scrutiny. She devoted particular attention to the organization of the manual recount. She commented on the tensions arising from disagreements among her canvassing board members and the stress of complying with recount orders from courts. LePore touched on the conflicting legal opinions given by Clay Roberts and Bob Butterworth and alluded to the reasons for taking Thanksgiving off. She provided candid views of the Florida Supreme Court decisions and the "partisan" activity of Katherine Harris. She complained of unfair media coverage and blamed them for over hyping events and for overstating the problems with the butterfly ballot, since 250,000 voters got it right. The toll that the 2000 recount took on her was evident throughout the interview.

Theresa LePore was interviewed by Pam Iorio, Former Supervisor of Elections of Hillsborough County and currently Mayor of Tampa, Florida, on February 23, 2001.

I: Let us talk specifically about what occurred in your county because your county was probably the most volatile of this entire election. First of all, tell me what your Election Day was like.

L: Normally, I am in the office [at] about 4:00 A.M. because I cannot sleep the night before. I am so geared up and the adrenaline is going and all, so I get in and I turn the phones on. I had known it was going to be busy prior to that, but I confirmed it when around 5:00 A.M. the

phones started ringing with people wanting to know if they were registered, where to go vote and all this. That started it, and it just went
downhill from there. We had about 60 incoming [phone] lines. We
had contracted with one of the high schools to help with the phone
bank. So we had them on the phone banks, plus our regular staff . . .
and they were constantly busy. There was just no stopping. The staff
was trying to get people on and off as quickly as possible. We never did
get a count of how many phone calls we had that day, but I am sure it
was 15,000, 20,000, easy.

About mid-to-late-morning, it all kind of runs together—a couple
of elderly gentlemen came into the office and were complaining about
the ballot, that it was confusing because we had used the facing pages,
since known as the "butterfly ballot." The media or somebody dubbed
it that: we never called it that. We thought it was just an isolated inci-
dent, because they were a couple of very elderly gentlemen. That was
the first we had heard that there may be a problem. Later on that day,
the phone calls started getting worse, and what we found out afterwards was that—I have not confirmed it, but a number of people told
me—the Democratic national party had commissioned a phone bank
group out of Texas, I believe, . . . to call all the Democrats in the
county and tell them their vote may not have counted, that they
needed to call the office to complain. With those calls coming in, it
made our phone situation even worse, because the regular people, plus
the poll workers, could not get in because [of] these people calling to
complain . . . and we could not get them off the phone short of hanging up on them. They wanted to come back and re-vote.

Then, about mid-afternoon, a contingent of elected officials came
in, Congressman [Robert] Wexler [and] . . . Representative Lois
Frankel, . . . and complained that they were getting a lot of complaints
from voters saying that there was a problem and I had to do something
right now. They wanted me to fax something to all the polling places.
I said, first of all, I have got 531 polling places, or precincts. It is impossible to send the fax. We would be here all night. Second, probably
99 percent of them do not have faxes, and if they did, I don't know what
the numbers are. So we kind of compromised. We had written up a
statement for . . . the poll workers to tell the voters. Basically, find the
name of the person you want to vote for [and] follow the arrow to
the punch number to the hole that you want to vote for. They [the
Democratic office holders] read it and said it looked fine. I made
the copies, and they agreed to distribute it because they had people in
all the precincts. I found out afterwards that [the statement] was used
against me because then they were saying, well, she knew she had a problem, so that is why she sent this out—a "she-screwed-up" type thing.

I: When the public officials came in and said, this ballot is confusing,
was that the first time that you were presented with this notion that
there was something wrong with the ballot?

L: It was the first time. We had mailed sample ballots out to all registered voters, about 655,000 of them. We always mail the ballot pages, the proof pages, to both party chairs, the whole set, because they want the punch numbers. Then we mail it out to all the candidates, their page, so that they can have their punch numbers. So they knew way back then what it looked like. On the presidential pages, we had put both pages on the same piece of paper, so it was obvious what it looked like. Nobody said one word about anything.

    They were going around saying the ballot was illegal, because they were looking at the wrong section of the statute. [In my thirty years] nobody has ever complained because the sample ballot did not show the punch holes. They were saying that the sample ballot that was mailed was not the same as the ballot that was in the precinct, because it did not indicate where the holes were. [T]he sample ballot is the ballot pages; it is not the machine or the equipment that you are using.

I: Explain how you came up with this ballot design.

L: The voting systems guy had brought me three or four different designs, and the one-page print was small. We have a lot of elderly voters in our county and I really felt that it would be a problem to them having the small print, so we went to the two-page facing page. Actually, he had recommended, and I probably should have listened to him, the one design where the left side of the page was the way it was, but the right side, because it had less candidates, was moved down, so it was off-center. Being the perfectionist that I am, I wanted it to look nice, to have everything all lined up.

I: Had you ever used this design before?

L: Yes. We had used it back in 1988 when we had a lot of constitutional amendments on the ballot.

I: You still did not realize, even at 4:00 A.M. on November 8, that you were going to be absolutely at the center of all this, did you?

L: No. It really took a couple days. Looking back, I really do not think it sunk in, and it really still has not sunk in, because I was sheltered from everything, if you will. I was not watching TV or listening to the radio or reading the papers or anything. I was putting in 18, 20 hours a day, 7 days a week. I was exhausted to that point, and then going through Election Day and then everything else, it was just the adrenaline kept going, and I never had time to crash and burn, if you will, to calm down, settle down, so nothing really, really sunk in as to the enormity of what was going on.

I: When you came back to work on November 8, and learned you were supposed to conduct an automatic recount, how did you all proceed, and what was the atmosphere like?

L: The atmosphere was very tense, because at that point, actually before we left from election night, early Wednesday morning, the attorneys started showing up, from all over the country, for both parties.

I: They were already in your office?

L: Yes, they were already there. I had heard . . . from several people . . . that the planes were chartered, the attorneys were on stand-by, and if Gore lost Florida, everybody was to move in to certain targeted counties, and Dade, Broward, and Palm Beach were three of them. I can't explain how these people all just materialized so fast. They were just there.

I: How did you decide how to proceed with the automatic recount?

L: We do everything in the Sunshine [Florida's Sunshine Law provides that all state meetings are open to the public]. We had decided to hold the meeting in the lobby of our building. The security people . . . had sectioned off a big section at a table there with the microphones, and we conducted our meeting in front of God and everybody. Our County Cable Channel 20, our local government channel, decided to broadcast everything live from start to finish.

[W]e had gotten the word down, that we need to do the automatic recount . . . and we decided to do it that afternoon. We met again on Thursday, and that is when the Democrats were asking for a manual recount, and the Republicans decided if [Democrats] are going to ask for a manual [recount], then we are going to ask for another machine count. So the canvassing board met again on Thursday and decided to honor the request to do the machine recount that the Bush campaign requested and to do the one-percent manual [recount] for the Gore campaign.

We did the machine count and simultaneously did the one-percent manual count, which was a complete nightmare. I have been through manual recounts a number of times, and we have never been [as] under the gun and under the watchful eye as we were there. Everything had to be equal; there had to be the same number of Democrats as Republicans in there and the same number of attorneys. We had observers at each of the tables, and we tried to follow the written procedures we had in our security procedures, but the way things were going, we were developing procedures as we were going, because nothing was normal about this. [I]t was decided to separate them all into the 12 or 13 different piles, the 10 candidates, plus the overvotes, plus the undervotes, plus the objectionables. The objectionables were ones that the party observers would object to. Or if it was an overvote or undervote and they didn't think that it should be, it would go into [the objectionable ballots pile]. Then the objectionables would go to the canvassing board to review.

That was a long, tedious process; something that should have only taken 4 or 5 hours ended up taking until 1:00 in the morning, and we started early Saturday morning [November 11]. We actually had three precincts that the Democrats had selected, and then one additional precinct that the canvassing board had selected, to come out to that 1 percent. The three precincts that the Democrats had selected were very large precincts that were very high in elderly population, and, of course, Democratic, with the chances that they would gain more votes, which they did. Because of that gain that Gore got [ed.: 19 votes], they extrapolated that into what it should be for the whole county, which was absurd, because the whole county does not have large Democratic precincts with elderly voters. You can't say, okay, you have got three precincts [where] you got 20 votes, so therefore that, times six hundred precincts, you are going to get whatever that comes out to. At that point, the state had sent down two people to assist, Paul Kraft, and an attorney by the name of Kerey Carpenter. They were, of course, lobbying for us not to have a manual recount. At this point, there was the discussion on the request to do a county-wide manual recount. Personally, I didn't want to do it because I knew what was involved in doing a manual count on a small level, let alone 162,000 ballot cards.

I:     Was there anything in that manual recount that, in your view, caused any alarm?

L:     Nothing out of the ordinary from what we had experienced in the past. We pulled the test ballots . . . and they all looked fine. They had no problems, so we determined it was not equipment; it was voter error that did it. At this point, things were getting really bad as far as people coming down; the press was just from all over the world, literally. [T]he sheriff's deputies were around me the whole time. There were 5 SWAT [Special Weapons and Tactics] team guys waiting there, because they had radioed down that we were coming down. They got around me, literally, practically carried me through, and people were pulling at me, calling me names, screaming at me.

I:     How did that make you feel? It is still hard to talk about, is it not, even after all these months?

L:     Yes. It was pretty scary. It was that afternoon that the top brass in the sheriff's office came in and said, we are following you home tonight, and you are not driving.

I:     Can you describe some of the media frenzy, because unlike any other supervisor, you really were at the center of that frenzy, over 500 media were there. Still, you had your job to do. So, how did you go about planning, and how did this manual recount actually commence?

L:     Let us see, we finished up Saturday, and actually it was early Sunday morning [November 12] when the canvassing board met again and released the results of the machine count. We obviously had not discussed amongst ourselves, because of the Sunshine Law, what we were going to do, if we were going to go ahead and grant the request for a full manual recount. I didn't know until I got out there, until the vote came up, what I was going to do. At that point, an attorney I know, . . . [Robert Montgomery] had volunteered to represent me, because by this time the lawsuits were fast and furious. The county attorney's office was using all of their staff, and they were just overwhelmed and suggested that we get outside counsel to help out.

All three of us [the canvassing board] were being lobbied very heavily by both parties to do a manual [recount or], not to do a manual [recount]. Probably because I was so exhausted, upset, and everything else, because really it had been a good solid week since I had any sleep, a lot of it just was not really registering. We had discussed about doing the manual count. We talked about getting an opinion from the Division of Elections. At first, I had voted to go ahead to the judge [Burton], as chair of the canvassing board, to ask him [Clay Roberts, Division of Elections], and then my attorney said, no, withdraw your second to the motion. So, I withdrew it, based on what my attorney was telling me, the outside counsel, not the county attorney's office. Then we went to the question about doing a manual count, and the commissioner [Carol Roberts] was very vocal about how she felt, that we should do the manual recount. Her and the judge got into a very heated discussion.

By then, it was just a mob scene, not only with reporters. It was just mass hysteria all over. They had to block off all the streets. And they were expecting a lot of problems. There were . . . police cars lining the street, as well as uniforms all up and down the street. They had snipers on the roof. The protestors were all over the place. They had surrounded the stage and were pushing into the stage. That is when the judge got upset because . . . it was starting to get really ugly, so at that point, they had to come up with the steel barricades to put around the stage to keep the crowds back.

We got to the point of asking about doing a manual recount and thought it was the best thing to do, because people just were not going to be satisfied if we did not. Not that I thought it was the right thing to do. I believe I made that clear, when I said that I am voting for it because it seems to be the will of the people, not because I think there is a problem with the tabulating equipment. It appears that the tabulating equipment is fine. The judge [Burton] got mad, not necessarily at me, but at the commissioner. It was very partisan, and he got real upset about the whole thing.

I: What was your assessment of Carol Roberts?

L: I think she had an agenda . . . and I have talked to my county attorney about this [and based on] some of the [partisan] comments that she had made prior to Election Day, that we probably should have asked her to recuse herself that Friday before the election. [She had] been active, had raised money, had gone to some of the dinners for Gore. Also . . . we thought it was odd at the time, but we didn't really press it, she has been on the canvassing board a number of times over the years. The judge we had, Judge Burton, was wonderful. He was very nonpartisan, was trying to abide by the rule of law during the whole thing. I can't speak for the judge, but I am sure he and I both feel that, as long as we were being as nonpartisan as we could, that it would be two-to-one on a lot of stuff.

I: How did it make you feel about the common assumption that Florida election officials would succumb to their party allegiance instead of their professional ethics?

L: It was very discouraging and disheartening and upsetting, because I know [that] the majority of the supervisors, probably all of the supervisors, when it comes to doing their job, try to be as nonpartisan as they can. Myself, in particular, when I first registered to vote, I registered Republican, because that is what my dad was. Then . . . I felt that I should be nonpartisan, so I registered Independent, which then became an organized party in the state, so I registered to change to No Party. I had been No Party up until the time my predecessor decided to retire and I had to pick a party. The county is predominately Democrat, so I chose Democrat. But I have always treated everybody equally, and both parties know that. For the longest time, the Democrats thought I was a Democrat, the Republicans thought I was a Republican.

I: Probably the one thing that most people will always remember about the 2000 election are all those scenes from Palm Beach of your canvassing board and all your workers holding up those ballots. How long did the manual recount take? What about the decision to take Thanksgiving off, which became an issue? And then get to the point where you did not quite finish in time for Katherine Harris.

L: When the canvassing board, very early Sunday morning, decided to go ahead with the manual recount, we all went home. I showered, changed, came back to the office. [W]e spent all day Sunday, into Sunday night until about ten o'clock, trying to figure out logistics and location. We finally decided that the EOC, Emergency Operation Center, might be the best place, because they . . . had about 100 seats that were built-in and set up amphitheater-style. Everything was there. It was all self-contained. We made arrangements to use that, contingent on the canvassing board's approval. Trying to figure out staffing [was difficult]. We did not want to use poll-workers, because we thought that there might be some kind of perceived conflict of interest with using them. We used the temporary employees we had in the office, we used county employees, and basically anybody we could drum up. We had the major task of trying to pair up Democrats with Republicans. We finally got all that worked out.

The canvassing board met Monday morning and decided to start the manual count the next morning, Tuesday morning. The counters, as we were calling them, were to report out there at 7:00 A.M. We had special badges for them that we issued, and then it was up to the parties to come up with an observer for each of the teams. We ended up with . . . maybe 25 teams, up to 35 teams, of 2, with the observers on top of that.

But we could not start because, that might have been the [Florida] Supreme Court lawsuit. The judge, on his own, on that Sunday, had asked for the opinion from the Division [of Elections], and I still have not read it, [but] I believe it said, unless there is a machine problem, do not do a manual recount. So the Democrats went to Butterworth and asked for the opinion from him, . . . and he, of course, had an opposing opinion. I think we had gone to the [Florida] Supreme Court to ask for clarification, which one to listen to, because we stopped and started. We got everybody there several mornings, and then we were not able to proceed because of lawsuits that were going on. So we really did not start Tuesday like we wanted to. We did not even get the ballots open to start. So, as far as actually starting, we had that delay. If we were able to start Tuesday morning when we had planned, we would have been finished in time.

As far as taking Thanksgiving, we were running shifts from 7:00 A.M. until 10:00 P.M. So we were running that long schedule, and by the time we got everything shut down, it was two, three o'clock in the morning. We had a discussion about Thanksgiving. It was the general consensus that all the staff, . . . who had been there from the beginning, needed a day to relax. We kind of calculated how many we had to do, and we honest-to-goodness thought we would get finished. I think, plus, at that point, the Supreme Court had said that if the secretary of state was in her office around 5:00 P.M. Sunday, that was the deadline; otherwise, it was 9:00 A.M. Monday morning. Well, how many elected state officials are in their office on a Sunday afternoon of a holiday weekend?

I: So, you assumed that you had until Monday morning.

L: It would be 9:00 A.M. Monday, right. Plus, at that point, when the Republicans saw what was going on, they were the biggest offenders. I mean, I don't want to blame it all on the Republicans, because they both were equally bad. We had gotten word that the observers were told to put as many in the objectionable pile as you could to bog everything down, slow the process. We figured the canvassing board had Friday, Saturday, and Sunday to go through all the objectionables. We started at seven in the morning and went late into the night each time, but because of all the objectionables there ended up being . . . more than half of a precinct that they had in the objectionable pile.

I: And then the canvassing board had to look at each of those.

L: Had to look at each of those, and when we were looking at them, we had three attorneys from each side behind us, watching what we were doing. They had a court reporter there recording everything. By Saturday afternoon, we realized that we were not making a whole lot of headway because of the peanut gallery, and we decided to work through the night that night. In the meantime, we were having to audit all the tally sheets against the printout from the last machine count that we did, and then put all those numbers into a spreadsheet. So, it was trying to get all that in, get that proofed, doing the audit sheets, comparing the audit sheets to the printout to make sure that the audit sheets were right, because we found in a lot of cases, again human error, that the counters were not recording the numbers in the right columns.

I: Did you handle most of that, or did you have key staff people doing that?

L: I had handled most of that. Unfortunately, and I probably shouldn't have done this, but I had told staff when they left Wednesday that I [didn't think we would need them] for the weekend, so a number of them went out of town, and I could not get a hold of them when we saw what was going on, to get them back in there.

I: How did it make you feel, on that Sunday night, when Harris opened the office at 5:00 P.M. on Sunday?

L: It was very disappointing, because our judge had been in touch with them several times that day, and I believe he even wrote them a letter, asking for them to give us until 9:00 Monday morning so that we could be finished, that we just needed a couple more hours, which we did. We were finished at 7:00 with everything.

I: I heard Harris give an interview the other day that said, no, that was not true that they were finished a couple hours later; they actually were not done until days later.

L: No. I will tell you what happened. [A]t 5:00, she went on and certified everything, and we sent her a partial [count] of what we had finished at the time, thinking maybe they will accept those and then maybe we can talk them into accepting the rest of them when we are finished. When she said she was not going to do it, we were all very disappointed.

I: Did you feel that the hand-count vote was more accurate than the machine count?

L: No. Because my feeling is, the voter has instructions to punch the hole clearly through. We originally used what the county canvassing board had adopted in 1990 [but] they [the Democrats] took us to court on that, . . . saying it was too rigid. So, we went and took part of that and the Broward County procedures and merged them together to be a little more lenient on . . . two corners broken and chad partially hanging or whatever the case may be. Some of the ones that were counted, I can't honestly say that if somebody partially punched it, and it did not go through . . . or [if] they just did not use proper [procedures], especially when the rest of the card is punched properly.

I: Were you counting dimples?

L: No. If the rest of the card, or the majority of the card, was dimpled, then they would count it. [I]f the majority of the candidates voted on were Democrats and it was a soft punch for Gore, they would count it as a Gore vote.

I: You did not agree with that.

L: No, because a lot of people do not vote straight party, and what if there is a soft punch on one and another hole is completely punched through? You call that an overvote. That bothered me, that part of it.

[A]t that point [after Harris had certified the vote], the general feeling was, because everyone was so disappointed, why bother finishing up the tally sheets and the spreadsheet when she is not going to accept it anyway? Everybody pretty much went home. [W]e had to deal with [lawsuits to inspect the ballots], so that took us [away] from doing the final audit. It was a couple days later . . . when we decided that, well, it can't hurt, we will just send it [the final tally] up anyway. If we would have known [Harris was] coming out and saying we didn't finish for several days, we would have sent it up Monday when we finished doing the checking and everything like that. I think we ended up with, like, three different versions, and each time we would send it up there to them saying, this is revised; sorry, but we found some typos, or whatever. I can't remember the exact date we sent the final, but Gore ended up gaining, I think it was, 174 [ed.: the total was 176], if it would have been accepted in the manual count.

I:    Judge Sauls ordered your ballots sent to Tallahassee. What happened then?

L:    [W]e had two days to pack everything up and send them to Tallahassee. We were trying to figure out logistics, how to get them up there, and we decided the best way would just be to rent a truck, load them up, and drive them on up there. People asked, how did you decide on Ryder? I pulled out the phone book and opened up the Yellow Pages, and Ryder had the biggest ad, and we said, let's call Ryder. And the rest is history, as they say. We got everything arranged, loaded them up, recorded all the serial numbers and what was in everything and shipped them off with a police escort in the front and the back. We got them out there on Monday, and that was a media circus. We loaded them into the truck, and I rode with the truck, with the helicopters following us up above and the police escort front and back and that whole nightmare. They had a secure room out there that we could put them in. We had to put evidence tape on the door. All the doors had to have evidence tape on it that we checked every time we opened the main door. Of course, we had a sheriff's deputy there 24 hours a day as well.

I:    Then the Florida Supreme Court said to manually recount these undervotes statewide. What was your reaction?

L:    My first reaction was that it was a partisan decision. I know several of the members on the Supreme Court, because they come from my county. I have known them for a long time, and it was very obvious . . . which side [they were on]. [A]ll of our efforts may have not been for naught, because now our numbers would have counted, because they had said to go ahead and count Palm Beach County, the numbers that we had submitted at that point.

I:    Do you feel that the media was fair to you personally?

L: What I have seen and what they have individually told me, I would like to think so, but to be honest, I still have not read all the news clips and stuff. I was totally secluded from everything. Every now and then, I will pick up and start to go through because I want to clip the stuff, and I start getting upset, so I just put it down.

I: Did you feel that the media fairly reported the events that occurred in your county?

L: I don't think they did. They just want to sell press-time, air-time, paper-time, whatever. I think a lot of things that were said were not true or taken out of context, particularly when we had . . . our celebrity observers. You know, they would come in, and everything was real nice and everything, and they would go out, and [claim] we were eating chads and throwing ballots on the floor and just all kinds of stuff. Of course, the media thought it was a hot story and . . . ran with it.

I: Do you think Florida in its election process was cast in a fair light?

L: From the comments I have heard, particularly south Florida, they came across as a bunch of bumbling idiots . . . it was the perception more than anything, which perception-ends-up-being-fact-if-enough people-believe it type thing. I think people really thought that Jeb Bush got the state for his brother via Katherine Harris. There are a lot of people out there who thought a conspiracy was going on.

I: Do you believe any of that?

L: No.

I: You had a high overvote and Duval County had a high overvote. What factor do you think ballot design played in this election?

L: I'm not going to be naive and say I don't think it did. I think it did, but, perhaps, at least in my county, not to the extent that people portrayed it—250,000 people did it right. The amount of people who claim they had a problem, did they really have a problem, or did they hear it so much that they think they had a problem? One reporter told me he was out at one of the condo developments in the morning the day after the election and asked this little old lady, how did you vote? Did you have any problem? No, I had no problem at all. [That afternoon the] same lady was sitting in the front row, crying hysterically, because she knows she voted for Buchanan.

I: The media attention may have blown it up a bit, though the numbers do show that there were higher overvotes in these counties that had unusual ballot design.

L: Yes. We did have a high [number of] overvote[s and] undervote[s].

I: On the overvotes, people would punch a lot of different candidates?

L: Four, five, six. We had some that punched every single hole. We had a number of them where they punched all the holes except Gore, so, of course, the Gore people would say, well, they wanted Gore; they thought they had to punch everybody else out.

I: What is the responsibility of the supervisor to have a ballot that makes voting as simple as possible and diminishes the likelihood of error, and what is the obligation of voters to understand the instructions and vote correctly?

L: As a supervisor, you need to make it as simple as possible. I tried to make the print bigger to make it easier to read. If we squeezed it all on one page, I would have gotten grief because the print was too small. So, you do have some responsibility, and the voter has to have some responsibility to find out who the candidates [are] and to vote responsibly. The punch-card, they are punching the holes, the instructions are right there, they are on the sample ballot, they are offered a demonstration when they walk in. Put the card in, punch it, take it out, check it and make sure. We had cards that were put in, and we could not figure out at first what had happened. Looking at the card, it is punched fine, and then they had two big holes in it about three-quarters of the way down. It finally dawned on us; the voter had put the card in upside down and forced the punched part of the card over the two red pins.

I: How do you assess Katherine Harris's role as the state's chief elections officer during this time period?

L: As I have said, as an elections official you need to have the appearance of being nonpartisan.

I: Your feeling, though, is that the Division of Elections had an agenda and that it was a Bush agenda.

L: Yes.

I: What impact do you think that the removal of the felons from the voter rolls had on this election?

L: If you believe all the conspiracy theories, the Republicans did it on purpose, but I do not honestly feel that it was an intentional thing. I had my concerns about DBT [Database Technologies, Inc., the company that did the revised felon list] from the beginning. The guy who owns it is very high up in the Republican Party as far as a financial backer. So, there were all these things that did not look right, . . . so I had my doubts about them just as far as accuracy. It just so happens that there were more African Americans on there than there were white people. I, personally, did not use the list . . . because I did not feel it was accurate.

I: Do you think that blacks encountered difficulties at the polls that whites did not encounter?

L: I can't honestly say I think that every precinct in the state was perfect, because we all know how poll workers are, and there are still unfortunately some areas in the state that are very prejudiced, including maybe some in my county. I would like to think nothing was intentional.

I: What do you think about this U.S. Civil Rights Commission and their work?

L: I think they are for the most part on a fishing expedition. From what I have heard, the complaints they have received . . . were not valid.

With regard to my case, we had most of the ones who claimed they did not vote, which I think there were almost 60 [complaints] out of 462,000. Most of them voted, even though they had sworn an affidavit saying that . . . they were denied the right to vote. I know we had one guy in the primary come in who registered at the DMV [Division of Motor Vehicles], who did not sign the application, a year and a half before the election. It was Election Day, he came in, he was not on the list to vote. His wife was, because she did hers right. Again, going back to taking responsibility. I have heard in some of the other areas, a lot of the ones who claimed they were denied the right to vote were because they had not completed the applications properly, or they did not even bother to register to vote.

I: Has this election caused you to view your job any differently?

L: Yes.

I: How so?

L: It's not fun anymore.

I: Do you think it ever will be again?

L: I don't think so. I think everything we do now in just my county is going to be under so much media scrutiny and public scrutiny that it is going to get in the way of doing our job and doing it properly.

I: How do you feel about the whole postelection media examination of the ballots?

L: I don't think it is a good thing, because, just from experiences we are having in our county, we had four different groups in there at one time, and [my] staff is telling me they are writing down different things for the same card, not paying attention, and of course they will not share their numbers with anybody. You know they came up with four different results, and they are just putting out more inaccurate information, plus they are dragging this on when it needs to be over. We need to have closure to this. We have got a new president, we have got to move on and live out the future. We can't go back and change the past.

I: What has been the personal and professional toll that this experience has had on you. How do you assess what kind of impact this has had on your life?

L: Physically, I have not had time yet to crash and burn, because I have not had any time. Personally, the verbal and probably written abuse I have taken, from people I had considered to be friends, . . . for them to be bad-mouthing me and [saying] I did this on purpose. People in my own party making all these accusations [saying that] I was paid off by the Republicans and just all this garbage, a petition going around calling for my resignation. It has hurt professionally, because I do not feel comfortable going out in public speaking to groups like I did before.

I: How are you going to describe this one day to a future generation?

L:    I think it is a good learning experience. They say of all bad things, something good comes. [We've got new] technology . . . and public awareness, voters hopefully understanding that their vote will count.

I:    Who do you believe won Florida?

L:    I don't know. Too many variables, so many factors.

PART IV

# INTERVIEWS: MEDIA AND PUBLIC INFORMATION

·

# ➤ LUCY MORGAN ◄

Lucy Morgan, a 1985 Pulitzer Prize winner for her investigative reporting of the Pasco County Sheriff's Department, is the Tallahassee bureau chief for the *St. Petersburg Times*. Morgan began her newspaper career while working as a stringer for the *St. Petersburg Times*. She later joined the *Times* as a full-time news staffer and eventually became a state-wide investigative journalist. In her career Lucy Morgan covered a variety of state and local stories, including drug smuggling, corruption in law enforcement, Florida politics, and the 2000 presidential election controversy in Florida. Her work has received recognition from the Florida Society of Newspaper Editors, the Florida Press Club, and the LeRoy Collins Distinguished Community College Alumni Award.

In describing her numerous activities and responsibilities during the 2000 election, Morgan recalled "the phenomenal invasion of the news media" in Tallahassee and the problems associated with the "constant turmoil of not knowing what the next event was going to bring." She discussed the tension between Jeb Bush and the Katherine Harris camp and how Ralph Nader and Pat Buchanan's candidacies impacted Gore's campaign. She commented on the problems with the butterfly ballots and the lack "of a good clear standard . . . to determine the intent of the voter." Morgan reacted to the advisory roles of Warren Christopher and Jim Baker to Gore and Bush respectively; the political, legal, and public relations wars associated with the "win at all costs attitude of both sides," and Jesse Jackson's accusations of racial discrimination in voting.

Morgan also addressed the influence of Mac Stipanovich, Attorney General Bob Butterworth's behavior during the recount controversy, and the charge that the secretary of state's office deleted or destroyed computer files. Morgan assessed the decisions of the Florida Supreme Court, Judge Sanders Sauls's performance, and whether or not the U.S. Supreme Court should have taken the case. She concluded her interview with observations on how the 2000 election will change the way people view elections in the future and how the recount controversy impacted her life and the city of Tallahassee.

Lucy Morgan was interviewed by the author on May 16, 2002.

P:  Explain to me what assignments you had and what activities you were involved in during the 2000 presidential election.

M:  I generally supervise our coverage of state government in politics and write some, so I was here on election night awaiting returns when we discovered we were not going to learn who won the election right away.

P: What was Tallahassee like during the 36 days?

M: I guess one of the earliest signs of the invasion [was] when we all woke the next morning and realized that we still didn't have a winner declared in the presidency. We prepared for a long haul. We dispatched people to Palm Beach and I and my staff were here. Slowly, as the first day after the election went by, we became a campground for out-of-town newspapers. The legislative officials decided very early to let them simply set up broadcast areas underneath the overhang of the Capitol and everywhere else around the Capitol grounds, so that we had a trailer and tent city that sprang up almost overnight. Everybody thought this might last a day or two, in the beginning. In the end, they were decorating the trailers and tents with Christmas lights, but it was a pretty phenomenal invasion of news media. The time I thought the bottom was falling was [when] I watched a Japanese TV group pitch a tent on the grounds of the Supreme Court, and they let them [do that]. The state, I think, was as bewildered as anybody. It was an almost surreal scene, where we had . . . chanting protesters carrying signs, trying to get in the background for TV. There was a moment where I was walking back to the office and passed a guy wearing a papier-maché Pinocchio head painted pink, with a long nose and the sign under it said "Jeb-nocchio," referring to the governor. I didn't even blink or look twice and decided that I had been overcome by the whole thing. It was just a ludicrous scene.

P: I talked to some other people who were in Tallahassee who said it was so crowded that it was difficult to get a hotel room and difficult to get in a restaurant.

M: I think Bill Hemmer with CNN was one of those who came down here thinking he would be here a day or two and wound up having to buy clothes, had to buy a coat. It was very cold. Many of them had to buy extra underwear and things to stay here, because nobody anticipated, in the beginning, that this thing would last 36 days. After all, how long does it take to count the votes? But as it got drawn out and you had more and more people coming in, we even had some of the big publications that . . . came in, in shifts, sending a second team down after the first team wore out, because it was an exhausting effort that went on, seven days a week. We had press conferences coming one on top of another, . . . and the way you knew who was about to have a press conference was by whose flags went up. The Democrats had a state flag and the U.S. flag, very plain, and if those were the two flags in back, we knew the Democrats were going to have a press conference. The Republicans decided that didn't look grand enough and they ordered a dozen flags with very ornate flag poles with gold eagles on top, so when the gold eagles started coming out with the flags, we knew the Republicans were about to have something.

The hotel room thing was hilarious, because you had national news media . . . ordered out [of their hotel rooms] for football game weekends. The Florida-Florida State [football] game occurred shortly thereafter, and I think these national news correspondents thought they were so important that nobody would kick them out for a football game, and many of them wound up having to move into private homes. This is a relatively small town by comparison to Washington, so . . . the TV networks had a problem. I believe it was CBS that had a big motor-home parked between the Capitol and the Supreme Court, but they didn't have enough room in it to set up a broadcasting studio, so they rented space at the Doubletree Hotel and they were constantly having to run videos back and forth between their two locations. There was a kid that did a sprint for them every night to make the 6:30 news, as they would get the stuff edited down there and have to run it up to transmit it.

P: What was your reaction to all of the celebrity politicians coming in to support both Bush and Gore? How did you approach their participation in this?

M: We interviewed them, we went to their press conferences. It became a situation where at noon every day, you would think, well, I know what the story for tomorrow is going to be, and then by 4:00 it would have gone totally the other way. Because we were so dependent on events that were happening in courts in other places; we often would start out in one direction, only to have a court filing or a court decision change the whole text of the day. We just were in a constant turmoil of not knowing what the next event was going to bring us.

P: How many hours did you work every day?

M: Probably from about 8:00 in the morning until 10:00 or 11:00 at night, almost every day, seven days a week. All of us, we looked dreadful by the time we got to the end of it. One of my reporters . . . one day announced that she was wearing her husband's University of Michigan boxer shorts because it was the only clean underwear in her house.

P: When you look back at this election, how fair and how accurate was the *St. Petersburg Times* in reporting, evaluating and analyzing these events?

M: I think we were as fair as we could be, given that we are a newspaper that had editorials that supported, generally, the Democratic candidates. I think our news stories were balanced. It's hard, when you're covering a breaking news event like that, to be sure that every day you dot every "i" and cross every "t" and still sort of reflect the color of the situation. The thing that bothered me more was to see things that were just flatly erroneous, which we saw from time to time. I had one of the [outside] reporters walk in here and say, "now, I know you wouldn't write this if you knew it, but don't you believe that Jeb Bush is having an affair with Katherine Harris," and I just died laughing because [Jeb] Bush detests Harris. He supported her opponent [Sandra Mortham] in the last election. Their staffs aren't even really on speaking terms. There is nothing cordial, except a sort of public veneer, about the relationship between them. So for those of us who knew the Capitol, it was laughable. I think for a lot of people that didn't know Florida law, or Florida's public-records law, there were people who were sort of feeling their way through it and made some really ridiculous mistakes. We were sort of the truth squad, half the time.

P: It must have been difficult keeping up with all the legal cases because something would happen in Palm Beach that would change the paper's lead for the next day.

M: Yes. We had cases in circuit court, federal court, and in the Florida Supreme Court here. Then we had cases in Palm Beach County, Seminole County, Martin County, Collier County, Broward County, Dade County. It became just a legal nightmare and it happened on a very fast track. You would have court cases where you would have the suit filed, an almost immediate trial, and then an immediate appeal, and rulings coming out of the appellate courts. Most of the appellate court rulings simply passed it on to the [Florida] Supreme Court, but it was the fastest track I've ever seen for court cases. The logistics of it were a nightmare for everybody.

P: When you assigned your staff, did you assign one group just to the court issues, and one to the political issues?

M: No. We did it more by what was going on, on any given day. Usually, Tim Nickens [*St. Petersburg Times* political reporter] and I took the courtroom, whichever of us wasn't doing something else, because I have extensive experience in covering courts and he has some. So we did it that way, letting our other reporters sort of monitor the ground. We had to keep somebody at the Capitol all the time because you would have these visiting notables appear and suddenly have a press conference with virtually no notice of it. In fact, it was one of the few times in my life where having the television turned to CNN, or someplace like it, was a tremendous advantage because people would tell the TV crews before they would announce: we're going to have a press conference.

P: David Cardwell, who has detailed knowledge of this issue, noted that it was clear that the automatic recount was not supposed to be a tally of the machine totals, but a recount of all the votes.

M: I don't think any of us will ever know what the true number would have been if we had had a complete and thorough recount 24 hours later. Now, the way a lot of counties recounted at the time was to simply recheck the totals that had come. But I am told by the election supervisors that every time you pass the punch-card ballot through the counting machines, the vote total changes because chads fall out of the ballot. That's why my inclination is to think that we will never know exactly how many votes were cast on that night for either candidate.

P: Dexter Douglass believed that Gore should have gone to the contest much sooner than he actually did because the Democrats eventually ran out of time.

M: I think that's probably, tactically, their worst mistake. I don't know what would have happened had we gotten in a contest sooner, it might have been that the two courts [Florida and U.S. Supreme Courts] would have done exactly what they did. In a way, I think the courts lost some credibility. I don't know whether it's deserved or not, but the opinion that came out of the Florida Supreme Court was exactly what you would expect a group of Democrats to give you. The opinion that came out of the U.S. Supreme Court was exactly what you would expect from a group of Republicans, and I'm not sure that either court's ruling was convincing to me that they had the correct ground underneath it.

P: How important was the candidacy of Ralph Nader in Gore's defeat?

M: I think clearly it was important in Florida. Nader and [Pat] Buchanan both took enough votes to have decided the election in Florida. I think you could logically assume that those votes would have certainly gone to Gore, had Nader not been on the ballot.

P: What about counting the overvotes? Occasionally there would be somebody who would circle Gore and write in Gore instead of blacking in the circle. The optical scan machine will reject that as an overvote, but if you looked at it as an individual, you could say that person wanted to vote for Gore. Should these be considered legal votes?

M: I think that if your standard, [and] we lacked a good clear standard, . . . is to determine the intent of the voter, then that would be a clear vote. One of the problems we had during the recount was [the] absence of a really clear standard for deciding those kinds of votes. I think in some counties those were counted and in others they were not. I remember the Bush people complaining that there were some ballots in Lake County, I believe, where they wrote in Bush, circled Bush, but because they voted twice, that county decided not to count them. I think that's one of the whole problems with what happened here. We had 67 different fiefdoms, if you will, each of them deciding how they were going to handle the recount. And it was legal for them to do that. The state had not taken a hold of this issue and firmly promulgated standards to determine how to recount.

P: Another issue that was discussed frequently was the butterfly ballot in Palm Beach County. Did you consider that ballot to be illegal?

M: No, I don't think I did, no. There is no question that it's confusing. As I recall, Cook County [Chicago], Illinois, had butterfly ballots and threw out 220,000 votes in this very same election. But [is it] illegal? Probably not. That county had used them before, without complaint.

P: I notice that 96 percent of the voters in Palm Beach County had no trouble with the ballot.

M: Right. I think there are a percentage of people that will have trouble with any instruction you give them because they don't pay attention to it.

P: Give me your reaction to the spokesmen for each side, particularly Warren Christopher for Gore and Jim Baker for Bush. How do you think they represented their clients?

M: I think each one did a credible job. They're both good talkers, if you will. They had enough prominence and background to represent the two [candidates].

P: The Democrats had a lot of criticism of Jim Baker. They thought he was too harsh and that he denounced and impugned the Florida Supreme Court unfairly. He had announced at one point, after the 4-3 Florida Supreme Court decision came down, we should not have an election that is decided by the courts, but then when the 5-4 U.S. Supreme Court decision was announced, you didn't hear that comment from Baker.

M: [B]oth sides were filled with a lot of very angry rhetoric. It was not the finest hour of politics in Florida. Depending on which way the courts were ruling, you had the other side trashing them from the very minute that Terry Lewis ruled in the very first case. And it did make the courts, I think, look much more political than they might have looked otherwise.

P: One argument was, and a lot of the Republicans I've talked to agreed with this, that the Republicans out-organized, out-spent, and out-worked the Democrats, and that may have been the difference in the recount.

M: It could be. For reasons that are totally unclear to me, I have never covered an election where the Republicans did not outwork the Democrats as to absentee ballots. Now, if you took merely the absentee ballots in this case, they would make the difference in the race. It's hard for me to say that one side worked harder than the other, out of what we saw here, because both sides were out there working. They were working a legal battle, a PR battle, and a political battle all at the same time. And it may be the only time . . . in our history that we've had this confluence of events, where you had a race that was just so close that they were waging all kinds of war, political, legal, and PR.

P: Jeff Toobin argued that the Republicans were willing to win at all costs while Gore was more concerned with public opinion.

M: I don't think so. I would disagree with that. I think both sides wanted to win at all costs. I think the best example [of how] that's not true of Gore is the military ballot issue. For the Democrats to even think about doing something to try to deliberately knock out the ballots of men serving in the military, I think, was the best example I saw of "win at any cost" in this process. This was for all the marbles, and that both sides knew it and that they went after it in that fashion.

P: One author said that the Republicans had the home-court advantage because the governor and the secretary of state and legislature were Republicans, and therefore, they controlled state law firms; they had significant resources that they could use.

M: Well, I think that's true, although in this state we have about 400,000 more Democrats than Republicans. Now, they don't always vote Democratic, but I think both sides had adequate forces in play.

P: Jesse Jackson had a rally here in Tallahassee, and the main point of his argument was later taken up by the Civil Rights Commission. He indicated there was some anecdotal evidence of racial discrimination. Did you see any of that at all?

M: I saw no evidence of organized discrimination. You could say there was anecdotal discrimination—there probably is in everything we have that goes on. I have frequently heard the argument that the poorest neighborhoods had the worst problems. Well, if you look at the per-capita income of Florida, I think nine of the top ten per-capita income counties in Florida used punch-card ballots, which were the worst system, and the least reliable.

P: One study indicated that difficulties at the polls probably had more to do with economic-educational levels, because there were a lot of African Americans voting for the first time. We see that in Duval County, where there were many overvotes.

M: I think that in those areas you probably do have more mistakes made by the voter and there is not much question that Florida had done very little to educate voters. There was virtually no money in the budget anywhere for voter education at that time.

P: If that is the case, that's not discrimination. If voters go to the wrong precinct or vote for all ten presidential candidates, that is not an example of discrimination.

M: No, unless you wanted to take that back to the root of discrimination, which would be the failure to educate poor people.

P: One of the terms used in the Civil Rights Commission Report, which was rather offensive to some experts, was disenfranchisement, which harkens back to a much more segregated society.

M: I also think that the Civil Rights Commission was the closest I've ever seen to a kangaroo court. That group is heavily Democratic; they donate to Democratic candidates. If you run them through the federal campaign database, you find that Mary Francis Berry, although she officially is an independent, donates to Democratic candidates. That commission has gone on to greater ignominy than it had here, but it is clearly a biased commission. Several of the members of it, in order to remain on it and get reappointed, shed their registration as Democrats and re-registered as Independents so that they could be reappointed to that commission, because it's supposed to contain a certain number of Independents, Republicans, and Democrats.

P: I also want to ask you about the issue of Highway Patrol stops on Election Day. The law enforcement checkpoint was Oak Ridge Road, which is in Leon County. They stopped 150 vehicles in an hour and a half: 63 percent were white, 37 percent black, 16 citations were given to whites, 10 citations were given to blacks, but African Americans argued that the very presence of the Highway Patrol was intimidating.

M: Given my knowledge of the Florida Highway Patrol, I would not be surprised if those guys didn't know there was an election going on and probably didn't know they were anywhere near a poll at the time, but I think certainly there would be people who would see troopers there and be intimidated and turn around and go back. I also suspect that a very small percentage of those people would have been voting at all. We looked into that when it happened and I've read the various reports that have come out on that stop. I would be really surprised to see, after all is said and done and all these suits are over, if anyone found any organized discrimination that was sanctioned by any government entity. I just don't believe that existed.

P: Would you assess the performance of Katherine Harris during this period? *The New York Times* concluded that every decision she made favored Bush.

M: Well, I think it did. I think the facts she had at hand probably led her to that at each moment. At each moment that she made a decision favoring Bush, the vote totals were that way. Fortunately, I don't think Katherine Harris had very much to do with the outcome. I think, on balance, she probably was not a very good public official, I think she didn't know anything about election law. She did very little to talk about what was going on, she had maybe one very disastrous press conference. I also don't think she had much power, given the fact that it was fractured into 67 pieces in this state. I think a lot of the out-of-state press thought that the state Division of Elections had more power than it actually did, when you look at the way an election operates in Florida.

P: Was the national press unfair to her?

M: I would be the first to criticize her competence and note the lack thereof, . . . but to criticize her looks is pretty sexist in origin and a little over-the-top. [Y]ou can make jokes about public officials and everybody thinks they're funny, [but] I didn't think most of that was particularly funny. I think part of the image that reflected poorly on the state and on Katherine was caused by the fact that she was not [some]one that should have been cast out into the middle of that and asked to explain something that she didn't understand. There should have been a public official, ideally it would have been the governor. In this case, it couldn't be the governor.

P: Mac Stipanovich was put in Katherine Harris's office to "give political advice." Who determined that he should be there and how influential was he?

M: Well, my guess is that Mac determined he should be there. Mac helped to run her campaign for secretary of state . . . so Mac would have naturally been the closest political advisor that she had at the time. I suspect that she was fairly isolated from the very beginning because none of the governor's people liked her.

P: Did you see the Jeb Bush administration trying to influence Harris?

M: Absolutely not. I think the role of the Bush people was to keep an eye on what was going on, and I would bet money that each thing they found out, they transmitted to the George W. Bush campaign. But I never saw, and we looked awfully hard for it, . . . that Jeb was influencing [her] and I don't think they put Mac [in her office].

P: Katherine Harris had very little extra support in the beginning except for her staff, and they were not political veterans. Clay Roberts had just taken over that job as director of the Division of Elections, had he not?

M: Yes, and he was a creature of the legislature. He was staff director for the House Elections Committee. He's an attorney. He's got a lot of knowledge of the elections law. As long as they were dealing with election law and counting votes, Clay was fine. He probably would have done better had they put him out front to answer questions, but I don't think their egos could ever let them do that. I just don't think [Harris] had enough really experienced political hands around her and Mac probably filled that vacuum very quickly.

P: You also investigated the charge that the secretary of state's office had deleted or destroyed some of its computer files.

M: We, in the end, found no evidence that had happened. We paid a bunch of money to a company [that] took apart all the hard drives and we found very little that we had not already found in public-records requests made at the time of the election. I guess the most serious offense, if there was an offense committed, was that she was doing a fair amount of composing political speeches on state equipment and things like that, but I suspect it's not anything that everybody in the building's not doing over there.

P: But part of the problem was, of course, and it is true of Bob Butterworth as well, that both were public officials who were part of either the Gore or Bush campaign apparatus.

M: Butterworth escaped a lot of the public attention, but I thought it was pretty outrageous that Butterworth was trying to intimidate that judge down in Seminole County [Corr: Volusia County: ed.], and we wrote a story about it. He was calling down there, trying to intimidate him into recounting those votes in a certain way, and sending him written opinions on it that were unsolicited and contrary to those being put out by the Division of Elections. The intriguing thing is that his own website said he didn't issue opinions on elections.

P: Let me go to the controversy over the military and overseas absentee ballots. I talked to Mark Herron, and he explained that the five-page memo he developed was merely outlining the law as it existed. The Republicans accused the Democrats of trying to prevent the military from voting. Why was this issue so significant?

M: I think, again, you have 67 different standards being applied here. In some counties, they wouldn't open up and go back and recount [the military ballots], and in others they did and each county that did used a different standard to count by.

P: *The New York Times* concluded that there were 680 questionable ballots, which were judged by markedly different standards in every case. In Escambia and Okaloosa Counties, they went back and counted votes they had earlier rejected.

M: Two very heavily military counties.

P: *The New York Times* reported that there was some intimidation. Republicans allegedly said, "look, you live here, it's a military base, are you going to deny soldiers the right to vote?"

M: Absolutely. It became a sort of *cause celebre* to count the votes. You had, all over the state, the parents of military people [coming] to testify at one of the election commissions about the military ballot problem. It became sort of a mom-and-apple-pie issue to count those damn ballots, whether they were legal or not, and in some counties they did.

P: I noticed that, having talked with the elections supervisor in Alachua County, a vote that was not counted in Alachua County would have been counted in Okaloosa County. Isn't that a violation of the Fourteenth Amendment?

M: Probably. I don't think there's much question that this was not handled equally. Nor do I think that there was any chance that it would be done equally without a single standard. When you allow 67 different places to set the rules, it's an invitation for this.

P: I wanted to ask you your views of the Seminole and Martin County cases. Did you see the actions of Sandra Goard and Peggy Martin as violations of election law?

M: When you're dealing with the request for the ballot and not the ballot itself, I'm not sure that [it] was. It certainly was odd. To say it was a violation of the law, I suppose there could be a lot of things that would violate the law, but not to the extent that they would overturn the results in the election. That was sort of the way I saw both of those cases. You could say, yeah, they probably shouldn't have done what they did, but do you throw out an election based on that? I don't think so. Mainly because nobody was tinkering with the ballot itself. We rarely have an election where there's not some sort of irregularity. It is extremely rare, as you know, to see one overturned and you almost have to have the presence of out-and-out fraud there to [overturn an election].

P: Let me get your reaction to the decisions of the Florida Supreme Court. The Republicans charged that they were a liberal Democratic court, but if you look at their decisions, they declared the Palm Beach ballot legal and they voted against Gore on any number of other issues. Did you see them as politically motivated in their decisions?

M: I don't know. I think that they were widely perceived to be political because of the way it came out. I thought Judge Lewis's initial decision was a correct interpretation of the law and I thought [the Florida Supreme Court's] response to it was not correct, that there wasn't enough [evidence] shown to overturn the results of the election. So I was surprised by the vehemence of that decision, the first decision they put out.

P: This is the November 21, 7-0 vote to allow the recounts to continue and to put November 26 as the deadline for certification.

M: I thought that Judge Lewis had reasonably interpreted what the law was and that they [Florida Supreme Court] were reaching when they reached that opinion to reverse it. I didn't think it was good for Florida or the country to have this thing drag out interminably, whoever won it. I just thought that they looked political, and I had not expected them to, I guess.

P: One of the problems that comes up later is when the Florida Supreme Court changed the certification date to November 26.

M: Yes, I thought that was wrong. When they start tinkering with changing it, I thought that was not a correct legal interpretation.

P: Did you ever expect that this would end up in the U.S. Supreme Court?

M: Yes, from the minute it happened. I knew that both sides would sue at the drop of a hat, because it was just apparent that this was for everything there was in the world of politics, and they had to sue. I just thought that was where it had to end up.

P: I thought Craig Waters did a thorough job of providing information from the Florida Supreme Court to the media.

M: Oh, yeah, the U.S. Supreme Court, the way they put it out was awful. I thought Craig . . . may have been the most professional and balanced in what he did, in the way he handled it. The [way] they put the pleadings on the Internet the minute they were out was inspired, because they would have never been able to meet the demand for copies over at the court.

P: What was your assessment of how Judge Sauls officiated the case when the Democrats moved to the contest phase. Did you agree with his decision?

M: Of course, the Democrats didn't like that decision at all and took great umbrage at it, but I couldn't argue with his decision in that case. I became convinced fairly early on that no amount of recount in those damn ballots was going to produce something that was any more accurate. It might have produced a different winner, but I don't know that it would have been any more accurate than what we had. I thought Sauls did a fair job. He was folksy, but he ran a pretty good courtroom, and he didn't let anybody run over him.

P: The Florida Supreme Court voted 4-3 to reverse Judge Sauls. Were you surprised by the decision or the closeness of the vote?

M: I was surprised both by the reasoning in the decision and by the closeness in the vote. The story I did that morning was on [Justice] Wells's dissent. I had never seen a dissent in that court as impassioned as that one that Wells put out, and I wondered if it didn't signal some really serious trouble for that court in the future. There was a lot about that decision that simply was not logical to me. Giving back some votes and not others, I thought was a reach for the court. I was just puzzled at where the hell they were coming from.

P: The Florida House of Representatives, led by Speaker Tom Feeney, voted 79-41 to seat electors for Bush if the legal issues were not resolved by December 12. Was this move constitutional? Was it a dangerous precedent?

M: When Feeney got this idea that they should get in the middle of it, I think most of us didn't really take him seriously at first; we thought he was just saber-rattling. But I think Feeney and those around him loved the notoriety they got out of it and they were out there pandering [to] the television cameras every minute of the day. It was interesting to see how caught up some of these legislators got in national publicity. A number of them who had probably never even been interviewed by a Florida television camera, were suddenly international news stars, if you will.

P: The U.S. Supreme Court steps in and they halt all the recounts. Do you think, if the U.S. Supreme Court had not stepped in, that the counties would have had time to complete the count?

M: Probably, yes. I don't know what it would have yielded. I think some of the studies since then have suggested it would have come out for Bush. To me, the only logical thing to do was to try to recount every vote in the state, but it did not seem to me that anybody wanted that. Certainly the Democrats didn't, although they stood up and said they did. All they had to do was file a written request for a recount in every county and they never did that.

P: Justice Ruth Bader Ginsburg, in her dissent, argued that the U.S. Supreme Court should never have heard this case to begin with, that this was a state case. Do you agree with this reasoning?

M: Actually, I do think that they probably didn't have the authority to take the state case, that the final authority on state law should have been the state court. Now the question you have here is [that] this is a federal election and it is through that door that they came, but I don't know how constitutional that ground is underneath them.

P:   I noticed that Justice John Paul Stevens said the *Bush v. Gore* decision would undermine the nation's confidence in the U.S. Supreme Court and was wholly without merit. That's a pretty strong dissent.

M:   Which is essentially what Wells said of the Florida Supreme Court case. But I think both decisions went to undermine the reputations of both courts and probably made most citizens see both of those courts as much more political than you and I expect them to be.

P:   Would you argue, as one critic did, that the William Rehnquist court was now an activist court?

M:   Yes, I guess you'd have to say they are. And certainly this court [Florida Supreme Court] is. The Florida Supreme Court decision came down after 9:00 at night with us just killing ourselves. The Internet crashed when they put it up on their website [because] there were so many people trying to access it. It was a mess to deal with. I could not, for the life of me, understand why either court thought this decision needed to come out . . . in the middle of the night. I think both decisions might have been better received had they put them out at a decent time to give people time to analyze them.

P:   How much long-term impact will the 5-4 *Bush v. Gore* decision have? The U.S. Supreme Court indicated that the decision applied just to the 2000 presidential election.

M:   I think it's hard to tell. I think it will change the way everyone looks at elections for a long time. For instance, before this, the news media, including us, did a miserable job of looking at the mechanics of the election. Almost nobody was looking at the method by which we voted, how well we educated voters, how many ballots were thrown out. There were elections that had occurred before this in Palm Beach where even more ballots had been thrown out than were thrown out this time because of obvious voter confusion. Even if you disregard the legal precedent that it may or may not have set for the future, I just think that people will look at elections differently. I suspect that it was a great civics lesson for the voter. I think in the end game here, even the average citizen understands the electoral process better than they did, and understands that individual votes do count much better than anybody ever [thought they] did.

P:   Do you think the national media was unfair to Florida? We remember Flori-Duh and all of the foul-ups, but other states had more overvotes and undervotes than Florida did.

M:   Illinois. Yes, I think that Florida was made something of a spectacle. We did a lot to earn it, but I think that you could have taken the same issues and questions to virtually any state in the Union and found the same problems. I think we were just unlucky enough to be in the middle of the storm where the election was so close.

P:   How did the experience impact you and were you glad to have had the opportunity to go through it?

M:  Well, I think all of us were glad. We felt like we were living in the middle of history and, in a sense, we were. But it was a really difficult time on all of us, physically and emotionally. Of course, we had editors who every day were picking up every paper in the world or seeing something on television, saying, "wait a minute, we need to have that." It was just a nightmare to get everybody out where you needed them.

P:  Do you have any special stories or comments about anything we haven't covered? Any particular events that stand out in your memory?

M:  It was rewarding in a sense that you felt like people were really reading and paying attention to what you were writing and doing, and yet [it was] totally exhausting. I hope never to have to suffer through another one. I have joined the ranks of Kurt Browning, who told me that for many years he went to bed on the night before each election praying for a landslide in every race. I now join Kurt in that prayer; I hope the next election is a landslide for somebody, I don't care who.

For many people in the world, it was the only view they've ever had of Tallahassee, Florida. I think it's recognized as a place, and there's some merit to that. I think a lot of the business people made out like bandits from it. I think a lot of people also found that it was a very hospitable Southern city. There were little old ladies who took cookies down to the news crews. It was a time when a lot of people here went out of their way to help all the strangers who were stranded here. It was interesting to live through.

# ➤ CRAIG WATERS ◄

Before serving as the Director of Public Information for the Florida Supreme Court, Craig Waters was an award-winning journalist for Gannett Florida newspapers. He earned his undergraduate degree at Brown University in 1979 and his Juris Doctorate from the University of Florida College of Law in 1986. He began working at the Florida Supreme Court in 1987 as a staff attorney and, in 1996, moved into administration as executive assistant to Chief Justice Gerald Kogan. During this period of time, he created the Court's first public information program as well as Justice Kogan's award-winning Access Initiative, which improved public access to the Florida Supreme Court. In September 1997, Waters was invited to serve as a faculty member of the Court Tech and spoke on the Florida Supreme Court's innovative uses of the Internet. As Director of Public Information, Waters deals with the press, maintains the public information press pages of the Court's websites on a daily basis, distributes opinions electronically, coordinates Court broadcasts with WFSU, and handles public information requests.

Waters began his interview with a discussion of Election Day 2000. Although he was expecting significant legal cases from the beginning, he "greatly underestimated what would come the [Florida Supreme Court's] way . . . and never imagined that it would become as big as it did." Waters talked of how he became so visible that his public appearances had to be controlled, especially when security became an issue. Waters discussed the negative image of the court, stating that "some of the best spinmeisters in the business . . . were trying to put a negative spin on what [the] court was doing [and] in many cases [were] really misinterpreting what had actually been done in opinions and doing so for their own political reasons." Because of this negative spin, Waters viewed the controversy "not primarily, as a legal battle, but as a battle of public opinion." Waters also felt that "Jim Baker was playing to a public audience" and the "the exaggerations he made about Dexter Douglass's influence over the court [were] just one example of the kind of thing that [the Republicans] were doing for their own political ends."

When asked about the positive aspects of this experience, Waters observed that "it showed for the first time on an international basis, how important it can be for courts to have a public information function and to communicate in a timely basis with the rest of the world." He noted that other states "revisited their own policies because of what happened." Waters also addressed the ways in which access to the hearings was determined, how he handled the media onslaught on a daily basis, the issue of security in the courtroom, the national media's treatment of the Florida Supreme Court and how the media was impressed with the openness of the Court, and the attitude of the Supreme Court Justices and the environment in which they worked. Waters concluded his interview with a discussion of the impact of the election controversy on the Court as well as how the recount affected him mentally and physically.

Craig Waters was interviewed by the author on October 3, 2002, in Tallahassee, Florida.

P:   What was Election Day, November 7, 2000, like for you in a personal sense?

W:   Election Day was really kind of off-the-radar-screen with me because I was in Orlando at a conference of the National Conference of Court Public Information Officers. It was our annual conference, and I, of course, had voted absentee and went down there. I was on the faculty, so I was giving a presentation. In fact, I gave my presentation the morning of the election, and the presentation was on using the Web to distribute public information to the media and to anybody who wants it. The conference ended, and I went to my hotel room after we had a dinner that evening . . . and went to bed completely ignorant of what was happening in the greater world at the time.

I got up early the next morning . . . and I turned on CNN, and they were saying that there had been this chaos going on in Florida. That they'd called it for Gore, then they'd called it for Bush, then they retracted that. When I heard that, I ran down to the front desk of the hotel, which had a stack of *Orlando Sentinel*s there. They had the latest version that said it was too close to call and that there had been all these problems in Palm Beach County and questions about other matters of the election. Shortly after that, I got a call from the Chief Justice's office telling me to get back to Tallahassee immediately because they were already getting inquiries from the national media and that I needed to be there.

We began preparing for what we thought would be a major event, completely oblivious that it would not be major, it would be enormous. I got together with the Chief Justice at the time, Charles G. Wells. [I] also met with our clerk of court and our marshal to begin putting together an emergency operations plan. It turned out that we greatly underestimated what actually would come our way. My estimate at the time was that, at the outside, it would last maybe two weeks. Yes, we'd have national media here, but it wouldn't be unmanageable. It would be a slightly larger version of the kind of controversies we get here all the time.

P:   So from the beginning, you were expecting some significant legal cases.

W: Yes, I was expecting them. Mainly because when I was a staff attorney here, I did do a lot of work on election cases. So I know something about election law in Florida. I had, of course, seen the controversy about the butterfly ballot. Quite frankly, my legal estimation of that at the time, which I, of course, did not share with the media or others, was that the butterfly ballot was not likely to be a meritorious case. There had been a number of cases in Florida talking about flaws in ballot design, and, essentially, there is some give-and-take there for technical errors that do not really call into question the entire election itself. Of course, that subsequently is what happened with the butterfly ballot case. What we did not know was that all these other cases would arise. Altogether, nearly . . . 50 cases involving some 500 attorneys were headed our way.

P: When you set up your website, I noticed at one point that you got up to 3,500,000 hits a day.

W: Right, and that was just on our server here, which is the "flcourts.org" server. That's the capacity, or was the capacity at the time.

P: So you had to put in a backup server.

W: Well, we have had a duplicate server at another location here in Tallahassee that was loaned to us by the Department of Education . . . and we've used it as backup whenever there were problems with our server. So we were actually diverting people onto this other server. Later on, as we maxed out the capacity of both servers, we did hire the services of a Web redistribution service . . . which literally has servers all over the world. They have the capacity to essentially duplicate any website and make it easier for people to access it. So ultimately we . . . were able to dispense, literally, hundreds of millions of documents worldwide on a continuous basis.

P: What was your function as the briefs and the cases would come in?

W: I created the presidential election page that we would use. It was a simple design that I've used. You use simple designs because they download quicker for any controversial matter. It was designed so that it would automatically check for new documents every five minutes, which was a feature that I found useful in the past. I could then tell the reporters to simply leave it on their screen, and it would reload itself and would tell when new documents were filed. I guess to show how naïve I was about what was going to happen at the time, I put my own e-mail link at the bottom of this page. [I] did not realize it until quite some time later, I had also put my cell-phone number at the bottom of this page. [I] was literally inundated with e-mails and cell-phone calls. Many times I had to turn the cell-phone off because it just became unusable.

P: I understand people called you late at night. What were some of the comments from your callers?

W: They were all across the board, everything you could imagine. Both extremes. People who were very unhappy with what the court had done. People who were cussing mad at what the court had done. People who thought that the court was the savior of the world. People who thought that our justices, or the majority of the justices, were the noblest species of human being on the Earth. Then [there were] those who thought the exact opposite, and everything in-between. It was something of a circus of responses. I think there was so much emotion going on at the time that people were really firing off responses, making telephone calls, and sending e-mails without putting much thought into the fact that, particularly with the e-mails, they are actually public record under Florida law and will be there forever.

P: How many e-mails did you get?

W: I got about 15,000 e-mails over the course of the 30 days. There certainly were a larger number sent to me, but because of the huge volume coming in, not all of them could jam through the bandwidth at the same time.

P: Give me an example of some of the more interesting e-mails.

W: I actually had, it was probably several hundred, people calling in various forms to suggest that I resign and call a press conference or whatever, and impugn my court in whatever way I could. I've been with my court through thick and thin and had absolutely no intention of doing anything like that, especially since the many conspiracy theories that were going around were wholly baseless.

P: Were there any threats?

W: There were a lot of threats, most of them veiled. I got a lot of e-mails with comments like, "Run while you still can." We got some others that were obscene in nature, but could be interpreted as threatening. I actually got a number of e-mails that could be construed as threats against some of the other public figures involved in this case, such as Katherine Harris and even President Bush's daughters. We handed [these] over to law enforcement authorities. So security was an issue. The marshal decided, at one point, that when I went out in public from then on until the controversy ended, I would have to have an armed security guard with me because of that.

P: Obviously, it was the same for all the justices?

W: Whenever they were in public places, yes. Although I can tell you, I certainly avoided going out in the public during all of this. Even when I went out to deal with the press in front of our building, people would stop me. I had people cuss me. I had people praise me. It was a very different kind of experience.

P: Jeff Greenfield, in his book, said that you became an internationally recognizable figure. I assume you didn't expect that.

W: No, I never did. It was something that I really had to be hit in the face with before I even realized it had happened, because I just thought it was so implausible. The day that it actually hit home with me occurred early on during that first week leading up to the first argument. I had been going out and briefing the press as I normally do. Our marshal had decided very early on that he was going to close the building to the public and the press, so the press began gathering on the front steps of the building. Many people actually felt that we staged this for the front steps of the building, but it evolved over a period of time. It evolved very rapidly. But that was where the press would gather, and I would go out and brief them periodically. In the first few days there were only a small contingent of reporters there. So I could go out and just mingle with them and brief them orally, which is what I was very accustomed to doing. Of course, we just never imagined that this would become as big as it did.

Then one day, it was probably about Wednesday of the week after the election, I got a call from one of the CNN reporters who had a question. She was having to make hourly reports on what was going on in Tallahassee. She said, at the top of the hour, I have to say something, and I don't have anything to say. Could you please come out and just talk with me? Just anything, I need anything. I said, okay, I will. I walked out there, and I was instantly surrounded by videographers and reporters with microphones stuck in my face. I started getting a lot of e-mails, probably about a dozen or two dozen, mainly from women who were very unhappy with me. I couldn't figure out why. So finally a reporter friend of mine . . . sent me an e-mail. [He] said that his mother-in-law had been watching her soap opera, and I had walked out on the steps. Dan Rather had interrupted the soap opera to say that Craig Waters had something to say, and then I appeared on television only to say that nothing new had happened. So his mother-in-law was very unhappy that I had interrupted her soap opera. That was when I realized that we were going to have to control my public appearances much more rigidly than I was accustomed to. It reached the point that even going out when I had statements to make, there were so many reporters later on, that I could not do them informally. So I talked to the five big news networks and asked them what they needed for us to make this work better. They said, first of all, we need a podium, and, second, you're going to have to go to some sort of mass briefing. So we brought up what became the famous podium. That's pretty much the way it remained, although later we did go to a pool system that reduced the number of microphones that were out there. The five big news networks, ABC, CBS, NBC, which is also, of course, affiliated with MSNBC, Fox, and CNN, rotated the camera and the audio-system out in front of the building on a daily basis.

P:    In many cases, Tallahassee was a mob scene.

W:   Oh, it was a tremendous mob scene out there. [I]f you were looking out back then, there would have been protestors in the streets. Two of the lanes of traffic were closed off to accommodate satellite trucks. There was a large tent sitting on the terraces where the news media had set up their tents as their command centrals. CNN had the tallest of all the tents out there, where they had Bill Hemmer, Greta Van Susteren, Larry King, and several others doing broadcasts from there. Of course, they had the Florida Supreme Court building in the backdrop. Then there were just mobs of partisans. The police tried to keep the Democrats on one side and the Republicans on another side so that they didn't get into fisticuffs over this. We also just had your run-of-the-mill kooks that kept showing up. We had people who came dressed in aluminum foil with satellite dishes strapped to their backs that were trying to channel energy toward the Court. One evening we had a prayer circle completely surrounding the court building. A security officer was actually showing me through the prayer chain so I could go home. We had a gentleman who owned an automobile museum who showed up here with one of the original Batmobiles [from the *Batman* television series or movie], driving it around the building and honking his horn repeatedly. We had a woman who showed up with a pet skunk that could do back flips, and she got her fifteen seconds on national television. That's the one interesting thing about an event like this, which is literally a 24 hours a day, seven days a week, news story, is that the networks are desperate for anything.

P:   Did you also distribute hard copies of court decisions?

W:   We did, and we were quite surprised. We had been distributing electronically since 1996, and the press corps here in Tallahassee is very accustomed to that. We closed down our newsroom, and even our opinions are distributed electronically via e-mail and over the [World Wide] Web. What we did not anticipate with this was the large number of out-of- town reporters who came here not knowing how we normally work. At the height of it, the police estimated that we had somewhere up to about 800 reporters outside the building. We had tremendous demand from these people for copies of our documents. That reached sort of a highlight during the release of the major opinion in November, when our high-speed fax machine liter-ally crashed and burned under the pressure of its use. We had to bring in staff from all over the building. They were using literally every photocopying machine in the building, and these are slow-speed copiers, to produce copies. The bottom-line was the people standing outside didn't get paper copies for about an hour and a half after they were released on the Web. Many of them would call their offices in New York and Washington only to find out that their people there had already read and reported what had happened in the opinions because they had gotten it quicker off the Web. After that, demand for paper trailed off tremendously.

P:   You were quoted during the 36 days as follows: "Access to courts and public trust in courts are closely linked. People distrust what appears to be secretive. They distrust government that operates in the shadows. Even people who strongly disagreed with the Florida Supreme Court election decisions sent e-mail to praise two things. One, the fact that all documents in the case were promptly posted on the Web, and two, the fact that oral arguments were available in live video. I repeatedly heard from people who said they were so glad they could read court documents without the media filter. This was among the most positive aspects of the presidential election cases." Do you still agree with that statement?

W:   Yes, I do.

P:   What kinds of people were accessing your website?

W:   They were all across the board. We had a huge number of attorneys and judges that were following it nationwide and a lot of people who were well-educated people, who were obviously reading the opinions and coming to their own conclusions. I still strongly believe in that. The major problem that was thrown our way was something that would have occurred anyway, whether or not we released opinions in this way. That was the fact that we had some of the best spinmeisters in the business who were trying to put a negative spin on what our court was doing. In many cases [they were] really misinterpreting what had actually been done in opinions and doing so for their own political reasons. That would have happened no matter what we did with the Web or the broadcasts.

[T]here were reports, for example, that the Florida Supreme Court had put the initial stay on Katherine Harris's certification without anything being filed here. That was not true, but that was an example of the kind of negative spin. There was a case that was pending here whenever the court issued that order. [The Florida Supreme Court ruled on an appeal as opposed to reaching out and taking the case.] I think that was the most cynical thing that I saw in all of this, realizing that there were people out there who were completely willing to misinterpret what this court had done, and doing so publicly, and repeating it over and over again in an effort to influence public opinion. Now, obviously, many of the politicians viewed this not, primarily, as a legal battle, but as a battle of public opinion. They treated it accordingly. That's nothing new in American politics, but it certainly was, I think, the first time this court had actually ended up in the cross-hairs of this kind of thing.

P:   What were some of the positive aspects of this experience?

W:   I think the most positive aspect was that it showed, for the first time on an international basis, how important it can be for courts to have a public information function and to communicate in a timely basis with the rest of the world. This obviously was an issue of worldwide importance, and if we had simply sat here and not communicated and stayed inside of our locked building, I think that would have been a far more damaging image than what was seen at the time. Even many people who disagreed with what my court was doing, in terms of the legal issues, actually e-mailed saying that they greatly appreciated the fact that we were so open, that we were not trying to hide. We were not concealing our rulings in the dead of the night. We were not leaving people to guess what had happened. We were being quite forthright. I think there's a great deal to be said about that.

Florida, of course, is rather unusual in that we have public-records laws that are written into our constitution, and are probably among the broadest in the world in terms of access. We've learned to live with that. Since the election cases, I've actually given speeches to state court systems in other states. Many of them are quite fascinated with what happened because they don't have that degree of openness in their states. Many of them expressed surprise that it worked so well in Florida. I have had a number of them who say that they have revisited their own policies because of what happened. Of course, we did have the famous episode with the U.S. Supreme Court, where they decided to actually distribute audio of the arguments immediately after the case was heard, which was unprecedented for them. Many people attribute that to the pressure that was put on them because of the Florida comparison.

P:     Do you think the U.S. Supreme Court should be as open as the Florida Supreme Court?

W:    I think they eventually will. That's something that they will decide in their own good time. There are arguments at the U.S. Supreme Court that they deal with cases of a different magnitude, and I think that's something that they do need to take into account. They deal with *Bush v. Gore* types of cases all the time. So that is something that I would certainly want to factor into the equation if I were the public information officer there because, I can tell you, that's very taxing to deal with, and you have to have the resources in place. Until you do have those resources in place, it certainly is not a good idea to try to do what we did here on essentially a permanent basis.

P:     How did you determine access to the hearings? How many journalists would you admit and on what basis?

W:    For the journalists we reserved 28 seats that were to be done on a lottery basis. When we decided on the lottery, we didn't realize what would happen because of the press of events going on because this was a 24–7 news event. The lottery essentially was conducted like this: we would put a box out on the front steps, or close to it, where reporters would put their business cards or a scrap of paper with their name and phone number on it. But the rule was this: by that evening I would, at a certain time, take the box away and would begin pulling names randomly from the box. The reporter had to be available at that phone number when I called. If they were not available, then that created an obvious problem. We had not anticipated the fact that on each occasion about half of the reporters were unreachable. What I did in that situation, because we had not anticipated that, is I exercised my judgment and replaced the half that were missing with people that I thought really needed to be in the courtroom, such as the major networks, the major Florida networks, and newspapers. So I used that to insure that we had a very good representation of the media, and that we didn't have people whose sole claim to journalistic fame was a web page that they operated from their home computer.

P: What about access for the attorneys?

W: The attorneys, of course, if they argued the cases, there was reserved seating inside the courtroom. We made a deliberate decision that we were not going to put folding chairs in the courtroom because of decorum, so we limited the seating to what would be normal in a routine court argument. There were about a hundred seats that were left for the public, and by public we meant anybody. We got a disproportionate number of journalists and lawyers who ended up being the "public" part of that, because they stood in line or hired someone to stand in line for them. In fact, a number of Florida State University fraternity and sorority members actually made some money by not only serving as runners for these journalists and others who were here, but also by standing in line and holding their places for the courtroom seating.

P: Once the hearings took place, what kind of security did you have in the courtroom?

W: We had a contingent of security officers. Not only our own, but we had also brought in those from local law enforcement, including the Leon County Sheriff's Department, Tallahassee Police Department, and the Florida Department of Law Enforcement. We had security at all the entrances to the building, watching the secure parking garages, and that sort of thing. Of course, because our marshal is a former full colonel in the Army, we had full perimeter surveillance already around the building, and our officers could watch what was going on outside.

P: What was your assessment of the media's treatment of the Florida Supreme Court?

W: The big problem with a story like this, when you have a state Supreme Court that is not well known outside of its state, is the media comes in and they instantly, in a very brief period of time, want to know who these people are. The danger there is in stereotyping, and I think that's exactly what happened with the court. It's probably unavoidable, given this type of news story, [and] given the fact that these justices were not well known outside of Florida. But they were stereotyped based on the governors that had appointed them [and] stereotyped based on their political affiliations. Even though, with many of the political affiliations, I didn't even know their political affiliations until they were being reported here in Florida.

P: The media called this the Dexter Douglass court, that Douglass had influenced Governor Lawton Chiles to appoint liberal Democrats.

W: Exactly, and Jim Baker actually gave a press conference in which he seemed to suggest that the court had essentially been appointed by Dexter Douglass. I had a chance to speak with Dexter about that. He told me that was one way of getting him moved to the second chair because it created an appearance of a conflict of interest that Dexter Douglass was unwilling to live with because of what it would have done to the court.

P: How do you think the media treated the state of Florida in general?

W: I think they treated the state as well as could be expected in this kind of situation. I do know that when they came here, they were awed by the openness because we had large contingents from the Washington and New York areas who had never dealt with this kind of openness. For example, when the big [television] networks first showed up here, I instantly was bombarded with fax letters from their attorneys at high-flying law firms in New York City saying, we demand access to the video, we demand access to your documents. I just called them back and said, listen, you don't have to demand anything, they're public record. We have our own video feed, our satellite feed, and you're welcome to downlink it if you want to. Many of them refused to believe me.

P: Is this the only state Supreme Court that operates this much in the open?

W: I wouldn't say that because there are others that, I know, webcast. To this date [however], the two cases in *Bush v. Gore* that were argued here remain the only appellant arguments that had been broadcast by all the major networks from beginning to end.

P: Could you give me some sense of what a typical day would be in the middle of all this, say between November 17 and December 8? What time would you get here? How late would you work?

W: Well, there really was no typical day because so much depended on what was going to be done. It was quite lengthy at times, because we often did not know exactly when opinions would be released and when I would be making the announcements. So there were some days when I would arrive at five in the morning, just in case we had to make an announcement at eight in the morning. There were days when I would sit around and the times would pass that we thought we were going to be making announcements. So then, it might be late in the evening. For example, the first major opinion was not announced until nine o'clock in the evening right before Thanksgiving.

P: Can you describe the attitudes of the justices during this time and how would you describe the environment in which in they worked?

W: Well, they were working constantly, and so were their staffs. I made a point of getting sleep every night because I saw too many exhausted people on television who were making fools of themselves. But for those of us in the building who did not have to have that public role, there were some of them that put in 24 hour days doing this work. So what I saw were people that had a tremendous burden on their shoulders, and they knew it. [They had] a tremendous amount of work to do in a very short period of time because of the deadlines that were imposed by the various laws, federal and state.

P:   It must have been extremely difficult to make decisions in two days when they would normally have two months to deliberate. How did they organize their staffs to provide the information that they needed to make their decisions?

W:   Well, there is a precedent for this kind of expediting of opinions, and that is when we have death warrants pending in the state of Florida. We have very tight deadlines for those. So most of our staff had been through those kind of experiences. They simply adapted that model to this, where you're going to have to work a tremendous amount of time, and labor would have to be divided up into ways that we might not normally do. You might have interns, for instance, going through the record and tabbing particular areas that needed special attention. Drafts being done by different offices and circulating. It would be a much more speeded-up process, but not one that is unheard of here at the court.

P:   How many staff members would each justice have to help them with all of their work?

W:   We recently moved to them having three, and I'm not sure exactly when that change occurred. I believe it was two, but I'm just not sure about that. But, of course, they also had interns who were working here from law schools as well.

P:   But if that's all the help they had under these conditions, obviously the justices had to do the major amount of work themselves.

W:   Right. We also have a central staff of attorneys though, and those were used very heavily for this as well.

P:   What was it like as you were waiting for the 4-3 decision in *Gore v. Harris* on December 8? Did you have any sense of either when they would complete their deliberations or what the outcome would be?

W:   I knew, the day before, that I was going to be making an announcement that there would be a statewide recount. [The decision] was not released until 4:00 P.M. when I made the announcement. So during that process, of course, I was waiting for them to come up with the final version of the opinion.

P:   What was the reaction of the crowd once you announced the 4-3 decision?

W:   There was a big moan that went up. Although I had a lot of people in the press corps tell me that it was them because they were now afraid they were going to have this case continuing on until the New Year. All during this, the police officers had been suggesting that I needed to wear a bulletproof vest. That night, and that afternoon in particular, they were more adamant, because the crowd was quite restless outside. It was a very large crowd. There were police snipers on the roofs of nearby buildings, although I didn't know about that at the time, fortunately. But the fact that they wanted to put a bulletproof vest on me really rattled me in a way that is hard to describe. We gave 30 minutes warning before we announced the result of opinions. That was so that all the reporters could be in place. The networks would be able to break into whatever their programming was, so that everybody had a fair shot, that was the main reason. We didn't want to leave anybody out. We didn't want to give anybody a scoop, an unfair advantage, over any other press.

P:    Plus you understood that this was a monumental decision, and that everybody in the world wanted to have this opinion.

W:    Right. So I took the opinion, drafted a statement, and it was edited and approved by the majority of the court in the 4-3 decision. Then I went and took my place waiting near the silver doors at the front of the building. We had a system worked out where, one minute before I went out, a representative of the Florida Association of Broadcasters would walk out. That was the signal, because he was well known by all the media, that there was one minute coming up. That was when they would break in. They would say, we have to break into programming. Then I walked out to this enormous crowd. The lights were fortunately rather blinding, so I couldn't really get a good feel for the crowd. When I first began my statement, something fell somewhere, some equipment or something, and, if you look at the video, I actually flinched. I was thinking that this was the bullet-shot and why had I not worn the bulletproof vest. Although I had deliberately decided not to wear a vest because it would have been visible, and because that would have become a news story all by itself.

P:    What's your opinion of the U.S. Supreme Court's decision in *Bush v. Gore*?

W:    I think many people agree that the majority opinion itself is a flawed analysis. I can understand that in the time constraints they were working under. It was something of a surprise, I think, to everybody. But the greatest surprise of all, to me, was when the stay order was issued. That was something that I never in a million years thought would happen. After the stay order, in particularly the language of [Justice] Scalia, I think it became less of a surprise what the U.S. Supreme Court subsequently did in its opinion.

P:    Were you surprised that the Rehnquist Court made a decision based on the Fourteenth Amendment? Certainly, that was unusual reasoning for them.

W:    Yes. I think a lot of people were surprised mainly because that issue had been mentioned only in passing here at the state level, and it became the major feature of the case at that level. That's very unusual.

P:    Some critics have argued that the *Bush v. Gore* decision was a "partisan political decision." How would you respond to that?

W: I have no reason to believe that. The fact that we had courts that were so evenly split at both levels tells me that this is an issue about which reasonable people could differ. In the law, that is an important point. There was a lot of partisan sentiment in the public that reminded me a great deal of how people feel about their football teams. That's fine and good. Politics in some ways is a lot like football. But when you get down to legal issues that kind of analogy really doesn't apply. The question on disputed legal matters is whether reasonable people could differ. I think it's quite clear, at both levels, that that was the case. In that sense, I would not at all be comfortable saying that either the opinions of this court, or the U.S. Supreme Court, were partisan.

P: What impact did all of the decisions have on the credibility of the Florida Supreme Court? You might remember that Jim Baker, after the 4-3 *Gore v. Harris* decision, had a lot of very strong, very negative comments about the Florida Supreme Court, as did other politicians. Do you think that, two years after the fact, Baker's criticism has had very little long-term impact on the status of the Florida Supreme Court?

W: It definitely has died down. You have to keep in mind that Jim Baker was not acting as an attorney in all of this, he was acting as a politician. He was engaging an active spin, and he was really quite the master of it. The Republicans, I must give them credit, are much better at that than the Democrats were. Jim Baker was playing to a public audience. The exaggerations he made about Dexter Douglass's influence over the court are just one example of the kind of thing that they were doing for their own political ends. And, yes, they did succeed in getting Dexter Douglass essentially removed from arguing the case. But I think that the vast majority of Americans realize spin when they see it, maybe not at the time it's being spun, but over the long-term I think they do.

P: How did this experience impact your life?

W: Well, it put me on the speaking circuit, which I never expected. [T]he election cases turned me into something of a national expert on crisis communications, using the World Wide Web, and broadcasting. I've also given a lot of speeches, essentially the same version of the same speech, which is just a humorous recount of the recounts, when I talk about the really funny things that happened here at the court during my period as the spokesman for the court during all of this. I'll give you just one of many examples. After the U.S. Supreme Court entered its stay order, they also ordered us to forthwith transmit the record to Washington D.C., which meant, essentially, we had one day to get it up there. The Chief Justice [Charlie Wells] had told me that I would have to try to requisition one of the state aircraft, which the chief justice can do. Unfortunately, there were Christmas parties all that evening whenever this all came about after the order. There were several of us manning the phones late into the night trying to find [one of] the pilots of the state aircraft. [I] called him at home, and he was home. I said, I know you're not the head of this agency anymore, but we're really desperate here. We have to get the record to Washington, D.C., and we need the state aircraft. He finally tracked down one of his pilots, one of his former employees, who called me on my cell-phone. We worked out the arrangements. I had him talk with my clerk of court, who was going to be taking the record up to Washington. We hung up and then the clerk turned around to me immediately and said, Oh, my God. I said, what? He said, I forgot to ask the pilot's name. Did you get it? I said, well, I didn't ask him. So I said, well, wait a minute. My cell-phone records phone numbers of incoming phone calls, so I'll just re-dial it. So I re-dialed it, and someone said hello. I said, this is Craig Waters at the Florida Supreme Court. I am really sorry. We were just talking with you about piloting a plane for us to Washington tomorrow, and we forgot to ask your name. There was this pause, and he said, Jeb Bush. I said, Governor? He said, yes? I said, well, someone just called me from this phone. He said, well, this is my personal line. Then he said, well, I'm having a party here for some FDLE [Florida Department of Law Enforcement] agents, let me see if I can find whoever it was who called. So he put me on hold and went around the party. [He] came back and said, Craig, I can't find whoever it was. They must have already left, and I swear it wasn't me. I said, well, Governor, believe me, I trust you implicitly. So that's how I ended up on the phone with Jeb Bush right before the big U.S. Supreme Court case.

P: How did the recount affect you mentally and physically?

W: I did not realize how exhausted I was until it was all over. You know, you work on adrenaline for awhile. You just don't feel the pain or the exhaustion or whatever because you're just constantly going. But the night that Al Gore conceded, there was a going away party at one of the local establishments here. All the major news organizations were there. I actually went to it. We were up late, of course, and I got up the next day, and I really began to feel it. Of course, we still had a few matters to be disposed of, and I was dreading going out on the steps and making the announcements. But that day, on the four-teenth, when we got out there and we went out on the steps, there was no one there. They were all gone. They were packing up, the tents were being torn down. The story was over.

P: Are you glad you had a chance to participate in such a momentous event?

W: I'm glad in a lot of ways, but, again, it's one of those events that you are far more glad to have in your past than in your future. I was coming into the office every day, literally knowing that there were a thousand ways to fail and that there were millions of people watching it live.

I can't tell you the kind of pressure you feel with that. There were times when my hands were shaking, and I was trying my best to keep that from being viewed. There certainly were things that I would have done differently in retrospect, but I was very fortunate that I did not make any major bloopers.

# PART V

# INTERVIEWS: POLITICIANS

# ➤ TOM FEENEY ◄

One of the more intriguing but often overlooked controversies during the Florida recount resulted from a much criticized decision by the Republican-dominated Florida House of Representatives. Under the direction of House Speaker Tom Feeney, the state legislature decided that they would vote in favor of the 25 Bush electors certified by Katherine Harris on November 26, regardless of any court decision or recount results. Feeney, like many other Republicans, feared that the delayed and chaotic recount could reverse the initial tally, thus sending Al Gore to the White House. In the end, this controversial move proved unnecessary, as the U.S. Supreme Court, on December 12, issued *Bush v. Gore* only a few hours after the legislature voted 79-41 to appoint the Bush electors. Feeney, now a focal point for the world media, based his decision on Article II, Section I, of the United States Constitution, which gave plenary power over elections to the state legislatures, not the courts.

Originally from Pennsylvania, Feeney was first elected to the Florida House in 1990. Riding the early waves of the "Republican Revolution" in the state of Florida, he quickly caught the eye of prominent Republicans throughout the state. In 1994, Jeb Bush selected Feeney as a running mate for his failed gubernatorial campaign. His state-wide candidacy for Lieutenant Governor put him in the spotlight and two years later, Feeney returned to the legislature and distinguished himself as an advocate of welfare and tort reform. Successes in the House led to his promotion to Speaker of the House in 2000, when, just days after accepting the gavel, Feeney had to face the chaos of the election controversy.

In his interview, Feeney described how he decided the state legislature should play a role in the recount process and, if necessary, select their own slate of electors. Declaring that it "was the Florida House that first recognized the potential role of the legislature," Feeney had no problem with choosing a set of electors prior to the completion of final recounts and judicial decisions. Feeney concluded that the Florida Supreme Court, in its ruling to extend the time for a recount to November 26, "had changed the law after the election," and felt he had a duty to act. "It was pretty obvious that the court was . . . not just stretching the law, but ignoring very specific deadlines and statutes." The Speaker firmly believed that the recount and legal challenges had created a crisis and a "constitutionally infirm moment of America's history."

As the recount continued, Feeney heard constantly from constituents urging him to take action lest Al Gore steal the presidency. Feeney admitted that they had an "uphill PR problem," but was not deterred and told supporters, "don't worry, the legislature is going to handle it." The state Senate, however, did not see the urgency and failed to vote on Feeney's proposal. The Speaker explained that, "the Senate never really did get to the point where a majority of them were anxious to go in and take any action." Although saved from final action by the *Bush v. Gore* decision, Feeney believed that had the legislature selected the Bush electors and Gore had won the recount, the legislature's decision would have passed constitutional muster.

Partly because of his activities during the 2000 recount, Feeney received a promotion from the voters in 2002 when he was elected to the U.S. Congress.

Tom Feeney was interviewed by the author on November 21, 2002.

P:   Give me a brief idea of what Election Day was like for you, and when you first realized this was going to be an extraordinary election.

F:   On Election Day I was campaigning here [in Orlando]. Of course, in order to become speaker, you need to have a majority of [members of] your party elected. I knew full well that I would be watching some very close elections that night. We have 120 members of the legislature [and] there were probably 45 genuinely contested seats. So, I fully assumed I'd be up late helping this candidate or that candidate in a state legislative seat, and that was my primary concern as incoming Speaker. I can remember watching the results come in [and] the networks making early calls against President Bush. [I remember] thinking that, while it was personally a great night [Feeney won election to the U.S. Congress], I was sad [because] the candidate that I felt would do the best job as President . . . was, it looked like, not going to win, or it was going to be very difficult to win without Florida. Then, late in the evening the networks pushed the presidential race, Florida in particular, back into the undecided column.

P:   At this point you were Speaker-Designate correct?

F:   [I was] the Speaker-Designate [and] this may become important later as we talk about the legislature's role in the judicial proceedings. The constitution of Florida really creates an infirmity on the part of the legislature for two weeks. Because as of midnight, while there are 120 certified members of the House, we've taken a position legally that at 12:01 you are a duly elected member and that swearing in is more of a perfunctory clerical chore, [but] you have no [leadership] organization. Under our [state] constitution, the legislature does not organize until 14 days after the election. So, in effect, while we had 120 members, we had no leadership, we had no clerk, we had no rules, and we had no ability to function. That's one of the reasons why the legislature was not represented in the first *Gore v. Harris* case, because only the presiding officers have the power to select attorneys, and there were no presiding officers because we weren't organized. So, I was Speaker-Designate because I had not been elected speaker and had no constitutional power, as I understood it.

P: Were you involved in the recount activities as they unfolded?

F: Well, I should tell you that in my view, and I haven't heard anybody say anything different, it was the Florida House that first recognized the potential role of the legislature. Within 48 hours of the election, . . . a lawyer on my staff named Don Rubottom came and sat down with me and we went over Article II, Section I, of the [United States] Constitution. He had come up with a theory . . . that . . . if the election [dispute] was going to continue to proceed, there may be a role for the legislature to be obligated to protect our [Florida's] participation in the election.

P: Because Article II, Section I says that the legislature is, in fact, responsible for elections.

F: [The legislature] shall determine the method. "Each state shall appoint, in such manner as the legislature thereof may direct, a number of electors." So, it's the legislature that directs the method. I asked him to go back and do some research. He did [and] he found Title III of federal law, which also is very important in all of this.

P: Let me clarify, that's Title III, Section 5 of the U.S. Code.

F: [Yes]. We were very interested in some of the provisions [of 3 U.S. 5] that basically said, if the electors were not ready to participate on December 18, [then] the legislature could go in and resolve the dispute. Those are my words [because] I don't have the language in front of me.

P: Title III said the legislature can resolve disputes concerning the validity of electors. If a state fails to make a choice by Election Day, because of, for example, recounts [or] court challenges, the law provides electors may be appointed on a subsequent day in such a manner as the legislature may direct.

F: That was the language, which is all in Title III. Once the Florida Supreme Court extended the deadlines [to November 26], . . . we felt very strongly they had done the wrong thing. We felt that they had changed the law after the election. We felt like they had violated Title III, that they had thrown the validity of any electors that [were] certified, or the secretary [had] certified, in doubt. We felt very clearly that Congress did not have to accept electors that were chosen in an election pursuant to rules other than the rules that existed on Election Day. At some point, as we went through this, I can remember asking Don [Rubottom] . . . to call folks in the governor's office, general counsel, [and] call people at the party [Republican headquarters] to make them aware we were looking into this.

P: Did you talk to Frank Jiminez?

F: I probably did talk to Frank Jiminez, but it more likely would have been Don going over the details with him. I probably wouldn't have been there for the machinations of what the law or the Constitution did or didn't [say].

P:  Did you notify the governor's office or consult them about interpreting the law?

F:  Oh, I think it was, at first, primarily notifying them. Don asked me for permission to contact both the Republican Party of Florida and the governor's office to tell them that we were looking into our potential responsibilities here.

P:  Let me ask you about the Florida Supreme Court's 7-0 ruling that allowed the recounts to continue and halted Secretary Harris' certification. What was your reaction to the decision to extend the counting and certification to November 26? Obviously, you believed that was making law as opposed to interpreting law.

F:  Yes, beyond that, it was ignoring the law. There is a sentence in the court's decision, something to the effect that they are not going to have a hyper-technical reliance on the statutory scheme. I can remember to this day telling people that meant the court intends to ignore the statute. They basically took authority that the legislature, under our constitutional authority, had vested in the Secretary of State. They undermined that authority and they did so in a fashion completely opposite [of] what the statute called for. Basically, the court, as I read their decision, acknowledged that. They said that they were going to give precedence to the Florida Constitution's will-of-the-people provision over the statutes. They basically acknowledged they were rewriting or ignoring the statutes. I became pretty comfortable with the fact that the deadlines were the deadlines. Title III said, if you're going to ignore the rules that were in place on Election Day, then your electors are, basically, subject to challenge, and may not be valid.

P:  Let me read your reaction, as quoted in the newspapers. "The court's ruling indicated the tremendous lack of respect the Florida Supreme Court has for the laws of the State of Florida and the legislature. The court continues to supplant its personal preferences over the statutory law of Florida." Did you consider this to be a partisan decision by a liberal Democratic court?

F:  Well, that would probably be shorthand for what I was thinking, yeah. Appellate courts have been accused, as long as there have been appellate courts, of being result-oriented. You know, adopt[ing] the reasoning to get you your result. This is nothing new. I felt in a case of this extraordinary importance and world-wide attention, that it was pretty obvious that the court was . . . not just stretching the law, but ignoring very specific deadlines and statutes. I felt that they were doing so because they had a goal that they wanted to achieve and that they were going to go through any manner of legal contortions to get the result that they wanted, the majority of them anyway.

P:  When you say a goal they wanted to achieve, was this the election of Al Gore?

F: I think if not the election of Al Gore, at a minimum, they felt strongly that we should take as long as it took to let the canvassing boards in Palm Beach, Broward, [and] Dade [counties], and elsewhere if necessary, just keep counting. Of course there's seven of them and each one of them [the justices] had a complex mix of motives . . . [and] maybe some of the justices just felt very strongly that it was critical that every vote be counted by the canvassing boards. Maybe they weren't so concerned with whether Gore or Bush became President as they were with the fact that every vote should be counted. I think that the court was really on a wing-and-a-prayer trying to keep the ball alive in a way that would a) keep Gore in play, and b) the count going. I don't think that they fully thought through the ramifications of some of the decisions that they made. There's a reason why games, or in this case political contests, come to an end and you have a time when you stop counting.

P: Justice Major Harding said that they were hearing cases and making decisions that normally might take two or three months, and they had two or three days. Obviously, they didn't have a lot of time to think through all of these decisions.

F: They were making momentous decisions of incredible constitutional complexity on very short notice. In their defense, I am confident that, if they had the luxury, they would have studied this case individually and collectively for not just days and weeks, but probably months, before issuing decisions in a different situation.

P: In your discussion of the 7-0 Florida Supreme Court decision, one of the things you mentioned was that the court, instead of resolving the issues, had created a constitutional crisis. What exactly did you mean by that?

F: I'll start out by saying, Justice Wells in *Harris v. Gore* II, basically says the same thing. I know Chief Justice Wells. He's a great guy, he's a friend, [and] he's a very thoughtful man. I have no idea why he issued that first *Harris v. Gore* opinion. I know the love he has for the Florida Supreme Court and the law, and my guess is he was probably led to join a majority opinion that he was uncomfortable with. We . . . had not had the opportunity to give the Florida Supreme Court the benefit of our study, things like the Federalist Papers, [in which] both Madison and Hamilton weigh in on the importance of having the legislatures involved. We read the *McPherson v. Blacker* case. The issue was whether the Michigan legislature could allocate presidential electors by district, rather than across the state as a whole. The U.S. Supreme Court ruled that the federal Constitution grants power to states to determine how electors are chosen and, if the Michigan constitution grants such power to the legislature and the legislature, through law, provides for electoral districts, then the people have spoken. We read the Constitution as basically saying that the legislature has plenary authority to select electors.

In the House, our view, along with our constitutional experts, the power [to select electors] came directly from the United States Constitution to the Florida legislature. It's one of the reasons we ultimately used a resolution, and not a bill, to select electors. We didn't think Governor Bush had the power to veto or be involved in anything we did. We didn't think that the court could, in any way, abridge or undermine our power. We didn't think the Florida constitution was able to modify [our authority], which of course, was the whole theory of the first [Florida Supreme Court decision].

P:   Let me stop you there. There was some conflict about whether a resolution could be used to seat electors, correct?

F:   No question there was. We went back and looked at history, and they used to select U.S. Senators, before the Seventeenth Amendment, by resolution. So, we used that precedent, but our theory, remember, was this is not a state power, this is a legislative power. So, we didn't want to use a bill that the governor could veto. We used a resolution, not because we were afraid Jeb [Governor Jeb Bush] [actually] would, but our whole theory was this is the legislature's [sole] power. The court can't abridge it, can't modify it, can't undermine it, and neither can the executive branch. The United States Constitution confers, under Article II, the power of the legislature to determine the method [of selecting] electors, and the court cannot review what we've done or how we've done [it]. Congress can. Congress has the power to strike the electors under certain scenarios in Title III, but the Florida Supreme Court was irrelevant. It doesn't say states should select electors, it says that the legislature [should]. If you go back and read *McPherson v. Blacker*, the *Blacker* case makes it very clear that the court can't modify or abridge what the legislature does. Now, the courts are not used to that. They're used to the *Madison v. Marbury* theory that they get to review what we do [and determine if it] is constitutional, [but] not in this case. By the way, the U.S. Supreme Court never actually got to that issue, although I think three justices clearly were prepared to [adopt our view].

P:   Some constitutional experts were critical of *Bush v. Gore* because they believe that there would not have been, technically, a constitutional crisis. Because even if two sets of electors had gone up, there's a procedure whereby Congress would have determined the President, and according to the circumstances at the time, Bush would have won.

F:   Well, I don't know that is correct. Let's assume for example, that the Florida Supreme Court had issued whichever appropriate writ, [a] *writ of mandamus* for example, to Secretary Harris. That she, pursuant to some vote count that might have turned out different than it did [and] that showed that Al Gore got the most popular votes well after the time for counting votes had stopped, and [they] ordered her to send the Democratic slate of electors to Congress. There's no question in my mind, because I have it on good authority from congressmen in Washington, that the U.S. House would have voted to object to the [second] slate sent up by Harris if it had been ordered by the court. There were, at that point, 50 Democrats, . . . who probably would have objected to the slate [Harris originally certified], and you would have had a constitutional crisis.

My theory is this [crisis potential is the] reason the U.S. Supreme Court ultimately jumped into a political question. I would have suggested [that the U.S. Supreme Court] . . . take note that the legislature can fix this in Florida anytime they want. I would have just basically declined to take [the] case if I'd have been a [Constitutional] purist. They had other considerations, and I think one of those is that they saw a constitutional crisis potentially coming.

P:  Apparently from around November 10, 11, and 12, you began consulting with prominent law professors.

F:  I asked Don to get us some of the best constitutional minds he could find. I wanted two things. Number one, I wanted a talking head on TV. I didn't want it to be Tom Feeney against the Florida Supreme Court or Tom Feeney versus Al Gore. I knew that I was going to have to potentially preside, at this point it became increasingly clear, over an historical occasion. I wanted to, insofar as possible, be an umpire, which is what, as speaker of the house, you have to be.

I was happy to answer questions from time to time [especially on precedures,] but I . . . shied away from the press. I wanted the constitutional authorities that would look good on TV, and more importantly, give us the best constitutional advice we can get. I did talk on the phone to Charles Fried, [a] former Solicitor General of the United States, a former Massachusetts Supreme Court Justice, [and a] brilliant man. He brought in Einer Elhague, who is, again, a brilliant man. We said, tell us what's wrong with our theory. This is well before I ever went out and made even the first peep of a comment to the press.

Within a day or two, they were . . . saying that, while all this was unchartered territory in modern times, they absolutely could not poke a hole in our reasoning, our logic, or where we talked about going. At some point, . . . when the Florida Supreme Court issued its (7-0) decision, a reporter from the *Washington Post* asked me about their decision. The reporter said, what happens if the vote count just keeps going and going? . . . This is the first time it was ever said publicly. [I said that] it is the state legislature that determines the method of selecting electors. The question is whether or not the Florida Supreme Court has any role whatsoever. If they try to interfere with our responsibilities, then we still have to fulfill them. [W]ithin 24 hours, I had 500 press requests and about a quarter-million e-mails and faxes. At that point, obviously, PR management became sort of preeminent as well.

P:  Immediately after you made that statement, the Democrats protested. Lois Frankel said it would be politically risky for the legislature to step in and overturn the will of the people. How did you create the sense that this was not a political issue, it was rather a constitutional issue?

F:  Well, in the first place, I think Lois was exactly right. I not only knew this was politically risky, but I fully understood that this could be my career, and the career of a lot of other colleagues, politically going down the tubes. If at any point, somebody had been able to laugh at or mock [our theory] in a thoughtful and responsible way based on constitutional law, then we were all political dead ducks. We had spent a lot of time studying and that's why I asked these Harvard law professors to poke holes in what we were doing. But again, we believed we had a constitutional responsibility and it didn't matter to me whether my political career was over. What mattered was that I had taken an oath at that point to do my duty, and that's what I started explaining to colleagues in leadership, and then ultimately to the membership. We had a couple of Republican members from districts that you would describe as politically soft. They were very concerned about how this vote would play in their district. I think the initial polls probably showed that no more than 25 percent of the people of Florida thought that the legislature should get involved in this. We weren't following the edicts of the polling trends, we were looking at our constitutional responsibility, [American] history, and federal law.

P:  Let me present an argument that some constitutional lawyers made after the fact. Their argument was that the plenary power of the legislature is to set the method of election. Once the method is set, then it switches to the will of the people. So, the legislature sets the date, the method and the standards for the vote, but the vote then becomes the crucial issue. If there is a dispute, these experts argued that then the separation of powers comes in to play and the Supreme Court of the state of Florida must interpret whether or not the law has been violated.

F:  We thought about that and I have two responses to that. Number one, it's a case of first impression. To my knowledge, it's never been resolved whether the plenary authority is to set the method of election, and then you're out of the system or not, but we could have argued that either way. [B]ut even if our only real plenary authority was to select the method of an election and then get out of the way, you still have Title III you have to deal with. Title III basically says, as long as the electors are not in place by December 18, and it talks about having all of the contests and controversies resolved, and then it goes on to say that the legislature has the authority to reconvene and set the electors. So, you still have Title III to get around if that theory is correct. The average time to resolve [a] contest in Florida is 17.7 months. The longest contest took 69 months. The shortest was 16 days. So, we basically felt like it was an absolute, given the fact that both sides were dug in, there was no way you were going to have all of the contests and controversies resolved by December 18.

The interesting question is on the margins of this. Supposing we have an election and the legislature just doesn't like it, can it just ignore the election results? Well, I can argue that, yes, and you do so at your peril. You can be tossed out on your rear end next election. Or [I can argue] no, that's not what the Constitution envisions, it envisions following the election results as long as there are results that are not contested.

P:  When did you begin considering calling a joint session of the Florida legislature? I assume that you talked with John McKay [President of the Senate] about this.

F:  I talked to John McKay on a fairly regular basis. The Senate was going belatedly [in the direction we had staked out]. The Senate never really did get to the point where a majority of them were anxious to go in and take any action, public or, let alone, organize [a special] session before [it became] absolutely necessary. Another professor came along to help in the Florida House, Professor John Yoo, from UC [Berkeley]. He was even more firm than our two paid lawyers that, not only could we act, but we had an absolute constitutional duty [to act, and] we would be derelict in our duty [if we did not]. Not only did we have to act, but Professor Yoo's opinion was the sooner the better. Because, if all the issues got resolved in terms of the contests and controversies, the Florida Supreme Court got things resolved, and everything worked out, [then] hunky-dory, fine, no harm done, at least to anything but our political careers, but [there would be] no constitutional harm done. To go in and say, the election has been held, our view is that the counting . . . stopped in accordance with the rule of law and the statutes in existence on Election Day, we're going to ratify this slate [because] it's already been certified by Katherine Harris, and our job is done. The Senate's legal folks never pushed that hard or were that assertive about the timetable. They did finally reach the conclusion we had the right to do, and ought to be prepared to do, this selection of electors, but we'll never know with certainty what the majority of the Florida Senate would have done.

P:  So, what you're trying to decide is, you don't want to wait too long, but you don't want to act too precipitously. You have to let some of the legal problems be ironed out, because by this point, I presume the U.S. Supreme Court is starting to get involved.

F:  Well, that's right, and there are two different timetables here. Number one is to make sure we're on firm constitutional grounds. The legal situation is changing hour by hour. I mean, this was an emotional roller coaster for everybody in America. I still meet people that tell me, [they] couldn't sleep, [they] couldn't eat, thank God [I] came on TV and said, don't worry, the legislature's going to handle it. We didn't want to act too early in declaring what our intentions were or what our options were because the legal landscape was changing every minute. The longer you waited, the more intelligent choices you would make. We had the uphill PR problem of explaining to America in an intelligent way what the Electoral College does.

The second issue was what the legislature's role was. I venture to say [that prior to election day] not 1 percent of Americans, me included, had any real understanding of the legislature's historic role in selecting electors. So, we had this extraordinary challenge to try to explain. I felt like one of the best ways to do that was for us to have a couple committee hearings where we would get these constitutional experts [to] come in and explain to the members what their duties were rather than Tom Feeney, again, standing up on TV and saying, by golly, here's what we're going to do. [W]e felt like we were on firm ground, we just had to help educate ourselves and America about what the responsibilities were. So, we selected the committee. I selected some articulate lawyer-types [to be] members of that committee. Rather than say what we're going to do, we invited constitutional experts to come tell us what we were either required to do, or had the right to do, depending on their theory.

P: You are organized and you are officially the Speaker as of November 21, correct?

F: Yes. Now I have . . . the authority to select lawyers to represent us in front of courts.

P: Let me go back to something you mentioned earlier. You got lots of e-mail. Could you give me some sense of their content? I know there were death threats.

F: It was the whole gamut. We had a lot of people telling us that they were praying for us, a lot of people supporting us, [and] a lot of people that were just interested in trashing Democrats, which wasn't very useful to us. We had some people that told us to keep our nose out of the business of selecting presidents and told us that we were trying to disqualify their votes, and we had death threats. My guess is I had a dozen or two dozen death threats, and a couple of them were credible enough that the FBI and the appropriate authorities weighed in. I had to have, as I suppose a number of the key players did, 24 hour protection by two FDLE [Florida Department of Law Enforcement] officers. [They] came and delivered me at home every night [and] they stayed with us in the office. We had some really funny stuff that my wife has collected.

P: Did you expect from the beginning that the U.S. Supreme Court was going to get involved?

F: I don't know when I thought the U.S. Supreme Court would get involved. I guess it was always my fear that the U.S. Supreme Court was going to leave us out there hanging until we had really a major constitutional crisis in the United States. I can't say that I ever really knew that the U.S. Supreme Court would act. I was delighted when they took cert [certiorari] in the first case and the second case.

I'll never forget the thrill when I was listening to, I think it was, the tape-delayed proceedings of the court. Sandra Day O'Connor basically asked Laurence Tribe, who by the way, is perhaps the fore-most liberal constitutional scholar in America and Vice-President Gore's main lawyer, whether the legislature had the authority to act under Article II, Clause I. Professor Tribe's answer was something to the effect that, well, I'm not sure. To me that was match-game-and-set because here you have the best constitutional lawyer that the Gore team's ever going to find, with a zealous obligation to represent his client, who, if he had said, yes, they can do what they're doing, would have basically forfeited the presidency on behalf of the Gore cam-paign. Yet he couldn't say no, either. If the answer had been no, if my theory had been wrong, we would have known at least that Professor Tribe thought I was wrong. [He] didn't necessarily think I was right, but he couldn't state on behalf of his client unequivocally that the legislature didn't have the authority.

The other great one was Justice Kennedy, who asked David Boies whether or not, after the fact, the legislature could just go in anytime it wanted and just change the legal method of voting. David Boies said, well, no, Title III prohibits you from changing the law after the fact. Justice Kennedy said, well, if the legislature, who makes laws, can't change the law after Election Day, how is it that the court, who is not supposed to make law, can change the law after Election Day? Now, remember, I can count, and you've got Thomas, Rehnquist, and Scalia, who I always assumed were going to follow the Constitution as I read it, and now you've got Kennedy and O'Connor considered the swing justices. So, I felt like the ball game was over. At that point, I was in one sense, at least in terms of confidence in our constitutional theories, more emboldened than ever.

P: In fact, when the U.S. Supreme Court accepted certiorari, you, and I guess the Senate as well, sponsored a friend-of-the-court brief which, I understand, was written by Charles Fried.

F: And Elhague. If you look at much of the reasoning in the ultimate decision by the U.S. Supreme Court, you will find that there is probably more from the legislative brief, in the ultimate opinion of the majority, referred to, or at least our arguments are incorporated [in the majority opinion].

P: Was this decision to file the brief voted on by the House, or was this a decision that you and the Senate president made?

F: Our rules provided it's the presiding officers that can select attorneys to represent the House or the legislature. We wanted to act jointly, we did act jointly, and so this would be John McKay and Tom Feeney selecting the lawyers to file the brief.

P: Did you consult, throughout this period, with the Democratic mem-bers of the House as to what you were doing?

F: Yes. We didn't necessarily tip off Lois [Frankel] two days ahead of time what we were doing, but we made clear, for example, before I appointed the committee of the house to take a look at our responsibilities. I told Lois what I intended to do. I was probably speaking to Lois at least a couple times a day.

P: Who came up with the idea of the Joint Legislative Oversight Committee on Electoral Certification Accuracy and Fairness and what was its major purpose?

F: Well, ultimately I would have approved it, but probably Don Rubottom and Paul Hawks, who was my chief policy coordinator; Dudley Goodlette, I expect was involved; Johnny Byrd, who's . . . just been recently selected Speaker of the House. This would have been a House decision. We would have been talking to the Senate because . . . we couldn't do anything without them and we knew that. We had to go at a pace that they were comfortable with.

It had a couple purposes. Through the committee I wanted the entire House, anybody who wanted to sit in and participate was welcome to sit in the audience and listen or hand questions to members of the committee, to really have a thorough understanding as best our legal experts could provide them with. Number two, I wanted, again, to invite opponents to poke holes in our theory. I really wanted to know before I acted, rather than later, that this idea was just not in accordance with any legitimate reading of the Constitution. I never heard any arguments that I found persuasive that I ought to change course. Number three, I thought it had the advantage, again, of helping to educate all of us, but also the world. Anybody who was interested in this matter or what the legislature's role is, what the Constitution calls for, [and] the fact that we were acting in accordance with the Constitution as advised by our lawyers [could watch].

P: When you started out, one of the purposes of the committee, at least expressed publicly, was to address voter irregularities. Did the committee ever get into election reform?

F: Actually, the follow-up to the committee really did, because we passed an historic election reform bill as a consequence of some of the things that this committee started.

P: This is the Election Reform Act of 2001?

F: Yes. Now that committee was broadened dramatically before we finalized it, but remember, the most immediate thing this committee had to do was to tell us how to get ourselves out of this mess before December 18, and how to resolve it in accordance with our constitutional duties. While they were at it, any ideas they had about avoiding similar miscues in the future were part of our long-term goal.

P: The Democrats complained that there were conservative Republican lawyers making a presentation, but the Democratic point of view was not presented.

F: Oh, they had two or three lawyers come.

P: There were eight Republicans and six Democrats on the committee. Obviously, there were more Democrats on this committee than the ratio in the House. Who chose the members of the committee?

F: I think I chose all of the members. My guess is that I probably asked Lois for some input as to a couple of the members. That may not be true, but that's certainly what I did after this. There were two Democrats on the committee whose districts voted for Bush who were conservative Democrats. I think [Will] Kendrick and [Dwight] Stansel were on the committee, weren't they?

P: Yes. The Democrats, as soon as these activities begin to take shape, are going to call you an extremist and accuse you of a power play to get Jeb Bush's brother elected. How did you respond to these attacks and what conversations did you have with Jeb Bush during this period of time?

F: Well, in the first place, my defense to those attacks was always, if you're mad at the Florida Legislature for following Article II, your quarrel is with the Founding Fathers and not with the legislature. We had fun responding because we kept taking them back to the Constitution. The more they used the *ad hominem* arguments, the more confident we were right on the law.

   I talked to the governor on several occasions. Most of our [later] discussions revolved around the time for going into session. I'm sure I had one or two early conversations with the governor to sort of tell him from our perspective what our obligations were, what we were doing mechanically in the House to set up a committee, what we thought the end-game may be if the courts didn't resolve this in time, to talk to him a little bit about the constitutional issues.

P: Was he encouraging you to call a special session?

F: No, I think it would be fair to say he was discouraging me from acting before he was confident it was necessary. Neither Jeb—and my guess is [this], I never heard from [them], certainly—[nor] the folks in Austin [the George W. Bush campaign] [wanted to act too early].

P: So you had no contact with Jim Baker or the George Bush campaign or Ben Ginsberg?

F: Ben Ginsberg is an old friend of mine. He does [a lot of Florida Republican legal] stuff, so I'm sure I talked to Ben. I talked to people in the Republican Party on a regular basis, and certainly my staff lawyers and constitutional lawyers were conferring with them. I never met with James Baker. I don't believe I ever spoke to him. I never talked to Katherine Harris about these issues during this time. I probably would have spoken to Ben about what our professors were up to, because he is a top lawyer that has done work for the Republican Party while I've been in [the] Republican leadership. But in terms of coordinating with the [George W. Bush campaign] or the governor's office, that did not happen in any direct way.

   I don't want to deny talking to a bunch of political operatives. You know, in Tallahassee, you couldn't turn around and get a sandwich [without encountering a political operative], but as much as anybody, I was a captive in my office. I couldn't go outside. I would have been mobbed by people that wanted to hang me and people that wanted to love me to death. I was going to die either way. I was captive, and I'm sure Katherine Harris was in the same boat. I think it's fair to say that Governor Bush really didn't want this election to hang on action by the Florida Legislature. He was hoping and praying it would resolve itself favorably in the courts because he could just see a two-year nightmare about Tallahassee's involvement in this. I understood that and I had the same concerns. The Bush campaign never ever encouraged us [for] a moment. Neither [did their] top leaders, until on television, at the same time the rest of the world saw it live. James Baker III announced that there was always the legislature that had a responsibility.

P: The Democrats argued that, since you ran on the ticket with Jeb Bush on his first run for governor, you were partisan, and that you and Katherine Harris were "taking orders" from Governor Jeb Bush and Governor George W. Bush of Texas.

F: Well, I'm guilty on the first part of that claim, I am a partisan. I'm a friend of Jeb's, I was Jeb's running mate, and I had as much interest in having the president of my choice elected as anybody in the country, but it would be wholly inaccurate to say that we coordinated, let alone got encouraged at any point, by either the governor directly or the President-elect or any of his top folks. Were Republican operatives giving us all sorts of advice, go, don't go, this, that? Yes. For the most part, people outside my office and outside my constitutional legal team were saying, go slow, slow this down. Remember, we had a two-week head start on doing our homework and studying this stuff. Even people that wanted to resolve the thing favorably in the legislature if necessary, they hadn't spent anywhere near the time we had on the constitutional or historical issues. So, if anything, Jeb and I had some earnest words [about his concerns]. I don't think Jeb ever took the position with me that he was opposed to acting if necessary. If anything, to an extent, we had, I don't want to say heated conversations, but energetic conversations. It was the governor's notion that we should do everything in our power to not act until absolutely necessary and [to wait] until every other potential resolution had been given time to work itself out. I think if I'd have told him we were going to act at one minute to noon on December 18, he would have said that might be a little too early.

P: On December 4, you and Senate President McKay announced that you were going to call a special joint session of the Florida Legislature to convene on December 8.

F: My records show that on Monday, December 4, our joint committee, both the House and Senate members of the committee, recommended convening a special session. So, we signed a proclamation on Wednesday, December 6, to call a special session on December 8.

P: In that resolution, what did you state as the purpose of the special session?

F:     Well, in the purpose we recited parts of Title III and the United States Constitution that we were relying on. We talked about how the election had been held in accordance with the law as it existed prior to election day. Therefore we were going to certify the 25 electors that had already been certified by Secretary Harris. So, in essence, rather than doing a new certification of new electors, we ratified the 25 existing electors.

P:     Did you have a specific date by which you felt you had to do this? Would December 12 be the last date for you?

F:     There was a lot of debate by the constitutional scholars. I think the Senate's position was, you could wait until the eighteenth, the very last minute. There's language in the Constitution that talks about 6 days before the date for convening [the electors].

P:     One thing I learned [while] doing a little research about the "safe harbor" clause, it is voluntary. It is up to the legislature to make that choice. I assume that the Florida legislature, controlled by the Republican Party, would have chosen that December 12 would be the final date to ratify the certification. In fact, you did take your vote on December 12, is that correct?

F:     Yes, on Tuesday, December 12, the Florida House cast its vote. So, we would have put the Senate in position, at that point, of deciding either later that night or any time through December 18.

P:     This was the same day, but prior to the release of the U.S. Supreme Court 5-4 *Bush v. Gore* decision, which came out sometime around 10:00 P.M.

F:     That's right.

P:     So you did not know when that decision was forthcoming.

F:     No, we didn't. In fact, I can remember, there are two TVs on the Speaker's podium, and throughout these processes, regardless of what we were doing on the floor, I was constantly watching one of the cable networks. If there was a decision by the Florida Supreme Court or U.S. Supreme Court that would have affected the processes, we would have stopped, taken a 20 minute recess, talked to our lawyers, and decided whether to go back. So, I was constantly watching to see whether a Supreme Court decision occurred while we were on the floor that day.

P:     What was the tally of the final vote and exactly what did the resolution that you voted on state?

F:     [The total was] 79 yeas, 41 nays.

P:     Two Democrats, Stansel and Kendrick, voted yea.

F:     There were 77 Republicans and 2 Democrats, so that sounds right to me.

P:     Specifically, you stated that you wanted to keep the citizens of Florida from being disenfranchised [and] that you wanted Florida's electoral votes to count, therefore the House was going to seat, in effect, the electors certified by Katherine Harris.

F:    Well, you have to remember this goes back to the old legislative intent theory. We had 79 yea votes on a resolution, [but] there could have been 79 diverse reasons. I felt not only did we want Florida to be counted, I wanted the right electoral votes to count. My theory was that the election had been held in accordance with the law of Florida. It provided for a time for counting votes, that deadline had come and passed, the votes had been counted and recounted. Any changes, either to that deadline or, just as pernicious, changes in which ballots did or didn't count [with the] standards for counting changing on an hourly basis from table to table in the four counties doing recounts . . . [were unacceptable]. Now there could have been some members that voted yea that just said, we have to get this resolved and be represented, but from my perspective, to get it resolved and get it resolved right.

P:    Why do you think the Senate didn't act at the same time you did?

F:    I think there were senators that wanted to act early. I think the Senate in Florida, like the upper chamber in most legislative bodies, tends to be a little bit more reserved. I think there were senators that didn't want to vote on this resolution. I think there were senators that were not just afraid of the political ramifications themselves, but I think for good reason felt that it might do damage to the working relations in the Senate. But there were probably senators that were afraid that it was a tough political vote one way or the other.

P:    In retrospect, do you wish you had now waited until after the *Bush v. Gore* Supreme Court decision?

F:    No. Knowing [now] what I knew then, I would have proceeded the exact way I did. I probably would have gone in earlier than we did. I would have sent as strong a message as I could, and I did, [at] every opportunity, to the Florida Supreme Court, that I thought they had trampled upon the rule of law. So, I wouldn't have done anything differently. Now, if the Supreme Court of the United States had issued its opinion before we actually took the vote, I would have held a recess, . . . but it would have been moot at that point. My guess is we would not have voted if we knew what the Supreme Court's decision was.

P:    The Democrats criticized the special session. Lois Frankel claimed it was ultimately a partisan act that was unnecessary, unfair, and unjust, and would cast a dark stain on the integrity of the legislature. How did you respond to that?

F:    Well, in the first place, as I always did when we heard these criticisms, I referred people back to the Founding Fathers. But secondly, I talked about how proud I was of . . . the legislature doing its constitutional duty. It wasn't popular, it wasn't easy, there were a lot of members put in tough situations, but that we took an oath to uphold the United States Constitution, not when it was fun or convenient, but all the time. I was really proud of the House as an institution. [T]he debates were largely based on the Constitution and the law. They were not redundant as you would expect in a situation where 63 brand-new freshman are thrown and thrust into the limelight.

P: Due to term limits over half of the House was voting on their first act as legislators.

F: Their first formal act, other than organizing, was selecting electors, which hadn't been done in the country in 120-something years. This was extraordinary stuff. We had adopted a new rule that hasn't been used for some time in Florida where we actually, as is done in Congress, give on great issues like this, each side a certain amount of time, and they have floor managers. That helped in a great measure, because people were able to prepare their arguments for and against and coordinate with other members, so that not everybody would address the same three or four issues. So, it was just really a wonderful part of American democracy to be part of. The arguments were cordial in the most partisan decision that any of us will ever make in our life. People treated one another with respect, they treated one another's arguments with respect.

P: Although the vote was pretty much on partisan lines.

F: It was on largely partisan lines. You know, I think that there were some legitimate arguments against, including [that] we ought to wait and see what the court does. But, of course, remember while we're describing partisan motives [that] one of the things that we Republicans believe is that the Democrats and some members of the court wanted to just keep on counting until December 19.

P: If the Senate had come up with a different resolution, then how would that have been resolved?

F: Well, we actually, in our resolution, I think we had agreed to the language of what was going to be [beforehand]. You have to remember that President McKay and I had a lot of disputes after this, but this was really the first significant difference of opinion. He was very reticent to act. Several times I thought I had an understanding with him about when we were going to sign that resolution, and it turned out that got postponed. There was always one reason or another why it seemed to me the [goal line] kept moving, and I was very uncomfortable and I didn't have the confidence in the Senate leadership to agree to something and then do it. So, I think in this resolution we agreed on the actual language. Anytime they wanted to pull the plug, they could have. While I believe there's a 90 percent chance they would have passed this resolution, I've spent the last two years after the fact [talking with the Senate], and I can't guarantee on any given moment what they're going to do.

P: You did not adjourn the legislature until December 14, and that was after Gore had conceded. So, you officially stayed in session until all of the issues had been resolved?

F: Well, there's some interesting twists about this. We wanted to extend it even further. While the legislature [was] in session, we felt like we were immune from process or service of process. Some of us were at least theoretically concerned that the Florida Supreme Court would issue subpoenas for us to come down [and] explain what we were doing to them. Remember, under our theory of *McPherson vs. Blacker*, we had a plenary power, and some of us would have thought long and hard about whether we had to respond to subpoenas. We were basically acting in defense of our institution. We didn't want to be stopped in the course of the proceedings, and that was one of the reasons we extended it. There are a lot of these little fascinating parts that we thought long and hard about.

P:    In *Gore v. Harris*, the Florida Supreme Court awarded Gore votes from Dade and Palm Beach County and ordered the counting of all the undervotes in the state. Let me read your printed response to this decision. "I am terribly saddened. Once again the Florida Supreme Court has changed the law and prevented a final determination of all contests by December 12." What was your major objection to their decision?

F:    I'm sure I had intricate thoughts at the time, but two years later, I can't tell you what my legal reaction was, . . . but my reaction in general, was that the Florida Supreme Court had a majority that was very result-oriented here. [They were] going to twist and turn and contort language so long as they thought there was a chance to get the result they wanted, which was [for] Vice-President Gore to become president.

P:    Let me point out something that Barry Richard mentioned to me. People talked about a partisan, liberal Florida Supreme Court, but this vote was 4-3, and as you know, Justice Wells had a very stinging dissent. The Florida Supreme Court voted against Gore on the butterfly ballot, against him on restarting the Dade recount and they voted against him on Seminole and Martin Counties, and of course, if they wanted to change the result of the election, Seminole County would have done it very easily. So, if you look at the overview of the decisions of the Florida Supreme Court, do you still see it as a liberal, partisan court?

F:    Well, I think it's an activist court, and just because courts are result-oriented doesn't mean they turned a blind eye to all reasonable arguments of the other side. Again, I'm not a psychologist, and for that matter I'm not really an expert on the makeup of the Florida Supreme Court, but if you wanted to cover your tracks, you would throw some victories to one side and some to the other, and you'd say, well, there's win and lose. But as long as you kept the vote going and allowing people to change the standards that were dominated by Palm Beach, Dade, and Broward Counties, the likely result is that you're going to be helping out Gore make up the 500 vote or whatever the vote difference is.

P:    537 votes. At that juncture, you indicated that because of this 4-3 decision, that the Florida Legislature should take a look at how the Florida

Supreme Court operates, and that you might consider imposing term-limits on the current justices. What was the thinking behind that statement?

F:   I don't know whether I said that *sua sponte*, or whether I was invited to talk about what I would call court reform. You have to remember that this wasn't the first sort of difference of opinion I've had with the Florida Supreme Court. On a number of issues, including a number of death penalty cases, . . . I essentially said that there are times when I felt like the court saw itself as a supra-legislature, and instead of just interpreting the law and Constitution, was looking for ways to achieve results that they wanted.

So, the *Harris v. Gore* cases were hardly the first time that I had taken differences of opinion with the court. [As] a matter of fact, I like to say that I would be thrilled, one day, to read an opinion by any of the justices, and I would come over and wash his or her car, if it would start out [by saying] those fools and imbeciles in the legislature have done it again, they have produced one of the worst pieces of legislation in the history of free government, but we find ourselves powerless to change what they have done because they are, after all, the legislative body and there's nothing in the four corners of the Constitution that prohibits this foolish piece of legislation. I think that would show the appropriate respect and deference to the policy-makers.

P:   Some critics argued that you did not really understand the separation of powers. Although the legislature has the constitutional authority to make laws, the Supreme Court of Florida has the right to interpret these laws.

F:   Well, I happen to believe in *Marbury v. Madison*. [But] I'm not the first legislative leader to complain that courts are making law rather than interpreting the law. But in the *Harris v. Gore* case, I think they made our case for us. This is a situation where they clearly, by their own acknowledgment, . . . were not going to have a hyper-technical adherence to the statutory scheme. We clearly believe, like most of the U.S. Supreme Court, that the Florida Supreme Court did in fact, change the law after Election Day, and they made [new] law to boot, which is two sins in my book.

P:   What influence do you think the closeness of 4-3 Florida Supreme Court vote had on the U.S. Supreme Court? One lawyer said that if the court had voted 7-0, the unanimous decision might have made a difference. Maybe it made it easier for the U.S. Supreme Court to overturn the Florida Supreme Court because the vote was very close.

F:   I really hadn't thought about it at that point. I think the U.S. Supreme Court was motivated by a couple factors. Most importantly [was] the fate of the Republic and avoiding any severe U.S. constitutional crisis. Secondly, the fate of the U.S. Supreme Court. Whether it's the Nixon tapes case or other key cases during constitutional crises, I think the

Court has wanted to act with a strong majority. They wanted to look for a decision that they could not have a 5-4 [decision], and [not have the] embittered four members dissenting and attacking the legitimacy of the Court itself. Because after all, the Supreme Court doesn't have control of the armies or police force [or appropriations process]. All it has as its resources is the legitimacy that Americans subscribe to it. I think . . . they were concerned about the public's response to whatever they came up with. It certainly had to be an opinion that Americans would acquiesce to and hopefully most Americans would embrace.

The U.S. Supreme Court's first decision [the remand] said, we have no idea how you reached your conclusion; [you need to] rethink it, and by the way, in the second part of that last paragraph, it says, while you're rethinking it, read Article II of the Constitution and read Title III. As I remember, the four-member majority of the Florida Supreme Court continued to sort of just ignore what is pretty clear language in the Constitution and in federal law. I think the three [dissenting] members got it right.

P:  An analysis from one Democratic lawyer alleged that Chief Justice Wells's dissent was so strong partly to try to alleviate what he feared was pressure from the legislature to reform the court.

F:  Well, I think that's wrong. I think Chief Justice Wells is an incredibly honorable man. I think he loves the Florida Supreme Court. He certainly loves his state and his country. I don't think that's what was motivating him. I don't think it was in response to anything that the legislature was doing. I think it was in response to some loss of patience, perhaps, with the reasoning of four members of the court.

P:  After Al Gore's concession speech, you were reported in the paper as saying it was an evil speech, and you called Gore a loser. What specifically did you mean by that? Most people thought it was Gore's best speech and that it was conciliatory.

F:  Well, in the first place, the next day I apologized for those remarks. In the second place, while they were probably accurate, we were in a fairly jovial mood celebrating the ultimate resolution of this. [It was the] first time I had been let out of the speaker's office to relax with a Republican victory party, and it was a mistake for me to say those things. In fact, Vice-President Gore's speech, especially given the difficulty of the times [and] the pressure on him from both sides, . . . I think his speech was important for the Republic. It was a mistake for me, even in what was supposed to be a private party setting—reporters are always lurking around Tallahassee—to even in jest be saying things like that.

P:  Let me go back to the 5-4 U.S. Supreme Court *Bush v. Gore* decision. Some experts have argued that this was really a 7-2 decision because seven of the justices brought up the issue of different standards as a violation of the Fourteenth Amendment's equal protection clause. Would you agree with that?

F: Well, yes. Ultimately there were seven votes to stop the recount, and two of those votes might have been for [a] largely practical basis. I understand their practical reasoning. I actually differ with using the Fourteenth Amendment as the ultimate resolution to this, but I do think that they were right. They were watching different standards being applied in the same counties from one table to the next, [and] even at the same table. They were watching standards change over time. All of the reasons why you do not have recount after recount after recount were brought to light as you watched these butterfly ballots get in worse and worse shape and continue to deteriorate. So I think the justices, for practical reasons, basically implicated the whole recount process in Florida, which I agree with. But I think that fundamentally the constitutional decision could rest on sounder ground. In my view, one of those grounds could have been that Article II empowers the legislature to resolve these issues.

P: Let me ask about the dissents to this 5-4 decision. Justice Ruth Bader Ginsburg argued that this was a state issue. Under no circumstances, said Ginsburg, should the U.S. Supreme Court have taken the case.

F: I respect her support of federalism and am enthused by it, will hopefully remind her of it if there's an opportunity, but remember that our reading of the Constitution was that the legislature had a plenary authority. It is the U.S. Supreme Court that interprets what Article II of the United States Constitution ultimately means. I disagree with her that this is just a state issue because it's a federal constitutional principle [of] who selects electors.

P: I don't know if you took a specific stance on the military absentee ballots, but a military vote in Alachua County was not counted while the same vote in Okaloosa County was counted. If a vote had different standards, even though a military vote, isn't that also a violation of the Fourteenth Amendment?

F: Well, I don't know what is or is not a violation of the Fourteenth Amendment under this new decision. It's one of my concerns about the rationale. But in Florida, we have 67 different supervisors of elections. Traditionally, each of them have had a different process for things like how you can acquire absentee ballots. As long as you can have a constitutional system that empowers supervisors to use different types of equipment, different recount mechanisms, different ways to request absentee ballots, or so forth, as long as the rules are applied equally to everybody within that county [and] as long as nobody has their ultimate ability or right to vote hindered, you don't have an equal protection problem.

P: Gore was saying count all the votes, but then he's trying to challenge some military ballots and to nullify the vote in Seminole and Martin counties. Some argue that's hypocritical. On the other hand, the Republicans were saying, we strictly adhere to November 7 as the certification date. Harris is right. But then on some of these military ballots, they changed their emphasis and concluded that it was okay to count them because we did not want to adhere to hyper-technicalities. So, both sides seemed to be a little hypocritical.

F:  Well, clearly both sides were trying to gain every advantage, but that implicates, once again, the recount process. The more you delay the decision, the more you recount, the more opportunities for fraud and for just clerical error occur. The human error potential is what you ought to try to minimize when you create an election system. It's what we've done in our elections reform package, I think, pretty success-fully. But there's no question that both sides had some hypocritical arguments. With respect to the military, there is a federal law that supersedes state law on that issue. Obviously, the federal government has imposed a statute that binds Florida to go out of our way to try to allow men and women in the military overseas to have their votes counted even after our normal counting deadline.

P:  I talked to Mac Stipanovich and he very candidly said that the Bush supporters, within the law, sought to do whatever it took to win the recount. He thought Gore paid too much attention to political issues and how a certain decision might affect public opinion. For example, backing off the military ballots because they didn't want to seem unpatriotic.

F:  Well, Mac's a hard-ball player, but let me tell you, I think it would have been devastating for the Democratic Party as a party to publicly and permanently take the position that if it takes disqualifying military ballots to win, then that's what we'll do. So I disagree with Mac that you do whatever, whenever, no matter what the PR cost is.

P:  In the Electoral Reform Act of 2001, the legislature got rid of the punch-card machines. One of the advantages of new technology is that there will be very fewer overvotes. So that reduced one of the problems. You still have undervotes, but you'll never get rid of those.

F:  No, and a lot of people deliberately undervote. I'm proof in point. In the most recent congressional election where I was successful, we waged a very expensive [and] I would admit, the nastiest campaign I've ever been involved with. We were the first race on the ballot, because we're the only federal race in my area. Right after us was the gubernatorial race. I think there were about 6,000 fewer ballots cast in my race than in the [Jeb] Bush/[Bill] McBride [2002 Florida guber-natorial race]. People weren't inadvertently skipping over our race. They came to vote for governor in 6,000 cases, and it wasn't because they didn't know my opponent and I, because we had only spent a cumulative total of something like $10 million telling people who each other were. I think that there were some people that were either undecided about who was the least of two evils, or just were turned off by the negative campaigning. Now fortunately 62 percent of the peo-ple that did vote endorsed me, but the point is [that] the first race on the ballot, with both candidates having 90 plus percent name identification, was skipped deliberately by 6,000 voters.

P: In Judge Nikki Clark's ruling in the Seminole County case, she determined that Sandra Goard had violated state election law, but it was a technical violation. It was the request for an absentee ballot, it wasn't a ballot, therefore, a decision to throw out all the ballots would have been draconian.

F: What she essentially ruled, in layman's language, is that there was harmless error [that] didn't have any impact, but I think that's right. Your last point is probably most important. The only remedy asked for in the lawsuit was to throw out all 16,000 ballots. Of the 16,000 ballots it might have been 2,000 or 3,000 that were as a result of these request forms that were missing an identification number. So even the plaintiffs . . . had to acknowledge that the remedy asked for was to disqualify 12,000 or so votes where nothing was wrong, either in the request form or the ballot. She just couldn't tell you which of the 16,000 ballots were infirm. So, that was disenfranchising people. By the way, even the people whose ballot request forms may have been technically wrong, as Judge Clark ruled, didn't do anything deliberately. They didn't do anything mischievous. They weren't trying to commit vote fraud, they were just trying to vote. So nobody did anything intentionally wrong, and 12,000 of them didn't have anything wrong with either their request or their ballot.

P: How did this experience impact your life, both personally and professionally?

F: I won't deny that I was convinced . . . that I was at an historic time and moment. I clearly believed that George W. Bush would make the best president, [and] I clearly believed that the Florida vote on November 7 had made him president. So, I felt as though, whether this was the end of my career or not, it might have been Providence that I was in that place where I could be a leader, or at a minimum, the mouth of the lion of the Florida House that roared. I felt it was an extraordinary responsibility, but I was up to it, regardless of what the personal costs were going to be.

P: Were you treated fairly by the press and the media?

F: On the whole, yeah. I really think I was. I think that I got beaten up a little bit, but some will say I injected myself and the House into this controversy. I think my critics had every right to take the shots they did. I mean, I volunteered to be speaker of the house . . . [and] I took the oath. I don't think there were too many cheap shots at me. I was more offended by some of the things said about Katherine Harris, for example.

P: As far as I can determine, there was no proven case of fraud, at all, in this election, which is to Florida's credit. You might not be able to say that about Louisiana or Chicago, for example.

F: I think that's a great point. I think that most of the close calls that were resolved by partisan people at supervisor's offices or elections boards were probably because we all see things through the shades of the glasses that we look. I admitted to my biases. Having said that, I am offended by the United States Civil Rights Commission, Jesse Jackson, and others, [who have] routinely accused people like Jeb Bush and others of everything from setting up police roadblocks, [and] have really tried to create a division in Florida as a consequence of this close election. [There are] all sorts of wild accusations based on . . . allegations that not only have not been proven, but to the extent you can disprove a negative, have been disproved.

I have read through parts of [the majority report of the U.S. Commission on Civil Rights]. It's just completely [filled with] anecdotal allegations that are unsubstantiated. Look, charging people with racism is one of the ugliest charges that you can [make]. It'd be almost like accusing somebody of being a Communist back in the 1950s. Where you find a racist, you ought to condemn him or her, but you've got to be awful reticent to make the charge. Then, when you are given responsibilities as a chairman of a commission designed to promote civil rights, I think you really make a mockery of your own cause and you really create a lot of backlash that's harmful. Now let me say, I've never been the victim of discrimination against racial or ethnic minorities, because I'm not one. There are a lot of things that go wrong in my life, that if I were African American or Hispanic, I may wonder. But bad things happen to all of us. What we need to make sure is that there aren't any conspiracies, especially any engaged in by government officers, to make bad things happen to people because of their race. There was absolutely no evidence of that and it's irresponsible for the people that are running around claiming so.

P:   What impact did the 2000 election have on the recent 2002 election? Clearly Jeb Bush won very handily in what was thought to be, in the beginning at least, a closer race.

F:   I would turn that around and say the 2002 election had more impact on the 2000 election. We have put, in Florida, the 2000 election to bed. There was not a whole host of voter-turnout to punish or to reward Jeb Bush based on what his brother did in Florida two years ago. I'm going to turn your question around and say, the good news is that 2002 basically said that 2000 is behind us as a state, and we're ready to move on and judge the quality of candidates and their policies.

P:   Let me end with a broader question. For the first time in the history of this state the Republican Party not only controls and dominates the legislature, but has the governor, and all cabinet positions. What has been the reason for the rise of the Republican Party in Florida, in, let's say, the last 20 years?

F:   I don't think you can subscribe it all to the electorate has moved dramatically right. I think there's been a slow, but probably steady, evolution to some conservative politics. But I think people's willingness to vote Republican has moved from the top of the ticket all the way down to dog-catcher. There's no question that, in most of the state, being Republican is no longer a liability. I don't think the fundamentals of the electorate have changed in this sense, I think there's forty percent of the voters out there that are going to vote Republican almost no matter what. Forty percent will vote Democrat almost no matter what. I think the 20 percent in the middle are more inclined, at the moment, to lean Republican. As long as we behave, don't get too far afield, don't let corruption seep in, or we don't promote an extremist agenda, I think that they're more inclined to vote Republican.

# ➤ MAC STIPANOVICH ◄

John McKager "Mac" Stipanovich, one of the most powerful lobbyists in Florida, is well known to both friends and adversaries as a tough negotiator and a skilled and effective opponent. He is also noted for his honest comments and colorful language.

Stipanovich received a B.A. in history from the University of Florida in 1972 and earned a J.D. in 1974. Following law school, he practiced law and has worked on political campaigns throughout Florida since the late 1970s. In 1979, Stipanovich supported Bob Martinez in his race for mayor of Tampa, and served as campaign manager when Martinez ran for re-election in 1983. He was campaign director for Martinez's bids for governor in 1986 and 1990. During Governor Martinez's administration (1987–1991), Mac became a principal policy advisor and chief of staff. From 1993–94, he was a senior advisor in Jeb Bush's run for governor. In 2000, he was dispatched to provide political advice to Katherine Harris during the recount controversy. Stipanovich, however, has refused to identify the higher authority who requested his services. During his stints as a political strategist, he continued to practice administrative law. He has represented clients before state government agencies, the governor, the cabinet, and the legislature.

Stipanovich began his interview with a discussion of how he became acquainted with Katherine Harris and how he became her advisor in the campaign for Secretary of State and in the recount controversy. He detailed how he assisted Harris in dealing with the media onslaught as she struggled with decisions on certification and recounts. Stipanovich discussed the decision to hire Joe Klock as Harris's attorney and how the legal decisions during the recount were made. Although a practicing attorney, Stipanovich "did not act as a lawyer, but probably more in the role [of] a surrogate for [Harris] and as a well-informed client." He recalled that the overall strategy when he first began to advise Harris was to "bring [the election] in for a landing with George Bush at the controls."

Stipanovich concluded that Al Gore's advisors, Bill Daley and Warren Christopher, were not as committed to Gore as Jim Baker and Bob Zoellick were to Bush. Stipanovich also discussed the public relations battle waged during the recount controversy and believed that Gore was much more influenced by public opinion than Bush and didn't fight hard enough to win. "They said we had to obey the law, they didn't say we had to fight fair." Stipanovich then talked about what would have happened if the Democrats had taken the lead in the recount and discussed whether or not it was a strategic error for the Democrats not to go to the contest right away. Mac reacted negatively to the Democrats' accusation that the decision by David Leahy and the Miami-Dade Canvassing Board to end the recount was due to intimidation from a Republican "rent-a-mob."

As both an attorney and a skilled politician, Mac presented a cogent and enlightened view on what he called "the partisan" 7-0 decision by the Florida Supreme Court. That verdict moved the certification date to November 26, which prevented Katherine Harris from certifying the election and allowed Palm Beach and Broward Counties to continue their recount. He felt that the court had "usurped the legislature's authority . . . and were totally off-base in the standard of review they applied." Stipanovich claimed that the Florida Supreme Court, with its harsh criticism of Secretary Harris, had, in effect, "basically bitch-slapped Katherine." He also talked about the military ballots, the Election Reform Act of 2001, the United States Commission on Civil Rights Report, and the impact of the candidacy of Ralph Nader. In response to Judge Sanders Sauls's decision in the contest, which unequivocally denied the Democrat's case, Stipanovich said that Judge Sauls "just clubbed them like baby seals." Ultimately, Stipanovich concluded that those in power must "stick to the scheme [for elections] that the legislature had put into law [and that] not doing so was the mistake of the Florida Supreme Court."

Mac Stipanovich was interviewed by the author on June 10, 2002.

P: When did you first get involved with the Secretary of State, Katherine Harris?

S: One of my colleagues, Jim Magill, was the director of Senate campaigns for the Republican Party from 1994 to 1996. One of the candidates that he helped, on behalf of the party, and to whom he introduced me, was Katherine Harris down in Sarasota. When she came up here after she was elected, I lobbied her, of course, on a number of issues and got to know her that way. When she decided that she wanted to run for Secretary of State because Sandy Mortham [Florida secretary of state, 1995–99] was going to be on Jeb's [Bush] ticket as Lieutenant Governor, . . . she asked me to help her. But when Mortham withdrew from the Bush campaign and said she was going to seek re-election, most of the people here in Tallahassee decided that discretion was the better part of valor and they were no longer very supportive of Katherine. I told her that I would help her and I kept my word and I did help her. I saw her on and off and . . . gave her advice when she asked me while she was secretary of state.

P: When did you actually come to her office? Was it the day after the 2000 election?

S: No, it was on Thursday [November 9]. I think the election was the 7th, a Tuesday. [O]ne of my partners, Ken Sukhia, was over in Gadsden County representing the [George W.] Bush campaign on recount issues.

He took exception to and didn't like some of the tactical decisions that the Bush campaign was apparently making about whether to protest these types of ballots that he was, in effect, appealing, so he wanted me to call somebody. I made a call to somebody and they said they would look into it, and then they asked me what I intended to do. I said, well, I'll help. I said, where am I needed? They said, Katherine Harris, as I understand, probably needs help. So I called over to Katherine's office and I got Ben McKay, her chief of staff. I said, Ben, could you all use help? And he said yes. So I . . . went into the conference room where they had it kind of set up as a war room.

Katherine, at the time, didn't even have a press secretary or a communications person. She had some good solid professional staff in terms of Clay Roberts, who's the Director of the Division of Elections, and Debbie Kearney, who was the general counsel. Ben McKay was a hardworking, bright, young guy, but she didn't have anybody on staff who, to use the old phrase from the Civil War, who'd ever seen the elephant. So I went over there to help them. All the media, literally, from the world, was outside trying to tear the door down, and they were unprepared for that.

P: Who decided to hire Joe Klock and his firm, Steel, Hector, and Davis to represent Katherine Harris during the 2000 recount?

S: We had a number of conversations and meetings. A number of large law firms were conflicted or tainted for several reasons. Steel Hector was, of course, on the list. We knew the folks at Steel Hector Davis, both the lawyers and some of the non-lawyers, . . . and they're a first-class firm. Equally because of their qualifications and sort of by default, they were the choice.

P: Did you choose them because they were primarily a Democratic firm?

S: That wasn't a principal reason, but it didn't hurt. It gave the appearance of balance.

P: How were the legal decisions made?

S: Typically, they [the attorneys] would come over and we would meet with them. We would explore options, they would make recommendations, [and] we would make decisions. At one point in time, they filed a motion in the Florida Supreme Court that was a fairly lengthy, detailed motion, but among the reliefs they prayed for was a consolidation of the cases here in the first DCA [District Court of Appeals] . . . and that any recounts be suspended until the consolidated cases had been heard here. That made it look like Katherine was trying to use the court system to stop the recounts, valid recounts, that were underway. We were pretty exercised about that and had a "come-to-Jesus" meeting with them about that.

P: I talked to Joe Klock and he said that the Bush campaign wasn't real happy with that decision. Didn't they file it late at night?

S: Yes, there was a lot of stuff going on. They did a yeoman's job and they had a lot of decisions. They probably didn't give any thought to the public perception and the political implications of that particular aspect of their motion. They're good lawyers, [but] that doesn't make them good politicians.

P: Was that your primary responsibility? Were you more interested in giving the Secretary of State political advice as opposed to legal advice?

S: I didn't give legal advice per se, but because I'm a lawyer, at least I have a degree and I'm a member of the Bar, I, perhaps more than some other non-lawyers in our office, was suited to ask hard questions and question their reasoning. I didn't act as a lawyer, but probably more in the role [of] a surrogate for Katherine and as a well-informed client.

P: The Democrats charged that whatever was decided in Harris's office had been communicated to her from Governor Jeb Bush. What contact did you have with the governor's office or Jeb Bush during this time?

S: This will probably not be very helpful for an oral history, . . . but there are three things that I've never been explicit about. One is who I talked to on Thursday the 9th who said, get over to Katherine's office. The second is if I was in contact with the governor's office or the Bush campaign and if so, with whom and to what extent, and I think I will stick to that. I think the universal suspicion is that I was in Katherine's office to make sure they didn't go astray and that I was in communication with the campaign or the governor's office or both, but I've never confirmed that.

P: I talked to Lucy Morgan and she thought that there was not a lot of good feeling between the governor's office and Katherine Harris.

S: I think that there had been some strain between those two staffs and, to some degree, on issues. Some of it was cosmetics, [the] presentation between Katherine's office and the governor's office. I think that's probably a fair statement.

P: Lucy said she looked very hard and they had not found any specific communications coming from the governor's office to the secretary of state's office.

S: That is true. Of course, they questioned all the public information available to them, as did *The New York Times* and others—phone records, e-mails, and those sorts of things—and were unable to uncover specific communications from them. *The New York Times* also requested my cell-phone records for November and I wouldn't give it to them. But I think it's true that they were unable to discover any specific [connection].

P: What was the overall strategy when you first got to Katherine Harris's office?

S: My goal was to bring the election to an end. At the time I arrived, there was a great deal of confusion. There was a great deal of speculation about how it all might play out with recounts. [I]n a phrase that I've used at the time that has been repeated in the media since, my principal objective and my principal advice to Katherine was to bring the election in for a landing, get it over with, finish it. Of course, from my perspective, I was not the secretary of state, I'm not the state's chief election officer, my goal was to bring it in for a landing with George Bush at the controls.

P: One of the issues that came up very early was the automatic recount. The secretary of state still has to send out a specific notification that the automatic recount will take place. She did that, but did not specify in that order, as I understand, precisely what was meant by a recount. As you know, many counties just ran the cards, ran the totals, but did not actually go back and count the ballots again.

S: That's an interesting point. [T]here was a question in some people's minds, [although] there wasn't a question in Clay Roberts's mind and in my mind, that the manual recount provision in the law, we believe, and I think it had always been the position of the department, only came into play in the event that a sample hand count gave evidence of a system failure, mechanical or software failure. The court subsequently ruled that wasn't the case. [I]f you were just going to do a recount, what other way could you do it than by just running them through the machine again?

P: On June 22, 2000, Clay Roberts said that "checking the totals is not enough. In order to do a recount, you should run every ballot through the machines again. The Secretary of State's office believes this is the only correct way to conduct an automatic recount."

S: Is that not what they did?

P: Some did, some didn't. Several counties didn't. Many election supervisors said they did not get any guidance from Katherine Harris as to what they were supposed to do. As you indicated, a lot of counties, traditionally, had just run the totals.

S: My assumption, if I were a supervisor of elections and you sent me a notice that said [to] recount, would be not to re-add, but to re-feed the ballots into the machine. To the extent that a county got a notice from the secretary of state's office saying, recount your ballots, and all they did was re-add the totals, I would think it would be a little disingenuous of them to complain of the lack of specificity in the instructions, that they probably ought to think themselves pretty dumb.

P: The Democrats asked for manual recounts in four counties. One of the issues for the Republicans was that Gore was talking about wanting to count all the votes, then it appeared that he was really cherrypicking, he just wanted to count in major Democratic strongholds. What was your reaction to Gore's initial request for manual recounts?

S: I, of course, thought the Gore campaign was doing exactly what the Gore campaign was doing, which was to try to count undervotes in counties where they would expect to do well, as opposed to Sarasota County. I think there was a theory that they wouldn't ask for a recount in Sarasota County [ ed.: a strong Republican county], but they would in Broward County, because you're going to turn up more Democratic votes in Broward County [than in] Sarasota County. I'm not sure that's true if you were to test it empirically, because my suspicion is that folks who vote incorrectly would have a greater tendency to be Democrat than Republican in any event, in any county. The margins by which that might be true might be greater in Broward County than Sarasota County, but I would still expect there to be a disproportionately large number of Democrats in any undervote situation, even in Sarasota County. Obviously, they wanted to count the counties where they thought they would get the most votes.

As for the phrase, "count every vote," and how that turns out to be inconsistent with the request for recount in four counties, one of the things I think we all ought to be careful of not falling victim to, is this broad hindsight that assumes that there was some strategy in place almost from the get-go that was only tweaked in small ways as the [recount] progressed. That's not true, at least from my perspective, which was up pretty close. There was never a strategy other than, for example, on the part of the Republicans, to keep them from counting and on the part of the Democrats, to make them count. It was tactics every day. When the Gore campaign asked for the recount in the four counties, they were going after enough votes to win. When those votes weren't getting counted to their satisfaction, they invented the phrase, which was a great media hook. [I]t was all tactics, there was very little strategy.

P:  I have talked to several of the Democratic lawyers for Gore and they indicated that Bill Daley and Warren Christopher didn't know Florida well, didn't know Florida election law and they were flying by the seats of their pants.

S:  I'm not terribly critical of those guys. Their top leadership was from out of town. In a sense, our top leadership was from out of town. I'm assuming that they were relying on local knowledge, just as Jim Baker and Bob Zoellick were relying on local knowledge here, . . . so I'm not sure that they were terribly disadvantaged by that. I'm just not sure that Daley's and Christopher's hearts were in it to the same extent that Baker's or Zoellick's were. These guys were Democrats, partisan Democrats, who cared about the outcome, but they probably didn't want to throw themselves under the bus to put Al Gore in the White House.

P:  Christopher left early, Daley didn't stay the whole time. Most observers indicated that Baker was more of a forceful, effective presence. How would you assess Jim Baker's contribution?

S:  I think Baker did an outstanding job. I think he did what you would expect someone of his stature [or] position to do, because he set the tone and then he didn't interfere with the field officers. He let us run the fight, he let us scuffle. If he thought that we were getting off-track or that the tone was wrong, he would, of course, correct it.

P: Did you talk to him frequently?

S: I never spoke to Secretary Baker.

P: Where was the central decision-making process going on? Was it in Texas?

S: No. Obviously, I think that probably Secretary Baker and Bob Zoellick and Joe Allbaugh were down here. I think the decisions about Florida would be made in Florida, probably . . . in consultation with Texas.

P: That is interesting because, having talked with the Democratic lawyers, apparently Gore made almost every decision.

S: One, [that] is inefficient. Two, he was disadvantaged by the fact that he wasn't here and didn't know the state. I think the people who could make a decision, Secretary Baker or some of his primary assistants, listened to [Ben] Ginsberg. He's been down here a lot, for reapportionment and stuff like that. The guys who could make a decision for the Bush campaign were on the ground here and they were listening to the people who knew this state well. There wasn't a Bush monolith, as some people might expect. Theoretically, for example, had I been in communication with the Bush campaign, the Bush campaign might have been overzealous in something they would want the secretary of state's office to do that I might have thought would actually harm the cause by publicly confirming Democrat or public suspicions that she was not being evenhanded and being fair.

P: How much of a problem was it that Katherine Harris was one of eight co-chairs for the Bush campaign in Florida and went to New Hampshire and campaigned for him?

S: There, of course, was a lot of hay made out of that, to the extent that this was . . . a public relations and a perception war. That certainly wasn't helpful. She didn't look nonpartisan and above the fray. The Democrats probably succeeded, to some degree, in characterizing the appropriate role for her. Katherine Harris is a partisan elected statewide official. The assumption, or the supposition, that she should have no feelings or no opinions or no preferences in a presidential race always struck me as being kind of odd. Bob Butterworth clearly had a preference, and he was the state's chief law enforcement officer.

P: But Butterworth backed off and became more neutral, particularly over the military ballots.

S: Yes, and I don't know exactly what that decision making was. I suppose my impression was formed of Bob's participation on the day that he, on his own motion, issued a written opinion saying that you did not have to have a system failure in order to do a manual recount. On that very day, if you went to the attorney general's [web]site and wanted advice on Florida's election law, they referred you to the secretary of state's office because they had no jurisdiction.

P: As the fight went on, the Democratic lawyers and the Gore people were very disappointed in him. They didn't think he helped them enough.

S: Well, that's kind of like Alex Penelas down in Dade County, where they're upset with him as well. When you lose, no one helps you enough. I'm not saying their criticisms of the attorney general or of Mayor Penelas are not valid, maybe those guys could've helped them more.

P: Almost all the books I've read have said that the Bush people were more loyal, more dedicated, more willing to fight for his election than the Gore people.

S: I can't speak for the Gore people, but all I can tell you is that, as far as I was concerned, it was a war to the knife. Loser leave town.

P: Was it a battle for public relations? Everybody, even the Democrats, will admit that the Republicans won the public relations battle. How important was that?

S: I think it was critically important because in effect—I guess I'm bad about military analogies—the public relations battle with Secretary Baker, I think, was so effective, "the votes have been counted once, twice, three times, and now again." The public relations battle was, in effect, the air cover for the ground war, which was the counting or not counting of the votes. Had the Republicans lost public opinion, some of the things that were done in connection with the lawsuits or in connection with the positions of the secretary of state's office might have been untenable.

P: Do you think the views of the public influenced Gore's thinking or decision making?

S: I think that it did. An impression I have [is] that, at some point, the Gore campaign, meaning the vice-president, I suppose, decided that if they could just buy enough time, they would turn up enough votes. What he had to do was not appear like a sore loser, that he wasn't a good American and he wouldn't take defeat gracefully; he had to convince people that it hadn't been a fair fight and he deserved more time to get a fair fight.

P: His critics argued that he didn't fight hard enough. Bill Clinton said he was too easy, too concerned with how the American people perceived what he was doing, and that, in fact, he should have taken a tougher stance on the military votes.

S: Had I been him, and this is why I guess that I'm not an elected official and certainly not a statesman, I would have done anything within the law to get in the White House, on the assumption that I would have four years to make it right.

P: He mentioned to several people that he didn't want to win a fight that might seem to the public that he had stolen the election. He was afraid he couldn't govern.

S: Well, good for him, I'm glad he felt like that. I think that if he wanted to win that fight, he should have fought with all he had. If he didn't think the presidency was worth his very best effort—and he may be right—he may be a better man than all of us, but I don't know, I'm not making that judgment. But it certainly hampers your ability to win if you're pulling your punches.

P: On Monday, November 13, Katherine Harris gave a legal opinion stating that the deadline for certification was November 14. In other words, she was not going to change the certification date. She also said that the only way manual recounts would be allowed would be due to a malfunction of the machines and, later on, to some extraneous event like a hurricane. The state law says recounts are allowed only due to problems with vote tabulation. What did you assume vote tabulation meant?

S: If you're referring to the statute when you say that, and I don't remember them by heart, my assumption was that the position of the Division of Elections was the correct decision after I had read the statute, which was that you could only undertake a full manual recount if a sample manual recount produced credible evidence that the machines had performed incorrectly, [and] that they had failed to count correctly. That's what I took tabulation to mean, that they didn't work, they didn't tabulate the votes correctly. Obviously, and of course I had a reason for wanting to believe this, but I did in fact happen to believe it. I thought system failure was a precondition to a manual recount.

P: Of course, the Democrats argued, why have manual recounts in the law if it's just due to a failure of vote tabulation? If the machines didn't read the votes correctly, then the canvassing boards could go back and be more accurate in determining the intent of the voter. What would be your response to that argument?

S: I suppose this is where we get into the subtleties where all the controversy [arose], if the machines didn't read the votes correctly because the machine was malfunctioning, I would agree with them. If the machines didn't read the votes correctly because you can't read a frigging sign that's as tall as a barn door telling you to check and make sure all your holes are punched correctly, then that's a different issue. The machine didn't fail there, the voter failed to perform his or her duty.

P: Judge Richard Posner argued that was where the Democrats were wrong. They looked at the issue as a legal issue over the vote tabulation, when the issue was really voter error.

S: That's right, that's my opinion. The undervotes that didn't get counted, if you assume that there were some significant number of Floridians who attempted to vote in the presidential race and failed to do so, is because of voter error. They didn't do what they were supposed to.

P: Was the butterfly ballot in Palm Beach a major problem for voters?

S: The butterfly ballot in Palm Beach could have made the difference, because in a margin this narrow, anything could make the difference. It's kind of interesting, I looked at the butterfly ballot in Palm Beach, and I have a dad who's 80 and a mother who's 73 and a mother-in-law who lives with me who's 72 and I can see how you can get confused. All I can say is [that] apparently something like 98.5 or 99 percent of the people in Palm Beach County understood the ballot.

P: I believe 96 percent voted correctly, but it was a confusing ballot.

S: Yes, it was confusing, but I don't think it was a conspiracy or anything like that.

P: Your argument is that if a voter does not vote correctly, that is an invalid vote. It doesn't count under any circumstances although Florida law says that it's the intent of the voter. Can a canvassing board determine the intent of the voter?

S: If all that matters is the intent of the voter, then you would count manually every election, because those damn machines, I think, are designed to assume like a 1 percent error rate. There's an assumed error rate in the engineering of the machines. If all that matters is the intent of every single individual voter, you wouldn't use machines, you would use people. I bet you'd get a bigger error rate than you'd get with a machine, or at least a greater suspicion of bias. At least I'll speak for myself, after watching them count votes in Broward County and Palm Beach County on television, I'd feel much better, regardless of the outcome, that I'd gotten a fair deal from the machine, which I think is why we went to machines . . . I think the machines are more accurate, but even if they're not more accurate, they're certainly less biased.

P: What about the overvotes? Overvotes didn't really get talked about very much.

S: Again, how would you ever define intent, even taking the Supreme Court's standard, on an overvote?

P: Let's say on an Optical-Scan machine you wrote in Bush and circled Bush, but you didn't fill in the bubble. If you looked at that vote, I think it'd be pretty clear that the person intended to vote for Bush. However, they didn't make the proper mark for that ballot to count. Should that vote count or is it an invalid vote?

S: That's an interesting question that I don't know that I've really given a lot of thought to. A classic case is out here in Gadsden County where uneducated voters would vote for Gore and then, when it came to the bottom, it said, "write-in candidate," they took that to be a command and wrote in Gore and the machine kicked it out. Well, they counted those in Gadsden County, and I guess, without being totally logically consistent, if the preconditions for a manual recount had been met and you and I were on the canvassing board and we came to a place where they circled Bush, wrote Bush, but hadn't punched out the hole, I'd give it to Bush.

P: When Judge Terry Lewis made his first ruling, *Lewis I*, he said that Harris must exercise discretion in deciding whether or not to accept these late ballots. What did that mean to you and the secretary of state's office?

S: Basically, what Judge Lewis said was, you have some discretion, you have to exercise it, which means you have to think about it a little bit and you need to have some reasons for thinking about it. The standard of judicial review there, which the Florida Supreme Court subsequently totally ignored, is that she's entitled to a huge presumption that anything she does is correct, as long as it's not arbitrary and unreasonable.

What we did then was kind of an interesting thing, it was one of Katherine's great contributions. We're sitting here in a meeting . . . in Ben McKay's office and we're saying, now we have to decide whether Broward County and Dade County or whoever is wanting to recount has good reasons for missing the deadline. Well, what are the good reasons? Joe Klock and I said, we'll go out and we'll review the case law and come back for your consideration with a set of criteria that might be applied. I said, well, once we have the criteria, how will we know what their reasons are? We're all sitting there just agonizing, our faces are all screwed up, Katherine says, well, why don't we ask them? I said, I beg your pardon? [She said], why don't we write them a letter and ask them what their reasons are? We said, geez, that's brilliant, we'll do that. We faxed them down a letter asking them, why can't you finish your recount on time? And their answer was, because it's hard; we're a big county and it's hard. That didn't meet any of Klock's criteria that Katherine adopted, so we said no.

P: Palm Beach County had something like 461,000 votes.

S: Let me give you an example. This is not as big a county, but when Volusia County decided they were going to recount, they sat down, they started counting, they didn't call anybody, they didn't ask anybody, they didn't need any advice, they counted until they were done, and they were done way ahead of time. Palm Beach County thrashed around like a fish out of water, complained, moaned, and took Thanksgiving off and never finished. And then they ask us for a binding opinion. They knew what the answer was going to be. We stopped them before they asked for the opinion because we had already told them all what the opinion would be, and they asked us for it anyway and stopped themselves.

P: Let me go back a little bit to the contradictory law which stated that late returns "*shall*" and in the next paragraph, indicated that they "*may*" be ignored. Katherine Harris said "*shall*" takes precedence, then Butterworth countered by saying that "*may*" takes precedence. Judge Charles Burton got these two conflicting opinions and the question was, for him, which ruling takes precedence? Is it the attorney general or is it the secretary of state? Obviously your answer would be, in this category, as indicated on the attorney general's website, the secretary of state.

S: Well, but see, from Judge Burton's perspective, one was "*shall*," which Katherine says is [November] 14, no matter what. The other was "*may*," which means Katherine can decide whether it's the 14th or not—and she said it was the 14th. Our position was, under either "*shall*" or "*may*," you lose. What Judge Lewis said was okay, but tell us why you made the "*may*" decision. We went back, developed criteria [as to] what would be reasonable to make that decision, [and] asked them what their reasons were. They didn't match the criteria, so we said, we meant no when we said no before. It's the 14th.

P:   Was part of the criteria a hurricane or a power outage?

S:   One of the problems we had was some institutional knowledge. The way that second statute that said "*may*" arose was after Hurricane Andrew. We knew it was intended to be a *force majeure* provision, an act of God, that would prevent people from going to the polls. If you were prevented from counting the votes because the election was held and then the warehouse blew down, well, then the secretary of state's going to give you a bye. If the Democrats didn't have enough votes in your county, we weren't interested in that.

P:   Kerey Carpenter was sent down to Palm Beach as a representative of the secretary of state.

S:   I think we actually sent "observers" to all four counting counties to provide them with technical assistance if they needed it, and advice. That did several things. One, it showed from her perspective that Katherine was on the case, paying attention and dealing with this situation, not just sitting there like a deer in the headlights. Two, it gave us eyes on the ground, at the location, that weren't Democrat eyes, that weren't Bush eyes. We were able to get real-time reports from the scene as to what was actually happening. Then three, because they were the representatives of the chief elections officer, if questions came up, we were able to influence the decisions.

P:   Who determined who would go? Some of the books report that they were sent down by Jeb Bush.

S:   No. The governor's office was not aware of that decision, the governor's office was not consulted by the personnel and all the decisions were made in the secretary of state's office.

P:   I talked with Palm Beach County Commissioner Carol Roberts and she saw Kerey Carpenter as someone who was specifically told to stop the recount, that was her function. Roberts claimed that Kerey was giving advice to Judge Burton and Burton was unaware that she was representing the secretary of state.

S:   Well, who did Judge Burton think that Kerey was there representing? I'm serious. She's the lawyer from the secretary of state's office. Assuming that Kerey did not misrepresent who she was, it's inconceivable to me that Judge Burton didn't know who she was or didn't ask this lady leaning in and whispering in his ear, who the hell are you?

P:   Was there a specific decision on the part of the Republicans to challenge every vote?

S: I think the Bush campaign's intention was, unlike the Gore campaign who was more worried about perception, was to fight tooth-and-nail, hammer-and-tong, over every ballot, and to try to get a standard that would produce the outcome they wanted.

P: On Sunday, November 26, Palm Beach made a request to extend the 5 P.M. deadline and allow them more time to finish their counting. Burton called in and said, we'll be finished in two hours, can you give us two more hours? That request was denied.

S: No. We were probably being a little disingenuous. The Supreme Court said, in its opinion in which they were so rude to Katherine, if the office is not open on Sunday the 26th, they will have until 9:00 A.M. on Monday to submit their ballots. If the secretary of state's office is open on Sunday to receive the manual recounts, then they shall be submitted by 5:00 P.M. Since the Supreme Court was so big on the difference between "*shall*" and "*may*," who would we be to correct their grammar?

P: The issue again is that she could have exercised her discretion and chosen to open up Monday and not opened up on Sunday and by then Palm Beach County could have finished their recount. By not waiting until Monday, she made it appear to be a partisan decision.

S: Probably. It did make it appear that way.

P: In fact, there were actually two different totals for Palm Beach County. One was about 215, one was 176, and, as far as I can tell, no one knows for sure today which one was the correct total. Also, I understand that Theresa LePore submitted partial recounts.

S: The state law says that if you make the decision to recount them by hand, you must recount all the ballots. You would not have conformed to the manual recount statute if you gave me a certification that was a partial recount, partially hand [counted] and partially machine counted, which is what Palm Beach was preparing to do. We had this big raging argument on Sunday afternoon about whether we would take the Palm Beach returns if we knew in fact that they were illegal, but on the face of it there was no way to ascertain that on the piece of paper. The decision, contrary to my position, was that we would have to. Then it became irrelevant, because Palm Beach sent us a certificate that was obviously flawed on its face. They specified, some are hand count, they specified some are such-and-such, and then they gave us the numbers from the machine rerun from two weeks ago that we'd already certified. The classic example of that would have been, what if Dade County had gone on and just counted the undervotes, the 10,000 undervotes? I believe that Katherine Harris would have thrown Dade County's votes out because they didn't count all the votes. You can't just count the undervotes.

P: Was it a strategic error for the Democrats not to go to the contest right away?

S: In retrospect, they frittered away the time they had, fighting on ground that was not favorable to them, when their time might have been better spent in a contest.

P:    Plus in a contest, there would be no challenges. The judges would do the counting and therefore it would be less problematic.

S:    He has all of these equitable powers where he's not bound by binding opinions of the secretary of state, he can do whatever he thinks justice requires.

P:    As a matter of fact, in Judge Lewis's second opinion, it's very clear in that decision that he's a little perturbed with the Democrats. He indicated that he didn't know why the Democrats were arguing over this, they had an option, they could go directly to the contest.

S:    Again, it's so easy to look back and say that, even if it was 100 feet off the ground, you should've jumped from the *Hindenburg* [the airship that crashed on May 6, 1937] before it exploded and burned. But I think it would have been very tough for them when they were always just a couple of hundred votes away from victory, to pull the plug on an effort they were heavily invested in, organizationally and otherwise, to begin a whole new effort, and bet everything on the turn of that card. They had been gaining ground. They whacked it and whacked it [Bush's lead] by like two-thirds and they had every reason and were justified in believing that if they could get done what they wanted done in Palm Beach and Broward counties, and ultimately in Dade County, they would prevail.

P:    If the Democrats could have taken the lead in the recount, that would have changed everything, would it not?

S:    I think that's right. I think it would have changed the psychology of it. Going back to something we were talking about earlier, there's also something that should be made explicit about the [November] 14 deadline. When that deadline came and passed, it wasn't as if all those counties were counting away and just got cut off. Dade County had decided not to recount when the 14th came and passed. Dade County didn't decide to manually count until after the 14th. Palm Beach County had decided to manually count, but wasn't counting at the moment. Broward County had decided to manually recount, but hadn't counted a vote yet. One of the things to be avoided is this idea that four counties were just counting away like mad and the clock ran out on them and the secretary of state's office did them wrong. That's not right. Nobody was counting when the deadline came and passed.

P:    One of the arguments made by the Democrats was that if the secretary of state has discretion, she has flexibility. Thus she could have waited until November 17 when the overseas ballots were due.

S:    She should've. That would have been the only hook where she could've stopped. One of the problems with saying, keep counting, is that once you let the deadline slip, you have to pick a time when you say, okay, now you have to be through. If it wasn't going to be the date that the legislature said, which was the 14th, another date that it might plausibly have been was the 17th, as you pointed out, when the military ballots were due. She could've done that and that would have been a plausible reason for stopping. But if she had reached out and just said 5:00 P.M. on the 21st, when 5:00 P.M. on the 21st came and Dade County had not finished being recounted and wanted to continue, what could Katherine say to cut him off? There was no place to stop, it was like a slide. There was no place to stop once you went past the 17th. I think that there's probably some manifestation of partisanship in not allowing a slip from the 14th to the 17th. Midnight [on] the 17th would have been a reasonable fall-back date. I would point out to you that Dade County could not have finished by the 17th. Dade County hadn't even decided to count until the 15th. They'd have never finished by the night of the 17th.

P:  The Democrats argued that the decision by David Leahy and the Miami-Dade County Canvassing board to end the recount was due to intimidation from a Republican "rent-a-mob."

S:  That's bull. Leahy is a first-rate supervisor of elections officer. I think he believed system failure was required and he didn't see any. He told them, forget it. Then, when they started recounting, they were just counting the undervotes. It was Thanksgiving weekend or close to it when Dade County decided to stop, when they had the little mini-riot down there or whatever. I'd spoken to Katherine about that. You can't just go count the undervotes. The law says you have to count all the votes. I think Leahy knew that. I don't believe that Leahy and a county commissioner and a judge from Dade County refused to count Dade County votes because they were afraid, physically or politically. I think Leahy knew that he couldn't count the undervotes and submit undervotes with machine counts on the other precincts.

P:  Let's discuss the November 21, 7-0 Florida Supreme Court decision. In that particular decision, the court prevented Harris from certifying the election. They went on to say that Palm Beach and Broward counties could continue the recount and the new deadline was Sunday, November 26. That new date seems to me, in retrospect, to be the crucial point of that decision. Why November 26?

S:  I don't know why they chose that date. Probably, if I were just guessing and speculating, . . . they too thought there ought to be some closure. So they picked some time in the future that they thought was a reasonable time to allow those counties to finish counting, and they were wrong. The counties didn't finish counting, at least Palm Beach County didn't finish counting.

P:  Did you, at this point, conclude that the Florida Supreme Court 7-0 decision was making law rather than interpreting law?

S:  I thought they had gone flat off the reservation. I thought that, and still believe, they took the entire state election law and just [threw] it on the scrap-heap and were making it up as they went. Don't misunderstand me, their system may have been better than the legislative system. The legislative system may have been a bad, unfair system. But that wasn't the issue. This is a separation of powers issue and I think that they usurped the legislature's authority.

P: Did you see this as a partisan political decision, part of the idea that most of the members of the Florida Supreme Court were liberal and had been "picked" by Dexter Douglass?

S: I did. I thought it was very much a liberal Democratic partisan decision, and again I'm not a big-deal practicing lawyer like [David] Boies and all those guys like that, but . . . I thought they were totally off-base in the standard of review they applied. I thought Terry Lewis did the best job, from a legal perspective, of anybody in this field.

P: On the other hand, the Florida Supreme Court ruled against Gore about four different times on the butterfly ballot, on his request to continue the recount in Dade County, in the Seminole and Martin county cases. So in some crucial cases, they ruled against Gore.

S: I think that's right. The butterfly ballot and some of those things, to me, those were throwaways. You're not going to re-vote in Palm Beach County after the election is over. Talking about the [Seminole County] thing or whatever, you're not throwing out 4,500 military ballots either. Some of those about which the national pundits on television waxed eloquent for days and days as they breathlessly awaited the court's decision were no-brainers.

P: Let me ask about the military ballots. The original law said ballots either should be postmarked or signed and dated no later than the date of the federal election, November 7. The state and the federal government agreed to a administrative regulation that allowed the overseas military ballots to arrive ten days after the election date. Apparently some of the election supervisors were very confused about exactly what the law was and whether federal law took precedence over state law.

S: Clay Roberts told me from the get-go, when I first asked him, and I never asked him again, . . . that the law was exactly what you just said, that you had until midnight to get the ballots in on the 17th, but they had to be either postmarked or signed and dated and notarized on or before the day of the election. You can't have people voting after the election's over. If you're going to accept ballots after the election's over, there has to be some evidence that they cast a vote before the election results were known. [S]ome of my lawyers worked on and tried the cases out in Pensacola and . . . didn't we end up counting some ballots that didn't have those dates and stuff on them? I think that's wrong.

P: Let me refer to a *New York Times* article. The authors concluded that there were 344 ballots without postmark, several postmarked after the election, 96 without a witness, 103 ballots mailed within the United States—of course that doesn't count since you're not over-seas—19 people who voted twice, and 5 ballots received after November 17. The issue for the election supervisors in Okaloosa, Escambia, large military areas, was that they felt pressured to go back and recount those votes, and in fact they did go back and recount.

S: As I recall, the Republicans would pound on the drums like crazy. It was kind of like Al Gore's, "let every vote count," which kind of got him in trouble on the military ballots as we all remember. It was a whole lot of chest-thumping, bloody-shirt waving, our-boys-and-girls-overseas-defending-ramparts-of-freedom, blah-blah-blah, and I say [it was] voter error just like in Broward County. If you can't vote right, we're not counting.

P: If the people in Duval County were "too dumb to vote" and the military's "too dumb to vote," neither one counts.

S: That's exactly right. If you're too dumb to vote in the military, you shouldn't be treated any different because you're wearing a uniform than being too dumb to vote in West Palm Beach.

P: There were at least, from *The New York Times* count, 680 disputed military ballots. No one knows how they broke down, but that could be the difference between winning and losing.

S: They would probably have to be at least 65 percent Republicans.

P: That's what one would guess. So that's a pretty significant percentage.

S: Yes. In that case, if you threw them out, 65 percent of [the] 700 [disputed ballots], you don't change the outcome. You don't get there, but it gets a lot closer. There was not a lot of discussion about military ballots in the secretary of state's office in my presence, and I was there continuously from the 9th through the 26th. I know that *The New York Times* spent six months and 20 reporters and they had to write a story, but there was no big discussion or conspiracy about the military ballots in the secretary of state's office.

P: In fact, I have Katherine Harris's statement after that article came out and she said *The New York Times* failed to accurately and completely report the facts. Did you help her with that news release?

S: I didn't help her with that news release after *The Times* story, no.

P: There is another intriguing issue in regard to the military ballots. Election supervisors, one in Escambia County and one in Alachua County, said a military ballot that was counted in Escambia would not have been counted in Alachua. Those are different standards. Isn't that a violation of the Fourteenth Amendment?

S: Probably.

P: But that never got any real attention.

S: No, all that was obscured, if not covered, by the bloody shirt.

P: Both Joe Lieberman and Bob Butterworth backed off of that issue.

S: That's a perfect example of losing your nerve. Maybe these men felt strongly that you ought to be able to vote if you're an idiot in the Marine Corps, but you shouldn't be able to vote if you're an idiot in Palm Beach County. Maybe they felt strongly that somehow putting on a uniform excused ignorance. If they didn't, if they were just afraid of the adverse publicity and the political blow-back from bouncing military ballots, then I would say that's the classic example of them failing to fight hard enough for victory.

P: You may not have been involved in this, but while Mark Herron had a five-page memo on the legal aspects of the military ballots, apparently the Republican Party had a 52-page memo which spelled out, in very precise details, about how to challenge the military ballots.

S: I think the Republicans mounted obviously an extensive and pretty effective campaign on the military ballots on the legal front.

P: Give me your analysis of the activities with Sandra Goard, the supervisor of elections in Seminole County, and Peggy Robbins, the supervisor of elections in Martin County. As you know, they allowed the Republican Party to come in and put voter identification numbers on the requests for absentee ballots. Peggy Robbins allowed them to take the ballot requests out of the office. They're not ballots, they're just requests, but some people perceived that as both a violation of public records law and a violation of election law, because once the documents were in her possession, they were public documents and should not have been taken out of the office. As you recall, in the two decisions by Judge Nikki Clark and Judge Terry Lewis, they claimed that while that was bad judgment, there was no harm done.

S: No harm, no foul.

P: You couldn't determine which of the ballots had been tainted.

S: That's what I was talking about. They weren't going to throw out all of those ballots because there might have been some that were tainted. Not tainted, as you pointed out, by some defect on the ballot that had been remedied, but rather a technical defect on the request for the ballot, with no indication that the ballot itself that was cast as a result of the request was invalid at all.

P: The Bush campaign filed suit in federal court, which gets up to the 11th Circuit Court of Appeals. The court voted against the request to stop the recounts and all during this time, we hear very little about the Fourteenth Amendment. Why do you think the 11th Circuit Court's decision was so different from the U.S. Supreme Court?

S: I don't know the answer to that. I'm not a good enough constitutional lawyer and a good enough student of the court to tell you that. I'll tell you this though, when I listened to the radio or the sound on the television, whatever it was, to the U.S. Supreme Court grilling those lawyers—theirs, not ours—I was really impressed, because I like smart people, and at how smart all those people were, no matter what their approach and their ideology apparently was. I would submit to you that it's quite possible that the U.S. Supreme Court just saw more clearly and analytically than the farm club down in Atlanta. Just like the [New York] Yankees hit better than the Monroe, Louisiana Yankees.

The Supreme Court had a difficult job, and I know the Democrats feel the same way about the U.S. Supreme Court decision as we feel about the Florida Supreme Court decision, that they were partisan. But if you give them maximum benefit of the doubt, I think the U.S.

Supreme Court may have thought that this thing had great potential for doing serious harm to the nation and to the political structure. While we all resolve our differences without violence and lasting, or at least debilitating, rancor; I think they probably wanted to bring this election in for a landing and found the best way they could to do it.

P: The Democrats finally go to the contest, and of course, this is a different process, and the contest was filed in Judge Sanders Sauls's court. Were you involved in that at all?

S: I watched it. That was kind of an interesting thing too. I couldn't really read it that well until he rendered his decision, and then he just clubbed them like baby seals. I have this terrible partisan bias, but I basically thought he was right and thought it was kind of interesting that he had the courage to say so unabashedly.

P: Judge Sauls concluded that the Democrats had to prove a probability, not a possibility, that the votes would change the outcome. The plantiff had to demonstrate that the canvassing board had abused its discretion. He said, there's no proof in either case. The Democrats, through David Boies, said how does he know? He didn't count the votes. They brought the ballots to Tallahassee and had them admitted as evidence, but Sauls never counted them.

S: I'm not sure I would agree with Boies on that, if I understand his argument, because if you count the votes, there's no need to determine probability or possibility. You'll know. If there's some question about what the eventual outcome would be and whether to count them depends on how you resolve that question, then that's the threshold question. I would submit to you the argument about systems failure. You have to adduce some evidence that something has gone badly awry and is going to produce the wrong outcome, not just that if we fooled around with these things long enough, we might get a different outcome. This is my characterization—what is the standard for a search warrant? Probable cause? If there's probable cause to believe there's been a miscarriage of justice? I think Sanders Sauls says, I don't see any probable cause to believe that.

P: The Florida Supreme Court, of course, on December 8, reversed Judge Sauls by a 4-3 vote. Were you surprised by that decision?

S: I wasn't surprised by the majority decision, I was surprised by the three dissenters and I was surprised by the tenor of Justice Wells's dissent, which pleased me enormously, of course.

P: It was a very vigorous dissent.

S: Now, that doesn't totally rehabilitate Charlie with me, but it went a long way. [Laughter].

P: It was a little surprising that Justice Shaw voted no. Barry Richard argued that this split decision demonstrated that the Florida Supreme Court wasn't as partisan as its critics had claimed.

S: My view on all this is totally distorted by partisanship, and some scholar standing back and looking at this might well say that the

[Florida] Supreme Court did a good job. I was shocked and still don't know why. Just on judicial restraint issues.

P:  Why do you think the Florida Supreme Court decided to count just the undervotes?

S:  I think that's exactly the difference, that under the protest scenario, the law requires that all the votes be counted. That law is not applicable in a contest situation and the Supreme Court was focusing on the fact that the only thing really at issue was voter intent on the undervotes. I think that's why they framed their ruling that way.

P:  Justice Wells, in his dissent to the 4-3 decision, stated that "there is a real and present likelihood that this constitutional crisis will do substantial damage to our country, state and this court as an institution." Was that overstated?

S:  No, I think he was right. I'm not suggesting that the republic was going to collapse or anything like that, but I'm suggesting, for example, that the Florida legislature was probably prepared to send their own slate [of electors] to Washington. I'm suggesting that, but for the outcome that did transpire, we could have had a first-class constitutional crisis that ultimately would have been resolved, I think, without violence, but I think it would have severely damaged the comity on which representative democracy in this country [is based]. People were angry enough as it was, but if it had gone to Congress on a partisan vote on three different slates up there, it could have just been really awful.

P:  Tom Feeney, speaker of the Florida House of Representatives, called a vote, decided 79-41 on party lines, with two Democrats supporting Speaker Feeney, that if the election controversy was not resolved by December 12, the legislature would present the Bush slate. In your view, was that constitutional? Would it set a dangerous precedent?

S:  I don't know whether it was constitutional or not. It was certainly dangerous and that goes back to what I saying a while ago. Had this not been resolved as it was, I am convinced that the [Florida] House, without trepidation, and the [Florida] Senate, with much trepidation, ultimately would have, given the stakes, sent a slate to the Congress and it would have been a tong war from then on out. We would still be recovering from it.

P:  After the 5-4 vote on *Bush v. Gore*, the Democrats argued that the Rehnquist court, which had not entertained the Fourteenth Amendment very often, was now an activist court.

S:  They may be right when our ox is in the ditch.

P:  Some critics argued that this was, from the beginning, a partisan political decision. David Boies said it was Catch-22, if the Florida Supreme Court had set a standard they would be making law, if they didn't set a standard, they violated the Fourteenth Amendment.

S:  I think Boies is probably right about the Catch-22. I really can't speak to the motivations of the U.S. Supreme Court, but implicit in Boies's point is the danger that I think that Katherine and the folks that worked with her saw all along, if you didn't stick to the scheme that the legislature had put into law, however flawed it might be, there was no place to plant your feet after that. It was all downhill from there. I think that was the mistake. When the Supreme Court of Florida decided they didn't like the harshness with which poor old ignorant Josephine-voter was going to be treated, everything just spun out of control from then on out.

P: Joe Klock said that the Florida Supreme Court 7-0 decision was very harsh towards the secretary of state.

S: It was very personal toward Katherine, they basically bitch-slapped Katherine. That's part of, I think, what gave rise to some of the feeling that it was partisan. You can make a purely legal argument that they'd exceeded their jurisdiction or they'd applied the wrong standard of review, but if they had used the normal, dry language of logic and legal interpretation, it wouldn't have had the same effect as what was basically an inflammatory attack on Katherine.

P: Justice Stephen Breyer, in his dissent, said that he thought there was still time, because he did not adhere to the December 12th, safe harbor date. The U.S. Supreme Court could remand the case back to the Florida Supreme Court and the Florida Supreme Court could set a standard and the votes could still be counted. Was that a possibility?

S: I think that it was a physical possibility in terms of sheer time before the electoral college met. It was probably a political and psychological impossibility. I just don't think anybody could stand it anymore. We just wanted to be through.

P: Judge Richard Posner said the decision was a pragmatic one, not a legal one, but it did save the nation from a looming political and constitutional crisis.

S: That's exactly what I was saying awhile ago, that the United Supreme Court did the nation a great service, if not the Democratic slate in that particular election, by finding the means to bring this election in for a landing.

P: I also want to ask you about the Election Reform Act of 2001. The bill eliminated all of the punch-card machines. They're going to put in a statewide database and they're going to provide a provisional ballot. Do you think that's going to do a lot toward resolving any of the problems with voting?

S: I think we ought to go back full-circle like we did. We have the technology now. You know how kids who can't count, all they have to do is punch the Big Mac [button] and it'll ring up the right charge? What we ought to do is go back full-circle and we'll put your picture on a touchscreen with a donkey by you, and we'll put my picture on a touch screen with an elephant by me, and that way idiots can vote.

This is not very democratic of me, but there was kind of an assumption that I've always [had]. I've been to a million meetings where people talk about low voter turnout and increasing voter turnout and voter apathy and stuff like that. Everyone should have the opportunity to vote, an equal opportunity to vote, but I'm not too sure that it would be good for us if everybody, in fact, voted. Just think about everybody you've met and talked to today, the sales clerk you dealt with, the guy you met in the filling station, the guy you saw in the parking lot and talked to, I mean, do you really want that rascal voting? It's not up to me to decide who should and who shouldn't [vote]. Everybody should have the same opportunity, but if you don't want to vote, I don't care.

P: The other element that's disputed is that the act did away with a second primary and, of course, the Democrats say that this was a partisan political move on part of the Republicans.

S: I think they're probably right. I think we probably hosed them on that one. We'll probably restore it after this election.

P: Comment on the U.S. Commission on Civil Rights Report. There was talk about discrimination at the polling places. In Leon County, for example, there was a highway patrol car stopping people near a precinct. Do you think there was any validity to those charges?

S: No, I don't. If there was a highway patrolman stopping people near a polling place, my suspicion would be that was poor judgment on his part, without thinking [of] the political aspect. Really, what he's thinking about, from the standpoint of his performance, is a ticket quota. I don't believe for a moment that there was any sort of conspiracy to deprive anyone of the opportunity to vote for any reason, whether it was race or otherwise. I think what happens a lot of times, particularly when you're on the losing side of a hard-fought contentious contest, is that you're easily offended. But I think a lot of people seek conspiracy whenever they aren't pleased with the way things work out.

P: I looked it up, and the highway patrol stopped something like 24 cars; 16 were white, 8 were black, and it really wasn't all that close to the actual polling place. From the African American point of view, Ed Jennings said it was intimidation. Even if the traffic stop is not close by, they see "the man" trying to prevent votes. I don't understand how they would know that the patrolman was a Democrat or a Republican.

S: Well, that's right, particularly in this county. He might be a Democrat and how did he know it was going to be a close election and those eight people—that's just so bogus. Race is an area where you're not allowed to say the obvious because it sounds insensitive and stuff like that, but that's just a bunch of whining and crying and there's just nothing to that.

P: How important was the candidacy of Ralph Nader?

S: I haven't done a statistical analysis, but if you assume, which I think is safe to assume, that half the people that voted for Nader wouldn't have voted because they were just disenchanted. If you wanted to assume that 70 percent of the remaining half would have voted for Gore, Gore would've won. When Bob Martinez lost to Lawton Chiles by 13 percentage points in 1990, I fell asleep and slept like a rock, because when you lose by 13 points, nothing you do could have made a difference. When Jeb Bush lost to Lawton Chiles in 1994 by less than 1 percent, then you worry the rest of your life, because almost anything could've changed the outcome. So yes, the Nader candidacy, I think, but for that, Gore could've won. But for two or three other things, Gore could've have won. But for the mistake in Jacksonville, Gore could've won. Almost any change could've produced a different outcome.

# PART VI

# INTERVIEWS: JUDICIARY

# ➤ Judge Nikki Ann Clark ←

Judge Clark, who presided over a crucial case in the center of the Florida recount maelstrom, became interested in the law while growing up in Detroit in the 1960s, a significant time for social change and political upheaval. She "fell in love with the whole court system" because the practice of law and the pursuit of justice made significant differences in peoples' lives. Before choosing a career in politics and jurisprudence in Florida, Nikki Clark graduated from Florida State's law school. Within four years she had risen to the position of assistant attorney general for Florida. After serving in that capacity from 1981 to 1991, she joined the Department of Environmental Regulation and later served a year as Governor Lawton Chiles's chief cabinet aide. These experiences afforded her the opportunity to "really learn about the responsibilities of being a public official."

Democratic Governor Lawton Chiles appointed Clark as a Leon County Circuit Court Judge in 1993, making her the first African American and the first woman to sit on that court. Asked if being the first African American woman judge in the Leon County Circuit put extra responsibility on her, Clark replied, "There was a lot of attention, but I don't think it added anything to the responsibility."

When she recalled her adjudication of the 2000 election cases, Clark emphasized the pressure on members of the judiciary from the media and the political parties. GOP activists with the Bush campaign tried to recuse her from hearing *Jacobs v. Seminole County* on the grounds that she was an angry African American woman who had been passed over for an appellate judgeship by Governor Jeb Bush. The reality was that the Republicans sought to recuse her because they assumed that as an African American woman appointed by a Democratic governor, she would be biased in favor of Gore. Judge Clark denied the recusal petition as legally insufficient and was surprised that anyone thought she would be so upset over failing to get the judicial post that she could not carry out her responsibilities fairly. Judge Clark found the media guilty of projecting a flawed perception of the judiciary. "It does a huge disservice to the public to make the public believe that the judges have one big fat voting machine up there we could just pull a lever on, as if we were substituting our judgement for the judgement of voters."

Judge Clark explained in some detail the reasons for her ruling against Gore in *Jacobs v. Seminole County* and discussed the time pressures as well as the security measures designed to protect her from some threatening telephone calls. Overall, Judge Clark looked back on her experience in the 2000 election controversy in a positive light. Letters and e-mails commenting on her performance were "85 to 90 percent . . . favorable." Harry Jacobs, who brought the suit and lost, praised Clark's performance during the trial: "She did an excellent job at conducting the trial and . . . was certainly in control of the courtroom. I think she did what she did for reasons outside any influence by the media whatsoever." For her part, Judge Clark praised Florida's open court proceedings: "I really think the value of this case was the civics lesson that was shared, as to how the court works." Clark thought the public witnessed "judges who had obviously read the law and knew what the law was." The public was "able to share with us our deliberative thoughts and see why we ruled the way that we did." Judge Clark concluded that the recount never reached the level of a constitutional crisis. "When they were able to watch how this case was resolved, I think they felt more comfortable about the way we resolve disputes in this country."

The author interviewed Judge Nikki Clark on September 25, 2003.

P:   How did you get interested in the law? I read somewhere that you had grown up in Detroit and had watched the riots and had seen that somehow the law was the way to change things.

C:   I did grow up in Detroit during the 1960s, which was a very significant time in the history of this country, especially in terms of social changes and social advancements. I was a teenager during this time, so, of course, I was taking all of this in and watching all of it and very much noticed that the significant social changes, especially as they affected African Americans, were happening in the courts. I went to court, and I must have been about fourteen years old, . . . and I was awestruck. I was mesmerized. I was in love with the law. As [the attorney] argued his case, I wasn't really sure what he was saying, but I . . . knew that what he was doing was making a difference in somebody's life.

P:   How did your professional experiences, prior to becoming a judge, influence your views and decisions?

C:   That is a good question, how those influenced me or affected my career as a judge, and I don't know if I can give you a direct answer to that, but I got very, very good training in what it means to have influence in people's lives. I knew from those experiences what an awesome responsibility I was taking on in coming on the bench. I had a chance to really learn about the responsibilities of being a public official. I had the experience of learning from public servants who were so dedicated to what they were doing and who were so committed to making people's lives better.

P:   In this circuit, as I understand, you were the first woman and the first African American. Is that correct?

C:   I was the first African American judge in the circuit, and the circuit is comprised of six counties. I was the first woman circuit judge.

P:  Did that put extra responsibility on you as you took your oath?

C:  I don't think it put extra responsibility on me, really. I mean, I was coming on to a very responsible job, so I didn't really see it as extra responsibility. There was a lot of attention, but I don't think it added anything to the responsibility.

P:  Did being the first black woman on the bench add to the pressure?

C:  I don't think it really added anything to the pressure. It was certainly a high-pressure job. When I started off, I was assigned to the criminal bench. What added to the pressure was the interest of the media. It seemed that every case I had suddenly became a high-profile case. I was on the criminal bench, so [I had] felonies, so all the cases I had were basically murder and mayhem. Suddenly, all my cases became high-profile cases. That added pressure.

P:  What was your reaction when you got the *Jacobs v. Seminole County* case?

C:  My reaction when I got that case, I guess, was pretty much, oh, darn! [laughing]. I had some other matters pending, and I had a trial I was about to start in another case, and we had to set all that stuff aside and pretty much just clear out my office and concentrate on this one. It wasn't a surprise. Like every other observer in the country, we knew there were more challenges coming.

P:  Judge Terry Lewis told me that when he got the Martin County case, which was, of course, a very similar case, he said to you, these are sleeper cases because everybody was concentrating on Palm Beach County and the punch-card ballots. In the initial phase, I don't think too many media people were paying a lot of attention to this. Is that correct?

C:  The media was not, but I never thought of it as a sleeper case, not in the least. You have to remember what a frenzy the media was in at this point, and so many people were getting their information just from the media. Of course, . . . we were watching the news and listening to the news. The media's description of it as a sleeper case didn't influence my opinion; I knew it was significant. The Seminole County case involved some 15,000 votes. If those votes were thrown out, that was going to make a huge difference. That would turn things around.

P:  At the outset of the case, the Republicans tried to have you recused, and their argument was, at least from my perspective, somewhat flimsy. They said that you had been turned down by Governor Jeb Bush for a judicial promotion and therefore would be angry toward Bush or the Bush family. Other people's reading of this is that they assumed, since you were African American, the black vote in the state was something like 92 percent for Gore and you had been appointed by a Democratic governor; you would be biased in favor of Gore. What was your reaction to that recusal motion?

C:  My reaction, first of all, [was that] I wanted to be able to rule on it right away. I took the motion, looked at it, . . . and decided really immediately that it was not legally sufficient. That one would not be selected [for the District Court of Appeals]—and note, I didn't say that one was turned down—for a district court of appeal position, is hardly grounds for one to get angry or one to feel vindictive or the other language that was in that motion. In fact, being nominated really was quite an honor, especially since most DCA judges don't get it the first time or the second time. A sense of disappointment in not getting it was by no means in my mind or, I think, anybody else's who has ever been through that process, a grounds for revenge.

P: I've talked to some Republicans, and it's very clear from them that the purpose of the recusal motion was because you were African American and "a liberal Democratic judge." Did that concept offend you, that they would assume that you would be biased?

C: First of all, the concept that I would not fulfill my role as a judge bothered me. If somebody thought I would put a case, no matter how significant, ahead of my responsibility to the people of this state to uphold the law, [that] was wrongheaded.

P: If I may read what you were quoted as saying: "I was surprised that someone in such a major case would think I would be so childish and upset that I would not be able to do my job. Either they had a very unfortunate misperception of what a judge's job is or they had a misperception that I wasn't able to do my job for some reason." Jessie Jackson defended you, and if I could read his statement: "They challenged her competence. Her compassion to be fair is outstanding and should never have been challenged in the first place. They sought to get her off the bench based on their own fears. Nothing is sacred." What is your reaction to that statement?

C: They obviously wanted me off the case. That the motion was legally insufficient means that they probably had some other reason for wanting me off the case. When you start making assumptions about people the way that . . . they were making assumptions about me, then you are always wrong. The minute you start assuming that somebody thinks a certain way because they look a certain way or that somebody is going to either not do their job or do their job well because they look a certain way, then you have just lost all credibility. I think the most bothersome thing about it was that they were seeking to impugn my integrity. I value my integrity.

P: I notice that throughout this, the press was referring to the Florida Supreme Court as the "liberal Dexter Douglass court," and they assumed that everybody on it was a Democrat, and they assumed that everybody would, in fact, decide cases in favor of Al Gore. On at least five occasions, the Florida Supreme Court ruled against Al Gore. Did the media have a flawed perception of the judiciary?

C: Absolutely, and I think that the public in some ways shares that perception. I really believe, though, that with our courts, our circuit court as well as [our state] supreme court, with us having everything out in the open, everything on television so people could watch the entire process from start to finish—they could see the legal arguments, they could see the evidence, they could be a part of it. I really think that we were able to show the public how the court system really works, what really happens when a case goes to trial. I sure hope and I really believe in some little small part of me that we did make a difference in showing people what the court system was all about. It does a huge disservice to the public to make the public believe that the judges have one big fat voting machine up there we could just pull a lever on, as if we were substituting our judgement for the judgement of voters. That never was the case . . . and that never would have happened.

P:  Of course, this is the most highly contested presidential election in American history. Emotions were running pretty high and both sides were trying very hard to win, and part of the battle was public opinion.

C:  Absolutely. Emotions were running high, but, again, you've got to keep in mind the role of the judge. I've got to leave my emotions at home. So, when emotions start running high, that's when I get even more intent [on] making sure that I don't bring my emotions into it, because the minute I bring my emotions into it I'm no longer an independent judge. Of course, in the back of your head you're going to have some visceral reaction to it, but it's not those visceral reactions that you get paid to share.

P:  Let's talk about the specific case, *Jacobs v. Seminole County Canvassing Board*. The essence of this case is that Sandra Goard, the supervisor of elections in Seminole County, allowed one man, Michael Leach, the Republican Party representative, to come into the supervisor's office and put voter ID's, which had been left off by the printer, on around 2,126 ballot applications. The issue to be adjudicated was whether or not this was a violation of Florida election statutes. Sandra Goard, the Supervisor of Elections in Seminole County, allowed Leach to put the correct ID numbers on the ballot requests and accepted these absentee ballot requests as valid. What were the crucial issues in this case?

C:  The gravamen of the irregularities in this case involved the people who added the voter identification numbers to the ballot request after they had been turned back in. So, there really was just that one issue. Clearly the statute says that the person requesting the absentee ballot should provide certain information. The statute lists off, I think it's eight or nine things that are supposed to be included in it. So, the issue really came down to whether or not the irregularity of allowing somebody else to fill in the voter identification number was so substantial in irregularity as to invalidate the entire ballot.

P:  In your ruling did you use a precedent like *Boardman v. Esteva*, or *Beckstrom v. Volusia County?*

C:  Absolutely. There was a whole body of law. This case was high-profile, it was emotional, it was hard-fought, but it wasn't a complicated case. It wasn't breaking any new ground legally.

P: According to the Florida Supreme Court, the canvassing boards and anyone making these decisions should err on the side of counting votes. In other words, the right to vote is paramount. These modifications to the absentee ballot requests, were, as some people said, hyper-technical violations.

C: I never did agree with that phrase, "hyper-technical violations," but the bottom line was that the sanctity of the ballots was supreme. The judge *had* to give effect to the will of the voters and couldn't throw any votes out on a technicality.

P: If you threw out all the votes that would be a rather draconian penalty wouldn't it?

C: Yes, it sure is, and then you disenfranchise people. Can I just read to you the crux of that case in terms of what the significance of it is? Here it is, and it's on page two of my order, "The sanctity of the ballot is as old and treasured as our democracy. This court is guided by the guiding principles set forth in the Florida Supreme Court in the *Boardman* case which reads," and I'll just read a portion of it, "'The real partisan interest here, not in the legal sense but in realistic terms, are the voters. They are possessed of the ultimate interest, and it is they whom we must give primary considerations.'"

P: The Democrats argued they'd been denied equal access and they had not had the opportunity to come in and change any kind of ID numbers on their requests for absentee ballots. What was your ruling on that issue?

C: My ruling on that was that they had not been denied equal protection and they had not been denied equal access. Certainly, they hadn't been given access to come in and correct things, but there was nothing for them to correct. What the Democrats had sent out was correct: it had the preprinted voter identification number. The Democrats never even sought access for that; they didn't need to [because] they had done it right.

P: Harry Jacobs, who brought the suit, thought what was truly dangerous about this was that Leach was in there for three weeks unsupervised and that he could have been tampering with Democratic absentee ballots. Of course, there was no evidence that that was the case, therefore it was not an issue, but you did come down on Sandra Goard for using bad judgement.

C: I sure did.

P: Did you see that as a violation of election law?

C: I basically said she violated the law. It wasn't my job to follow up on that, but I sure put in my order. I also talked about her bad judgement.

P: Technically, she could have been prosecuted for violating the law, could she not?

C: As far as I'm concerned she could have been prosecuted for that.

P: But obviously was not.

C: Not that I've ever heard.

P: How would you assess the ability of the lawyers and their presentations in this case?

C: That was some of the finest lawyering I've ever seen. They were terrific lawyers to work with, every one of them. They were well prepared, they were courteous, they were professional. There were a couple of times when lawyers on both sides had to be reigned in a little bit so as not to turn the court case into a press conference.

P: Harry Jacobs evaluated your performance during the trial. He said, "She did an excellent job at conducting the trial and came across as a very strong individual. She was certainly in control of the courtroom. I think she did what she did for reasons outside of any influence by the media whatsoever." That is a pretty strong endorsement from a person who lost the case.

C: It sure is, thanks. [That is] a nice compliment.

P: In the process of dealing with this case, how aware were you of the public attention, of the intense pressure, of the extraordinary importance of this case? How did you manage to make a decision in a much shorter period of time than you would normally have?

C: I was very, very aware of the intense pressure. There were demonstrations going on outside the courthouse. Of course [there] were hundreds of reporters here, there were scores of cameras here. When I went home and would turn on the TV for five minutes all the talk was [about the recount], so I was very, very aware of the pressure. I had to stop by the grocery store one afternoon to pick up some eggs or something, people in the grocery store were bugging me. One lady pulled me inside and said, honey, I've been around for a while, let me tell you what's really going on. People would just gratuitously make comments to me about what I should do or what I shouldn't do. I didn't shop anymore until the whole thing was over.

P: What kind of security did you have in the court?

C: We . . . have real experienced bailiffs. The bailiffs really had to be with us almost every minute, it was just unrelenting. I remember one time I was in this suite of offices . . . and we didn't have a bathroom back here. For me to go to the ladies' room I'd have to go across the hall. The media attention got so frenzied, there were cameras that tried to follow me into the damn bathroom. That's how intense it was. My bailiff was with me the entire time from when I got out of the car until the time to go home. In fact, they took me home a couple of nights because of some phone calls that I had gotten, but they were very good, very professional. The SWAT team guys walked me out to the car a couple of nights. For a couple of days . . . sheriff deputies would drive me home to make sure there weren't any protestors on my front lawn, or media on my front lawn, and to make sure everything was okay. They offered to just sit somebody out there around the clock. I didn't want to do that. So, the compromise was they'd have somebody drive around every 20 minutes or so just to make sure I wasn't being hassled.

P: Did you get specific threats?

C: I got threats and I got just some of the most incredibly nasty phone calls and notes ever. I think that was the most shocking thing. Because it was controversial, I expected people to disagree with me, I mean that's part of it, but I did not expect people to write nasty, nasty notes to me or to make horrible, horrible phone calls to my home. I had been on the bench at that point, I guess seven or eight years. I always had my number published, it just wasn't a big deal. But during the midst of that case, I had my number changed because of the phone calls I got.

P: Were there death threats?

C: I didn't get any death threats. I got some threats [by] people [who] wanted to do some pretty horrible things to me.

P: In your case the plaintiff had to prove "substantial non-compliance" with the law and/or fraud or malfeasance. These were absentee-ballot requests, so there was no indication of deliberate tampering with the ballots themselves, is that correct?

C: That's right. I mean there were certainly irregularities in allowing the requests to be completed by somebody other than the person request-ing the ballot, but there was not substantial noncompliance with the voting laws.

P: I know Judge Lewis said that the remedy in this case was not to throw out the votes. He said, if you wanted to prosecute Sandra Goard or Peggy Robbins for doing these things, the state had a right to do that, but that was not the remedy for this problem.

C: Exactly.

P: Judge Lewis told me that, as soon as he got his case, he went to you and he said, look we've got very, very similar cases. What was your reaction to his initial statement to you?

C: I don't really remember what my initial reaction was, but we had sim-ilar cases and surely what we did was talk about the existing body of law. At that point what we both had was allegations of some pretty serious wrongdoing. None of us had had any fact-finding sessions yet, we hadn't had a trial. We didn't know what the other version was.

P: You were just discussing the applicable law in this case.

C: Yes.

P: You and Judge Lewis used the same courtroom so Barry Richard and other attorneys could do both trials. How did you organize that?

C: I did not really concern myself with which courtroom at which time. I was concentrating on the legal aspects and I let the other folks concentrate on the administrative aspects. As long as I had a court-room, then I could work.

P: You were certainly aware that the process needed to be expedited?

C: Absolutely. It was very, very clear that we had to work real quickly. We had some constitutional deadlines looming. It wasn't like we could take up until the last day and say okay, that's it, that's a decision, live with it. We all wanted to make sure that whatever decisions we rendered had time to be appealed so they could be final. In fact, part of the case was getting the case not just decided but to make sure the record was good and clean so that when it went up for appeal the appellate judges were ready for it.

P: In this case did you expedite testimony?

C: [I] expedited everything. [I] expedited testimony, expedited discovery, expedited the time for the defendant to answer. Normally, even a case that you kind of hurry would take a year. Even in a case [in which] there is not much dispute would take six months. We had two weeks to make sure everything was done and up to the Supreme Court, and we did it in much less than two weeks. I think we did it in a week.

P: When you made your decision, as I understand it from Judge Lewis, you wrote your decisions separately, but you discussed it with him.

C: I don't really remember if I discussed it with him or not. I'm thinking [I did] not. We wrote our decisions independent of each other. We have different styles of writing, we have different styles of judging, [but we had] that same body of law. I'm sure, without a doubt, we talked about those cases ad nauseam, but we didn't really compare drafts or notes. It wasn't necessary; we weren't trying to mirror each other. We weren't even trying to make sure we were consistent. This is the way I'm ruling, however you rule, however you see it, go for it. But we certainly talked and said this is how I'm seeing it.

P: You did make the announcements at the same time.

C: Actually, we didn't make the announcements. We . . . gave the orders to the court administrator, [who] was the one directly involved with working with the press. She would have press conferences at certain predetermined hours. I was not concerned at all about what those hours were. I was not releasing my order until I was releasing my order. I didn't care what CNN thought; I also wasn't going to rush my order to accommodate the media.

When I . . . [finished] with my [decision], my JA [judicial assistant] gave it to the court administrator. Apparently, when Terry got done with his, his JA also gave it to the court administrator. She chose to release those at the same time.

P: It would be convenient for the press to do them both at the same time.

C: Yes, absolutely. She [the court administrator] had asked at one point that I give her a very brief summary so when she announced it she could announce what that ruling was and I did do that.

P: This was appealed to the Florida Supreme Court and they ruled very quickly, and in their decision, they upheld your ruling. So, it's pretty clear that they had the same view of the law that you did.

C: It didn't take them very long at all. In fact, I'll tell you what they did. In their nine-page opinion they quoted extensively from my order. Page three through page seven or eight is a direct quote from my order. So, what they essentially did was say yes, what Clark said was right.

P: When the Florida Supreme Court ruled 4-3 to count all the under-votes, the responsibility for setting up the procedure fell to a judge in this circuit.

C: Right.

P: The first person up, according to the rotation, was Judge Sanders Sauls. For obvious reasons, since he'd been overturned by the Florida Supreme Court, I think he turned it down. As I understand it, you were next on the rotation and you chose not to take it.

C: I don't think I was next on the rotation. I got a call at home asking would I take that case. I asked was I next on the rotation and I was not, so I volunteered not to take the case.

P: Could you give me an example of some of the interesting letters you received, both pro and con? What percentage would you say were favorable as opposed to unfavorable?

C: I'd say 85 to 90 percent were favorable. A lot of people wrote even before I made a decision. A lot of people wrote, . . . sharing their prayers with me. One lady even called Doris [judicial assistant] and said, I see your judge is coughing, tell her to try some lemon and honey. She had a home remedy for me because she could tell I wasn't feeling well. I got lots of letters thanking me for the way that I ran the court, thanking me for my courage to stand up and take the case and not be nervous. I got a couple of notes from judges from across the country, judges that I don't know. Here is one, for example, from Judge McGuire who is a judge in Kentucky. He says, I'm thinking of you, you really distinguish yourself in how you've run your court. He says, you clearly distinguish yourself *and the independence of the judiciary* [Clark's emphasis] in rendering your decision. It's a very complimentary letter. It goes on, I honor your character and your integrity. You, madame, and Judge Lewis, are to me shining examples of what all judges should be.

P: I remember reading at one point, one of the Democratic lawyers in the hearing said, that in your verdict, you needed to send a message. Your reply was I'm not here to send a message, I'm here to do justice. I think that resonated with people who were watching this on televi-sion. They saw a judge who was not going to fall prey to all of this media hype and pressure.

C: A few of the letters I got mention that exact phrase and said they were glad that I had said it.

P: I don't recall the newspaper but an editorial praised you for reaffirm-ing the belief that judges can be objective and follow their profes-sional responsibilities instead of yielding to pressure exerted by various special interests. That may be, as much as anything else, the importance of this case in the long run, isn't it? People all over the world watched this case, watched you and Judge Lewis. Both of you judged on the law, not on the basis of your personal political affiliations or emotions. That really reenforced a belief in the fairness of the judicial system.

C:   When it's all said and done, I too think that's the importance of this case. I think it gave people a chance to see, again, firsthand, what happens in a court. In Florida we've got a very open system. I think [because] people [could] watch it from start to finish, we really did reaffirm, or in some cases, affirm, what the justice system was about. So many people who don't know the justice system think that you've got influential lawyers who come in and somehow influence the judges in ways that are not [visible] in open court. I think a lot of people also thought in the beginning that we were just there to agree or not agree with whichever candidate we voted for in the election.

I really think the value of this case was the civics lesson that was shared, as to how the court works. On the one hand, they were able to see all the demonstrators, to watch Jessie Jackson having a press conference, and then, the cameras would come to court. Hopefully, what they saw was a very orderly and dignified presentation of the law and the facts. Hopefully, they saw judges who had obviously read the law and knew what the law was. They were able to watch us actually deliberate on that process through our whole Socratic method of asking questions and getting additional information by asking those questions. They were able to share with us our deliberative thoughts and see why we ruled the way that we did. I really think that's the key to this case.

P:   And that was done under the most intense pressure imaginable.

C:   [It was] under the most intense pressure imaginable. Somebody else mentioned to me that this was the first nationally observed case since the O. J. [Simpson] trial. Of course, after O. J., people were so disgusted with the system. They watched a judge that didn't really control his courtroom. They watched lawyers who were totally out of control. They were actually watching lawyers having press conferences on the steps criticizing the judges. Hopefully, what we did was to bring back that sense of decorum and dignity to the court system.

P:   Plus, I think it's also important to know that people all over the world watched that. They watched, if we can use this term, a democratic system at work.

C:   I think you're absolutely right. The media was very fond of portraying this situation as a constitutional crisis. It never was a constitutional crisis. In fact, that's the whole point of our judicial system. We have disputes and we have methods of resolving those disputes. We didn't have a constitutional crisis, but that's what people all over the world were hearing. When they were able to watch how this case was resolved, I think they felt more comfortable about the way we resolve disputes in this country.

P:   What was your view of the first 7-0 Florida Supreme Court decision where they stated that Katherine Harris had to extend the certification period? They picked a new date for certification, November 26. The

Republicans would argue ultimately, to the U.S. Supreme Court, that the Florida Supreme Court was making the law. Did you see it that way?

C: No, not really, I didn't. I didn't see that they were making law, I saw that they were trying to create a solution. As judges, we are sometimes in a position of having to try to create solutions. Oftentimes a law will give us a solution, but oftentimes it won't. Oftentimes a law will just tell us what's acceptable and what's not acceptable, what's allowed and what's not allowed. I mean that's why judges have discretion about things, and that's why it's so important to make sure that you've got good judges who have good sense, because we are often called upon to create solutions.

P: The Florida Supreme Court said we need to fashion a remedy, and of course a lot of people jumped on that statement and said, well, now they are taking on the responsibility of the legislature, they are in fact determining who's going to get elected. The state law says that the certification date was to be seven days after the vote and they were going to extend that. Did you see that as an error in terms of how they presented their judicial decision?

C: They had to do something. I didn't really see it that way, that by extending the date they were creating something that the statute had not authorized. I still saw them as trying to create a remedy to a problem that was brought to them. It wasn't like they looked for the issue. I saw the reason they had done that and, quite frankly, I agree with the reason.

P: What was your reaction to the U.S. Supreme Court 5-4 decision in *Bush v. Gore?*

C: As a judge, it's hard for me to criticize a U.S. Supreme Court. I mean they are the U.S. Supreme Court, so what they say is right. I can't really analyze their decision. What they say is right, whether I like it or not. I think that what their decision did, though, really took away from the confidence this country has in the U.S. Supreme Court. The Supreme Court was roundly criticized, as they would have been, no matter what their decision was.

P: As Justice Harding said, it showed the system worked, because the U.S. Supreme Court made the decision, George Bush W. became president, and there were no tanks in the street.

C: The problem was resolved. You may not agree with it, but you have to agree that we've got a process in place that resolved disputes. Whether it's a dispute between two neighbors and what their property line is or whether it's a dispute about who should sit in the White House, we have a system in place and people have confidence that we've got that system in place. They may be upset and they may be angry, as they were with me some, as they were with [the Florida] Supreme Court, as many were with the U.S. Supreme Court. But I think any undermining was short-lived because people still appreciate the fact that we have a system. Just because we have a staunch disagreement about something incredibly important doesn't mean we're going to be out there shooting each other.

# ➤JUSTICE MAJOR HARDING ◄

In controversial cases before the Florida Supreme Court, Justice Major Harding defied any political categorization of his judicial philosophy. Despite his nonpartisan approach to the law in the *Bush v. Gore* saga, the press labeled Harding and his colleagues on the high court "partisan, liberal Democrats."

A native North Carolinian with law degrees from Wake Forest and the University of Virginia, Major B. Harding began his career in Florida jurisprudence as an appointee to the Duval County juvenile court in 1968. He subsequently sat on the Fourth Judicial Circuit, rising to the position of chief judge. When Governor Lawton Chiles tapped him for service on the Florida Supreme Court in 1991, Harding was dean of the Florida Judicial College. From 1998 through June 2000, he held the office of Chief Justice before relinquishing the post to Charles Wells.

In his interview, Harding revealed a sense of fairness and moderation in his decisions as a judge. He recalled when, as an appointee to the Florida Supreme Court, a reporter asked him to name his favorite U.S. Supreme Court justice. Instantly, "it flashed into my mind, Byron "Whizzer" White, who had distinguished himself on the Supreme Court for a number of years and had avoided successfully being labeled."

In explaining his judicial philosophy, Justice Harding noted that precedent should be important in decision making and that judges "should be controlled by precedent except in very rare cases." Questioned about judicial restraint, he emphasized a pragmatic rather than ideological approach to the law. Asked about the media's harsh criticism of the state supreme court's alleged liberal bias, Harding replied that such accusations disturbed him "only to the extent that it reflects on the independence of the judiciary." A calm presence with 34 years of experience on the bench, Harding confided that "you quickly get over it and move on."

He described the rather chaotic scene that unfolded as the election cases were heard by the Florida Supreme Court. Juggling two death penalty cases, setting case schedules for the trial courts, disposing of those cases, and dealing with the issues arising from the 2000 election required hard work by the court. But, as Harding explained, "there was a certain peace, a sense of purpose that we had to resolve the issues." He and his colleagues recognized that the court had to decide at least 15 crucial cases much more expeditiously than it would have done under normal circumstances. Nonetheless, under intense pressure and with the world watching the televised hearings, Harding "thought the opinions of the court, whether I agreed with them or disagreed with them, were thoughtful and well done and represented . . . a lot of effort in a short period of time."

The justice explained the court's voting process and inner workings. Harding emphasized the judicial body's commitment to informing the public and applauded the court's clerk for speedily placing the complete trial transcripts on the Internet for immediate use by the media and casual observers. By providing the public with information and access, the court ultimately exposed itself to both criticism and praise. Members were inundated with e-mails, phone calls, and letters telling them how to vote. Some communications praised their "fair and honest decisions" while others were derisively addressed to "The Seven Dwarfs." One pejorative letter referred to Harding as an "evil, Godless Democrat."

Harding also commented on the court's security procedures and the importance of an open system that required that all proceedings be televised. When recalling some of the key cases, he praised the performance of the attorneys who appeared before the court and claimed, "they were extraordinarily helpful in our decision making."

Harding stood by his rulings and his dissent in *Gore v. Harris*. Reflecting on the election controversy in its entirety, Harding deemed it a "wonderful opportunity to be a part of what makes America so great." He concluded that the recount was "just such a significant milestone in the fact that we can resolve our disputes, and we can do it peacefully in a respectful and dignified manner. Whether you are right or whether you are wrong, the people have exhibited their faith in the decision-making process of the court. The president was inaugurated."

The author interviewed Major Harding on August 20, 2003.

P:  Would you talk very briefly about your appointment to the Florida Supreme Court by Governor Chiles in 1991 and try to give me some sense of your judicial philosophy during the time you were on the court?

H:  I was a circuit judge in Jacksonville and had been for 23 years. I was for two years a juvenile court judge and then in 1970 was appointed to the circuit bench and served there until my appointment to the [Florida] Supreme Court in 1991. The nominations came out, and I was on the list, and I was fortunate enough to have been selected. I, of course, had been a judge for so long that I have been referred to as a political eunuch because we could not participate in any political kinds of things, and I had no political clout whatsoever with either Governor [Bob] Martinez, who was just going out or Governor Chiles, who was just coming in.

As to judicial philosophy, I don't know how I could be characterized. I guess one of the things I recall in the announcement of my appointment, one of the reporters asked me who my favorite supreme court justice was, and instantly it flashed into my mind Byron "Whizzer" White who had distinguished himself on the Supreme

Court for a number of years and had avoided successfully being labeled. I thought that was a wonderful attribute and if I could have been thought of in my trial court career and in my judicial time on the supreme court, as being a judge who listened and who evaluated the law and ruled in accordance with it, then I would have been a success.

P:  How important was precedent in your decision making on the court?

H:  Precedent should be very important to every judge, and we should be controlled by precedent except in very rare incidents. It is very hard not to find some precedent for something, but when you look at the law from a holistic point of view, you generally get some lines or you generally get some traditions established that can give you guidance to a precedent, and you should follow those precedents unless it has been determined that the precedent just does not work.

P:  What is your view of the concept of judicial restraint? Justice Antonin Scalia would argue that courts should interpret, not make, law.

H:  And Justice Scalia is an originalist, and he advocates that the Constitution should be interpreted by the intent of the framers at the time it was written. That is a very easy concept, and as he has indicated in speeches that I have heard and things that I have read, that puts you sometimes on what is labeled the liberal side and that puts you sometimes on what is labeled the conservative side of the issue.

I was confronted on the Supreme Court of Florida one time with a case in which a man and woman on their way to the airport to return to Argentina after a visit in Dade County, got off on a bad exit from the interstate, and they were robbed. The police caught the robber and the robber went to trial, but the people were in Argentina and for whatever reasons could not come back to Miami. The judge there set up a satellite connection between a courtroom and Argentina and the courtroom in Miami, and the testimony of those people was transmitted instantaneously by satellite to that courtroom in Miami. The people were placed under oath. The jurors had an opportunity to see the witnesses, the judge, and all of the attorneys and the defendant. But, of course, the issue of the right of confrontation came up and whether or not this fit within the concept of the right of confrontation.

If I had been an absolute originalist, I would have, of course, said that was not consistent with the right of confrontation because the founders had no intent and no knowledge of the communication skill that would be available 200 years later. So, I determined and the court issued an opinion approving what the trial court had done, and said that it was consistent with the right of confrontation, and as I recall, that issue was sent to the Supreme Court of the United States and they refused to take the case.

P:  Was the decision thus more pragmatic than ideological?

H:  To that extent, I think that my view is probably more pragmatic, but certainly we could not have done that had we taken an originalist point of view.

P: What is your political affiliation?

H: I am a registered Independent. No political party. In 1968, I was a registered Democrat, and I was appointed to the [circuit] court by a Republican governor. Subsequently, I registered Republican, and I was appointed to the supreme court by a Democratic governor. When I got here, I said, I am tired of living too close to the edge, and I am going to register "no party," so I am an Independent.

P: I noted that several members of the press stereotyped the Florida Supreme Court. They said it was the Dexter Douglass court, that this was in fact a liberal Democratic court. How did you react to those kinds of assessments?

H: First of all, at the very beginning, I recall that Craig Waters indicated that we had a request for a disclosure of our political affiliations, and so all of the members of the court disclosed how they were registered. I disclosed I was a registered Independent. But it was very rarely mentioned. I think the picture painted was that all of the members of the court had been appointed by Democratic governors, and for that reason, we were all Democrats.

P: What was the political breakdown, do you recall?

H: I am not positive, but I think the rest of the people were registered Democrats.

P: Does that in any way disturb you, that observers assumed that in the court your decisions would be influenced by your political affiliation as opposed to your legal judgment?

H: It disturbs me to the extent that it reflects on the independence of the judiciary. The independence of the judiciary is the hallmark of what has kept this country together for 225-plus years in its history. I guess it is a very difficult thing for the average public reader to separate that a person can make a decision not consistent with his or her political affiliation. But we have to go back only to 1876 [Rutherford B. Hayes-Samuel Tilden presidential election that was decided by a special commission]. There were three justices on the Supreme Court of Florida who were Republicans, and I think they were unabashedly Republicans, who voted that the votes in Florida should go for [Bill] Tilden, a Democrat.

There are lots of times a judge, if he or she is writing on a clean slate, would make a different decision, and this falls into the discussion on precedent. But, you know, we don't write on clean slates. We write on the basis of the laws that have gone before and how they have effectively governed us. To some extent, you just have to understand that the general public is going to think that a court is going to rule consistent with its political leanings or affiliations, and I don't think that is fair, but I understand that it is a reality.

P: In the recount of 2000, two judges thought to be Democrats, Judge Nikki Clark and Judge Terry Lewis, made rulings against Al Gore. Barry Richard concluded that the court was not liberal because, on at least five major cases, the Florida Supreme Court ruled against Gore, when any one of those decisions could have given him the presidency.

H: That is exactly right. In the last case, Justice Leander Shaw and Justice Charlie Wells were Democrats and thought that the decision should have gone the other way. Your question is, does it bother me? You know, I was a judge for 34 years, and, of course, when these things come out, . . . [it] tends to bother you, but you quickly get over it and move on.

P: Would you describe the circumstances in the court during the 36 days when the 2000 presidential election recount was going on in Florida? If I may quote from a statement you made: "Within the court and the deliberations, there was a certain peace and a certain sense that we had a job to do. We have a short time to do it, and we are not ruling on political issues; we are ruling on legal issues."

H: That is a fair statement in my recollection of how things were. We were fortunate because of communications; when these cases were filed in the circuit courts around the state, the clerks of those courts sent our court the pleadings, because . . . in all likelihood, these cases were coming to our court. So, we were able to get somewhat of a heads up on what the issues were. Of course, we couldn't know what the facts being presented would be and what the ultimate ruling would be, but at least we got a sense of what the issues would be. We had a lot of long days, early mornings, and late nights, because in all of this, we still had cases to write and vote on and issues that needed to be resolved. We could not allow the exigencies of these election cases to totally undo our schedule.

P: And didn't you have one or two death penalty cases?

H: And during that course, the governor [Jeb Bush] signed two death warrants, and we scheduled oral arguments on those, set scheduling for the trial courts, and we had to dispose of those. They were scheduled on successive days. The first one took place, but we could not get to the resolution of the second one, and that had to be put off for a week.

Needless to say, we were busy, and needless to say, everyone was working very hard. But as I indicated in that comment, there was a certain peace, a certain sense of purpose that we had to resolve these issues. We discussed our agreements, and we discussed our disagreements, and ultimately, decisions were made, opinions were written, and votes were cast.

P: This must have been a very difficult time because, as I recall, the supreme court ruled on something like 15 cases. Normally, this might take several weeks or longer, and you were having to hear oral arguments and make decisions in the space of 48 hours. Isn't that a little unusual for the court?

H: It is very unusual for the court to have to get decisions out as quickly as we did, but we realized that the exigencies of these circumstances required that we do it. I thought that the opinions of the court, whether I agreed with them or disagreed with them, were thoughtful and well done and represented a lot of work . . . in a short period of time.

P: How did you utilize your staff? You would have had law clerks and there was a central staff of attorneys for the court to call on.

H: We have a central staff, and each justice has a staff of law clerks. I think at that time, we had three. We would put them to researching certain issues and also to checking records and transcripts of proceedings below. It was a collective effort in each office as to how the law was viewed and [how] the ultimate decisions were made.

P: Could you explain the process by which the court voted? Does the chief justice have any extra influence?

H: Oh, no. From just a procedural matter within the court, if you are asking how the votes take place, when an opinion is circulated, there is a vote sheet with that opinion, and you have all the choices of concurring or concurring in part, dissenting in part, concurring in result, dissenting with an opinion, without an opinion. You have all those options, and those votes are then sent back in to the clerk and ultimately tabulated.

P: I talked with Craig Waters, and because of the website and the technological ability of the court, reporters were getting the pleadings and the decisions almost instantaneously, and that was rather extraordinary, particularly under these circumstances.

H: Yes. As I understand it, the first case was filed in our court at like 3:00 in the morning on November 15, and the clerk put that on the Internet by 7:00 A.M. It took a while, but as the reporters wanted to get that information, they were told where they could get it. They soon learned that they could get more information quicker off of the computer screen than they could coming to the courthouse. That solved a great deal of problems because of the security that we had imposed on us during that period of time and the restrictions on access to the buildings. So, you are right. They were not only able to see the opinions, but they were able to see whatever pleadings were filed, the briefs, and it was just a remarkable experience in modern technology. I thought it was not only good for the press to be able to do that but, you know, the general public was able to do that. We got just random letters from people out there in the world who felt like that they had an opportunity to see the court in action and the decision-making process, and they felt good about it.

P: And unfiltered because the press had not commented. They could see that themselves.

H: That is right.

P: I think Craig Waters said there were something like 3.5 million hits a day on the court's website. That is a huge number.

H: After it became obvious that the supreme court was going to be involved in the case, we started getting lots of phone calls. Of course, soon people were wanting to indicate how they wanted us to vote on these cases, but particularly after each opinion was released, the phone calls were phenomenal. The clerk had to put, I understand, more than four people just answering the phones in his office, and the phone lines were tied up so badly in the clerk's office that the judges couldn't communicate with the clerk, the lawyers couldn't communicate with the clerk, and I understand they had to put in separate telephone lines in order to accommodate that.

My secretary would just not answer the phone after these opinions were released. People would put their messages on the voice mail. Then periodically, somebody on the staff would empty the voice mail and I would have a little list of the calls. But my secretary . . . came in one day and said, Justice Harding, I am not old enough to listen to a lot of the comments that are being made on the voice mail.

P:  Would you comment on these calls and the thousands of emails and letters you received? I know at one point, you had mentioned that some of the emails were quite derogatory, for example, "Justices are rednecks who can read."

H:  First of all, we got some really wonderful letters. I got a letter here from a guy. The subject of his email was, "You make me proud. I am an immigrant from Ireland who became a Marine Corps infantryman and spent 34 years in the service, serving in both Vietnam and the Gulf War. I followed the Bush/Gore case on television and have read all of the relevant documents on the Internet. I am honored to have played a part in my life in fighting for a system which is capable of such judicial action. The entire conduct of the Florida Supreme Court in the Bush/Gore case was exemplary. The dignity of the court and penetrating questions asked by the justices, the ethnic and gender diversity of the justices and everything made me proud. It is the kind of advertisement for America that I hope is seen overseas. I have read the decision twice and find it truly worthy of Solomon. Regardless of how this election turns out, you have played a key role in restoring a sense of dignity, intelligence, fairness and respect to the rule of law." Then he concludes by saying, "Again as a fellow American, thank you and may God bless you, and as they say in Ireland, 'May the wind always be at your back.'"

Then I got a personal note from a fellow in Palo Alto who said, "I just want you and the other justices of the Florida Supreme Court to know how much I appreciate the fair and honest decisions you have rendered during the recent presidential elections. Of course, these were decisions that were characterized in favor of Bush and those that were characterized opposed to Bush. Though not an attorney, I read a lot of legal documents, and the clear logic of your decisions was inescapable. Somehow, this nation is going to benefit from all of this, probably with a strong dose of election reform. I voted on a punch card ballot in California and hopefully with a different method next time."

Then we got a letter from a person in Memphis who said, "Major B. Harding, you evil, liberal, godless Democrat. How dare you think you are above the law? You need to stop and think about where you will spend eternity. I pray for you."

And then this one from Omaha, Nebraska. It is addressed to the Florida Supreme Court (The Seven Dwarfs), and it addressed to the chief justice, "Dear Doc, It has been said that a lawyer in Florida is sometimes just a redneck that can read. It has also been said that a judge in Florida is sometimes a lawyer who has failed in private practice." He went on and a copy was sent to Sleepy, Happy, Grumpy, Bashful, Sneezy, and Dopey.

Then we got a letter from a fellow from Whitehall, Pennsylvania. "You may call yourself a judge, but you are in reality one of seven dung heaps of injustice." He said, "You are so ashamed of your biased ruling that instead of facing the media, you sent out a clerk to read one paragraph of a 42-page report." I am sure he is referring to Craig Waters who went out and gave a prepared statement that had been approved by the court to the press. But this fellow continues, "You someday will be judged by a 'higher authority.' I pray that God will banish you to burn in hell. There is no justice in the Florida Supreme Court."

So, what was happening did create a great number of emotional responses. We recognized that it was a political issue and it was being resolved by the courts, and we recognized that this was a natural part of a fallout of this. But we also recognized that as [Mitchell] Berger said in his law review article, when these issues came up, they went to the law, not to the generals, to resolve them. And do you know that the case was decided, the president was inaugurated in January. There were no tanks in the street. Nobody died a violent death. I have had a conversation with the marshal at the supreme court who tells me that there was not even an arrest made during all of that time with all of those people on the grounds and across the street at the Florida Supreme Court.

P:   Did you get any death threats?

H:   No.

P:   Did you have a security guard with you in public?

H:   No, but there were times when we had additional security. We were aware that they had extra security in our neighborhoods, and once or twice, we came home and found a police car in our driveway. They were just checking around and making sure everything was okay. We were offered whatever portion of security we thought would be appropriate, and as I recall, none of us felt any fear. They would stop traffic so we could get out of the parking lot area under the supreme court. But, you know, I never felt physically threatened in any way.

P:   Another thing that was important about this event was that Florida carried out its deliberations under the Sunshine Law. I would assume without knowing specifically, except perhaps for the state of Washington, Florida must have the most open court system in the country. People were able to watch all the proceedings, and some had never ever seen a trial, let alone a supreme court proceeding.

H:  I think you are right. I don't know of any system that is more open. Of course, I was a trial judge during the time when the issue of whether or not the court should be open to television and photographs [was being debated]. I never have felt during the course of my entire judicial career that the openness that the supreme court inaugurated was a problem. I thought it was always the best thing for the system. I never felt like anybody ever played to the cameras or anything like that during the course of any of the trials I presided over, and I just think it is a wonderful thing. I have nephews who lived in Ethiopia, and they went, as I recall, to the American embassy and were able to watch the proceedings at the embassy. I had a lawyer friend in Jacksonville . . . watch it from Chile. So, people from all over the world were able to see the court in action.

P:  How much television did you watch, and how much press coverage did you read during these 36 days?

H:  We didn't watch much television because we were busy. Actually, it was really not until after the case was over that we sort of had an opportunity to decompress. I guess we were aware of the headlines. We got some letters at home during the course of this from people I had considered to be friends for years there in Jacksonville. Evidently there was a letter-writing campaign in my old neighborhood and Rotary Club. People wrote and said some very unpleasant things and, I guess, in effect severed friendships that I had known and enjoyed for many years. Of course, I really didn't have an opportunity to dwell on those until after the election was over. Those kicked in some other issues that I had to deal with, like the issue of forgiveness, and whether or not I was going to allow these issues to determine the quality of my life.

P:  Were you aware, for example, that Jim Baker was highly critical of the Florida Supreme Court, particularly after the 7-0 decision in *Palm Beach County Canvassing Board v. Harris*?

H:  Sure. I was aware of that. There was a segment on NPR [National Public Radio] with a panel of some former press secretaries, . . . but they all agreed that Jim Baker was the master [political] spinner. I thought to myself, that was what he was a master at, and that is what he did after that case.

P:  Baker said: "The votes have been counted, recounted and counted again."

H:  "And they [the Florida Supreme Court] have moved the date [of certification to November 26]." But, you know, we understand that in those difficult cases where people's emotions are high, there are going to be those who seek to inflame the emotions. I have heard it wondered [about] the impact of Jim Baker on the decision of the

Supreme Court of the United States to take that first case because it was a state law issue and ruled on by the state court. You don't know what goes through their [U.S. Supreme Court] minds, but when they got it, they obviously had second thoughts and sent it back without ruling on it, except to stop the voting recounts.

P: In many of the cases you took, the district court of appeals passed those directly through to you. This is called pass-through jurisdiction. They knew that it would be in your court eventually.

H: It is not as nice a word as "pass-through." It is a "throw-up." The district court of appeal here in Tallahassee was the natural place for those cases to go, and they realized that they didn't have the luxury of hearing the arguments, ruling on it, and getting a decision up to us before the time ran out.

P: So, it was expediency.

H: It was expediency, and I don't think that anybody thought that any other process would work.

P: Would you comment on the performance of the attorneys who appeared before you, and how important their oral arguments were in helping you make your decisions?

H: The attorneys were just extraordinarily helpful in our decision making. Barry Richard was just a master, and David Boies was just phenomenal. When we learned later from articles in *Time* or whatever that David Boies was dyslexic and . . . we all marveled that he could get up there and speak without notes, but of course we realized upon reflection that he had to accommodate and adapt that. There were lots of local lawyers involved, Dexter Douglass and John Newton but primarily the lawyers were David Boies and Barry Richard. We were very pleased to have them appear before the court.

P: Would there be an occasion that you would make a decision prior to oral arguments?

H: No. You can't get a case, read the briefs, look at the record, and then do some research and check out the case without having a preliminary predisposition about the case. In all of my time on the Supreme Court of Florida, I never knew of our going into an oral argument with a preset result in mind. Many times, I have heard in conference, wow, [after that] oral argument, I am really 180 degrees from what I thought I would be when the arguments were concluded. I know somebody wrote a book and said that somebody had made an announcement that we had decided the case [before the oral arguments]. I wish I knew that had happened because it would have saved an awful lot of time and effort that we spent after the argument.

P: I think that was in Jeffrey Toobin's book, *Too Close to Call*.

H: They were inaccurate, and if anybody had made a decision, I didn't know about it.

P: Let's discuss some of the key cases. The first one of some importance was *Fladell v. Palm Beach County Canvassing Board*, the butterfly ballot case. The court ruled rather quickly on that, and I think the way you put it was, that although there may have been some problem with the ballot, it "did not amount to substantial non-compliance," which is what the statutes say. Another issue, it seems to me, was that there really wasn't a remedy. In a presidential election you can't revote, can you?

H: I don't know. I can't at this point in time go back with any degree of specificity and give you anything other than what was contained in the opinions as to our reasoning for that. I know that there have been people who have criticized the court for deciding this during the protest phase when they thought it should have been decided in the contest phase. The remedy is certainly a significant issue. The remedy would have been to reprint the ballots, have another election, and, wow, would that have created all sorts of legal issues.

P: But under the United States Constitution, in a presidential election, the vote has to be November 7, just that one day.

H: So, you know, whatever remedy was available, it would probably have been not able to be accomplished.

P: Also, I noticed that a lot of times, the court cited *Beckstrom v. Volusia County Canvassing Board* and *Boardman v. Esteva*, which were cases where there were minor problems—in one case, the envelope of the ballot had been mangled, and the court ruled that the hyper-technicality should not override the will of the voter. Was that the essence of your opinion?

H: Well, you know, we are almost three years after, and I think that the best answer that I can and should give to you on that is that the opinions should speak for themselves. Needless to say, we have been voting in America for many years, and also needless to say, there should be confidence that the votes that are cast are appropriately counted and that the one who gets the most votes wins the election. When we first started our research, we found it interesting that so many elections had been subject to judicial scrutiny over the course of the years to include the election of 1876. But we just did not have the luxury of that type of scrutiny in this type of case when there had to be a determination of who won the election under constitutional guidelines.

P: One issue that came up over and over again was the validity of a ballot, and Judge Posner argued that the Democrats had confused voter error with tabulation error. The question is, if a voter does not properly vote and the machine does not pick up the vote, can you go back and with a human being determine the intent of the voter? One could argue that the vote is invalid because you didn't punch out the chad properly.

H: I called the supervisor of elections here in Leon County. He indicated to me, as I recall, that the voting machine ballots and punch-cards had been in existence since the 1950s and . . . the statutes authorized recounts of those machine-cast votes manually under certain circumstances. When those circumstances existed as determined by the local supervisor of elections, you manually recounted the votes. That has been done for 50 years. He said that you are able to determine what the voter intended many times by looking at the ballot manually as opposed to what happens when it is run through a machine.

P: So, for example, if somebody didn't punch Bush but circled Bush and wrote in Bush, you would assume that they intended to vote for Bush?

H: I'm not up on all of the actual procedures, but his comment was that you can tell how those votes were intended. So, it was not anything new. Of course, it took on all sorts of political overtones when Secretary of State [Katherine] Harris and the state election board determined that she and it were not going to receive manual recounts.

P: Section 101.5614 of the state statutes indicates that no vote shall be declared void if there is a clear indication of the intent of the voter as determined by the canvassing board.

H: Right.

P: So, that is pretty precise. In *Miami-Dade County Democratic Party v. Miami-Dade County Canvassing Board*, the Democratic Party asked the canvassing board to resume the manual recount. The Florida Supreme Court concluded that based on the Dade County Canvassing Board's decision they could not complete the count in time, that the court could not order them to do something they could not accomplish in the time allowed.

H: I am not sure exactly of all of the details. You will have to excuse me for that. Except I think we denied the writ. Isn't that correct?

P: That is correct, yes. The court could not compel the performance of an act that was futile or impossible to perform.

H: Right.

P: When the Miami-Dade Canvassing Board ended the recount, that was November 22, and by that time, they had until November 26 to complete the count. When Judge Terry Lewis finally went and counted some 9,000 votes, they were able to count them in half a day. I just wondered, in retrospect, was the key issue for the court the decision of the canvassing board, that you had to rely on their judgment that they could not complete the count on time?

H: I think that common sense would indicate that was the case. A *writ of mandamus* is a discretionary writ. The court, in denying it and not taking that, determined that it would not exercise its discretion to get involved in that. There had been a decision by the canvassing board, and those are the people whose decisions over the course of this the court tended to honor.

P: I noticed that in *Gore v. Harris*, Justice Charles Wells was arguing that it was up to the canvassing boards and the voters to make these decisions, not the courts.

H:  Right, but nonetheless, the courts have been involved. I have not done a study of this, but my recollection of a lot of that research is that where the courts could support the decision of a local canvassing board, they were supported.

P:  In *Palm Beach County Canvassing Board v. Harris*, obviously this is the first prominent national case, the court by a 7-0 vote decided to extend the certification to November 26. Statute 102.111 said that the Secretary of State "shall" ignore late returns and 102.112 indicated that she "may" ignore late returns. Obviously those two statutes are contradictory. How did the court decide which statue took precedence here?

H:  I think it ought to be pointed out that as late as 1999, the legislature was dealing with these statutes. During the course of this, the speaker of the House and many people in the legislature acknowledge that the statutes were conflicting and confusing. Rightly or wrongly, the courts have been, since the beginning of this country, cast in the position of resolving conflicting statutes. As the opinion indicates, we determined that in the state election, Secretary Harris had inappropriately stopped the recounts and the extension was only the amount of time that they would have had to get the recounts in had she not stopped them.

P:  So, that was why you picked November 26? Just the number of days the canvassing boards had lost in recounting?

H:  That is the way, I think, it worked out, and as I recall, that day was on a Sunday and [the court] gave her the choice of taking them that day or the day after.

P:  Many observers were puzzled about that because the court decision said 5:00 P.M. Sunday if she is open or 9 A.M. on Monday. Well, of course, she had never been open on a Sunday. I presume the court, since you decided on the November 26 date, also decided that opening Sunday that would be an appropriate choice for her.

H:  Yes. We gave her the choice. If she wanted to accept them that day, that was good, or if she wanted to accept them the next day. I think that is what the opinion [stated].

P:  It seemed to me that you made clear in this decision that the court was interpreting legislative intent and not making law. Immediately after this decision, Republican spokesmen said, well, as soon as they changed the date, then they had changed the law.

H:  And that is the point, as I recall, that Jim Baker made: they have rewritten the law, they have changed the law. George Will wrote an article that was in the Sunday, November 26 opinion section of the *Tallahassee Democrat*. He wrote an article that called us a lawless court and [claimed] that we had been legislating by rewriting Florida election law and applying it retroactively.

P:  In the *Gore v. Harris* decision, by a 4-3 vote, the supreme court ordered that the 9,000 undervotes in Dade were to be counted. Also

Gore was awarded 168 votes in Dade, 215 in Palm Beach, but not the 51 votes in Nassau County. My reading of this case was that the majority saw that under the contest statute, if there were irregularities that could have changed the outcome of the election, the judges had to correct that. Secondly, that even though the ballot might not have been properly filled out or punched, again, if it could be determined that this was the intent of the voter, that vote should count. For example, the votes in Miami-Dade and the votes in Palm Beach. You dissented. You agreed with Judge Sanders Sauls's opinion, but you dissented on two major issues.

H:   Well, the opinion speaks for itself, but I just didn't think that he [Judge Sauls] got it right as far as his assessment. He applied the wrong standard, as I indicated in my dissent. He, I think, used the abuse of discretion standard, and I pointed out in my opinion that was not the appropriate standard. He was to look at it from a *de novo* standard.

P:   He had to look at all the ballots fresh.

H:   Yes.

P:   If there has to be a counting of the votes, at least as it appears in the contest statute, then the count should be statewide, not limited to four counties.

H:   That was the way I interpreted it.

P:   Were you surprised that the United State Supreme Court took *certiorari*, and were you surprised at the remand?

H:   This is in the second case?

P:   Yes.

H:   No. I left for Jacksonville on Saturday, but I called my son in Jacksonville on the Friday night that we released the opinion and I told him what the results were. I said, but I bet you by the time I get to your house tomorrow, the Supreme Court of the United States is taking this case to stop the recount. About five minutes before I got to his house in Jacksonville, we were listening to NPR, and they broke in and said the Supreme Court had taken the case and stopped the recount.

P:   Let me go back to this remand of *Gore v. Harris*. When the U.S. Supreme Court remanded back to the Florida Supreme Court, the U.S. Supreme Court said, we are not clear about how you took into consideration the legislative authority of Article II and 3 U.S. 5. I don't think the Florida Supreme Court's response to that remand came out until December 22.

H:   That is correct.

P:   Why didn't the Florida Supreme Court immediately answer the U.S. Supreme Court?

H:   We got that case back, I don't remember the date. But, you know, we had a week of oral argument, we had these other cases, we had to prepare for the oral argument in the last case, and it was just a question of being able to prioritize our time. I know Justice Sandra Day O'Connor in the audiotapes of that case wondered why we had not responded. We just had a very full plate, and we could not get to it effectively until then.

P: And ultimately, as you know, in *Bush v. Gore* the U.S. Supreme Court reversed the Florida Supreme Court. David Boies expressed the view that maybe Judge Lewis or the Florida Supreme Court, somebody should have set a standard. David Boies said, well, if the Florida Supreme Court had set a standard, they would be making law; if they didn't set a standard, they violated the Fourteenth Amendment, so it was kind of a Catch-22.

H: That is right. It was a Catch-22.

P: In the stay, which you obviously anticipated, it was pretty clear from Justice Scalia's opinion that Bush ultimately would win. Scalia wrote about the question of irreparable harm and saw harm to Bush if votes of questionable legality were counted, and that would threaten his legitimacy. But Justice Stevens replied that the key was the state law, that the U.S. Supreme Court should respect the state law, and how could you do irreparable harm if you count votes?

H: I didn't understand the argument that Scalia made in light of the fact that, of course, if a person received less votes, they would be irreparably harmed in that they could not take office. But the number of votes is the determining factor, without getting into the legality or his thought processes. I just quite frankly did not understand.

P: Is that the standard for granting an injunction, irreparable harm?

H: Yes. If something is going to happen and you can't undo it, that is a standard.

P: Give me your reaction to the 5-4 *Bush v. Gore* decision by the U.S. Supreme Court.

H: They had the right to make the last decision, and I'm not in a position to say they are right or they are wrong beyond the fact that they were last. That is the way I have always viewed appellate review of any of my decisions. I don't think it is appropriate to begin questioning motives or personal implications. I certainly didn't think it was appropriate for that to be done for those of us on the supreme court. I have had the privilege of meeting and being with, on a number of occasions, justices from the Supreme Court of the United States and found them to be decent and honorable and wonderful people, and I have a great high regard for them.

P: Were you pleased that you had a chance to participate in these events?

H: Yes. Upon reflection, it was a wonderful opportunity to be a part of what makes America so great. I just think that this experience was just such a significant milestone in the fact that we can resolve our disputes, and we can do it peacefully in a respectful and a dignified manner and without any violence. Whether you are right or whether you are wrong, the people have exhibited their faith in the decision-making process of the court. The president was inaugurated. So, yes, to that extent, it was a very wonderful opportunity to be a part of a historic American election.

P:   Is there anything that I have not asked you that you would like to discuss or talk about?

H:   I think you have been very comprehensive, and I have been very successful in avoiding answering your questions.

P:   [Laughs]. Well, I understand your position completely.

# ➤ JUDGE TERRY P. LEWIS ◀

Prior to the 2000 election controversy, Florida Circuit Judge Terry P. Lewis had ruled adversely in several lawsuits brought by Governor Jeb Bush. Republicans, therefore, accused Lewis, a Democrat, of partisanship before he heard a single case in the 2000 recount. However, despite his alleged liberal bias, Judge Lewis twice ruled against Gore, dealing a severe blow to Gore's hopes of winning Florida.

Democrat Governor Lawton Chiles appointed Lewis to the Leon County Circuit Court in 1998. Lewis, known for his easy-going approach on and off the bench, was typically regarded as a fair, open-minded judge and a pragmatic and nonideological jurist.

Volusia County, in *McDermott v. Harris*, asked Judge Lewis for an injunction ordering Harris to delay certification until they completed their recount. In essence, Lewis had to decide if Secretary of State Katherine Harris could be forced to accept vote counts after the initial certification deadline. Lewis did not have a difficult time ruling on a case that proved to be pivotal in the recount process. "The way I saw it is, it's her job to make that decision, not mine." In his initial ruling, *Lewis I*, the judge concluded that Harris had to exercise discretion and to look at the facts as to why the recounts would be late. She had to make a rational decision and could not automatically certify the vote count. In *Lewis II*, the judge decided that Harris had used discretion in refusing to delay certification. This decision was overturned by the Florida Supreme Court, which extended the recount until November 26.

Judge Lewis also had to make another controversial decision in *Taylor v. Martin County Canvassing Board*. Lewis determined that the elections supervisor had used "bad judgment" in allowing Republicans to place voter identification numbers on absentee ballot requests, and that they probably broke election law. Since there was no way to tell which of the absentee ballots had been modified; it would have been "a very harsh remedy" to throw out all the absentee ballots and deny Martin County voters their franchise.

Judge Lewis was not intimidated by the glare of world attention and by the thousands of e-mails and phone calls, some of which contained veiled threats. The responses ranged from a critic who wrote, "I hope you burn in hell and have a long, miserable life prior to that," to an admirer who referred to his "luxurious mustache" and called him a "fine-looking man." Lewis had no problem taking any of the highly charged election cases: it really was not that much different than what he did every day. The only difference was that there were a lot of people interested and a lot of people watching. However, Lewis found it disheartening that many observers assumed that judges would rule in a partisan manner based on their political affiliation. Those representing the Republican Party "were a lot more vocal and strident in making those kind of insinuations or outright claims."

Lewis also discussed, in some detail, his responsibility for overseeing the recount of the undervotes as ordered by the Florida Supreme Court. Lewis was surprised that the U.S. Supreme Court took the case and puzzled by the reasoning behind their order to stay the recount. He insisted that the recount of the undervotes would have been completed on time. It is instructive to note that all three of the decisions rendered by this so-called liberal Democratic judge went against Al Gore. A reversal of any one of Lewis's decisions might arguably have made Gore president.

Judge Terry Lewis was interviewed by the author on December 19, 2002.

P: Would you talk about how you first got involved in the court cases in the 2000 presidential election?

L: I didn't even really think that we would have the cases, to tell you the truth. About ten o'clock, the Deputy Court Administrator came in the back of the courtroom and kind of waved to me to get my attention. So I took a break and then he showed me the pleadings that had been filed. This . . . was on behalf of Volusia County only [*McDermott v. Harris*], where they were asking for an injunction to be able to continue their counting.

P: Judge Michael R. McDermott was chair of the Volusia County Canvassing Board. This brief was asking for declarative relief through a temporary injunction, even though Volusia would ultimately get their recount done on time. They insisted that the Secretary of State consider the certified results from Volusia and Palm Beach Counties even if they were filed late. Is that your understanding?

L: That's the way I understood it, yes.

P: I know from talking to Dexter Douglass and Barry Richard this was a very hastily called hearing. I don't think either one of them had time to even prepare a brief.

L: I guess it was [done] fairly quickly because the time frame was fairly pressing. On that Monday, that would have been the 13th, it was the day before [vote certification] was due. The secretary of state had said, no ifs, ands, or buts [about it]. I'm not going to count any late [election] returns, so you better get them in. That's what prompted the suit.

P: The crucial issue in this case is Florida statutes 102-111 and 102-112, which state that late returns "*shall*" be ignored or "*may*" be ignored. How did you deal with the issue of these particular statutes, which were obviously not clear?

L: It was a typical statutory interpretation. I went to see if there were any case law that would help me. There wasn't anything that I can recall of significance. It was really kind of, let me look at the statute [and] see what I think the proper interpretation is. Of course, one of the principles of interpretation is, if you have a conflict, the more recent statute is going to prevail.

P: In your ruling, you indicated also that if the canvassing boards didn't get the returns in on time, there was a $200 fine. The assumption would be, if there were a fine for getting the returns in late, then the counties must have the option to turn them in late, otherwise that portion of the statute would be meaningless. In other words, if the law allowed the secretary of state to ignore all the late returns, there would be no reason to have a fine in the statute.

L: That's a good argument. That's the way I saw it. You could make an argument the other way that there should be a fine anyway because they've messed up the election. But it's true, why fine them every day until they are in?

P: You ultimately ruled that Secretary Harris was not required to ignore late returns. She had to use her discretion and look at the reasons and the facts before she made a decision.

L: Right.

P: What argument did the Republicans make?

L: Well, at this point I guess Bush would have been a defendant, but I think most of the argument came on behalf of the secretary of state. The argument basically was for a strict construction [of the statute], and of course [the argument was], "judge, that's not your job, that's the secretary of state." You know, don't interfere with the executives' job. There was a dispute about it, so of course I was going to have to make some declaration about it. Their argument was simply [that] they're due at 5:00 and she has every right in the world—every duty— to declare that they [late returns] won't be counted.

P: When I talked to Barry Richard, he said it didn't matter about the construction, "*shall*" or "*may*." She still can decide not to allow late returns. Your argument was simply that she had to make a choice, and therefore she had to take into consideration the facts and come up with a specific reason for her choice.

L: I agree with Mr. Richard's argument there.

P: Could you have ordered her to wait until November 17, when all the absentee ballots came in? I notice that at one point in the hearing you brought up that issue. You're going to be certifying, but it's not a final certification until November 17.

L: Yes.

P: Could you have ordered her to wait until November 17?

L: Well, theoretically I could have done a lot of things. According to later events, according to the Florida Supreme Court, maybe I should have. But my view of that was just like Barry Richard said, that's really the secretary of state's call. The only thing I was saying was that she had already made the call without viewing any of the possible reasons that might justify an extension. The way I saw it is, it's her job to make that decision, not mine. But she had said ahead of time, I'm not going to count it, period. No ifs, ands, or buts. My only point was that you really can't do that. You can't say ahead of time because you have a duty to exercise your discretion. It'd be like me: I have discretion in sentencing. If I made a statement and said every DUI offender is going to get ten days in jail, [people would say], now, judge, you can't do that, you have to exercise your discretion on a case-by-case basis. That's the way I saw it.

P:     Another issue that Dexter Douglass brought up was, why would the legislature pass a provision for recounts if it were not possible to use that portion of the law?

L:     Right. You mention the questions that I asked of the attorneys . . . about why don't you wait until the 17th. There's a difference between good policy and legality. What's the big hurry here? You're going to have to wait [until November 17] to officially certify it. When you're deciding whether you should count these votes or give them some more time, shouldn't that be a factor? I didn't feel that, as the judiciary, I could come in and tell her, you have to do [it in] a certain amount of time. At that point I would figure, well, if she has abused her discretion, if she has made an error and not included things that could have been a justification, then that was, to me, something that would be brought up in a contest, not in a injunction to keep her from certifying the results.

P:     Dexter Douglass indicated that you implied exactly that. When these issues came up, then the plaintiff had the right to go to the contest. Was that a hint that going to the contest might be the best thing for Gore to do?

L:     Well, I don't know if it was a hint that it was the best thing for Gore to do. When I was looking at the statute, I [said], well, there's a provision for recount [and] there's also a provision for contest. The way I saw it, [it] must have been the intention [of the law] that if a particular canvassing board . . . had what they thought were the criteria to require a recount, then they should do it. They had a duty to do it, irrespective of what the secretary of state said. I don't care if she said, I'm not going to count them; to me, they had a duty to count them, Now she had another right—the authority—to not accept it, but they should have kept counting, as far as my interpretation was. Why would you use that if not for a contest later?

          I always say, if somebody comes in asking you for a remedy, I think you've got the wrong remedy here. If you want me to tell the secretary of state, who exercised her discretion, that she can't do it, you're barking up the wrong tree. There is a remedy for you, if you think she's done what she's not supposed to do or hasn't done something she should, and that's the contest. That's right there in the statute and it specifically says in there, if you don't count legal votes, that's a pretty good reason to file a contest.

I remember seeing Dexter Douglass sometime after that and making some comment about, why didn't y'all, instead of appealing my order over to the Supreme Court trying to get some extra time and going through all that and wasting a lot of time, just come back, amend it, and contest it? He told me, "that's what I advised." I'm not saying that would have helped them one way or the other, but in terms of resolving the issue quicker, that's where it was going to have to end up. There was no way that they were going to let one particular area of the state recount their votes, and not everybody else, when the vote was that close, and it was an election of that importance. So they should have, I think, gone that way anyway, but that wasn't my call either.

P:   As a matter of fact, if the Democrats had done that and had amended it, it would have been back in your court, would it not?

L:   Yes.

P:   How would you have felt about hearing that case instead of Judge Sanders Sauls?

L:   It would have been fine. That's what I do. People have asked me about getting these cases, and, of course, you're of a mixed mind [about it]. You don't want to appear to be arrogant or whatever and say, I can handle that kind of thing, but it really isn't that much different than what you do every day. The only difference is, there are a lot of people interested and a lot of people watching. I don't know that I've got the right answer, [but] all I can do is do my best and listen to both sides, both arguments, and look at the law and try to come up with a solution. I would have had a quick hearing, and we would have gotten to some resolution of it before they did.

P:   What was your reaction to Judge Sauls's decision in the contest, and would you have made a different decision?

L:   I have to honestly say I don't know, because I did follow it, but not as closely. So I don't really know, . . . would I have ruled the same way or not? That's not fair because I wasn't there, [and] I couldn't judge the demeanor of the witnesses. I know that the basis for his ruling was something my wife, who is not a lawyer nor a constitutional scholar until this came up, said, that's not the right standard, is it, when she heard him read his [decision]. I forget now what it was.

P:   Sauls ruled that Gore had to demonstrate the probability, not possibility, that the recount would change the outcome of the election and also prove that the canvassing boards had abused their discretion. Justice Major Harding, although voting to uphold Judge Sauls, said abuse of discretion was the standard for the protest, as opposed to the contest.

L:   She picked up on that. So I said that may be coming back [to Sauls] if you apply the wrong standard. Now all these findings of fact and stuff, that's up to him and he can do that. But when he uses the wrong standard. . . .

P: Let me get back to your first decision. So, in effect, for Volusia County, you grant in part, but deny in part, their request. Obviously, now Florida and Tallahassee are the focal point for the world media and the comments on your decision were very interesting. Barry Richard and several other people commented that you came to a decision that nobody else had thought about. You didn't take the options that either side gave you; instead you came to a decision, if I may quote, that was "Solomon-like." You took a little bit from both sides and really, in effect, turned it back to the secretary of state. Would that be a fair assessment?

L: Yes, because I think the one side wanted me to tell the secretary what to do, and the other side wanted me to back off and don't do anything. Again there wasn't a whole lot of precedent and it was a short-term [solution], but I just had to look at the statute, and that's just the way I read it.

P: Dexter Douglass said he thought your ruling was reasonable, but you had a reasonable basis to rule the other way, for Gore. But then he said, the one guy I know as a judge, and he was talking about you, that would have loved to rule the other way thought the law required him to do what he did. I think he was referring to the fact that you're a Democrat, but ruled against Al Gore. He intended that as a compliment.

L: Yes, I take that as a compliment. That was not an uncommon remark that I heard or read about that decision, especially the second one, when I came in and said she [Harris] can exercise her discretion. As a matter of fact, there was a very nice article written by a guy in the *Baltimore Sun*. He said some nice things about [me]; he's considered to be liberal in his social views and decisions if pushed, but he had the courage . . . to do that. But actually that's not necessarily true when people make that assumption. I guess I'll take whatever label they give me if they ask me a specific issue, but if it comes to wanting to rule a particular way on this, absolutely not.

P: At the very beginning of the recount, and of course this is a political, public relations issue as well as legal contest, the Republicans are denouncing, even before they file suit, the Florida Supreme Court as the Dexter Douglass court. They said it's a liberal Democratic court, that you were a liberal Democrat, that Judge Nikki Clark was a liberal Democrat, and, they're going to kill us if we get in their courts. However, the Florida Supreme Court ruled against Gore four or five times, you did three times, and Clark did once. So it appeared that these so-called liberal Democrats, who could have given Gore the presidency had they been partisan, ruled on the basis of law. Is that a fair statement?

L: Yes, I think so. I think that one of the things that came out of that [recount] was really kind of disheartening, in terms of the public perception of the courts, is this notion that the judges are partisan, that whatever their politics are [determines] how they lean and how they're going to rule. That was egged-on by some of the participants, and especially, I have to say, the Republican side of it. They were a lot more vocal and strident in making those kind of insinuations or outright claims.

P: Particularly Jim Baker?

L: Yes. I've always said that what that means is, if you are such an ardent partisan, you expect everybody else is. It's sort of like a pathological liar. You think everybody else is lying because that's the way you see it. So it never occurs to you that somebody actually would not make a decision based on that, that they'll set that aside. I know that at least most of the judges that I work with . . . [are] always going to try to find in good faith what they think the law would require them to do. Now sometimes obviously you can't escape your personal backgrounds. When equities are nicely balanced, then, of course, your personal experiences are probably going to have some influence on that, but generally speaking, I think most judges are going to try to . . . apply the law as best they know it by the facts, and reach a decision.

P: The *New York Times* said your first decision was good common sense and "a rebuke to the partisan misreading of Florida statutes by Harris, who has blurred her twin responsibilities as chief arbiter of the state's election law and co-chairperson of the Bush campaign in Florida." Did you conclude that she was arbitrarily reading the statute that way because she was a Republican?

L: I have to be honest. I didn't know, and still don't know [about] Katherine Harris. I've heard things, accusations back and forth, and also defenses of her and from her as well. From a policy standpoint, it's obviously not good. [Ideally] you would just never be in that situation where you're having to make a decision [in which] you have some opposite interests, [where you're] biased . . ., but that happens all the time in executive and legislative branches, so you can't judge them by that same [standard]. If I were to have to guess, I would certainly be optimistic and hope that she was trying to do what she thought she was supposed to do. Again, subconsciously, who knows, but I would certainly hate to think, and maybe I'm naïve, that she [would say], okay, let's see how we can maneuver these rules to get my guy to win, to hell with the law.

P: One assessment concluded that this was simply politics as usual. The secretary of state was an elected office, Harris was a Republican, and it wouldn't be unusual if she were partisan. But under circumstances like this, with such intense scrutiny, it would seem to be an error in judgment to try to misread the law deliberately, would it not?

L: Yes.

P: Surely her legal advisors, like Joe Klock, told her you can not get away with that.

L: That's what I would think. I did hear that whenever my first order came out, she contemplated not doing anything about it, you know, not obeying the order, [but] they said, you don't want to do that.

P: That's correct. I talked to Mac Stipanovich and Joe Klock. What they advised her to do, and this was apparently her idea, was to get written opinions from each of the canvassing boards as to why they needed extra time. Once she received those requests, she denied their petitions. Did that help you in your second decision? The solicitation of the written opinions demonstrated that she had gotten the necessary information and made a judgment.

L: She got good advice. Instead of just throwing your nose up or thumbing the court order, you say, how can we comply with this? You can be cynical and say, they were just finding a way to do what they wanted to, but obviously she had made a decision. A lot of judges get accused of finding a way to do what they want to do, too.

P: The Democrats in *Lewis II* didn't present a lot of evidence to demonstrate that Harris had abused her discretion. I don't think they brought many witnesses.

L: They didn't bring any witnesses.

P: So they didn't have a particularly strong case, did they?

L: No.

P: What you essentially ruled in *Lewis II* was that she did not abuse her discretion.

L: I think that's the way that's interpreted. Like we were saying earlier, if she abused her discretion, I think the remedy would be to challenge [or] contest the election. What I said first of all was, she had to exercise her discretion. She had not exercised any discretion, [she] just said, I'm not going to do it. It's the same analogy that we used before in my court. If I have discretion in terms of a sentence of a criminal defendant, and I say ahead of time I'm going to give everybody a certain amount of time, that's not an exercise of discretion at all. I'll be reversed. But if I exercise my discretion, and I say, you slouch when you stand and you don't say "Yes, sir" to me, so I'm going to give you five years instead of two, well, I've exercised my discretion. But if it were appealed, it probably would be considered an abuse of discretion because that's not a logical, reasonable basis to enhance a sentence.

Similarly here, that didn't mean that I agreed with what she did or that I thought that was a proper decision, that there weren't other factors that she should have considered had I been her, but I wasn't. So when they came back and said she abused her discretion, . . . that's a pretty high standard. She set forth reasoning. She sent out letters [asking], what's your reasons, [and said] I don't find those to be sufficient. But that's her call. If she is appealed, in other words, if there was a contest later, a court like me might very well say, no, you exercised your discretion, but you were wrong. You didn't count some legal votes, and we're going to count them now. I think people interpret that as [my] saying she didn't abuse her discretion, [but] I wasn't even looking at whether she abused her discretion so much as I was whether she exercised it or not. If you wanted to pursue the abuse of discretion, you need to file a contest.

P:  In fact, your first order stated as much.

L:  Right. They didn't listen, did they?

P:  So she, in effect, complied with your order, [and] therefore there were no grounds for you to make any other judgment, correct?

L:  Yes, because they [the Democrats] were basically saying, she disobeyed your order, judge, and you need to tell her to do something else. [I told them] no, what I told her was to exercise her discretion. She's exercised her discretion [and the] case is over.

P:  By the way, isn't it unusual for circuit court judges to overturn decisions made by state officials?

L:  Yes, and if you talk to Barry Richard, that was his argument. I take that very seriously. I'm a judicial branch. Unless there's a real good reason, I'm not sticking my nose into what the executive or the legislative branch is doing.

P:  I want to mention one of the things said by Dexter Douglass, and this is vintage Dexter Douglass. He said that when Harris refused to accept Palm Beach county's late returns, and then the Florida Supreme Court allowed them to continue, she issued a second opinion that said the recount was too late because the deadline had passed. I quote Dexter Douglass, "Sort of like a traffic cop asking you to stop and pull over and then give you a ticket for blocking traffic" [laughing].

L:  [laughing] That's pretty good.

P:  Which is a good anecdote, but not evidence.

L:  Right. They came in and made an argument, but they didn't present any evidence to me to show that she was being completely unreasonable. They just kind of wanted a feel-good let's go in and get the judge to stop her because we don't like what she's done. That's just not the way you operate. You've got to have some evidence; got to have a record on which to base it.

P:  The Florida Supreme Court, on November 21, reversed you in a 7-0 decision, and allowed those three counties to recount the ballots. The court then chose November 26 as the day for certification, giving the canvassing boards five more days to complete the recount. What was your assessment of that decision, and where did the November 26 date come from?

L:  I have deep respect for all of those folks on the Florida Supreme Court and know a lot of them personally, don't question their integrity at all, but I think that was a mistake. I know this was a unique situation because of the time frame, but generally speaking, an appellate court will say, trial court, you erred, let me send it back to you to consider these things. You applied the wrong law, you overlooked the evidence, or . . . [somehow] you made an error, and [then would] correct that error in the trial court. But what they did was just say, "Oops." And remember, . . . there wasn't a record, [and] there was no evidence of anything to pick that day [November 26].

How did they come up with the day? That's just something an appellate court should never do. I'm sure they had their reasons. They never shared those except in the written opinion, which I disagree with, but that's the way our courts work. As a matter of fact, I saw Major Harding after that, [because] he's in the same Rotary Club. He said something about, we're not last because we're right, we're right because we're last. I reminded him of something I heard him say one time when he was asked, how did it feel when, as a Florida Supreme Court justice, you got basically reversed by a federal district court judge. He said, well, they have just as much right to be wrong as anybody. He laughed then.

P: By choosing a new date for certification, the Florida Supreme Court, according to some attorneys, made law rather than interpreted law. Did you agree with that?

L: Well, I thought that was a mistake because I didn't see why their judgment about a date to extend [would be] any better than the secretary of state. I think they could have very validly said, no, I think the reasons the secretary of state gave are insufficient [and] it's abuse of discretion. Then you get a question: well, what do you do there? My thought was, you contest it.

P: The 7-0 decision was a very harsh denunciation of Katherine Harris and the court characterized her decisions as "arbitrary, unnecessary, contrary to law, unreasonable." They argued that the right to vote was paramount and that what you do first is count the votes, otherwise you violate democracy. Isn't that a little unusual for the supreme court to be that personal in a decision?

L: Probably. I don't know if it's personal. I've seen strong language like that before. But I don't know, perhaps they were trying to give a basis for why their opinion should be accepted as right, so they had to say something fairly strong. Again, they don't come out and discuss it, so I don't know.

P: Let's go to *Taylor v. Martin County Canvassing Board*. How did you happen to get that particular case?

L: It was just straight rotation.

P: When you got the case, what was your general thought process as you came to a decision?

L: Nikki Clark had the Seminole County case, which had even more voters affected. When she got that case, I came down and commiserated [with] her and said, Nikki, they're all looking at what Sandy Sauls is doing, but you may have the sleeper case. This is 15,000 votes here, and if those get thrown out, we're counting 9,000 votes down in Dade County that [aren't] going to mean anything. The pressure's on, basically. So when I got the Martin County case I said, hmm, same issues [and] very similar facts. I met with her and said, what have you come up with in the law? She had the law clerk working on it, so I got on that and did my own research. I thought the law was fairly straightforward, and [it was] just [a matter of] applying that law to the facts. If the facts were as alleged, they were going to have to show me something other than what was done was done.

P: So, basically, they would have to show something like either violation of the law or substantial noncompliance with the law or fraud?

L: Yes, . . . but as I recall, the most important thing was, were the people's votes that should have been counted, not counted? Was there something that interrupted the will of the people? Was it thwarted in some way in what they did? If that wasn't done, even if there were illegalities, that's a very harsh remedy, to throw out somebody's vote because somebody else did something that wasn't quite right.

P: Plus there was really no way to tell which of the absentee ballots might have been tainted by this process. The only option would be rather draconian: to throw them all out. I know the Democrats came up with an alternative proposition. They had some experts come in and propose a mathematical allocation of the votes. If this county is primarily Republican, we can determine that there would be so many Gore votes and so many Bush votes. Did you agree with that argument?

L: No, it doesn't appeal to me. It seemed to me from the evidence that there wasn't any intent or intentional wrongdoing in terms of trying to change a vote or give a fraudulent vote. What they did was not proper, it was improper; nobody should condone it, but when all the dust was settled, there wasn't any real suggestion at all that people who wanted to vote didn't get to vote and that their vote was not counted for the person they wanted.

P: Your decision was very similar to Judge Clark's decision. I believe that you determined that at the very least, both supervisors used bad judgment. I presume both of you ruled that it was a violation of state law, is that correct?

L: I think so. Definitely, I think it wasn't something that should have been done. I don't know if it was saying a criminal law was violated or anything, but it was not in accordance with the proper legal criteria or legal procedures.

P: Under Florida law, it's a felony for an unauthorized person to request an absentee ballot. It has to be done either by a guardian or the individual or the family, but this is not exactly a request for an absentee ballot, it's modifying that request. Some people argued that it was not only a violation of election law in Martin County, it was a violation of public records law, because she allowed those requests out of the office.

L: Yes, I think that was argued, and without a doubt it should never have been done. It shouldn't be read to condone that, but in terms of discounting the votes that were cast as a result of that, as far as I could tell, it was a no-brainer.

P: Because the key is still the will of the voters.

L: Right.

P: Was there any penalty on either of these two individuals for violating the law?

L: [I] don't know. That's why we have state attorneys [to determine if] there has been a violation of the law. The people that were involved didn't strike me as . . . intentionally doing something [wrong]. That doesn't mean they didn't violate the law, it just didn't seem like a nefarious conspiracy of great proportions either. But even if it had been, the remedy would be to prosecute them, not to throw out the people's votes.

P: What was your reaction to the Republican's attempt to recuse Judge Clark? I know, for example, Barry Richard refused to sign the recusal request.

L: I have a word for it, but it wouldn't go on here, and the word starts with "chicken."

P: Do you think this is an example, as some Democrats have argued, that the Republicans were willing to do whatever it took to win? They were playing hard-ball. If they thought they could get an advantage by recusing a so-called liberal Democratic judge, they would do that.

L: I don't know. Of course, we talked earlier about the fact that to me it seemed like the representatives on the Republican side were more strident—as you call it, hard-ball. They were more likely to be aggressive in terms of what they wanted. I've heard that from the Gore side, he was very much insistent that they not criticize the courts, [that they] be gentlemanly. As long as they play within the rules, that's part of our adversary system. If playing hard-ball is legal, well, you play it hard-ball. In those kind of tactics where you say, we're going to try to recuse the judge, I don't think they had a grounds for it and obviously it didn't work. Those kind of things could backfire on you, [but] Judge Clark's not like that. She's not going to rule against you because you tried to recuse her, but it doesn't look good for you. Barry Richard said, I'm not going to sign that, and I think that's what should have been done. You shouldn't do that as a lawyer. You shouldn't try to recuse a judge. That's not playing within the rules, as far as I'm concerned, unless you have a legitimate reason. I'll give them the benefit of the doubt and say somebody thought they did. Where do you draw the line between zealous advocacy of your client and being an officer of the court? A lot of people have a hard time drawing that line.

P: Of course, at that point, and I think you mentioned this earlier, these were stealth cases. They were under the media radar and all of a sudden people are saying, hey, if Gore wins either of these, he's president of the United States. Were you aware of the extraordinary burden in making a decision like this?

L: Yes. Like I said, . . . if we rule this way, that's it. Had it been a lot closer, it would have made it a lot harder, obviously, but Judge Clark and I both agreed. We met and talked and came to the same conclusion.

P: Is it unusual for two judges in different but similar cases to sit down and discuss their decisions?

L: That's a little unusual, because you wouldn't have the cases that were that similar all the time, but it's not unusual at all, for example, for me get on the phone and call someone and say, listen, I've got this case, here are the issues, you know anything about it? [And for them to say], well, I had a case like that, you might want to look at this case, or this is how I would interpret that statute myself. Now if you go to a judge for factual information, you can't do that. You can't go to anybody else without letting all the parties know that, listen, I've got this article written by Judge So-and-So that I'm going to consider and y'all need to . . . brief it. But that's not unusual.

P: Both your and Judge Clark's decisions were very similar, particularly in the law. The facts were a little bit different. Did you specifically sit down and discuss the issues or did you write your opinions separately?

L: [We] wrote them separately. We . . . got together and basically said, I've looked at the law in this area [and] this is what I think they mean. They mean this, this, and this. I agree with you, that's the way I read it too. I said, your issues are very similar to mine, so we agreed to share our draft of our opinions with each other, but I know that I didn't change mine. They were very similar because the law is very similar. Like we talked about earlier, she had a couple things maybe that were important to her that she put in her opinion.

P: How did you deal with the incredible pressure, since time is of the essence here and the world is watching, of trying to make these kind of decisions in one day and having shortened hearings? How does that affect the ability of the court to make a judgment when normally, you might have had two or three weeks to sit down and consider your opinion?

L: Obviously, that's a factor. It's not a good factor. It's a negative, generally speaking. There's a point, of course, [at] which more time is not going to do you any good. It might make it worse because things get forgotten or a little more hazy. This did have to be done quickly. [The Martin and Seminole County cases] weren't that complicated. The case law wasn't that extensive. You read it and you applied it.

P: You and Judge Clark announced your decisions at the same time?

L: Yes.

P: Why?

L: They were the same issue, and we figured it would be better to do it sort of like a joint announcement. A statement, [and then], here are the decisions. Get the lawyers together at the same time. We were going to be close together anyway, so why bring them in again three hours later for basically the same thing? [It] just seemed to be administratively more convenient for everybody.

P: Talk a little bit about how the courts were able to organize both cases. I understand the courtrooms were right across from each other, and you started early in the morning. Was this primarily to accommodate Barry Richard and the other lawyers so they could go back and forth from one courtroom to the other courtroom?

L: Yes. Actually, we ended up using the same courtroom. We figured [it's the] same lawyers and I can't go while she's going and vice versa. She had hers scheduled for 8:30 or something, [so I said], we'll start it early, we'll go till she's ready to start, then whenever she's finished we'll come back and finish ours. They didn't have to move their stuff around.

P: I understand that one day Judge Clark finished a little earlier than you expected her to. You were out shooting some hoops, I guess to sort of settle down, and your wife had to come get you.

L: Yes, that was one of the funny stories. My wife, she's a little more excitable than I am. But yes, I was down playing some basketball because [Judge Clark] was not supposed to be through until 8:00 P.M. or something like that. She [my wife] comes running in [saying], they're done, they're done, they're waiting for you, they're waiting for you. So of course I had to rush down.

P: And the Florida Supreme Court approved your decision on the Martin County case, I think within 24 hours, with very little comment. So, I assume their approval demonstrated that you were correct.

L: Well, like I say, sometimes I agree, sometimes I don't have to agree with them on that. If they'd have said no, obviously I'd look at it and see why, but I thought it was consistent with their previous decisions.

P: Let me ask you a question that doesn't exactly relate to this case, but there's an interesting point that came up. I forget which lawyer brought it up, but one of the issues is going to be the plenary power of the state legislature under Article II of the Constitution of the United States. A Democratic lawyer argued that if it were unconstitutional for the Florida Supreme Court to extend that deadline to November 26, because they had no power to do so because that was up to the legislature, wouldn't it have also been unconstitutional for the governor, the executive branch, in this agreement with the federal government, to extend by ten days the date of the receipt of absentee ballots?

L: Good point. Actually, that came up in the first hearing we had. I wasn't familiar with it. It's not an area of the law that you get a lot of, so when they mentioned this thing about a consent decree [for] ten additional days for overseas [ballots], I said, where's that in the statute? [They answered,] well, it's a consent decree. [I said] well, what does that mean? If you can consent to that, why are we going to have to bother with this right here? I don't understand. Nobody ever really gave me a good explanation. That was a consent that the state, I guess, agreed to. I don't know whether the legislature has to affirm that or ratify it or something, or whether they did.

P: Give me your opinion on the Florida Supreme Court decision in *Gore v. Harris*. In that 4-3 decision, the court gave Gore 168 votes in Miami-Dade, 215 in Palm Beach County, and they sent the case back to Leon County Circuit Court and directed, I guess in the beginning it was Judge Sauls, to count all the undervotes. He decided that he didn't want to take that case. He recused himself. Was that out of pique or frustration, or do you know?

L: I've never talked to him about it. I think he was upset, that was the report I got down the hallway, so he recused himself. So it just went to the natural rotation, which would have been Nikki Clark.

P: And she recused herself.

L: No, she said she was not available.

P: What's the difference?

L: If you go into the cycle, because it had to be done, it goes to the next judge. But if they're not available [it goes to the next judge], and what's "not available" is in the eye of the beholder, I suppose, but she had gone home. In her defense, she had a hard week because they had that recusal stuff, and she had gotten some threatening phone calls or something. So she was home, and she really didn't want to take it. I, unfortunately, happened to be in my office at the time thinking everything was done and relaxing and, it's 5:00 in the afternoon. [Then] Judge Clark's not here and you are next to hear this [case]. [I said] okay. I actually told Judge Reynolds, he was the chief judge, maybe you should take it, because it really looks like it's not something you have to make a legal decision on so much as it is administrative.

P: To carry out the order of the Florida Supreme Court.

L: To count votes. He said, no, I don't want anybody thinking I took the case. It's going to go the natural rotation. Now if you say you're not available, I guess . . . I said, well, I'm not going to say I'm not available. I'm here, I'm ready, give it to me, let's go.

P: While we're on that subject, did you get a lot of e-mails and threatening phone calls?

L: I didn't get any really bad threatening phone calls. I got a lot of e-mail stuff, some good, some bad.

P: Can you give me some examples of some of the more interesting ones?

L: Most of them were very good; they were very complimentary. Of course, even before I entered *Lewis I* they were telling me, people like Rush Limbaugh [were saying], he's a liberal Democrat, just giving me a hard time. Then as soon as I entered my ruling on *Lewis II*, it's, he's an American stallion, a hero. So it depended on your perspective. All of these partisans don't look at the process. They don't look at it in terms of, did he do a good-faith effort to decide what the law is. They say, do we like how he ruled? If we did, he's a hero; if we didn't, he's a goat.

P: In fact, even Jim Baker praised you. He said you upheld the rule of law. But his kindness towards the Florida courts didn't last very long.

L:   Right. You have to kind of discount [some things]. You know you're going to get those. Like I say, I think the bulk of them thought that I had applied the law and used integrity. I think a lot of it is, as we talked about earlier, the perception that you may not have agreed or you didn't like the result, but you were willing to do what you thought was right. Of course, I had some that were saying, this is why they burned Atlanta, and we're coming to Tallahassee. Probably the best one was the lady who had called our office several times talking to my JA [judicial assistant], and she was from Louisiana. She had a real thick accent. She basically said something to the effect of, I hope you burn in hell and have a long miserable life before that, and something about my anatomy, too. But my all—time favorite, which I kept, was a card from a lady from Kentucky who started off and said, you are one fine-looking man, and then talked about that luxurious mustache and asked me a lot of questions. So I kept that. That's in the scrapbook. My wife likes that one.

P:   In their 4-3 vote, why do you think the Florida Supreme Court said just count the undervotes? I know that in the hearing you held, Joe Klock argued the law says you have to count all the votes. Do you think that they misread the law, or was it a question of meeting the December 12 deadline for certification?

L:   I don't know. When I read that, they talked about no votes and undervotes. Of course, the issue came up later about overvotes. I wasn't sure, and I've been asked before, what were you going to do about overvotes and things like that? I said, nobody argued it to me, but . . . I've indicated my gut tendency would be that the intent was to count those votes that the machines did not count, if you could determine the clear intent of the voter. An overvote, to me, would be the same as a no vote because it just doesn't register as a vote. So overvote, undervote, whatever you call it, it's an undervote because maybe they didn't press the thing hard enough . . ., but there are a lot of overvotes where they voted for two people and it didn't count. But if you look at the actual ballot, sometimes it was easy to see that they, for example, circled two and the machine couldn't tell the difference, so it wouldn't count it, but they X'd through one of them and they wrote in the name of the other one. So it's pretty clear who they wanted to vote for.

P:   Some voters bubbled in Bush and then wrote in Bush's name. Technically, that's an invalid vote, but the argument made by the Florida Supreme Court was that if you could look at that and ascertain the will of the voter, it should be counted. But the Florida Supreme Court didn't order the counting of the overvotes.

L:   I don't know why.

P:   Your job was, in essence, to supervise the recount of the undervotes. Do you think the Florida Supreme Court made a mistake in not setting a more specific standard than the intent of the voter?

L:   No. I think they did what the law required. I think perhaps they and I could have handled that better. You mentioned earlier that when the

Florida Supreme Court . . . set that date of November 26, they were making up the law, that's nowhere in the statute. In defense of them not giving more specific standards or criteria in terms of determining the clear intent of the voter, that's all the statute says. It doesn't give you, do this, do that, [or rules for] hanging chads. That's not in the statute, so they would have been rightly accused or subject to the accusation, you're making up the law [because] it's not there. People have asked me would I do something different. What they said was, we need more criteria. Well, you've already asked the Supreme Court a couple of times to give [you some] and they haven't. This is what they said will be the standard and that's what I've got to go by. Everybody goes, oh, lack of standards. That's what the U.S. Supreme Court complained about, but I analogize it again to jury verdicts.

P:  The reasonable man standard.

L:  Right. And negligence cases are reasonable doubt. Have you ever tried to figure out what reasonable doubt means in a criminal case? You may try a case with very similar facts in Miami and one in Tallahassee and get a different verdict. That doesn't mean that it is illegal or it's violation of equal protection; that's our jury system. So you have a canvassing board with the criteria of, is it clear what the intent of the voter is? If it is, we count it; if it's not, we don't count it.

I had a good sound bite and didn't use it. My wife suggested, [along the lines of] "if in doubt, toss it out"; "If the glove doesn't fit, [you] must acquit." [a reference to Johnnie Cochran's defense of O.J. Simpson] But that was a common-sense thing and I could have done that. I could have said, . . . if you want a little bit of common-sense guidance, if you can't tell [by] looking at that thing real quick, then it's not clear. So if it's not clear, you don't count it.

P:  If you took the *Bush v. Gore* decision to the logical conclusion, to avoid a violation of equal protection, there would be one voting machine and one standard in all 50 states.

L:  Right, and that's exactly what I've said. Well, in that case we should throw the entire election out because the voting machines in Dade County aren't nearly the same as the voting machines in Leon County. There's been evidence in the record already that, as opposed to a 98 percent accuracy rate, you're going to have 75 percent or something. If equal protection is going to be the basis, we're in trouble.

P:  Justice Wells made a very strong dissent to the Florida Supreme Court's 4-3 decision and said it had no foundation in the law, that it was going to create a constitutional crisis. He said this is not going to withstand scrutiny. And Justice Major Harding and Leander Shaw also dissented. Were you surprised that the decision was 4-3 and that they had those three dissents?

L:  No. It's not that this is not a proper thing to do, I think [Chief] Justice [Charles] Wells's observation was a little too critical because obviously there's no precedent for this. But they were interpreting the law, and that's their job, and he may disagree; obviously he did, that's in the dissent. But there's a basis for them to conclude, we've got a state contest. There's no real guidelines on how to do that, so here's how we're going to do it. But I agree with Harding and Shaw to the extent that what they basically said [was that] we don't have enough time to do this consistent with due process. If somebody made that argument, I can accept that, because we were doing everything lickety-split. To conclude that everybody can't be heard in arguments in a manner consistent with due process is fine; I just didn't buy the equal-protection problem.

P: Apparently the Florida Supreme Court's failure to respond immediately to the first remand from the U.S. Supreme Court may have hurt them a little bit. Do you think that was a factor?

L: Yes. It's always easy, hindsight being 20/20. But obviously I think that hurts. In that period of time you've got the U.S. Supreme Court in there. That's why I said, that first opinion [*Palm Beach County Canvassing Board v. Harris*], I think, didn't help. Maybe they had a good reason, [but] I just personally disagreed with it. I think it hurt because it was perceived to be arbitrary and a "making up the law" kind of thing. So once you do that, you've almost got a reputation with the U.S. Supreme Court, oh, here's the Florida Supreme Court folks again, and you're almost prone to believe they're doing something they shouldn't again.

P: You were charged with implementing the 4-3 Florida Supreme Court decision. You required that the Dade County ballots, which were already in Tallahassee because Judge Sauls had ordered them up, to be counted beginning at 8:00 on Saturday [December 9]. You called for judges to help you. How exactly was that set up? Did the judges do the counting? Did you do the disputed ballots?

L: In Leon County, yes, it was set up so that we had two judges per team. They had the clerks of the court actually doing the counting and putting them over there in a pile if there was some question about it. The judges were supposed to agree [on these]. If they couldn't agree, they put it in a pile for me to look at.

P: Did you actually look at any of the ballots or did the stay by the U.S. Supreme Court stop you before you got a chance?

L: I never got a chance.

P: Would you have finished counting all the undervotes by the end of December 9?

L: Yes. I think we would have had the reports from most of the counties by the target date.

P: Which was 2:00 Sunday, December 10.

L: Yes.

P: In your order, you specifically stated that there could be observers, but they could not verbally object. Is that correct?

L: They can make their notes, and if it came to it later, I could hear it all at one time.

P: When you implemented the Florida Supreme Court decision, did you actually issue a formal order to each county?

L: No, I entered just one order and relied upon the secretary of state to get it to all the canvassing boards.

P: You also asked that each county send back to you a plan for counting these votes, but some counties apparently never sent back an outline.

L: I didn't do a count, but it seemed like I got reports from just about everybody.

P: One of the counties that had some problems was Duval, because they had to separate the undervotes from the rest of the ballots. It's possible they might not have finished because of that.

L: That was the one significant county that I knew might be a problem.

P: I understand that Bay County sent you a fax and said, we're not going to do the recount since we'd done it right the first time. Do you remember that?

L: I know there were at least one or two counties who had actually already counted manually. Of course, I told them no, you don't have to count it again. I think it was Bay County that sent me a fax that said something to the effect of, we're not sure that we're going to do it because we're not sure you have the authority to order us to do it. I think that was Bay County. I . . . made a copy of the Florida Supreme Court opinion that said, we're going to tell the canvassing boards to do it. I said, that's the only authority I have. If that's not good enough for you. . . .

P: One of the problems was that you were running up against the "safe harbor" deadline of December 12, and that was a reason why you had to get an expedited count.

L: Right. I wanted to get something, have some tally, [and] let them go appeal it, which I knew they were going to [do].

P: All through this the Republicans are saying, there are inconsistent standards again, and there are judges counting in Leon County and nonjudicial personnel in other counties. Did you see that as a delaying tactic?

L: Well, obviously, they're the winners. They don't want anything to change that, so they're going to do whatever legally they can . . . do. I think I remember one person commenting that they were making their arguments to the U.S. Supreme Court when they were outlining all that stuff to me.

P: As a matter of fact, Phil Beck said that specifically. He even said that you ought to set a standard. He had no intention of having you set a standard, he just wanted to use that as a basis for appeal to the U.S. Supreme Court. That argument seemed very perceptive.

L: Yes, . . . that's what I would be doing. Obviously, the Florida Supreme Court wasn't going to give them much help.

P: Were you surprised when the U.S. Supreme Court issued a stay on the recount?

L: Yes. I was.

P: What was your reaction? I understand at one point that you got a fictitious telegram from Justice Rehnquist telling you to stop the count.

L: Yes, I got a fake order. But when it was directed specifically to me, I knew it was false.

P: It had to be directed to the court, obviously.

L: Yes. I was surprised that they took the first case because, generally speaking, that's state law [and] we're not going to fool with it. But to do it [wasn't normal]. So I guess I wasn't as surprised as I might have been. Before the Supreme Court got involved, the 11th Circuit [Court of Appeals] issued an order that said, count but don't certify the election or anything like that until we have a chance to review. I thought that made more sense.

P: Allow the counting to proceed. The 11th Circuit court, which voted 8-4 on that decision, was known generally as a fairly conservative court. They didn't seem to have any interest in the Fourteenth Amendment as a basis for a ruling. The major issue here, in my view, was when Justice Scalia wrote the opinion in the remand. He said that there would be irreparable harm to Bush and that you can't count the votes and then determine if they're correct. But it was hard to see irreparable harm if Bush were in the lead.

L: Yes, that's what I said. I didn't see the rationale. I didn't see why they would stop the vote. I didn't see any irreparable harm. Everybody seemed to be so concerned that this might get into the Electoral College or it might have to go to Congress.

P: But there's a constitutional basis to resolve that.

L: That's the way things work. If we can't resolve it the way the state legislature said, and we get up to the deadline and they have to do something, they say, sorry guys, but y'all didn't resolve it. That gets back to what I said I think Major Harding and Justice Shaw were saying: well, you've run out of time, we can't take it, we're going to take the electors that were there. You tried to contest it [and] you couldn't get it done, [so] we'll take those. Or, we're going to take it up and resolve it in the Electoral College.

P: Based on what you know about the count of the undervotes, do you have any sense of how the election would have turned out, had it been completed?

L: No. All I know is I've read the various consortiums of newspapers that have done it. I do remember, what I thought was fairly ironic, was the conclusion that, if they'd have counted the way Bush wanted, Gore would have won and vice versa.

P: Perhaps if Gore had gone after the overvotes he might have won, but the Gore team never asked for that. There was another remedy, of course: they could have asked for a statewide recount.

L: That's what I think should have been done. Like I said earlier, there was no way just a few counties or districts were going to be counted. If this thing was going to change, it was going to have to be everybody is going to be counted. They should have gone right to the heart of it and said, . . . we have evidence that legal votes were not counted. They should have had a statewide recount. They could have been doing that while the contest was going on.

P: So they could have proposed a statewide recount at the same time they were in the contest?

L: While the contest was going on. In other words, I think there's fairly broad powers for the presiding judge on a contest. Just like Sauls said bring up the ballots, I think he could have said, just like we did at the end: counties, I want you to go through, and any vote that wasn't counted by the machine, I want you to count them if you can. If you can't, don't count them, [and] let's see what we've got. If you get to the end and you listen to the evidence and there is grounds to have a contest, obviously the remedy is not to revote, so you count them [the uncounted votes]. Who knows what would have happened. The point is you wouldn't wait until December 9 or 10 to start doing that.

P: What was your reaction to *Bush v. Gore*, the 5-4 decision by the U.S. Supreme Court?

L: I have to admit that I didn't read it carefully. I watched a lot of the news reporting on it. After the stay, I pretty much knew what was going to happen. My only comment was, as I've said before, to the extent they based it on equal protection, I just don't understand it.

P: Do you see that decision as partisan? Justice Stevens, in a very strong dissent, said that it was a blow to the credibility of the Supreme Court because it looked like, from the public's perception, a partisan decision by a "conservative Republican court."

L: Yes, and similar to the Florida Supreme Court's earlier decision that I mentioned. I don't know any of those people, so I'm not going to presume that they had any bad intentions, motivations, ulterior motives, or whatever. But when you look at it in the legal community, . . . law professors . . . say that just doesn't ring true, that doesn't persuade me in terms of the reasoning. You can't escape the perception [that it was partisan], and that hurts. That hurts the courts whenever that is. Every time something like that happens, people [say], see, I told you. Cynical folks say, it's all politics and they're all going to do what [is in their interest]. So that just knocks us down a few steps and you have to build that trust back up.

P: Judge Richard Posner said *Bush v. Gore* was not a strongly argued constitutional decision, but it was a pragmatic decision. Do you think the court at this point just wanted to end it?

L: I've heard that and read that. Probably so. It was a very pragmatic thing [to say], enough of this, we're stopping this. But like we talked about before, what are you stopping? You're stopping the natural, legal resolution of this. If we count them and you don't like what happens here and you don't have enough time to appeal and it goes to the Electoral College or the legislature sends it up, so be it.

P: I noticed that Justice Ruth Bader Ginsberg had a really strong dissent and her argument was, basically, we should never have taken the case to start with. Then Justice Stephen Breyer said, let's send it back and have them finish the count. If the U.S. Supreme Court said, we'll send it back to you guys and you set a standard or whatever and finish the count. Could that have been done?

L: Sure. Both of those are very valid arguments, a lot more persuasive than the majority [opinion], to me. On the one hand it's we shouldn't get involved in this, and I said earlier I was surprised that they did. I consider myself a very conservative judicial person in that extent, so I would agree with the concept that you don't get involved in something if you're not supposed to, [or] if you don't really need to.

P: In your decisions, did you come down on the side of the intent of the voter as opposed to strict adherence to the law?

L: I'm probably in the middle. Since I'm a trial court, I'm going to follow what the [Florida] Supreme Court [says]. Again, it's hard to give a blanket statement about where you fall, except that . . . if it's an irregularity that's fairly innocuous, that doesn't threaten to affect the credibility of the whole system. In other words, you can't let people just vote any way they want to and not follow the rules just because we know what they want to do. On the other hand, you shouldn't let form overrule substance. Yeah, maybe they put the stamp in the wrong place. But geez, they substantially complied. [That] is a term that's often used.

P: If they voted for all ten presidential candidates, clearly, that's an invalid vote. The Republicans argued that if they don't punch it through or they put it in upside down, their vote should not count.

L: Just because they didn't follow the directions quite right, it's not like they did anything illegal. So you have to look at every factual situation. It's the kind of thing where some people would be saying, well, if they're too dumb to figure out the directions and vote, then they shouldn't have their votes counted. Well, I guess that's a policy or philosophical thing to do, but I think, generally speaking, these are people that are fairly well educated. You know the butterfly ballots and all the things they had down at Palm Beach. These are not people that are fourth-grade educated people, these are smart people that didn't figure it out. We all make those kind of mistakes. So if it's an innocent mistake, I'd be more inclined to say it's not an illegal vote, it's a vote that wasn't counted by the machine. That doesn't make it illegal, it's [still] a vote. You could be too picky.

P: How would you assess the performance of the attorneys who appeared before you, understanding the pressure they were under?

L: I thought, almost without exception, all the lawyers that appeared before me were very professional, prepared, made good arguments. Even though, as we talked about, [there were] some tactical, strategic things that were done, for the most part everybody agreed to cooperate, in terms of getting the issues presented. If somebody wanted to, they could have jammed things up pretty easily. I thought the caliber was very high.

P:   Do you think that changed the public's perceptions of attorneys?

L:   I don't know. I think the public still saw that as here come all the lawyers trooping down to Florida. Although compared to the O. J. Simpson trial this was a beauty pageant. I mean, seriously, if you're going to compare the legal system and you look at this and you look at the O. J. Simpson trial, which got a lot of publicity, it's got to be a higher opinion.

P:   What's your view of the Sunshine Law and the fact that all of these trials were literally instantaneously seen all over the world? Do you think it affects anybody's performance in court because they're on camera?

L:   Maybe marginally. Florida's been doing it for awhile, so I think the Florida lawyers are pretty much [used to it]. I think once you get going, it's almost out of your mind. You don't even think about it that much. Perhaps, in some instances [they are aware]. Like we talked about Phil Beck, he knows other people are watching [and] not just getting a transcript somewhere else. But that's okay. Considering the entire picture, I think it's much better to have it open than it is to have [it] like in the U.S. Supreme Court [with] an audiotape in there and pictures of the people.

P:   How did this experience change your life?

L:   I hate to say it didn't change my life. Anything you do always changes your life, but it's not like [I was this person and] all of sudden I'm this person. I don't think I've changed at all. It was a very interesting time, and I'm glad I was involved in it. I'm glad I got a chance to hear the issues and do what I do. It's intellectually challenging, so it was good. I had my 15 minutes of fame, so to speak, because my picture was plastered on newspapers and people recognized [me]. But that died down pretty quick.

P:   When you look back at your decisions, is there anything you would have changed or done differently?

L:   I probably would have talked about the standards a little bit and given some direction, so that not only the general public, but also the appellate courts, could have seen it's not just willy-nilly. We do have some standards, we're going to get it done, it's going to be as fair as we can get it. That's why I wanted to use judges [in the recount of undervotes], [so] we don't have partisans.

# PART VII

# INTERVIEWS: ATTORNEYS

# ➤ Dexter Douglass ◄

Long before 2000, Dexter Douglass was one of the most colorful and well-known attorneys in Florida. Described by *The St. Petersburg Times* as the "distinguished white-haired guy," Douglass exhibited a down-home sense of humor and a political shrewdness in the courtroom.

A native Floridian, Douglass earned both his B.S. and J.D. at the University of Florida. While attending the university he was a member of Florida Blue Key and the University of Florida Hall of Fame. After graduation, Douglass fought in the Korean War and opened his own law practice in 1962.

Over the last 40 years, Douglass has achieved success in trial and appellate cases in both federal and state courts. He has represented clients in a variety of civil cases, including personal-injury and medical-malpractice cases, legal malpractice, challenges to ballot initiatives, land management, and zoning. Douglass has also practiced criminal law and litigated cases involving constitutional issues. From 1995 to 1997, he served as general legal counsel to Governor Lawton Chiles and, in 2000, as chief Florida counsel for Al Gore's legal team during the recount controversy.

In his interview, Douglass recalled the legal machinations surrounding the recount controversy in Florida and how, when first approached, he had reservations about joining Gore's legal team. He then commented on the first hearing in Leon County Circuit Court Judge Terry Lewis's court. At that juncture, Douglass argued that Gore should end the protest phase and move to the contest phase. Douglass observed that public relations was a huge influence on Gore's reluctance to move to the contest phase, since it appeared that the Democrats were trying to "steal" the election from Bush. He also discussed Ralph Nader's candidacy, what he viewed as the partisan activities of Palm Beach County Judge Charles Burton, the reason that the protest phase would not result in victory for Gore, and the controversial butterfly ballot. He then reflected on the problems in determining voter intent as well as Gore's offer to the Bush team to recount all of the votes if they would agree to end all litigation.

Douglass lamented Jim Baker's diatribe against the Florida Supreme Court's 4-3 decision. He discussed the legal strategy of Bush attorney Barry Richard and Katherine Harris's counsel, Joe Klock, and explained why the controversy over military votes became such a difficult public relations problem for the Democrats. Douglass talked about his high regard for David Boies and Boies's influence on the Gore legal team.

He assessed the Florida Supreme Court's 7-0 decision allowing for the continuation of the recount in Palm Beach and Broward Counties, and conjectured on whether or not the Gore team could have won the lawsuits in Martin or Seminole Counties. Additionally, he commented on Gore's increasing influence in making legal decisions and House Speaker Tom Feeney's attempt to seat Bush electors in the event that the election had not been decided by December 12.

Douglass also discussed the 4-3 Florida Supreme Court decision to count the undervotes and his view on why the court did not set a standard for the recount. He commented on Chief Justice Charles Wells's "blistering dissent," in which Wells stated that the undervote decision had no foundation in law and would lead to a constitutional crisis.

When asked about the accusations of discrimination against minority voters, Douglass referred to those making the charges as "just seeing ghosts." He pointed out that the worst thing the Republicans did was to make the argument that "if you don't have sense enough to vote, your vote shouldn't count." Douglass countered this argument by calling it "absolute poppy-cock, because there [are] a lot of very, very intelligent Republicans that don't have sense enough to vote." Douglass concluded that Gore's biggest problem was that "he was indecisive in the way [he] approached the litigation," since he was too concerned about how it appeared to the general public. He closed the interview by revealing that Gore had called him after the 5-4 *Bush v. Gore* decision by the U.S. Supreme Court, obviously wanting to continue the fight. Douglass told the vice-president that the highest court in the land had ruled against him and that the conflict was over.

Dexter Douglass was interviewed by the author on October 30, 2001.

P:　What was your official position with the Al Gore campaign?

D:　I was engaged as the chief Florida counsel in connection with the election lawsuits.

P:　Who first contacted you?

D:　I was first contacted by Mitchell Berger, the lawyer from Ft. Lauderdale who is very close to [former] Vice-President Gore. He [Berger] had worked for him, he had known his family growing up, had been a long-time friend, and is a very outstanding lawyer from south Florida.

P:　When you accepted this role, did you have any idea of the extraordinary amount of time it would take?

D:　Originally, I told [Berger] I didn't want to do it. I felt that I just really didn't want to devote the time to it that it was going to take. I had been in some litigation involving elections before and they are not very satisfactory from a lawyer's standpoint, [on] either side.

P:　When you started, did Gore specifically explain to you what they wanted your role to be?

D:　I'm not sure. I think it just sort of evolved, because after I agreed to do it, the next day we filed a suit and I thought the hearing would be a day or so later. I got a call from Barry Richard, who I knew was on the other side, he said, look, we got a hearing at 1:00 today. This was about 10:30 in the morning. I said, I had it down that we would do it tomorrow—when they called, I thought they said it was Thursday. He said, no, it is at 1:00 today; I didn't think you were aware of it, so here we go. So we go over and have the first hearing before Judge [Terry] Lewis.

P: What were the legal issues in that first case?

D: We were urging the court to extend the time from the very beginning [in order] to allow the protest to be completed in the counties that were involved. [The Gore legal team] had selected the remedy before I got in the suit, to [file under] the protest statute in Dade, Broward, Palm Beach, and Volusia counties. They had concluded, based on the returns and the votes that had been thrown out and not counted, that if those [votes] were counted properly that they would have enough votes to put Vice-President Gore in the lead and therefore to win the election. After the first hearing, my first reaction was that I thought that we were using the wrong remedy. I thought we should go, and I think most other people that had dealt with this [thought too], that we should go under [statute 102.168]; let them go ahead and count the votes.

P: This is the contest phase.

D: Right. We would have a contest; then we would be in court and we would have the entire proceeding under the jurisdiction of a judge here.

P: That would probably have been Judge Terry Lewis.

D: We could have amended our complaint then, [and] later on, as it went along, he [Judge Lewis] invited us to do that. When he finally ruled, that while we were correct that she [Katherine Harris] could extend the time, it was discretionary. She had the right to use her discretion and then he would review it to see if he thought it met the standard of an abuse of discretion. He, in effect, told us that he thought our proper remedy was a contest and invited us to do that.

P: Perhaps Judge Lewis thought his initial ruling didn't matter so much since he figured you could always go to the contest.

D: I can't tell you what his thinking was, but I would assume that he probably reached the same conclusion that I did, and others; I was not the only one. Mark Herron, who is the Democratic Party lawyer, [is] probably as knowledgeable in the area of Florida election law as anybody, had written a memo and had taken that position. Mitchell Berger did. All of the Florida lawyers, I think, did.

Early on, maybe right after I was employed, Secretary Christopher and William Daley asked me to go with them over to her [Harris's] office before we filed a suit. Of course, I knew Harris and knew everybody over there. I went, and that was a waste of time, a photo-op, whatever. I do remember, I thought Christopher was pretty cool.

I liked him. We came out and they [the press] said, do you think the fact that Katherine Harris was one of the co-chairman in Florida for Governor [George] Bush would have any effect on what she is doing? He said, you will just have to let the facts speak for themselves. I thought that was a nice way of saying, you betcha.

Anyway, we came back and filed the suit. Actually, the team leader was Ron Klain. Ron had been Chief of Staff to Vice-President Gore, he was a *Law Review* editor from Harvard, a very bright, very capable lawyer. There were others there of course, but he was the major person dealing directly with the vice-president and with whoever was the brain trust in Washington.

P:    Who do you think made the decision to continue the protest?

D:    I think Gore did, ultimately. He may have had a lot of advice. My impression, whether it is correct or not, was that Daley agreed with us [and he was not optimistic about success]. Anybody that had ever been in an election contest [was] concerned that the protest would be a way [for him to overturn] the election without "contesting" the election, so that it would not appear that Bush had been declared the winner in Florida. He [Gore] therefore was going to court to over-throw it. They put, obviously, a lot of emphasis on this from a public relations standpoint. They didn't want [it] to appear that we were try-ing to take the election away from Bush when he had actually already been counted in.

The position that most of us took . . . was that this was not the way to handle a case, because no matter what happened, if you contested the election, everybody thought you were doing that already in the protest. I don't think anybody caught the nuance of that. The nuance they were thinking about was when Katherine Harris would get up and say, I hereby declare George Bush the winner, and then we would go to court and say no, you are not. I think they were putting a lot of emphasis on that, which I think just doesn't make sense, because in an election contest, it does not matter what you call it. If you are behind when you start counting the votes, everybody says, well, he is trying to overturn [the election]. Your people all are saying they stole it, and their people are all saying you are trying to steal it—they use all this kind of language. When it is over, whoever wins is president.

As it turned out, here is George Bush who is president, who [received] a minority [of the votes], he did not even get a plurality of the votes; Gore did. And [Bush] is president. Now he acts like he has got a mandate and the public has forgotten how he got in, [and] the fact that he didn't really win the election at all, [as] if losing the pop-ular vote is a mandate. They seem to take that attitude—we have got a mandate to reinvent government by demolishing it because the public wanted it. If you figure the reason Gore lost ultimately was because he had [Ralph] Nader in the race, . . . [he] is not exactly a right-wing, tear-the-government-down guy, you know? If you counted the votes on the basis of the philosophy of the candidates, [Bush] not only lost, he lost big-time. Probably the one person who elected Bush was Nader; the votes that he got pretty clearly deprived Gore of winning, in other states too, I think.

P: Most of the experts I have interviewed indicated that a crucial factor at the outset of the recount was that Bush stayed in the lead.

D: That was the political view. The legal view should have been, we are behind, let us get in the lead, and let us get there the way that would be the most efficient and the most well supervised way. The real thing that blew this thing up is when they allowed the Republicans to send all of these operatives in from Congress, from New York—some hoods that call themselves lawyers. They caused the protest to be a joke. You have got the wrong judge in Palm Beach County. You have got a guy that was a [Jeb] Bush appointee who was playing to the world [that] he was this intellectual sort of guy that was ruling this way. What he was doing [was] just making sure the votes didn't get counted.

P: This is Judge Charles Burton you are talking about?

D: Yes. On the other hand, you had pretty good judges in the other cases. They were more even-handed. Of course, the real reason this protest wouldn't work was [that] they got all hung up on how to count the undervotes. If we had been in a contest . . . we . . . would have had a month to count the entire state and we could have done it the way we were about to do it, by having a judge supervise it [and] rule on the issue of how to count these machine votes. That was 42 percent of the vote [punch-card machines]; everybody forgets that the other 60 percent were optical[-scan] and one county, Union, was a paper ballot— probably the most accurate count was at Union County. Here they were arguing machines were more accurate than people. You come back and say, is that why you take your car to the shop, is that why it breaks down on you, is that why it runs out of gas, why do airplanes crash? Human error, sometimes, but [it is] nonsense about machines [being] more accurate than people; they obviously are not. We sought a ruling that would have adopted the Texas standard, which would have put Gore in the lead, unquestionably.

P: That standard counted dimples?

D: Yes, indeed. The Texas statute, which George Bush signed into law, lays it out step-by-step.

P: One thing that puzzled me was when the Gore team hired all these Florida lawyers, who were very knowledgeable about Florida law, and sometimes when you made a recommendation, he ignored it.

D: I don't know that they ignored it, but they didn't accept it. That is their right. We are just lawyers, we don't call the shots ultimately when it is a policy decision. I think the thing that we kept coming back to, and we did this all through, I think we recommended that they . . . let Gore . . . contest the entire state. In the first instance, if we had contested, the judge would have probably required a recount of all the overvotes and undervotes. Where Gore really lost votes was on the overvotes. I think everybody was aware of that, because in Jacksonville, they essentially had the overvotes thrown out in the black precincts, which were heavily for Gore. That was a hard county to deal with because they were controlled by the Republicans and by the secretary of state. You just could not get anywhere in those counties, except with a judge.

P:   I have talked to several election supervisors, and there is no question that if you use intent of the voter as a standard, a human observer could have determined that if the voter circled Gore, but did not fill in the bubble, or wrote Gore in the write-in box, that would have been a valid vote.

D:   [There was] a lot of that. Over in Gadsden County, where they recounted them the night of the election [with] the overvotes, Gore added 100 votes in that county, just over here. That was an optical[-scan] county, of course. That was true in a lot of others. It turned out in Lake County, Gore had an extra 280 [vote] margin that they didn't even count on the optical votes—somehow or another it was excluded from the count. You can't say it was dishonest; you certainly can't say it was honest. You just say they didn't do it. The same [thing happened] over in Nassau County. They had recounted and given Gore an extra 100 votes or so [ed.: 51 votes]. When we got to it, they said they didn't have a proper meeting, [but] they were advised by the secretary of state's office [that] they did not have to [accept the recount]. They had a woman sitting there who was [a candidate] in the election, which is contrary to the statutes. She was sitting on the [canvassing] board. However, if we had been in a contest, that wouldn't have been singled out, it would have been dealt with on the [same] basis on all the rest of the [cases].

P:   The judge could have ordered them to count those votes.

D:   Correct. I think probably, if we had a contest, those votes would have been properly counted, and I think probably Gore would have gotten those votes. What they did is just left out a bunch of votes.

P    At one point, Gore publicly said that if he and Bush would stop litigating the legal issues, Gore would agree to count all the votes in the state.

D:   Count all the votes, recount all the votes if you will agree to it, and whoever wins will win, and then that is the last we heard of it. I was in [on] the conference call when that decision was made. He [Gore] wanted to know what we thought. I said, make that offer, make that offer. I said, they are not going to take it, because they will not let you recount all the votes, but make the offer and stick with it. That was about the only time I got to really tell Gore directly at that point something that I thought should have been done. That would have gotten us back to the point we were trying to get to and he did that.

When Bush said no, whatever his advisors said, the [Gore team] dropped it.

P: Should they have pursued that?

G: Absolutely. [He was] to . . . say, look, we have offered to recount all these votes and they will not do it because they know they have lost, and just hammer that in like [the Republicans] did with the issue they had. They were masters at saying the same thing over and over, even though it was totally off-the-wall, some of it. The worst exhibition in the whole thing was by Jim Baker, who should have known better. He got up and made the personal attack on the Florida Supreme Court. I think if he [had been] acting as a lawyer, he would certainly have been disciplined for that, because he was clearly out of line.

P: I noticed that Baker was very upset and said the Florida Supreme Court 4-3 decision was a disgrace and that a court should not decide elections.

D: Then [he turned] around and made sure his court [the U.S. Supreme Court] decided the election. I have a feeling they already knew they had the five votes, the way it turned out, [but] that is guessing, of course. The same people who spent most of my lifetime talking about an activist court doing things that were beyond the law were the people that were saying "what a wonderful, courageous legal decision" [5-4 U.S. Supreme Court decision in *Bush v. Gore*], which just goes to show you that politicians have no interest in fairness in the courts. What they are interested in is their own decision. That is true with most litigants, truthfully, and probably [for] me, too, for that matter, but I learned early on that you keep that in the [privacy of your] office. When you think somebody really did something that was totally wrong, you have got a right to bitch about it one time and you have a right to appeal it if you can, and you have a right to say you don't agree with the opinion, but you don't have a right to say they did it because they were crooks or they were political whores or whatever.

P: The Republicans repeatedly accused the Democrats of saying they wanted to count all the votes, and then they said the Gore team just wanted to count them in the counties in which Gore did well.

D: If I had been them, I would have been saying that too. We were saying, we just want to count the votes [and] count them all. In fact, when they did count, we were picking up votes in Bush counties. Gore had picked up 58 votes and all of those counties were Bush counties.

P: The *New York Times*, in their recount analysis after the election, found that where they least expected it, in Bush counties, Gore was getting votes.

D: I tended to think it [was] because the votes [that] were excluded were [votes of] blacks or old people. The most mistake-prone votes that were thrown out were made by people that were not aligned with Big Oil and Big Tobacco, they were concerned with their civil rights or Social Security. Those votes were primarily going to Gore.

P:    Let me ask you about the controversial butterfly ballot. The initial lawsuits were not from the Gore campaign, they were brought by local attorneys. Were they supported by the Gore campaign?

D:    No. I looked at that, too. I think a lot of us did. The problem with the butterfly ballot cases is you had to object before the election. The ballot had been approved by the local Democratic people, and once that occurs, I think the issue of the ballot being contested, by the Democrats particularly, was a loser. We were in a different legal position there. I think someone else had to contest that other than Gore.

P:    Was that lawsuit a waste of time?

D:    No, it wasn't a waste of time. From a political standpoint, it was clear that [Pat] Buchanan got more Jewish votes than he did in the whole world in Palm Beach County. It was clear they were Gore votes. From the standpoint of saying who won, Gore can say, and Buchanan said, he didn't get all those votes. When you looked at it, there was just no way that you could effectively do anything with that. It was great political fodder and it was really an illegal ballot, but so what? You weren't going to get any remedy that could reach the problem.

P:    Another important issue was the automatic recount mandated by an election with a margin of less than one-half of 1 percent. Some of the elections supervisors were unclear about what exactly was meant by a recount and several counties merely retallied the machine totals. They didn't actually recount the votes.

D:    That happened in several counties and I don't think we were aware of that until we got into the contest. See, that is where the contest would have come in. We would have discovered that immediately. When we were doing the protest, we were not concentrating on these other counties. Nobody was, particularly.

P:    In the contest, could the judge have set a standard for counting ballots?

D:    Yes, sir. He probably would not have. Nobody wanted to, for some reason. I kept wanting to revisit that in the [Florida] Supreme Court. When we went back the last time, I wanted to argue that the court should set a guideline for the machine ballots. If they had followed what the Massachusetts court did, the Illinois court did, [or] the Texas statute, then the votes would have been counted differently. They [the ballots] were not counted again, so it did not matter.

P:    In the beginning of the legal maneuvering, what was the strategy of Barry Richard and Joe Klock?

D:    Just completely obliterate the thing so that nobody could get a handle on what was going on. We played right into their hands by having these big shows going on in Dade and Palm Beach Counties. It looked like one big mess and there was no way anybody could ever tell what was going to happen. I think that was where we were in bad shape.

P:    At this point, did you anticipate that the conflict would end up in the U.S. Supreme Court?

D:   Yes. Sure did. Once [the U.S. Supreme Court] came in and intervened [and] told the Florida Supreme Court, tell us why you did this, I said, we are on the way to [the U.S. Supreme Court].

P:   In the first Bush appeal to Judge Donald Middlebrooks, the judge was very clear in his ruling that the recount was a state issue.

D:   He denied [the injunction to stop the recount] and they raised every issue in the world down there that they could, I think, and Middlebrooks ruled against them and the Eleventh Circuit [Court of Appeals] did.

P:   That is the other interesting thing: the Eleventh Circuit Court didn't accept the Fourteenth Amendment equal protection argument.

D:   [That] happens to be the most conservative circuit in the country. All of the scholars, everybody [said] this is clearly a state issue. That was what everybody thought, even the Eleventh Circuit. You would have thought those states' rights people on the Supreme Court would have reached the same conclusion. They did not. They are the ones who reached the conclusion that it was a federal issue. I don't want to pound the [U.S.] Supreme Court; we have got enough people doing that.

P:   I will give you a chance to do that later.

D:   I don't have to, they have pounded themselves.

P:   When Katherine Harris decided on certification, she said that the law was very specific and that she really had no discretion on certification, that it had to be done seven days after the election, which was November 14. Do you think throughout this period she was acting in an unbiased manner?

D:   Of course not.

P:   Would you expect otherwise since she was a Republican?

D:   No. I would not expect otherwise, she was George Bush's campaign manager. I will tell you a story. The first night, we were sitting having dinner with [Ron] Klain, [Warren] Christopher, [Bill] Daley, and Jeremy Bash, I think. We were discussing this and somebody [asked], what is it she wants? I said, you know, the rumor in the press is she wants to be an ambassador. Daley said, as long as there are 40 Democrats in the Senate, I do not know whether that will work or not. Christopher, God bless him, said, I don't know. What you want in an ambassador is somebody that can take orders and carry them out, and she is a very good soldier. I think we would have to all agree that she was a good soldier and that is why she is so popular with the Republicans. I like Katherine, but she was doing what she felt she was elected to do by the Republicans.

P:   One of the arguments you made against her decision on certification was that she did have flexibility. She could have waited until November 17 when the overseas ballots came in.

D:   She could do that or she could actually extend the time. She said, we have only done it when we had a hurricane. My argument was that this is as momentous an event as a hurricane and can be a bigger disaster. The [Florida Supreme Court] held that was true, that she had the discretion, and she did. She could have extended the time for certification until they finished counting the votes, but that wasn't to be.

P: I don't believe that you filed a suit to block the certification.

D: We didn't. I know the Republicans were counting on [being able to say that] it has been certified, . . . and the [Florida Supreme Court] came in and set it aside. What [the Florida Supreme Court] would have done is order Jeb Bush and Katherine Harris to undo [the] certification, and if they didn't, lock them up for contempt. The court clearly had jurisdiction to do that. My view was that once the court set [certification] aside and forced them to retract it, they couldn't call it a certification, it was no longer one. The court had voided it.

P: Prominent Democrats like Jesse Jackson, Sr., were in Palm Beach advocating for Gore. The Republicans countered with their own supporters and these commentators attracted a huge press presence. The Republicans claimed that with all the arguments going on and the changing of standards, that the entire process was chaotic.

D: They made it chaotic and we contributed, I guess. Of course the other side had all of their people running around. They brought in the governor of Montana [Mark Racicot], that highly populated state, to tell us in Florida how to run our business. I thought somebody should have really lambasted that nonsense. They bring [George] Pataki down from New York. New York has some of the most corrupt elections, locally, [of] any state, and here he is down here telling Florida how to do this. I think we didn't handle that very well; we could have made points out of that. This Montana governor didn't know what in the heck he was talking about. He was reading what they told him to.

P: Why did the controversy over the military ballots become such a difficult public relations problem for the Democrats?

D: I think we had a good point when they wound up counting votes that were mailed after the election and all sorts of things, it turned out, and got away with it. I don't know why everybody was afraid to contest the military vote because a lot of [them were] not military votes. Overseas votes were not all military. If they were illegal, they were illegal. The man in the military doesn't have any more right to vote than anybody else. Don't you remember Lieberman? How are we going to contest them [military ballots] after he gets up and says, we are not contesting the right of the military to vote. That sort of was the end of that.

P: Then General Norman Schwarzkopf came out and accused Gore of being unpatriotic.

D: He is a big Republican and he is a political person. They have a right to say all these things. I don't want to indicate that I don't think they were doing anything wrong by saying all of this. Legally, I think they were wrong, but politically, that was fair game. Again, if we [had] been in a contest, they would have all been done by a court.

P: Let me go back to this November 14 decision by Judge Terry Lewis. He ruled that Katherine Harris had discretion in her decision for certification, but he did not give her a specific order to accept the recounts. Why not?

D: What he said is she has discretion, she has not exercised it, [and] the court's duty is to send it back and say you applied the wrong law, now exercise your discretion. In retrospect, I have no argument with his decision. I thought it was one of the better-reasoned ones. What he said was, basically, you guys are right, she has got discretion and that is what I am holding and I am going to tell her to exercise her discretion, but I can't tell her what to do. Bring it back after she does it and then I will review it, which he did. He said she was within her discretion to do what she did. Then he suggested, rather subtly, that we file a contest. I was reading him pretty good. That was where I got in trouble, I think, with some of the [Gore] people. I was not chastised, but my influence [changed] because I got quoted in the *New York Times*, somewhere, as saying—and I didn't realize I had done this, I'm not sure I did, but you never can deny a [quotation]. [A reporter] heard [Mark] Herron and me talking and we said, we ought to be in a contest. He comes up and says, what do you mean? Why are you in this protest? I said something like, the decision was made by the people in Washington because they didn't want to make us look like sore losers. They put that in there. I think when they read that up there in Washington, whoever the brain trusts were, said, shut that guy up.

P: Do you think it was improper for Katherine Harris to have Mac Stipanovich and other Republicans in her office offering advice?

D: I don't want to judge that. Politics are politics and she has held a political office. She was elected by those people. I have been around long enough to know that the people that elected you can get ahold of you and talk to you.

P: How would you assess Governor Jeb Bush's activity during this period of time? He did recuse himself from the state elections commission.

D: I don't know that Jeb was more in it than others. He was a focal point because he was the governor and he had the ability to have a political organization and certainly that was used. He obviously was involved and he obviously was very interested in getting his brother elected and he was successful if it was him, but it was more than him; it was the whole bunch. I don't know that anybody could ever say that he was not talking to them and putting in his two-cents-worth about what they ought to do. I think that was true, but I'm not sure that I fault Jeb Bush for that. He was elected, too, and his brother was running. What would you expect him to do? Go lay down in a back room and not do anything? I would have been very shocked if he had not been involved in decision making. I don't think there is anything wrong with it either.

P: You decided to appeal Judge Lewis's decision allowing Secretary Harris to certify of the election.

D: Right. Let me intervene there. David Boies . . . thought that we wouldn't appeal it. We thought we would file the contest. I think David thought that too, [in] the afternoon. Then the word came down, we are going to appeal. So David and I both started on the appeal. We have got to say that she did not exercise her discretion properly, she abused it, and that they should have extended it [the vote counting]. Now we have got to figure out, how we are going to get the court to extend it, and how long? We have got to get the votes counted. So, we started to work on briefs, everybody did.

Honestly, I think we all thought, when we heard that [Judge Lewis] had ruled, which he had reasonable basis to do, [that] he had reasonable basis to rule the other way, too. In fact, the [Florida] Supreme Court overruled him. Here I am thinking that the one guy that I know as a judge that would have loved to rule the other way did not, because he [Lewis] thought the law required him to do what he did.

P: Who picked David Boies as legal counsel and why?

D: I presume he was picked by the brain trust, whoever it was. Christopher, I think, was involved in the picking, and Daley to some extent, but actually it was Gore, I guess. [Boies] is a very visible, good lawyer. He had just beat Bill Gates [CEO, Microsoft] and if you watch the deposition of Gates, he just did a super job. He was the best lawyer in the whole bunch. I thought he was outstanding in that he was so accustomed to fame. He didn't go around telling you he was the best lawyer on the earth, which a lot of them do . . . I immediately said that he should be the lead counsel, particularly in the overall aspect of it. Truthfully, the lead counsel was a group somewhere up in Washington, I think, as far as calling what we ultimately did. That is the client's prerogative.

P: Do you think Gore listened to Boies's advice?

D: Yeah, but he would listen to a lot of others, too.

P: I understand that not only was Boies a quick study, he tended to memorize all of the facts about a case.

D: He does not memorize. What he did is he sat and he did all of his [work beforehand]. Great concentration is what he had. Before he went up and before he got there, he would go over and go over and go over [the notes]. Then he would put them down and he would go up there and he would know pretty much what they were going to ask him. It was very impressive. He will be the first one to tell you that he doesn't have a photographic memory. His secret is concentration. I think he was a learning-disabled child and that is how he created the ability to just shut everything out and sit there and do it.

P: What was the essence of your argument to the Florida Supreme Court to overturn Secretary Harris's certification?

D: Basically, that she hadn't properly exercised her discretion, which was shown by the fact that she got the letter [from Judge Burton requesting an extension] an hour later without considering anything. [She] just overruled it. The word "*may*" made it discretionary and she abused her discretion.

P: And, in effect, according to your argument, disenfranchised voters.

D: Correct. [The] presumption was to count the votes. That was our argument. Now, I didn't argue in oral argument. I sat at counsel table. I am going to tell you why. That weekend before we had that argument, John Thrasher made a statement to the press. He said to several members of the press [that the Republicans] were probably going to have trouble in the Florida Supreme Court because Dexter Douglass was going to argue the case and he appointed six of them. He was general counsel to Governor Lawton Chiles, but [Douglass] is the man that selected the judges—which is bullcrap if anybody knew Lawton. Lawton selected whoever he wanted to. The trouble with his statement was, it was absolutely a lie. I wasn't general counsel when any of them were appointed. None of them. I had left when the last two [were appointed] and the other four were appointed before I went over as general counsel. I was nothing more than Lawton's buddy or friend and also was co-chair of the 1995 inauguration. I said, Thrasher is at it again. He is like John Shebel [lobbyist for Associated Industries of Florida]: if he told the truth, he would go back and correct it. That is his style; he just says whatever comes to his mind.

So then *The Wall Street Journal* prints the article, and they write this editorial, the lead editorial, in which they spend the whole editorial skewering the Florida Supreme Court and me, saying that it is the Dexter Douglass court. Here I am fixing to go over and argue. Some smart-ass reporter asked me if I was going to argue the case after this came out. I said, I don't know whether I am or not, but I will be at the counsel table, which was correct and I was. I felt with that [statement] being on the table and out in the form of an editorial that it would be embarrassing to the court [and the] bar if I got up there and made the argument, or a significant part of the argument at all, because it would appear as an absolute political thing. I thought that I was in the position of not being able to do anything [other] than sit there and introduce Boies because he hadn't been before the court. That is why I didn't make an argument.

P: Give me your assessment of the first Florida Supreme Court 7-0 decision, which ruled that Palm Beach and Broward County could continue the hand counts and set November 26 as the new certification date.

D: I thought it was a correct decision.

P:  Where did the new deadline of November 26 come from?

D:  In oral argument.

P:  Who made that argument?

D:  David [Boies]. He didn't make it quite like that. He said, this is the real hard part of the decision and we want to help the court arrive at a conclusion. He did a great job on this and he let the court sort of make the decision in his oral argument.

P:  A blow to Gore's attempt to get ahead in the count was when the Miami-Dade Canvassing Board discontinued their recount on the basis that they could not finish in time.

D:  That is because they had all those people out there screaming and yelling, [and as it] came out in the trial [before Judge Sanders Sauls], none of them were from Miami. One of the ones that got up there and testified was a lawyer from New York. Kendall Coffey asked him, had he ever taken the Fifth Amendment in an election case, and it blew up the whole courtroom. Of course he had. Anyway, Kendall comes back and he said, were you out there when all this was going on? [The man] said, yes, I was there and all these people were being very orderly and I was there and I was being very orderly. [Kendall] flashes this picture up on the big screen in there. He said, see this guy right here? This guy [says] yeah. And it was him [laughter]. [The picture showed him] screaming and yelling and all these people trying to push this door down and get in. Coffey said, I see, is that you? Yes, he says. Coffey says, I don't think I have any more questions for you. I thought Kendall killed him.

P:  Discuss Sandra Goard's actions and the Seminole County and the Martin County cases.

D:  We weren't in that. We weren't in it because Gore told us not to be in it.

P:  Should you have joined the suits?

D:  We recommended that.

P:  Could you have won the Martin or Seminole County cases?

D:  Probably not. [With] singled-out [cases], we couldn't. If it was in the whole state we could. The law . . . on absentee-ballots [is] unless you can show that the absentee ballots that were actually fraudulent were voted in such a manner that it would affect the outcome of the election, then they do not [warrant voiding the election]. The way you had to show that here was by taking the statistics of what the absentee ballots were and then saying, this many of them would have been for Gore and this many of them would have been for Bush, and therefore it does affect the election. That was the argument you had to make and it was made well, but the court didn't buy that.

P:  As the recount progresses, how much influence does Gore have over the legal decisions? Are you aware that he was involved in all of these decisions?

D:  Yes.

P:  Was he constantly in contact with you and David Boies?

D: Not with me. He talked to me once or twice and then later on, toward the end, he talked to me several times. He was in contact primarily with [Ron] Klain.

P: Tom Feeney and the Republicans in the Florida legislature got involved in the recount. They argued that they had to protect Florida's electoral votes and if the legal conflict was not cleared up by December 12, they would seat a slate of Bush electors—and in fact, they did vote 79-41 to do so. What was your reaction to that decision?

D: They didn't know what the hell they were doing; they were doing what they were told. Feeney doesn't know a constitution from a morning walk. I think what they were saying was [they had] the power to do this. [They were] going to send a slate up, which [they] have a right to do. The history of the Electoral College is [that] the legislature sends the slate up. They do designate the electors. Except our statute says they have to designate the group that ran on [the slate chosen by the voters], but they wind up designating them.

P: The election was formally certified on November 26, so you filed suit to challenge the certification, which is known as the contest. What was your reaction when you found out Sanders Sauls would be the judge in your case?

D: It wouldn't move quickly and we would lose.

P: Why didn't you ask to recuse him?

D: There weren't any grounds to recuse him. The client has to certify, in order to get a recusal, that he doesn't think he can get a fair trial. I don't think that we had grounds at that point for saying that. I felt that way because I knew Sandy Sauls well, had known him a long, long time. He is very conservative. I said, in my opinion, that he was probably one judge who philosophically was opposed to our position 100 percent. He didn't want us to win. I wasn't saying that he would be dishonest in any way, but maybe if we drew [a judge] that wanted us to win [things would be different]; that is the way life is. He tends to run the court slowly. I knew the other side was going to do everything they could to drag it out.

P: What was the thinking behind Sauls's decision to have all the ballots from Dade County and Palm Beach County brought to Tallahassee?

D: Well, that was where we were going to count them.

P: You thought it would save time if you had them already there?

D: Correct. Also, we would get them out of that mess down there [Palm Beach County and Dade County].

P: Did you assume at any point that Sauls would count them?

D: No, no. I don't know. We kept hoping he would. David would get up and say, the votes are here, judge, count them. I would get up and say, judge, if we count the votes, however you rule will not make any difference. Actually, it gave us one of our best points on appeal—how can he rule against them? He never looked at them. He didn't know what was in them. Thank God for unanswered prayers, right?

P:    How did you manage to keep up with all of these lawsuits? You are having to prepare briefs with 48 hours notice.

D:    Actually, it was really divided, we had people that were doing nothing but writing briefs. They would be preparing it in case we won. Then there was one [prepared] in case we lose. We would come back to the office and they would have all this done. All we would have to do is edit. Sometimes the editing was really tough, [but we] had to do it. I remember the last brief we filed, I guess, it was given to us with 65 or 70 pages. I said, say you are on the court and somebody files an 80-page brief. Are you going to read the thing when you have got to make a ruling in two days? You will not even do it if you have to make a ruling in six months, most of the time. Go in and . . . cut it down. You do that and you probably [have] a better brief when you get through.

P:    While you were planning legal strategy and writing briefs, was the Gore team working out of your offices here in Tallahassee?

D:    I [have] a whole space back in there [Douglass's law office] which we outfitted for them. We had 14 or 15 [high-speed] outlets for computers, we had cable TV in every room. We had about 40 people in there.

P:    Give me a thumbnail analysis of Judge Sauls's decision.

D:    It was 100 percent against everything that we asked for. The only thing that we got acknowledged on was the fact that we represented Gore. Which is incidentally, the best way to go up. When the judge rules against you on everything, you know something is wrong.

P:    You have a viable appeal.

D:    Well, somebody is going to look at it, because how could we be that wrong?

P:    He said that there had to be a probability that the outcome of the election would be changed rather than a possibility, that also he found no proof that the individuals at the canvassing board had, in any way, abused their discretion.

D:    This was a contest—, the canvassing board had nothing to do with this. He didn't read the statute. Or if he did, he didn't read the right part. That didn't have anything to do with the contest. What the canvassing board did doesn't matter. At that point, you are going to count them *de novo*. That is what a contest is; [it] is a recount. The canvassing board doesn't do it, judges do it.

P:    So you knew, at this point, that the trial before Judge Sauls had been, in some ways, a waste of time.

D:    In my mind, it was all a loss of time. What he ruled was so wrong that I knew we were going to get to count these votes under the contest statutes.

P:    The U.S. Supreme Court got involved when they vacated the November 21 Florida Supreme Court decision, which ruled that hand recounts must be included and moved the certification date to November 26.

D: We weren't expecting that to happen, really. We thought it might, but we weren't expecting it.

P: Why do you think the U.S. Supreme Court vacated the Florida Supreme Court decision?

D: Because they wanted Bush to win. Five of them did.

P: In that initial remand, they did not comment on the Fourteenth Amendment, the equal protection clause.

D: No, because they hadn't decided how they were going to get there. The five people that ultimately decided it, if you will recall, concurred in [Antonin] Scalia's little opinion, when he says, to allow the recount to continue would somehow or other affect the president-elect's legitimacy.

P: He said it would cause Bush irreparable harm.

D: He is saying in effect, the president-elect is George Bush. When I read that, that was my interpretation. I said, hell, Scalia says they have already decided Bush is it. Now we can't count the votes. But they didn't say anything about [an] equal protection argument. They never had in the history of the world. The five that ruled that way were always against federal courts interfering with state issues.

P: At this point, did you know that the election was over?

D: No. I thought so, but I remember sitting in there with David [Boies] back in that office. I said, David, we have got five people; you have got to get one of them in the oral argument. At that time, they were still trying to decide if they were going to let Tribe argue. I said, I have been raising hell with Klain and [others]. I want you to argue it because you know what to argue. He said, I don't know if I want to argue or not. I said, yeah you do. You have only got to convince one of those five. He said, that is a 20 percent chance. He said, [those are] not bad odds when you are on the gambling table. We thought he had a chance that O'Connor or Kennedy [might rule in our favor.] It turned out, we didn't know about O'Connor's statements that came out later, how she was so disappointed when it looked like Bush had lost, because she could not retire or some comment that was quoted all over. [In] their [previous] decisions, they had nearly always gone with the idea that state issues are state issues, and elections were always state issues. We thought that [with] those two, [we] might have a chance to switch them over.

P: The Florida Supreme Court, on December 8, voted 4-3 to order Judge Lewis to count all the undervotes.

D: Actually, they ordered Judge Sauls, who was the judge. They reversed his case and sent it back to the judge. In that case, Sauls then recused himself. We didn't know this at the time. We thought we were going to have to go back and face him.

P: The case finally ends up back with Judge Terry Lewis.

D: Lewis is assigned the case when it comes back, which is where we should have been all the time.

P: Were you surprised at the 4-3 Florida Supreme Court decision? I have talked to some journalists and they were shocked.

D: I wasn't surprised. I wouldn't have been surprised if it had been 4-3 the other way. I felt from the oral argument that we had three and probably four and maybe five [on our side]. I thought [Leander] Shaw might have gone with us, but he didn't. I figured the Chief Justice [Charles Wells] was not [going to go with us]. Harding, I figured, would go with the Chief Justice.

P: So you thought you had Pariente, Quince, Lewis, and Anstead on your side for sure?

D: Well, I wasn't sure about Lewis. I thought we had about the same chance of getting Lewis as we did Shaw. After we did oral argument, I felt that Lewis' questions indicated that he was looking at a way to square his idea of the law with having us do the recount. I thought we had a good chance of winning when we left. I think I made that comment privately. I thought we were going to win either 4-3 or 5-2.

P: Why did the Florida Supreme Court decide to count just the undervotes?

D: Because that was all we asked for.

P: Should you have asked to count all the ballots?

D: Yes. The reason we didn't do it, and I'm not sure that we ever really had much of a chance to consider this, we didn't figure we had time to do it.

P: Did you expect that the counting of the undervotes would be enough to put Gore ahead in the recount?

D: I think it would have [been enough]. Regardless of what all these after-the-fact things show, if it had been properly counted by judges, we would have won on the undervotes.

P: Why did the Florida Supreme Court not set a standard?

D: I don't know. In that argument, we didn't ask them to. I argued that we should because we argued [for] it in the first case, and they did not. I would have raised it again in oral argument. I said, David, we need to argue the standard. He said, no, we don't want to argue that, we don't have time, the judge has his hands full. I don't think we will argue it. He [Judge Terry Lewis] may set a standard. They [Florida Supreme Court] left the ruling to the trial judge and the reason they did it is because there is no uniform way to do it; it is different in each county.

P: Judge Lewis immediately began the recount. Could all the counties have finished in time?

D: Yes, the only one that was dragging their heels was Duval [County].

P: They had a problem separating the undervotes.

D: That is what they said; they had to write to Saudi Arabia to get the software or something. They could have borrowed Miami's. They weren't using it.

P: Was the argument that the court was a liberal, Democratic court undermined by the close, 4-3 vote?

D:   The argument that it is a liberal court is undermined by all of its decisions. They are very consistent in attempting to reach a consensus on the legal issues. They don't stray much, they really don't.

P:   What did you think of Chief Justice Wells's rather blistering dissent, in which he said that the Florida Supreme Court decision had no foundation in law and would lead to a constitutional crisis?

D:   Wells is a good judge. He is very focused and believes he is right when he believes he is right. I don't have any problems with him saying that. He was in the minority. Minority [of the] minority; nobody else said that. There is one thing too, that needs to be [talked about]. If he [Wells] was going to rule politically, if he was going to rule [for] Gore and [against] the Republicans, he had to face, as Chief Justice, the legislature. He is the one that has to go over there and sit down with [Tom] Feeney and whoever. They [the Republicans in the Florida House] are . . . trying to gut them [the Florida Supreme Court]. They don't think you ought to have a court. They don't know anything about the separation of powers, [they] totally ignore it. There is nobody in this administration that seems to have any respect [for] or even concept of what the separation of powers doctrine is.

P:   In fact, Tom Feeney said the 4-3 decision showed a tremendous lack of respect for the legislature.

D:   So that any time you declare a law unconstitutional, it shows a tremendous lack of respect for the legislature. What it shows is a large amount of respect for the constitution.

P:   Why did David Boies replace Larry Tribe as lead attorney before the U.S. Supreme Court?

D:   One of the reasons was that [I] and others argued strongly that he should. He knew the case, he had done a great job arguing it in the Florida Supreme Court, and he was the best possible person for us to have. You don't want but one person arguing the case. I think there was a feeling that Tribe hadn't done a particularly good job in the first case. I think they thought David would be a new face. He would be bringing in a different point of view.

P:   How did David Boies do in his 45-minute presentation?

D:   I thought he did extremely well, particularly recognizing that he had five people that were after him. Scalia, particularly, is always going to be after everybody.

P:   The crux of Boies's argument was, essentially, what you have been arguing all along, that the votes had to be counted. The Republicans argued that the different standards were a violation of the Fourteenth Amendment and Title 3 U.S. Code Sec. 5 and the changing of the certification date was making new law.

D:   I don't even know that they did that much arguing on the equal protection. That came from the bench, as I recall.

P:   What is your assessment of the 5-4 *Bush v. Gore* decision in terms of its legal and constitutional basis?

D:   It will stand there by itself like Dred Scott. They may cite it, but they will never follow it.

P:   Justice Breyer, in his dissent, said he thought the case should be remanded to the Florida Supreme Court to resume the recount under a uniform standard. That was obviously a minority opinion. Was that a possible remedy?

D:   Yes, but it wasn't an effective remedy. It wouldn't have made any difference.

P:   Because of the December 12 safe harbor date?

D:   Or December 18, whichever one you chose. It was going to wind up in Congress.

P:   Let me make some general comments about the court's decision and get your reaction. One argument was made—and I think both you and David Boies made this statement—that it really did not matter what the Florida Supreme Court did. The Florida Supreme Court was trapped in a Catch-22. If they had in fact, set a standard, they would have been legislating, therefore the court would have overturned them. By not making a standard, the court violated the Fourteenth Amendment.

D:   If they [the Florida Supreme Court] had come in and set the standard, the [U.S. Supreme Court] would have said that was a job for the legislature and you have overstepped your bounds, like the [Bush lawyers] tried to [argue] in the first instance by saying you didn't interpret the statute, you made new law. That is what became a PR deal for the [Republicans] and this is what Baker was yelling about,— you are writing the law—unbelievable. The [Florida] Supreme Court made a decision when they [interpreted the law]. They have the right to do that.

P:   David Boies argued that courts had been applying the reasonable man standard for almost every death penalty case. Why did the court not accept that, the intent of the voter, as a standard for the recount in Florida?

D:   [The U.S. Supreme Court] would not have been able to reverse it.

P:   Did Boies have a legitimate argument?

D:   Yes. But they ruled the other way, so now we have a special standard that applies to elections.

P:   The high court said that *Bush v. Gore* applied only in this case.

D:   That is right, which means, we wanted George Bush to be president.

P:   Let me read some comments about the decision. Some academics said that the decision was flawed and the *New York Times* wrote that the Rehnquist court overlooked the bedrock principle that every vote should be counted and thus ended up eroding public confidence in the court. Do you think that was a fair judgment?

D:   It probably is, but the one thing they all overlooked is that, under the rule of law, once they have decided, that is it. We can complain about it, but that is the way it is and you might as well say Hail to the Chief to George W. and wish somebody would teach him to read better.

P: What was your reaction to Justice John Paul Steven's rather strong dissent? He said the decision was wholly without merit and also argued that the decision undermined the confidence of the public in the court.

D: That was his opinion and I think it was shared by a lot of people. Obviously, you are disappointed that you lost the case and you think you were right. I have been very careful as a lawyer in the case not to really take on the U.S. Supreme Court on the basis of personal [opinions]. I can criticize the majority opinion, I can criticize anything else about it and say that I like Breyer's opinion. I loved Ginsberg telling them they were all SOBs. She got her dander up pretty good.

P: Let me read you the comments of Jake Tapper, a journalist who wrote a book on the controversy. He said this was an election that brought out the ugliest side of both political parties. He wrote that the Democrats were capricious, whiny, wimpy, and incompetent and that the Republicans were cruel, presumptuous, indifferent, disingenuous. Both were hypocritical, the media was lazy, and there were too many hired-gun lawyers.

D: He is a sore-head. He just didn't like anybody. [He took] a little truth and made it into a nontruth. Nobody was all that bad. Obviously, the PR battle cast the Democrats as whiny. They lost that battle with the Republicans, who *were* mean, and they didn't hesitate to lie and they didn't hesitate to say bad things and send people down to disrupt the counting. I don't think I would go as far as he did. It was politics as usual, as far as the two parties were concerned. You have got to be able to take it if you are going to be in politics. As [for having] too many lawyers, there probably were too many lawyers. There were not too many on our side; we didn't have that many.

P: One conclusion by the experts was that the Republicans outworked, outspent, and outsmarted the Democrats, partly because they were more committed to Bush than the Gore people were committed to Gore. They thought they were fighting a holy war. Is that a fair assessment?

D: I don't think it is a fair assessment of Gore; I think it is a fair assessment of the Republican people. They considered it a holy war because it involved their money. They had to get people like Clinton out of there. What he was doing was saving the government, reducing the debt, and still taking care of the poor.

P: One Republican said, literally, we are fighting for a righteous cause.

D: Yeah, well, so is Osama bin Laden. All wars are fought for a righteous cause. I always loved Lincoln's [quotation]. I think it was Lincoln. Somebody asked him, is God on our side? He said, I do not know but I sure hope we are on his side.

P: African American voters complained of discrimination. In Leon County, for example, there was a highway patrol stop that some have said was an attempt to keep voters away from the polls.

D: That was just seeing ghosts. In Leon County, that was certainly not planned to intimidate voters. You probably can't say anybody set out to disenfranchise them, but it certainly worked that way. If you stop and think about it, the poor, uneducated people and old people who can't see or [have] lost some of their faculties are the ones whose votes are going to be spoiled anyway, [or] more [often]. There are a lot more African Americans that don't read well, don't write, don't follow instructions. Some of them have no education because they were not afforded any. The worst thing you can do is take the argument they [the Republicans] did, if you don't have sense enough to vote, your vote shouldn't count. That is absolutely poppy-cock, because there [are] a lot of very, very intelligent Republicans that don't have sense enough to vote. Consequently, the idea that people don't have sense enough to vote is nondemocratic.

P: Let me ask some overall questions about the recount. Are you glad that you had the opportunity to participate?

D: Oh, yeah. I originally turned it down, then I got to thinking about it. Hell, I am 70 years old, I have not had a chance to be in anything quite like this. I have been in a lot of stuff, but this is something that would be interesting and you could never duplicate. From that standpoint, I am certainly glad I was in it.

P: How has this changed your life?

D: I quit practicing law as much. I love to go make speeches now. You know, one thing . . . happened in this case that I will remember. I was the last guy to talk to Gore the night before he announced that he was pulling out. He had not decided to pull out. Klain called me and he said . . . the vice-president wants to speak to you in private, on the phone, after you have read this U.S. Supreme Court decision [*Bush v. Gore*]. He wants you to give him your opinion of what could be done by the Florida court and the prospects of it. Fine. So about 1:00 in the morning, maybe it was later, I was sitting right here. I called him, he answered the phone. We talked. He really, I could tell, wanted to keep going. He was wanting me to give him some hope. I said, . . . I don't think the Florida Supreme Court is in a position to keep the case going to the extent that it could result in your election. [If they came] in and set up some system whereby they counted the votes and you should succeed and then they ordered that this go up, you are still going to have at least two slates going up. That is going to put it in Congress. When it gets in Congress, you win the Senate, you lose the House and then the House elects and that is it. In response to the question about the Florida Supreme Court, I went over each one of them with him and how I thought they would respond. I pointed out to him that the chief justice was under difficult political pressures, in my opinion. He had to deal with the Republican legislature, who was attacking the judiciary. He was torn with doing [his] duty to preserve the system of the court, the institution, and [to] preserve the third branch.

Then we talked on it for a while. He said, thank you, I am going to decide and I will make my announcement in the morning. He called and Klain got us all in there. He told us what he was doing and how much he appreciated it and all that. Then everybody packed up and went home.

P: Some observers concluded that Gore's concession speech was his best speech of the campaign.

D: It was. I don't know about the best speech of the campaign, but it was the best speech that had been made in a hell of a long time.

P: If he had campaigned like that, he might have won.

D: Well, that is what they always say. If a bullfrog had wings, he would not bump his ass. I think Gore's biggest [problem, and] this is certainly not an expert opinion, [was that] he was indecisive in the way we approached the litigation. We were always worried about how it looked. That meant his advisors were worried about how it looked. It was kind of like [if] you [have] a boxing match and one side is really stronger, but he fights by the Marquis of Queensbury rules. And the other side is not as strong, but he kicks you in the [groin], he hits you in the kidney, he does everything dirty, and he wins. That was about the way this thing came down. They were street-fighting, which used to be the Democratic strong[point]. The Democrats were acting like they all went to Harvard. Maybe they all did, I don't know.

The other thing that I thought that really affected this was that the people that were telling us what to do had the Washington Beltway as their vision. These [were] Washington lawyers. Bush, on the other hand, was sitting down in Texas, [staying] out of it, not making any decisions. He was in the perfect position because he had people like Baker on the scene here making all these tough statements. He had whoever was down there advising him, telling him what to say and when to say it. Gore was making his own decisions, but he had too many advisors. As a result, I think that is why he ultimately lost the election and this lawsuit.

P: Do you think that Gore should have used President Clinton more?

D: Absolutely. Clinton was very popular. Still is. When they do a poll, you will always see [that]. And guess who likes him? The women, because he is a real warm guy. He has a knack. The blacks love him. He just has a [way with people] and it kills the press and everybody else. One thing they can't accept is a guy with talent.

P: Describe what Tallahassee was like, with all the media people. It was difficult to get a place to stay, they couldn't get into restaurants.

D: Everybody had a good time. The press did. They always do. It was rather exciting. They liked Tallahassee, it was kind of an odd place for them. It has the small-town atmosphere. It's Southern, but it isn't. I thought the press was really pretty good. I thought they went out of their way to be polite to us and to not intrude on us. Particularly the major press, the major networks, and so on; they were very considerate of our position as lawyers. They were nice to me in *Time* [magazine]. I was "courtly," whatever the hell that means.

P:   It means a distinguished, white-haired southern gentleman.

D:   It was kind of funny. I got a lot more credit for doing things than I [actually] did. I didn't do that much, really. I was cut out of the inner-circle pretty quickly because of my nonagreement with things. Towards the end, I think Klain and I probably became much more attuned to each other, and I really like Klain. He was probably the major lawyer in the case that you didn't see, but was very, very much the head lawyer. I think if I had been a little more assertive that I would have had a bigger role, but I didn't feel like it was my place to do that, one. And two, I might have wound up doing more than I wanted to do.

P:   Do you feel, at this point, vindicated by your position on moving to the contest sooner?

D:   Oh, yeah, I have felt that way all the time. I don't think I ever made any secret of that. Anybody that read and knew Florida election law would just about agree with us, if your decision was to win and not worry about the PR stuff. Actually by going to PR [tactics], they got their tails beat. The Republicans beat the stew out of us in PR. They figured out the longer it drug out, the weaker we were. The more they said they are trying to steal the election from George, the more the public decided we are trying to steal the election from George. We should have had somebody up there, say, the governor of the Canal Zone, to match the governor from Montana, saying these crooks are lying. We didn't win that battle.

# ➤ BARRY RICHARD ◄

W hen the Bush campaign sought a lawyer to represent their interests in the Florida recount, Florida attorney Barry Richard stood at the top of a long list. Prior to the election controversy, Richard had represented everyone from the Republican Governor Jeb Bush to U.S. Senator Bill Nelson. Richard's experience in Florida ran deep and frequently crossed political boundaries. He successfully argued three cases in front of the U.S. Supreme Court and had appeared dozens of times before the Florida Supreme Court. In the mid-1970s, Richard was elected to the Florida legislature and later served as the state deputy attorney general. With Richard on board, the Bush team had gained an experienced attorney with a reputation as one of the state's leading constitutional lawyers.

Richard came to the Bush team with some political baggage. He had been a Democratic candidate for attorney general and that did not make everyone in the Republican camp happy. Because of his political affiliation, Richard believed that he did not enjoy complete support in the early days of the recount, commenting that there were "some who did not want to give a Democrat a high profile that might enable him to become a candidate for a higher office against a Republican." Despite these reservations, Richard's work for the Republicans proved instrumental in the election of George W. Bush.

In his interview, as the lead Florida attorney for Bush, Richard gave an astute, knowledgeable, and comprehensive analysis of the Bush legal strategy. Barry Richard indicated that he spoke with George W. Bush on only two occasions, and never about legal strategy. Except for some input from Ben Ginsberg and other attorneys, he called the shots. This scenario, according to Richard, was significantly different from the set-up of the Gore organization, in which Gore was apparently a hands-on candidate who made the final judgements on key issues.

Richard admitted that he would have worked for either side, but the Bush team called first and, after checking for conflicts of interest, he agreed to represent George W. Bush. Despite his experience, Richard found managing all 47 lawsuits simultaneously a daunting challenge. According to Richard, he felt like "these jugglers who spin plates on a stick and have to keep them all spinning." The stress did not bother Richard, who enjoyed the challenge. Logistics turned out to be the most difficult problem. "I was attempting to argue all of the actual arguments myself, largely by telephone." Often, after arguing a case in front of the judge, Richard excused himself, walked down a hallway and into another courtroom to argue another case. According to one observer, Richard had to perform a "marathon and a triathlon" at the same time.

Throughout the recount process, Republican operatives complained that the Florida State Supreme Court was a Democratic, liberal court and that it would almost certainly rule in favor of Gore. Richard, however, debunked the charge that the court was a bastion of liberal judges. He pointed to at least five court decision in which the Florida Supreme Court ruled against Gore. In a "number of decisions . . . the Florida Supreme Court . . . could have elected Gore president," but "they unanimously ruled against him. So I think the Florida Supreme Court received more criticism for being pro-Gore than they deserved." Indeed, Richard found all of the Florida courts to be fair in their judgments.

As the two sides fought in the Florida courts, time became a crucial enemy for the Gore team. Richard described the complex legal maneuvering in the race toward the December 12 "safe harbor" deadline. He thought the Gore legal advisors could have elected to go to the contest sooner, but Richard did not believe there was ever a route to a Gore victory. No matter what Gore's lawyers attempted, Richard believed the case was "still going to end up with the [U.S.] Supreme Court saying . . . the Fourteenth Amendment was violated."

Richard recalled that, over the 36 days of controversy, each side fought long and hard while accusing the other of hypocrisy and worse. In the end, Richard understood that both sides "were going to do everything that they thought was legal to elect their candidate President of the United States." The fight may have seemed political to the media, but Richard contended that from his perspective the issues were all legal. "There were no political agendas in what we were doing." The U.S. Supreme Court's 5-4 *Bush v. Gore* decision did not surprise Richard. The inconsistencies and the lack of a uniform standard found in the vote counting process across the state made this an "elementary Fourteenth Amendment equal-protection" case. "It was perfectly consistent with what the U.S. Supreme Court has always done." In Richard's eyes, "there was never a constitutional crisis, because at every stage of the game there was a mechanism to resolve an impasse."

As a former politician, Richard understood the nature of this contest. "Elections are a messy business; democracy is a messy business. This is an extraordinary illustration of how a complex society, [a] multifaceted society, can resolve its most fundamental disputes without anybody ever considering disregarding the system."

The author interviewed Barry Richard on October 10, 2002.

P:  Who contacted you first to be an attorney for the Bush legal team?

R:  Frank Jiminez, who was legal counsel to Governor Jeb Bush. At that point, I don't know if he was still in the governor's office. I know he took a leave of absence to work on his campaign. He called me about 7:30 in the morning on the day after the election.

P:  What was his general pitch to you?

R:  Would I like to represent George W. Bush in the anticipated litigation stemming from the race? I said, sure.

P:  If the Gore people had contacted you first, would you have gone to work for them?

R:  We had to run a conflict check with Bush. If there were no conflict, [and] then we had agreed on terms of engagement, I would have. Sure.

P:  Was your firm, Greenberg-Traurig, hired as well?

R:  The firm is always hired when individual members of the firm are hired. Over the course of this, not continuously, but [over the course] we had about 102 persons in the firm who worked on it. I don't remember the number of lawyers now, it seems to me it was 50-some . . . lawyers in and out of the case.

P:  That made it a lot simpler, in terms of plotting strategy and dividing up responsibilities, since you knew the people you were working with.

R:  Yes. They hired me, and then it was left to me to decide who in the firm would be on the team. I put together a structure which we added to as we needed it in various offices.

P:  So you were the one who was coordinating all the attorneys on the different cases?

R:  Yes, on the state cases.

P:  And Ted Olson was going to handle the federal appeals?

R:  Right.

P:  What was the substance of your initial meeting with Jim Baker and Ben Ginsberg?

R:  The meeting was actually with a roomful of people. It was probably 30 or more people in the room, among them, Ben Ginsberg and Secretary [Jim] Baker. George Terwilliger, I remember, was in the room, really everybody who was a key member. I went over to the campaign headquarters and was ushered into a large conference room . . . and [was] introduced around the table. I didn't meet Ted Olson until later that evening because . . . he arrived later. I just had a personal conversation with him.

P:  What was that meeting about, in general?

R:  They had already indicated to me that they wanted to engage me [as legal counsel]. It was largely a matter of their asking my opinions of the lawsuits that had already been filed. I think there had already been several filed in Palm Beach County. They asked my opinion of the probability of success of the butterfly ballot, which at that point was the major thing. They asked me for my opinion regarding the legal substance and the procedure and the strategy with respect to recounts. They asked me about the Florida courts, about my assessment of the different courts, federal [and] state.

P:  What was Ben Ginsberg's job during the recount?

R:  Ben was the overall coordinator of the recount activity, as far as I could tell, other than Jim Baker, who had . . . a day-to-day operating role. I think that Ben was, as I understand it, the general campaign counsel.

P:  Did you speak with your client, George W. Bush, at all during this time?

R:  Yes, but not with respect to the management of the cases or the strategy. I understand that Vice-President Gore had a very active role. George W. Bush did not. He called me three times. The first time was the night after the first Florida Supreme Court argument, when I had a relatively short participation, about five minutes. He called that evening to thank me. My wife answered the phone and she yelled across the kitchen, if this guy's for real, it's George W. Bush. [laughing] I took the phone, and it was him. He had called himself or at least he got on the phone before we answered it. He apologized for calling me at home in the evening . . . and thanked me. Said he thought I had done a good job. Then he asked me my assessment of the Florida Supreme Court, and the various strategic options that we had. It was a discussion that took about ten or fifteen minutes.

The second time he tried to call me was after one of the other televised arguments. I was in court all day, and he never did reach me that time, so we didn't talk. The third time was right after the rulings in the Seminole and Martin county cases, when I was in a room with several of the other lawyers. He called on somebody's cell phone and talked to all of us, thanked us.

P:  Did he talk at all about the possible involvement of the U.S. Supreme Court?

R:  There was no discussion of anything with regard to the U.S. Supreme Court.

P:  When did some of the outside lawyers come in, like Phil Beck and Fred Bartlit? Did you request them, or did Ben Ginsberg?

R:  It's easiest for me to give you a background so that you know how it developed up to that point. When I first met Ted Olson the evening of the 9th, Ted and I started working together on the case. He and I discussed the constitutional issues. We absolutely saw eye-to-eye. We both had the same reaction to things. I hope that Ted was as impressed with me as I was with him. I went home that evening and I said to my wife, you know, it's one thing to talk to somebody who understands all of the federal constitutional issues, but this guy can rattle the cases off. [He's] also a really nice person, very easy to deal with.

Either later that evening or the next morning, there was a session. The group had begun to split up. There was a group that was going to handle any briefing that was being done. There was, . . . what I consider, the political group. But there was a small group of people who were making the legal strategy decisions, and we had a meeting in which we were deciding whether or not we should file a lawsuit to stop the recounts from taking place. If so, where to file it, federal or state court. So the decision was made to file it in federal court, and Ted and I began working on the complaint. Shortly after that, the state cases mushroomed so rapidly that it became necessary for us to just go our separate ways. I undertook to manage all of the state cases. We would get three cases one day, nine the next day, twelve the next day. Ted actually went back to Washington to manage the federal stuff from there.

The question you had asked me was when lawyers were brought in. What happened was, they began to bring lawyers in from all over the country who were volunteering to help, but I didn't have much to do with them. A lot of them were housed at the headquarters in a big conference room, working on briefings. They were working 24 hours a day because briefs were . . . due everywhere all the time. I was unable to write a lot of them, so I would meet with the briefing team. We would talk about what direction would be taken, and then they would send me segments of briefs while I was sitting in hearings, and I would look at the briefs and send [them] back with my notes. So that was one group. Then I had my own group that I had put together in this office, and also, fortunately, we had an office every place that [there] was anything significant happening. We had to put lawyers at every canvassing board because the canvassing boards were meeting all day and having hearings.

Ben [Ginsberg] called me on my cell phone and said that he was concerned that the trial before Judge Sanders Sauls was quickly approaching, and that I was going to need more help because I was spreading my firm very thin. I had so many lawyers in so many places, and he thought it would be a good idea for him to bring in some additional, experienced lawyers. He knew I wasn't going to be able to be taking depositions and preparing witnesses. I told him I thought that was a great idea. As a matter of fact, I thought I had been doing a pretty efficient job of managing the cases. If there was one thing that I had not done a good job of, it was anticipating that crunch that was about to happen with the Sauls case, and it was fortunate that he said that. We did not meet again as a group until the night before the Sauls hearing. I think people who watched that trial thought we'd been working together as a team for the whole month, but we had only those two meetings. But that's how that developed.

P:  Overall you were involved in 47 different cases.

R:  Correct.

P:  How did you manage to keep all of them straight?

R:  Have you ever seen these jugglers who spin plates on sticks and have to keep them all spinning? Well, that's what it was like. I happen to like that. I would rather have 47 cases in 36 days than one case that goes for three years. I like a high-pressure situation. I like the organization and the management. The answer is that we put together a good structure, a good organization. I had good people working for me. I had a paralegal in this office who . . . created an Excel grid to keep track of every case. Every time there was a new filing, he would analyze it and he would bring me a summary of the filing, and it would go in the grid.

It's always difficult to have multiple lawyers handling multi-jurisdictional litigation on the same issues because the biggest problem is consistency. You run the risk that somebody's going to take a position in one court that's different from where you want to go. That's always a problem, but in this case it was a particularly acute problem because there was no time to train people. And because issues were coming up on the spot, there was no time for anything. Nobody had time to even read things. As soon as a case was filed, there would be an emergency hearing scheduled that afternoon or the next day, and there would be an order a day later.

So what I was doing in order to avoid the risk of inconsistency, I was attempting to argue all of the actual arguments myself, largely by telephone. One day I was arguing before Judge LaBarga from my office, and I had the associate, Sean Frasier, in another office holding another judge on the line. When I finished the argument with Judge LaBarga, I excused myself, went to the other one, and argued in there. So I did attempt to argue as much I could myself for that reason.

P:    Phil Beck said he'd seen lawyers do marathons and triathalons, [but] he'd never seen both at the same time.

R:    That was nice of Phil to say that. It felt like that at times, but it was fun.

P:    Who made the key calls on the legal strategy? Would you say it was Ginsberg or Baker?

R:    It was probably Baker, but you have to understand the way we were operating, which was substantially different than, I understand, the way the Gore team was operating. We didn't have very many strategy discussions. The campaign left it to me. We had an overall understanding of what the issues were that we were going to assert, and what the postures were we were going to take, but I was left to run the state show. I called Ben Ginsberg periodically to give him an update when something happened. Secretary Baker spoke with George W. Bush every day, and would call me. I would say I probably went over there every other day or so in the morning to give him an update, or I spoke to him on the phone, which he then would pass on to George W. Bush.

But we didn't have any discussions of what we're going to do in this case, when we're going to do it, and how we're going to do it. I did my cases. Ted Olson did his cases. The only real strategy session we had after that first one, that led to the filing of the federal case in Miami, was the night before the Sauls case where I met with George Terwilliger, [Fred] Bartlit, [Phil] Beck, and [Irv] Terrell, the lawyers who were involved in this, Daryl Bristow [as well]. We had discussed some of the strategy of the presentation of witnesses. The only other strategy decision that I recall, after the Eleventh Circuit granted *certiorari* and agreed to hear the appeal from Judge Middlebrooks in Miami *en banc*, [was] we made a decision not to assert the federal constitutional issues in any state court. That was a group decision. Other than that, we had no discussions.

P: Did you assume, at that point, that the dispute would end up in the U.S. Supreme Court?

R: The speculation [that] was the goal, and that's what we were assuming, is absolutely incorrect. We worked on the assumption that it was a long shot that we would ever get in the U.S. Supreme Court. But it was not so much the U.S. Supreme Court as the Eleventh Circuit. The Eleventh Circuit rapidly placed it on a fast track, and of their own volition agreed to hear it *en banc*, which as I'm sure you know, is extremely unusual to hear it *en banc* in the first instance, before they've had a panel at all. We were concerned about the fact that if we presented the federal issue to any state court, and it was adjudicated, that that would immediately divest the Eleventh Circuit of jurisdiction to address the same issue. The only route then would be if the U.S. Supreme Court would grant *certorari* if we didn't like the state result. So that's why we decided to reserve the federal issues.

P: Plus, the Eleventh Circuit was known as a fairly conservative court.

R: Well, it was a conservative court, but it was also another option for us if the state courts didn't go the way we wanted to. So regardless of whether we're conservative or not, I agree with you, but we wanted another option.

P: The first significant case was the Palm Beach County butterfly case before Judge LaBarga. Was that particular ballot invalid?

R: I thought that the ballot was valid. The law is pretty clear that the fact that a ballot might be confusing is not a sufficient reason to overturn the election. If the ballot had a name and then an arrow pointing to the wrong dot, so that the ballot was just erroneous and you would vote for the wrong person, it would have been an invalid ballot. But it didn't do that. The ballot was technically correct. So I thought we could uphold that ballot in court. But what I was concerned about is that these plaintiffs . . . had filed these suits, which, by the way, we felt that the Gore legal team supported and was probably assisting behind the scenes. They [the Gore legal team] were unable to help them overtly because they were taking this public stand that every vote should be counted, and those cases were seeking to throw out votes. So, they were unable to take it overtly, but we always believed that they were, if not coordinating, certainly strongly assisting them. What I was concerned about is that they wanted to put on a circus down there.

There were several things wrong with that. The first one was that we certainly didn't want to have that kind of a show in the hotbed of

Gore support and all of these people who were being whipped into a frenzy. But the second thing was, from a very personal standpoint, it was too critical for me not to handle it and I didn't want to be removed from the management of these cases by having to be stuck in Palm Beach County, and Ben Ginsberg didn't want me to. So our first goal was to try to head it off at the pass, which ultimately, we successfully did.

P:   I think Judge LaBarga decided there was no remedy, that you couldn't revote.

R:   This was interesting because this was the hearing with the packed courtroom when six judges recused themselves, and the chief judge kept . . . coming in and saying, well, I have to get somebody else. He said, I have only one judge left, and he's at lunch, so I'm going to have to ask you all to wait. It was Judge LaBarga, who, fortunately, had the courage to take the case and not be influenced by the public debate that was going on.

They were asking for a briefing schedule, for a discovery schedule. I asked Judge LaBarga to have a hearing first as to whether or not there was a remedy. I argued that one by telephone, and of course, he held there was no remedy and dismissed the case. So we never reached the issue of whether or not the ballot was valid. Ultimately, as I imagine you know, the Florida Supreme Court unanimously affirmed Judge LaBarga on the basis of the fact that without a hearing, they thought on its face the ballot was valid. So they would ultimately have reached that conclusion anyway.

By the way, and I want to digress from your schedule [of questions]: it was one of a number of decisions by the Florida Supreme Court that could have elected Gore president, in which they unanimously ruled against him. So I think the Florida Supreme Court received more criticism for being pro-Gore than they deserved.

P:   As a matter of fact, I have a copy of your article in the *National Law Journal*, in which you argued that on at least five decisions they voted against Gore.

R:   They were all critical. They all were decisions that would have made him president.

P:   One salient point: 96 percent of the people in Palm Beach County voted correctly. So when you are arguing about a confusing ballot, it seems difficult to make that case when only 4 percent appeared to be confused.

R:   You know, I think that the ballot could have been clearer. I don't know how many people were really confused, and how many people convinced themselves they were confused later because they didn't like the result. I heard a lot of people say, now that I think back, I think I voted for the wrong person. We know, everybody knows, that there was a much higher percentage of voters who voted for [Pat] Buchanan than made sense. Even Buchanan said that. So there's no question that there were people who voted for the wrong person. It very likely was because of that ballot.

I think we have to recognize that elections are a messy business. There probably has never been an election, certainly not an election on a statewide basis, where there haven't been errors, screw-ups, and confusion in a number of precincts. If we undid an election every time that happened, we would never have finality in our elections. The election law courts have always recognized that, and there's a fairly high hurdle you have to overcome. You can't simply say there were some people, some place, who were confused. This received more credence than it would have had we not been dealing with the President of the United States and such a close race, and everybody fighting tooth and nail with all of the legal talent they brought in. I think the Florida Supreme Court, when they made their final decision on the butterfly ballot, recognized the traditional law that there is a higher burden you have to overcome than just showing that the ballot's confusing and that a lot of people voted for the wrong candidate.

P: Judge Richard Posner said that the Democrats confused machine error with voter error.

R: I think that's correct. That's my point, I guess, when I say that the ballot itself was not erroneous.

P: In arguing against a recount in Palm Beach, I think you brought up a Louisiana case, the *Love* case. Louisiana held a separate election after the official date, and the court ruled that Louisiana could not hold a separate election since the Congress of the United States sets the date for elections.

R: Yes. Whether or not you can overturn an election, you couldn't overturn this one. It's not just that Congress selects the date, but that the election of the president, as with Congress, must take place in the entire country on the same day. I know the U.S. Supreme Court has never addressed this, but the law is quite clear that we all elect our members of Congress and the president on the same day. So you can't have another election. That was the basis for Judge LaBarga's decision dismissing the case.

What was interesting . . . was that in that case, as in the Seminole and Martin County cases, you won't see it if you look at the briefs of the main parties, but there was an *amicus* [*brief*] in that case that was arguing that you didn't need a new election. They had an expert witness who filed an affidavit and testified that statistically you could determine how many votes were remiss, how they would have broken between the two candidates had the people voted the way they wanted to, and you could reallocate the votes appropriately. They had a case from another state, I don't recall right now what state it was, where that methodology had been used in a local election. That's what they were arguing to Judge LaBarga, although he just ignored it. They argued that to Judges Clark and Lewis in the two county [Seminole and Martin] cases. They both rejected that as an option. By the way, if that had happened based upon that experts' testimony, Gore would have been president.

P:   Later on, Judge Jorge LaBarga allowed the Palm Beach Canvassing Board to begin a recount. Did you argue against that?

R:   No. The next strategic move they [Gore attorneys] made was to try to loosen up the standard that was being used. First, they went to Palm Beach County, and the canvassing board voted against doing that. ·Palm Beach continued to use a relatively conservative standard. So they tried and appealed to Judge LaBarga. In the first case before Judge LaBarga, he ordered that the canvassing board couldn't use a stringent formula like that. They were required to consider the totality of the circumstances [look at the chads and determine if they revealed the intent of the voter]. So when the canvassing board, under the chairmanship of Judge Burton, using the totality of the circumstances, still continued at a fairly conservative pace, they [Democrats] went back to Judge LaBarga.

It was at the second hearing that I personally went to Palm Beach County because it had become really critical at that stage. They were trying to get Judge LaBarga to order the canvassing board to use a more liberal standard. That's when I argued, and he refused to do that. That's when David Boies went to Broward County . . . and he convinced them to adopt a very liberal standard. The end result of these two things by the way, was what ultimately led to the U.S. Supreme Court's decision. It was just kind of interesting because he was successful in Broward County, but it was a pyrrhic victory.

The end result was that—my numbers might be off—the rate by which Palm Beach County was retrieving votes, in other words, they were picking up votes that had been rejected by the machine and counting them, was something like .002 percent. In Broward County, with the more liberal standard, it was 12 percent. Whatever the actual numbers were, the percentage by which Broward County was counting votes was 60 times the percentage in Palm Beach County.

P:   So this was a violation of the Fourteenth Amendment equal protection clause due to different standards?

R:   Exactly.

P:   Let's discuss Judge Donald Middlebrooks' decision. Who decided to file this emergency injunction in a federal court to halt the recounts?

R:   It was Jim Baker's decision. We were waiting, [and] he came in that evening and said let's file it. We had decided to file in federal court, that was a joint decision. It was my opinion that's where we needed to file. I thought we needed to file there for a number of reasons. One of them was it gave us a broader reach. If we had filed in state circuit courts, we would have had to file in every state circuit court where there was a recount taking place, whereas the federal court could reach all of them. The second reason was that we wanted to have another forum in case things didn't work out favorably in the state courts. They [Bush and Gore supporters] were involved in this battle of who would be the first to invoke the judicial side of the debate. It was Jim Baker who made that decision, I presume after he spoke to George W. [Bush].

P:   Who wrote the brief for the appeal of the Middlebrooks' decision?

R:   I believe that all the federal briefs were written in Ted's office in Washington. The briefing team that was working in the headquarters here was writing the state briefs. I was too involved in the cases and the management. I just was not very deeply involved in that.

P:   The reason I was asking was because this is the first time, at least in a brief, that there was a mention of Fourteenth Amendment, First Amendment rights, and a violation of Title 3 U.S. Code, 5. Was this an attempt to include all the salient points in the brief just to cover any constitutional issues that might come up later?

R:   Well, it was the first time. It was the first brief. It was the first case that was filed, and the answer is yes. We were going to cover all of the federal constitutional issues in that case to preserve them. My opinion was that there were two issues. I thought [the] First Amendment [argument] was weak: I thought the Fourteenth Amendment [argument] was strong; and I thought that the other issue, which was the sudden discovery of an obscure federal statute that had been passed in the 1870s, was a very interesting one.

P:   This is Electoral Count Act of 1877?

R:   The [act that established] safe harbor. But you know, that thing passed and was dormant, and nobody even knew it was there for all these years and then suddenly it came looming to the surface.

P:   Explain a little bit more about what the "safe harbor" means and whether or not there is, in fact, a specific date. Everybody talked about December 12. Boies accepted that date early on, and then, as the recount dragged on, he changed his mind. He said, well, it could be December 18.

R:   It was more than accepted . . . [by Gore's team]. They urged it upon the Florida Supreme Court. You look at . . . their first brief to the Florida Supreme Court, where they're urging the court to take it and put it on a fast track. They state in there, time is of the essence because this must be finally decided by December 12, or words to that effect.

     The answer to your question is that with respect to what it says, it says that if a state finally determines the makeup of its electoral college delegation, according to rules in existence prior to the election, that decision is set in stone and can't be monkeyed with by Congress. The constitution doesn't address what happens if there's a dispute as to which delegation is the proper one in the Electoral College. Anything that's not specified in the constitution is left to Congress to flesh out.

The constitution tells us very little about the details of what happens in this kind of a dispute. What happens is the constitution says that when a delegation is certified by a state, that certification goes to the archivist, who presents it to Congress. If there's more than one delegation certified by state officials purporting to have authority, then the archivist sends both of them to Congress, or however many there are, go to Congress. That's how Congress got into a bloody debate in 1876 that ended at 3:38 in the morning two days before the inauguration, and they were at an impasse. So they passed this law that said, now look, if a state finally decides it, . . . at least six days before the Electoral College is to meet, . . . then Congress can't monkey with that decision. Now the way it gets convoluted is . . ., it's not a mandate, they don't have to do it. But there's another provision of the constitution that says that the manner and time of elections leaves those issues to the state legislatures. The U.S. Supreme Court has construed that to be very specific. It doesn't mean the states; it means the state legislature. No other body in the state has the authority to monkey with that decision. So the question then becomes, is it the legislature's intent that the state abide by the Safe Harbor provision?

The way that this got interesting was, in the first appeal to the Florida Supreme Court, the Gore team argued to the Florida Supreme Court that Florida did want to abide by that. That's the reason that the Florida Supreme Court needed to take this immediately and put it on the fast track and order a recount. At that time, it served their [Gore attorneys] interests to take that position. In the first decision by the Florida Supreme Court, . . . the court says this must be decided by December 12, because that's what the Florida legislature intends. Later, when it no longer served their purpose, the Gore team reversed their position, but it didn't have a lot of credibility because they had taken the prior position. So all of the business that we all heard after the recount wasn't completed by the 12th, that we can go to the 18th, was just rhetoric. The fact is that every party, the Gore team, the Bush team, and the Florida Supreme Court, unanimously agreed that the 12th was the deadline.

P:  The Electoral Count Act also said that any controversy had to be settled by "judicial or other methods or procedures by December 12." Weren't the two candidates still in a controversial judicial procedure at that point?

R:  Yes, that's correct. But what the U.S. Supreme Court said in its final decision was, because we had not decided it by December 12, it was out of the state's hands. Here's what they said, and what I think was a well-reasoned opinion. First, we decide whether or not Florida intends December 12 to be the cutoff date for them to select their delegation. We looked to the Florida Supreme Court's decision, and they said yes, that the legislature made that decision. If the legislature had made that decision, then the courts can't change it any more, that's the deadline. December 12, to use their words, is upon us, therefore the courts cannot continue to meddle with it anymore, it's finished. So that was their judgment.

You can argue in any of these things from now until doomsday on both sides. I don't think you could take that judgment by the U.S. Supreme Court and say that [it was corrupt], as a number of writers have said. To say it was a corrupt decision is just completely unfair to that court. That decision can be sustained by any legal scholar. You can argue against it, but there's no basis for saying it's corrupt.

P: Joe Klock and Katherine Harris, on their own, filed a suit late one night with the Florida Supreme Court to stop the recount and to consolidate all the cases in Leon County. Why do you think they did that?

R: I don't know why they did it, but I can tell you an interesting sidelight to that. There was a lot of suggestion and speculation that Harris was a stalking horse for the Bush team, and that she was acting at the Bush team's behest or under its direction. From my perspective, I can tell you that was absolutely untrue. Our reaction, and when I say our, I mean the whole Bush legal team, was to raise our eyebrows when she did it. We were not happy about that . . . they never told us about it, we had no idea they were going to do it. We were not happy about it because we thought that it was not going to be successful, it muddied the waters, and we were concerned that it might invite statements from the [Florida] Supreme Court that would haunt us later. What it was doing, it was assuming a greater burden than we had to assume to win.

We never knew what that office was going to do. She was acting absolutely independently. In fact, the word that had gone out to our entire team was that nobody was to contact that office unless it was the lawyers on a strictly professional basis within the case. We were very nervous not only because we didn't want anybody suggesting that we were in cahoots, but because Katherine Harris was very independent and we didn't know how she would react if anybody tried to tell her how to do anything. So there was absolutely no communication between the two camps.

P: How would you assess Katherine Harriss's performance? Do you think she obeyed the law, or, as the Democrats charged, that she was partisan in favor of George W. Bush?

R: Well, I know this isn't the question you're asking, [but] she obviously was personally partisan. She was, as I recall, one of his [George W. Bush] campaign managers. I think she took a lot of abuse she didn't deserve. I think that what she did was clearly within the scope of the law. I can't imagine that their attitude was, we're going to do everything we can to elect George W. Bush and invite a reversal by the [Florida] Supreme Court. I think they were trying to do what was right. After Judge Lewis's first decision, which I thought was a very well–thought out decision, I think that they tried to abide by exactly what he said. I thought she was in a bad place at a bad time. Whoever was in that position would have taken that [abuse].

I don't think she was going to do anything to hurt him [Bush] if she didn't have to. Look, every person who has any political ideology who serves in public office, which is almost every person, if not every person, is going to have a desired result. Anytime any political person makes a decision, they can be accused by the side that doesn't like it of partisanship because that's what they would like the result to be. That's the law of physics. I don't know how you change that.

P:   You mentioned Judge Lewis's first decision, *Lewis I*. He said that Secretary Harris could go ahead and certify the votes if she used her discretion. Exactly what do you think he meant by that?

R:   First let me tell you that I think Judge Lewis is intellectually one of the brightest judges on the bench. He's very independent as a thinker. You can't assume that Judge Lewis is going to limit himself to what the lawyers on both sides tell him are his choices. He often doesn't, and this was one of those cases. His ultimate decision was not one of the options that either side gave him. I think what he said was pretty clear. He said that the statute imposed upon her the duty to exercise discretion in any given instance as to whether or not the date for submission should be changed. But what he said was, that she didn't read the law as giving her discretion, she read the law as being absolute. By doing that she had failed to perform the function the law imposed upon her, which was to exercise a judgmental decision. So he was returning it to her to reevaluate the situation, consider all the circumstances, and exercise her discretion.

She, in turn, I would guess with the help of the Steel Hector firm, did what I felt was pretty reasonable. They did an analysis of all of the cases addressing the question of when the date appropriately should or should not be changed, or anything that could indirectly affect that. Based upon those decisions, she arrived at a conclusion. They took that back to Lewis, and, of course, he said what you did is exactly what this statute says and what I told her. Again, we didn't know what she was going to do, but I thought that she would have no difficulty justifying what she did, and he basically said, it's your decision but you have to make a decision.

P:   Harris said that the only reason for a recount would be a hurricane or machine malfunction. Therefore, since that had not happened, there was no reason to accept recounted votes.

R:   That's correct. Let me tell you, by the way, that I think that interpretation of the statute is a very rational interpretation of it. These statutes as everybody knows, which were passed over a period of many years, are a mess. It was not a well-integrated statutory scheme.

P:   In *Lewis I*, Judge Lewis hinted that the Gore attorneys had another remedy, they could go directly to the contest. Why do you think that the Gore legal team did not choose that option?

R: I understand . . . , and I would be surprised if this were not true, that there was considerable amount of debate within the Gore camp as to whether or not they should go directly to the contest. I think they didn't do it because, like our team, nobody knew the consequences of what was happening. We had no road map here. I would think there probably were a number of concerns that they had. One of them might well have been what the end result would be. The problem is this: because the federal law says that the archivist must submit to Congress all of the delegations that have been certified, once she certified a Bush delegation it was going to Congress no matter what happened. So even if you had a recount in which the Florida Supreme Court said either Gore won and we are certifying the Gore delegation or instructed her to certify the Gore delegation, if it occurred after December 12 then you would have had two certifications to Congress. The law then says that both houses have to agree in order to select one [slate of electors]. I guess you could assume that there was a possibility that the Senate, which was close to being evenly divided, might have gone for Gore, particularly since he [as president of the Senate] would cast the deciding vote. But they didn't have a pipe dream that the House was going to do that. So the result was, the best that they could hope for at that point was a Congress that was split, which throws it to the governor of the state to make the decision, which is Jeb Bush. So for them to have allowed certification to take place for the Bush delegation was a dangerous game. Because then if it went one day past December 12, they were going to lose. It was out of everybody's hands.

The second [of the concerns] one may have been, which I think is an important one, just the psychology of the certification having taken place. What I was told, and I frankly am not being evasive but I don't remember who told me, by somebody in the Gore camp, was that Gore himself made that decision because he didn't want it to appear that he was bucking the tide of public opinion. Once the certification had . . . tak[en] place, he would be cast in the position of a rogue who was trying to beat the system. The only thing that favored their going the contest route was time. That, of course, is a very important element. In retrospect, we can look back and say they would have been better off if they had done that, but we don't know that. I mean, the analogy I used in a speech I gave was that this was like we were all on a high-speed sailboat race in high seas in the middle of the storm, and we couldn't see over the next wave. So we were making snap decisions as best we could with very little to go on. Nobody knew how these things were going to be construed.

P: Plus, they had gotten some votes in the protest phase and had narrowed Bush's lead.

R: Yes. They were fighting two things. They were fighting time and they didn't want to end up in the state legislature, before the state governor, or before Congress. They wanted this decided by the state courts, which meant that it really had to be decided by December 12.

P:   Dexter Douglass told me that he thought they should have gone to the contest right away because then the judges would be counting the votes. He stated that Gore and his advisors didn't always heed the advice of their Florida lawyers.

R:   Dexter has told me that. I have very high regard for Dexter and I can't dispute that. In retrospect, you can look at it and say, well, Dexter was probably right. But then, we don't know what would have happened if they had gone that route. So it's difficult to criticize any of the judgments that were made as a Monday morning quarterback. I don't know. If they had gone the contest route immediately, they would have saved, I think I counted, 19 days. Theoretically at least, but they didn't know how the courts were going to rule on that.

At the same time that the litigation was going on, there was a press conference battle going on between Baker and [Christopher and Bill Daley]. You could say, what are they doing?, the election is over. But the fact is that both sides were playing to public opinion because of the belief that public opinion could sway Gore's willingness to continue. I can tell you the Bush camp believed that if public opinion got tired enough of this, Gore was always subject to influence from Congress, and if he began to lose enough support in Congress and was pressured enough, he would have to get out to save any chance of a future run for the presidency.

P:   So he wouldn't be a sore loser?

R:   Well, he has to keep the support of the Democratic Congress, the people he's going to have to turn to, and the party, in order to get another nomination. We know that it reached a point where there was an increasing number of Democratic politicians who were becoming disenchanted with it. It was a continuing effort by the Republicans to increase the pressure on Gore to get out. Gore was making a continuing effort to shore up his support. I think that influenced a lot of the decisions, including the decision as to whether to go the contest. Their core argument [was that] the choice of the people has been defeated. I think they felt that, if it turned out that they could show a sufficiently overwhelming vote in Florida for Gore, the public opinion outcry would be so great that the Republicans would have to give in.

P:   What if Gore, in the protest phase, had somehow taken the lead, in terms of the votes? How would that have changed the strategy on both sides?

R:   I don't know. Some of it has to do with when he took the lead. If he had taken the lead before December 12, and the count had been fully completed. I still don't know that it would have made a difference. You were still going to end up with the U.S. Supreme Court saying the standards were different, and, therefore, the Fourteenth Amendment was violated. So the only way he could have done it is if the Florida Supreme Court had adopted standards and sent it back [to the U.S. Supreme Court]. But then you ran the risk that the U.S. Supreme Court would have said, you've changed the rules after the election, and, therefore, you still don't get the safe harbor. As a matter of fact, they kind of hinted at that in the U.S. Supreme Court's first decision where they said, you'd better be careful, because if you change the rules it's going to change things.

P: Didn't both Justice Antonin Scalia and Justice Sandra Day O'Conner indicate that? That point of view was in the remand.

R: That was in the first remand, correct. That paragraph, I guarantee you, had a lot of scrutiny from both camps when they made those comments. I don't know whether there was any scenario, in retrospect, by which Gore could have won. Because if you go back and plotted from any direction—we didn't know it at the time, of course— he ends up with a difficult problem. If you look at everything that ultimately happened, what it teaches us is, it might not have been possible, under the Florida statutory scheme, as it existed, for him to have done it.

P: Almost everyone I have talked to said that the Republicans won the public relations contest, particularly because Jim Baker was very effective in his presentations, saying the votes have been counted, counted again, recounted. But I did notice very early on, in one of his press conferences after one of the unfavorable Florida Supreme Court decisions, he was fulminating against an activist Florida Supreme Court. But I didn't hear those comments after the U.S. Supreme Court decision in *Bush v. Gore*. Is there a touch of hypocrisy there?

R: I wouldn't call anybody hypocrites in this thing. What we were dealing with here, despite the rhetoric, was two men who wanted to be President of the United States. Fortunately, . . . we live in a country where we abide by the law, [and] they were going . . . to play all the hands they had available to them that were legal and ethical.

As I indicated in an article that I wrote, I don't really think it's fair to call the U.S. Supreme Court's decision activist. In my mind, it was perfectly consistent with what the U.S. Supreme Court has always done in these types of election cases, contrary to what other people have argued. I don't know that "activist" is the word I would use for the Florida Supreme Court. I think that the majority of the Florida Supreme Court rendered what I would call a populist opinion. They had earlier case law, in which they had said that ensuring that people get to make a choice takes precedence over a super technical interpretation of the statutes. This was consistent with those decisions. Those people who don't believe that the court should stray very far from the letter of the law will say that's activist.

In terms of the political commentary, I stayed out of it. In my first meeting with Secretary Baker, he asked me to go with him to the first press conference, and I made a request of him that he keep me out of the political fray. I said, I am happy to address the legal issues that are pending or that we are intending to advance, but I will not make political statements.

P: I failed to ask you about Judge Don Middlebrooks's decision, in which he said that this was essentially a state issue. He also said, and I paraphrase, well, of course there are different standards, there are 67 different counties, that's the way it has always been. The court presumed that the canvassing boards made competent decisions and they did not abuse their discretion. What was your reaction to the Middlebrooks decision?

R: Well, you know, I'm an advocate, so I could argue either side. The one I would have made in this case and, frankly, [it] is the easier argument to make because I think it's more accurate. You can say that, if you're dealing with a local election, it makes no difference if every county has a different standard for counting votes in the election of its county officials. But we're dealing with the selection of the President of the United States, same as a U.S. Senator, [and] every person in this state has to have an equally weighted vote. That's the essence of the Fourteenth Amendment. If the U.S. Supreme Court hasn't said that previously, I think that they needed to say it. Because if that's not what the Fourteenth Amendment is all about, I don't know what it is. Now, when you have a situation in which the voters of Broward County have 60 times the percentage of chance that their rejected vote will be counted over those in Palm Beach County, then you are [not] giving the voters for one candidate . . . equal treatment under the law. To me, that's elementary Fourteenth Amendment, equal protection of the law. So I think it's perfectly sustainable.

P: Who wrote the brief for the November 20 hearing before the Florida Supreme Court? That was the hearing where Michael Carvin, I think, presented the majority of the argument, and you spoke briefly.

R: Instead of answering the question you asked me, if you will permit me, I'll tell you how it happened. You asked me also about the brief. The brief was a joint effort, like all of our briefs. It was being written by a briefing team over at the headquarters. By the end of the week before, by Friday, David Boies and I had begun to get so much publicity, and the press had begun to portray this as a Boies-Richard battle, that the assumption that was being made by the press generally was that Boies and I would be doing the arguments. The assumption that was being made on our team was that I would be doing the argument.

I told my wife on Saturday evening that I was not convinced that they were going to let me do the argument. She asked, why? I told her there were a few reasons. One of them was that I was a Democrat. People who do this, politically, think very politically. They always want to know . . . the political affiliation of the governor . . . who appointed every judge. They retained me because I had . . . ended up doing a lot of representation of prominent Republicans in Florida, including Jeb Bush. They [Republicans in Florida] urged that they retain me. But I think there wasn't a high comfort level with the fact that I was a Democrat, and I suspect that there were some who didn't want to give a Democrat a high profile that might enable him to become a candidate for a higher office against a Republican. Added to that was the fact that I was an outsider with a close group of Washington lawyers who had worked together for many years: Mike [Carvin], Ben [Ginsberg], and George [Terwilliger]. They all had been part of the Bush team from day one. Ginsberg had very little experience with me and had never seen me in a courtroom. He had a high comfort level with Mike.

I was over here preparing for the argument on Sunday morning and I got a call from Ben [Ginsberg]. He said, I'm coming over to your office. He had never come to the office before, so I knew he was coming over to tell me that he wanted somebody else to do the argument, which he did. He asked how I felt about it. I said, well, obviously, anybody in my position wants to do the argument. It's going to be a little embarrassing for me that I'm not going to do it since the media has been [assuming that I would]. We're going to have to be prepared to explain it to them, but you're the client, it's your decision. Of course, my wife was very upset. My partners were very upset.

I think [Mike] Carvin was put in a very difficult position because he had not been . . . preparing for it. It was a no-win [situation] for him because he could only be criticized. He became very agitated over the preparation. He was up practically all night the night before. It just put him in a very tough situation.

P:    Partly because he was not a Florida lawyer.

R:    [He] wasn't a Florida lawyer, [he] didn't know the court. I just accepted it. Monday morning . . . I started thinking, there's no reason for me to give up on this altogether. Mike was sitting at this table when I got in, going through his notes. I said to him, what would you think of my taking a small role? Because this is my turf, this is a court that I'm familiar with, they're familiar with me, and we should have [a] Florida lawyer up there arguing. He said, well, I'm very comfortable with that. I can't give you more than five minutes because of the way I've structured my argument, and that would be fine with me, but I can't make that decision. So George Terwilliger and Ben [Ginsberg] . . . came in this conference room. There was a conference that went on with a long distance call for about . . . 30 to 40 minutes. I have no idea what went on in that call. That's one of the things that made me suspect that there were some people who felt uncomfortable, politically. But they decided to give me five minutes, which we informed the court of. That's what catapulted me into a more prominent position.

P:    Explain the argument that you and Carvin made before the Florida Supreme Court.

R: Mike [Carvin] had a very rough time. The court was merciless with him. I counted the number of questions, at one point, from the transcript. I can't remember exactly, but it was something like 43 questions that he got. We had a half an hour, so in 25 minutes he had about 43 questions. He became hopelessly entangled in the defense of statutory construction. He was arguing the minutiae of statutory construction against Boies [who was] arguing a high-principled argument about letting the people vote. It was a disaster in terms of appealing to any high court. You never want to have the other side appealing on high principle and you are talking about minutiae, which was not Mike's fault.

P: What did you think of the Florida Supreme Court's 7-0 decision in *Palm Beach County Canvassing Board v. Harris?* Where did that November 26 deadline come from?

R: Fortunately, we had decided to . . . break from Carvin to me. I think, first, because they had vented on Carvin, and, second, because I have a long history. Some reporter asked me [and] I counted, I had been before the court 60 some-odd times. Not these same justices, but I'm over there a lot. I think they were giving me some slack. They allowed me to, basically, get the issues out before they started on me. So I was able to articulate a little bit of a principled posture, which is "separation of powers" and "this is the job of the legislature." Having done that, they obviously rejected that. I was not as disturbed, or as disappointed, in the first opinion as I was in the second one.

After that decision, my feeling was that they had simply come down on the side of what they saw as a principle over a super-technical interpretation. They were basically consistent with earlier decisions in which they said the election laws and their dates are directory and they are subject to modification when the circumstance is justified. The overriding issue is, can the public be given the maximum opportunity to be heard without doing undue damage to the system? That was the basic philosophy. If you accept that philosophy, then that's it.

P: When they changed the deadline date to November 26, did you, at that point, assume that they were making law rather than interpreting law?

R: Well, I thought they were making law when they didn't accept the statute for what it said, but once they said, we don't consider the date to be mandatory, then, after that, it's like I said to them when I was arguing, any date is going to be arbitrary. The question is, who gets to choose the arbitrary date, you [the court] or the legislature? So once they said, we get to choose it, it doesn't matter. The way they got to the 26th [of November], as I recall, was that they began by accepting December 12th as the deadline, because the Florida legislature wanted us to have the safe harbor, and then they counted backwards to the latest date at which, according to the supervisors, there would still be time to get the ballots out and meet the December 12 date. That's how they came up with that date.

P: Discuss Gore's appeal of the contest before Judge Sanders Sauls. How did you react to Judge Sauls hearing the case? When the Democrats discovered it was Sauls, at least one lawyer was very upset and thought he was the worst judge they could have gotten.

R: You know something, these people are all funny. When you talk about Democrats, you've got to distinguish between the lawyers and the political camp. When we got Judge [Nikki] Clark, the Republican camp thought it was the worst judge they could have gotten. She fit the demographic groups that had gone strongly for Gore, and, two weeks earlier, she'd been passed over by Jeb Bush for elevation to the appellate bench, so, to them, it was a horror. It turned out she was a great judge.

P: Which you already knew.

R: Yes. The only two documents in all of the litigation without my signature on them were the two motions to recuse her, because I refused to do it. But I digressed from your question. Dexter Douglass, who has a long, personal, friendly relationship with Judge Sauls, I think he considered Sauls to be a more conservative judge than they might have gotten, but I doubt that he felt seriously concerned about it.

P: How did you feel about Judge Sauls getting the case?

R: Well, first of all, I don't react, and I don't think most trial lawyers react the same way that political people react to a judge. It doesn't matter to me whether a judge is what you might call conservative or liberal. What matters more to me is the judge's intelligence and the extent to which he feels free to deviate from statutory language. I've been before Judge Sauls many times. I don't perceive Judge Sauls to rule on cases based upon whether he's a social conservative or liberal. The other thing about Judge Sauls is, I think he's a pretty bright guy. People who don't know him will perceive him, sometimes, as being a country bumpkin. I didn't mind when Judge Sauls got the case. I didn't have any read on him. I didn't know whether he was a Republican or a Democrat. I didn't know how he felt about national politics. My experience with Judge Sauls, over the years, has been that he calls them like he sees them.

  You know, if you go by the liberal/conservative attitude, they [Democrats] probably would have felt pretty good with Judges Lewis and Clark, who both ruled against them [and] gave them some of the worst rulings that they had. So I don't think you can call judges on that basis, and I didn't. I thought that Judge Sauls would do a good job on the case, and he did. [H]e kept it moving. Of course, they didn't put on much of a case, because . . . they were in a big hurry. We were surprised at the limited extent of their case because we didn't realize what their game plan was, which was to get out of that level as fast as they could.

P: What was your reaction to the Gore team's request to bring the disputed votes from Dade and Palm Beach county to Tallahassee. I don't know whether it was you or another member of the Bush team who said, if we're going to bring any of them, we're going to bring all of them. What was your thinking behind that decision?

R:    I know the media kept looking for ulterior motives. Their theory was that we were trying to delay the case as much as possible. Of course, the Bush camp wanted to see the case move slowly because they wanted to get past the December 12 date, but delaying the case was not an element of the legal team's management of the case. First of all, it's not the way that I do business, and, second, we weren't going to be given the ability to do that anyway. Any effort that we made to do that was going to . . . irritate the judge.

    For example, [David] Boies . . . was arguing to Judge Sauls [that] we should begin the counting immediately. I said to Judge Sauls, he's asking for the remedy before he proves he has a case. I was trying to make the point that they had a burden to overcome before they had a right to count anything. That was a very critical distinction between the two of us. So that's why I didn't want them to start counting, not because I was trying to delay them, although I'm sure my client was perfectly happy with that result.

    I don't know if you saw that argument, but at one point I got up and got very animated. People asked me later whether I lost my temper or not. I never lose my temper in court, but sometimes it doesn't hurt to look like you're losing your temper. I was sitting there practically falling asleep, and I was watching Boies. Judge Sauls made a ruling, and then Boies tried it from another approach, and Sauls made a ruling [against Boies]. [I] got very animated and said to Judge Sauls, three times you've ruled and three times he's ignored you. I remember Sauls said, alright, let's all calm down.

P:    What about the use of expert witnesses before Judge Sauls? Phil Beck just totally embarrassed Nicholas Hengartner, and then Steve Zack did almost the same thing with John Ahmann. It appeared to me that the use of expert witnesses had very little to do with this case.

R:    Experts are always the risks for lawyers. They're the biggest risk, I think, generally, of any witness. I don't ever like experts. You have to use them. I don't like them because they're a risk and because it's problematic what their value is going to be anyway, when they're both just disagreeing with each other. I also believe that every time you put a witness on the stand, you take a risk. That's why [after] one of the few strategic discussions we had, we had several more witnesses that we didn't use. I was vigorously opposed to using them because I said every time we put one on the stand we run the risk, which we encountered with our expert [Ahmann].

P:    In your presentation before Judge Sauls, you argued that the Florida Supreme Court had already ruled that the recount was up to the discretion of the canvassing boards. Then you contended that the canvassing boards had not, in any way, abused their discretion, therefore, Boies did not meet the burden of proof.

R: That's correct. What happened was, Boies was trying to argue that the two things, the protest and the contest, were entirely disconnected and that it didn't make any difference what the canvassing board did, [that] you started with a clean slate when you went to the contest. I was arguing that made no sense—why would the legislature have done that?—and that it was inconsistent with the absolutely long-established principle that, when an administrative agency [a canvassing board] is charged with a fact-finding function, that has a presumption of correctness, and you've got to overcome it.

P: As I understand it, if you recount under the contest, you are supposed to count all the votes, not just the disputed votes or the undervotes.

R: Right.

P: Obviously, you were pleased with Judge Sauls's opinion.

R: [He] adopted everything I said. That opinion was a slam dunk for me. I was thrilled with it.

P: Judge Sauls also indicated that the law said there had to be a probability that the outcome would be changed by a recount, as opposed to a possibility. What Boies argued was, well, how can he tell? He didn't count the votes.

R: The statutes were not written for this kind of a race. They were written for local races. The big case that they were relying on . . . was an old, old case, that said the judge has to look at the evidence and the evidence is the votes. That case involved like 25 ballots total. It had no relationship at all to state-wide hundreds of thousands of votes.

Any election lawyer who's ever challenged an election knows, you have to show that there is evidence that enough ballots were affected. Generally what happens is the court will say there were 1,500 votes that were not counted that should have been [counted], and the election was decided by 1,220 votes, and, therefore, we have to do it over again because it could have changed the election. The argument we were making here is, there was no proof of anything. Judge Sauls did say a substantial probability, and the Supreme Court said, that's the wrong rule, it should be a possibility that it would have affected it, but my argument was, it doesn't make any difference because they proved nothing. All they did was bring in an expert to say, these are the problems that could occur, you could have a pile-up of chads. They didn't bring in a single person to say that a single machine didn't work right anywhere, much less show that there were enough votes that would have made a difference. [T]he argument I made to Sauls was, if this is enough, then you have to have an automatic, court-supervised [count]; the judge will have to count every vote in every election.

P: In other words, I think you said that in that case you could just do away with the canvassing boards and let judges do all the counting.

R: That was my point.

P: Judge Burton testified before Judge Sauls and I assume your purpose in getting him up there was for him to inform Sauls that the Palm Beach County Canvassing Board had, in fact, very carefully considered all of the votes. Therefore, they had not abused their discretion.

R: I put him on there for two reasons, [and] that was one. The other one was [that] I wanted the judge [Sauls] to know how difficult the task is. What we were talking about was not something that a judge was going to be able to do any easier than the canvassing board did. I wanted him to understand that this is very subjective and that this wasn't a matter of a judge looking at it and seeing what it was.

P: One of the criticisms of the Democrats, as we discussed earlier, was that Gore continued to make political decisions as opposed to legal decisions, whereas the Republicans, on most occasions, were making legal decisions. In the end, it was a legal contest, not a political contest.

R: Yes. I do know that Gore, because I've been told by the Gore people, as well as read [about it], that Gore was in constant touch with his legal people and was involved in every decision. [O]nce they gained a degree of confidence, they [Bush team] didn't tell me what to do, they didn't ask me what I was doing, they didn't tell me how to do it. They basically set me free to run the state cases and they set Ted [Olson] free to run his cases. There were no political agendas in what we were doing.

P: Let's talk about your presentation to the Florida Supreme Court prior to their 4-3 decision in *Gore v. Harris*. In the beginning of the hearing, Justice Charlie Wells asked if the Florida Supreme Court had jurisdiction over the case of *Gore v. Harris*. There seemed to be some controversy about this.

R: The argument that would be made was that the U.S. constitution says the state legislatures shall set up the rules for elections, and that when you read this statute, the Florida Statute, it says that challenges, contests, shall be submitted to the circuit court for determination. So the argument is that because the legislature just said "circuit court," that therefore, no other court had jurisdiction. That once the circuit court, Judge Sauls, made his decision, they didn't have any jurisdiction. That's the question that he [Justice Wells] posed to me. My answer was, I do think you have limited appellate jurisdiction. I said limited because I thought the only jurisdiction they had was to determine whether or not he had abused his discretion, and no more than that.

P: Did you expect this issue to be raised?

R: No, but one of the reasons I do what I do and I enjoy it, is because I always [am ready]. You have got to have such a thorough picture in your mind at every moment of exactly what your case is, and exactly where everything falls into place, that you don't need a lot of time. You don't have time before an appellate court to figure [it] out.

So I knew what was happening when he asked me that question. First of all, I didn't believe that they were without jurisdiction, and it's always dangerous to argue from a position that you don't believe is accurate. Second, I didn't believe there was any way in creation they were ever going to say they didn't have jurisdiction. If I had answered that, I guarantee you, if I had said no, I never would have gone to another issue. I would have spent the rest of the argument exactly where Carvin was, being peppered with questions from that court about their jurisdiction. That would have been the end of the discussion, and they would have ended up saying they had it.

P: Although there was a Republican brief that was presented that held the Florida Supreme Court did not have jurisdiction.

R: Well, that's another issue which we got slammed on. It was embarrassing for me. You do not [change] when you are standing up in the middle of an argument and you have a well-conceived, defensible position. It's like you're out there after a shipwreck. You have a nice, sturdy life saver and you see some flotsam floating by. You say, hey that looks pretty good, I'm going to abandon this and I'm going to jump over there. But to do that I would have had to abandon some much more secure positions, and I wasn't prepared to do that without thinking it out. The third thing was, I still had Martin and Seminole Counties sitting out there waiting for a decision. Now, what if I had gotten the court to say, whatever the circuit court does is law, and either one of those judges had ruled against me, and Gore would have been president. Then, how was I going to say that they were subject to an appeal? So it just made no sense for me to have said [to the court], you have no jurisdiction.

P: You were very quick on your feet to be able to think in those terms.

R: Yes. Well, I wasn't unfamiliar with that issue. It was not something I thought I was going to have to tackle. The other thing is, I don't buy the argument, that's what the legislature meant. We've got lots of statutes that say that the circuit court has jurisdiction over something; that doesn't mean it's the only court. The circuit court is part of an integrated system in Florida in which the Supreme Court can do anything.

What happened was, after we made it, there were people in the Bush camp [who were] twitching . . ., hey, hey, he gave us an opening. We got to make that argument; we got to make that argument [that the Florida Supreme Court did not have jurisdiction]. They wanted to do it, and they were going to do it. But it was a mistake, and we got slammed in that footnote. I was never happy with it, and I think it was wrong.

P: I talked to Kendall Coffey not too long ago, and he said you established great credibility when you agreed that the court had limited jurisdiction. Also in a personal aside, he said he thought it was a good example of honest lawyering.

R:    Well, I'm flattered. But he makes an interesting point there. One of the reporters, I think, for *Newsweek*, told me that he interviewed all the judges and asked them about all the lawyers. He said he found it interesting that two of the judges, Clark and Lewis, both had the same comment about me, which was that one of the things they liked about my arguments is that I was never reluctant to concede issues. I think Coffey is right. There's nothing that gives you greater credibility than the willingness to concede an issue; [it] also gives you a greater air of confidence in your own case. But you have to know when you can concede it without undermining your case.

P:    Also Coffey said the very fact that you got three votes in this decision, the 4-3 decision, really helped the U.S. Supreme Court in their 5-4 decision. Had it been 7-0, he argued, that would have made it much more difficult for the U.S. Supreme Court to overturn the Florida Supreme Court.

R:    I absolutely agree with him. What's more, I think the very vigorous dissents, particularly Wells's, but the two dissents, helped them. I thought that made it much easier for them to do that. Wells was angry. I think it was probably the strongest dissent in the history of that court.

P:    In your presentation before the Florida Supreme Court, most of the tough questions came from Justices Anstead and Pariente. I think the question Anstead and Pariente were trying to pose was, if you can count the undervotes in Palm Beach and Broward, why can't you count all the undervotes across the state? Of course, that's eventually what they decided to do. Did you sense, at that point, that you were going to lose this case?

R:    It seemed pretty clear that Pariente was tending to be more favorable to their [the Gore team's] case. Quince, to a lesser extent, but Quince seemed like she pretty much was [favoring the Gore team]. Anstead is difficult to read because Anstead is tough on lawyers, that is his approach. I thought that Lewis was undecided. I felt that Wells and Harding seemed to be positioning themselves pretty much for me. I will tell you that . . . we thought we were going to win it. The debate was whether it was going to be 4-3 or 5-2, not whether we were going to lose.

P:    Evaluate the 4-3 decision that reversed Judge Sauls. Hand tabulate 9,000 votes in Miami–Dade. Include the 215 Palm Beach votes and 168 Miami–Dade votes for Gore. Then count all the undervotes in the state. Why would they count just the undervotes?

R:    I don't know.

P:    Time?

R:    Well, I think the reason was time. I think they thought that it would be impossible to do all of it, but I don't know. The reason that it was difficult wasn't just because of the number of votes, but because they had to find the votes. They had no methodology, in most of the circuits, for culling the rejected votes, the undervotes and overvotes, out of the total. I don't think they would have made it anyway.

P: If the Florida Supreme Court had set a standard, would that have improved their decision in the eyes of the U.S. Supreme court?

R: It's hard to say. Obviously, they [Gore's lawyers] couldn't have won it without a standard. If they had set standards, then that raises the second issue, which is that they changed the rules after the election.

P: David Boies said it was Catch-22.

R: He's absolutely right.

P: Let me ask you about the Seminole and Martin County cases, which were initially under the media radar but were crucial, because if Gore had prevailed in either case, he would have won the presidency. One election expert held that they violated state election law because once these documents were in their possession, then no one else had the right to add or delete anything from these documents. How did you deal with that issue?

R: Well, we already had the Supreme Court saying that you don't give a super-technical interpretation, especially when it's going to result in denying a person the right to vote. My argument was, they haven't really suggested that there's anything wrong with it. It would be one thing if we were dealing with ballots, but all we were talking about was applications. There was no evidence that any ballot was not a correct statement of what the voter wanted to do or that anybody voted twice or anything like that. It was truly technical. It didn't jeopardize the vote. They kept talking about, this was such a horrible thing, you let somebody in there. But there were no ballots there at the time, so there was nothing to jeopardize.

The second thing was, this was not something out of the blue. It had been done traditionally by supervisors. There was a time when that number was not even on the applications. The argument was made, at one point, you did it for the Republicans but not for the Democrats. My response was, [that's] because the Democrats didn't screw up. The Democrats had the numbers printed on all of them. It was only the Republican ballots that were a screw up. I really do think that was a tempest in a teapot. The problem was though, that if you had a judge who had ruled for them, and the Florida Supreme Court wanted to, they could easily have said, we're throwing those [votes] out.

P: Peggy Robbins, the Elections Supervisor in Martin County, allowed Republicans to take the documents outside her office. That act could be considered as not only a violation of election law, but also a violation of public records law.

R: Maybe it was a violation, but it was not something that should result in people's votes being [thrown out]. There is a body of case law that says that if there is an error by an election official, that the innocent voter shouldn't be punished because of it. So essentially what they'd be saying here is, there's no evidence that any votes were miscounted, but because the supervisor's office screwed up, let's punish these voters by not letting them vote. Which is just blatantly contrary to a very clear line of cases.

P: The circuit court staggered their hearings on the two cases which were heard at the same time. Judge Lewis was hearing the Martin County case, and Judge Clark was hearing the Seminole County case. They alternated times partly to accommodate you. Is that correct?

R: What happened was, the first day, he [Judge Lewis] started early in the morning and went from 8:00 to like 10:00. Then, she [Judge Clark] picked up there and went until about 7:00 at night. Then, he picked up at 8:00 and went most of the night.

P: Did you use the same arguments in both cases?

R: Yes.

P: Were you surprised by the decisions?

R: Not at all. I felt it was the right decision. Both those judges are very sharp judges, and I was very confident that's how they were going to rule. I wasn't surprised at all. I would have been very surprised if they had gone another way.

P: Did you expect the U.S. Supreme Court to grant *certiorari* on Bush's appeal?

R: I think every lawyer who has done U.S. Supreme Court practice is surprised when they grant *certiorari* in anything. But not particularly, . . . they took it on the equal protection [clause], which seven of the justices expressed concern over.

P: In the very first Republican brief before Judge Middlebrooks, you find the Fourteenth Amendment argument. You do not hear about it again until the *Bush v. Gore* 5-4 decision. Why?

R: That's because we took it off the table. As a matter of fact, Carvin, when he was asked a question by the Florida Supreme Court, said, we are not making that argument before this court. He was very clear about it. It was not in our brief. Because again, we didn't know that the U.S. Supreme Court was going to take the case. We knew the Eleventh Circuit had it, and we didn't want to divest the Eleventh Circuit of jurisdiction.

P: Some people argued that it was unusual for the Rehnquist court to make a judgment based on the Fourteenth Amendment.

R: I don't think there was probably any justice on the Florida or the U.S. Supreme Court who wouldn't have been perfectly happy to stay out of this battle. The U.S. Supreme Court has traditionally stepped in when there has been a significant dispute between the other branches of government, or between the states and the federal government, that really requires their attention. They have not hesitated. It's true that they have stayed away from election cases, but you're not talking about election cases of this magnitude, involving issues that go to the foundation of this system. They've never shied away from those kinds of cases. You can't take a case like that and say, well, they don't traditionally get involved in this . . . , but this particular court never had a case of this magnitude involving a state election before. This was not a state election, it was a national election. I think, if the U.S. Supreme Court had refused to step into this case, it would be criticized historically in future years as being a lack of courage on their part to look at the case. I think the U.S. Supreme Court would have stepped in no matter which way it had come to them.

I think the more important issue is just the fact that this involved fundamental issues. It involved every branch of government and both levels of government. It was as fundamental as you can get. I think that's when the U.S. Supreme Court should be heard. Again, I think if this had come the other way, if the ruling in the Florida Supreme Court had been for [George W.] Bush, they still would have taken the case. I really, truly believe that. They were not going to remain on the sidelines. Everybody has a sense of history when they sit on the U.S. Supreme Court, and nobody wants history to look back and say they didn't have courage to take a stand in this thing. I also dispute the argument that they don't get involved in election cases. In my article I gave a whole list of major cases that they've decided that were election cases.

The real decision by the five [justices] was to end the drama. I think that's true because I think, by that time, that really was the issue. I think they must have known that if they let this go on it wasn't going to be decided by the 12th. It was going to Congress. It was going to be a donnybrook in Congress. I'm sure that affected their decision. It was clear to me, and, I think, probably to the Gore camp, by the time the Florida Supreme Court decided, that the likelihood that there was any scenario by which Gore would become president was practically nonexistent.

P:   Justice Breyer, in his dissent, said that what he wanted to do was remand it back to the Florida Supreme Court. He said there was time to go ahead and finish the count because he was not counting December 12 as the final date. Did that opinion have any validity at all?

R:   I didn't agree with his conclusion that December 12 didn't matter. It's like I said, everybody agreed early in the case that December 12 was the drop-dead deadline date in Florida. I read what he said, but I don't know what the foundation was for that.

P:   Justice John Paul Stevens had a very strong dissent. He thought that the court should not have taken the case in the first place. He argued that the decision was wholly without merit and was going to undermine the confidence of the public in the Supreme Court. Do you think that has happened?

R:   No, and I have the same reaction that I had when reporters kept saying to me, do you think that either of them will be able to govern after this? Do you think that the American public will have any confidence anymore? I think that kind of a question is a failure to recognize the resilience of the American public. I'm not trying to make a patriotic speech here, but what I was telling reporters, I said, look, I think the Monday after this is over everybody's going to go back to work secure in the belief that we have a system that works fine. That is exactly how this country works, and that is exactly what happened. That's one of the great strengths of this country. I think people believe that our fundamental institutions are sound, and the Supreme Court is the Supreme Court.

I think the most important thing that came out of this, I'm not the only one who says this. People said, well, this was embarrassing. I don't think it was embarrassing at all. I said that elections are a messy business; democracy is a messy business. This is an extraordinary illustration of how a complex society, multifaceted society, can resolve its most fundamental disputes without anybody ever considering disregarding the system. I mean, every court accepted the decision of every higher court. Every lawyer accepted the decision of the next level of court. Every politician accepted the decision. And when you hear people talking about a constitutional crisis, there was never a constitutional crisis, because at every stage of the game there was a mechanism to resolve an impasse. It really was an awesome thing to watch work.

P:  Were you treated fairly by the media?

R:  Yes. You know it was interesting, people being interviewed look smarter when you're getting smart questions. First of all, we had the cream of the crop up here. The questions they asked were very well thought-out questions, and they were very courteous. During working hours, if I walked out of this office, walked to the courthouse, walked to the capital, I was surrounded by, what I refer to as, the swarm, which was that 60, 70 reporters, blue mikes, you know, people walking backwards. When I left the courthouse in the evening, I could walk by a hundred reporters and nobody bothered me. And nobody ever called me at home without making prior arrangements. They were very courteous, very professional all the time, and I thought their reporting was very fair.

P:  Speaking of professional, Chief Justice Rehnquist, after the case ended, addressed the legal community. He thanked the lawyers for exemplary briefings under very trying circumstances. Several other people, judges and opposition attorneys, said that they were really impressed with the quality of the lawyers and the courtesy of the lawyers all the way through at every level. Would you agree with that?

R:  Yes. I don't think people even understand the extent of it, because we waived all of the rules with each other. We were handing each other briefs and memoranda in the courtroom as we're about to argue. Everybody was cooperating.

I think it's a combination of things. First of all, I think that we're dealing with a very high caliber of lawyer. People were saying to me, do you think the lawyers were acting this way because they realized the importance of it? My response is, that's the way lawyers almost always act in the cases that I am involved in. My cases are complex commercial litigation and constitutional law, and the lawyers who practice in those fields tend to be very professional and highly courteous to each other. I think there's a mutual respect among them. I've known most of those lawyers for years. I think they're very fine lawyers. I enjoy watching a good lawyer work, even when he's on the other side. The first thing [David] Boies said to me when I shook his hand, which was in front of the Sauls courtroom the day after the first argument, . . . was, you made a great argument, I just really enjoyed listening to it. And I felt the same way [about him]. I think everybody [did].

P: The *New York Times*, in a rather exhaustive study, found that some military ballots were not cast until November 17, some arrived on November 21, a few lacked signatures or didn't have a witness. They were obviously not legal votes, but were counted. A military ballot, the same kind of vote, was counted in Escambia County and not in Alachua County. Isn't that a violation of the Fourteenth Amendment?

R: Well, I think it could be. I think that if anybody's vote wasn't counted, it should have been. That's wrong. It was not an issue, it was not made an issue. I don't know anything about the facts of the case.

P: Well, voter error is voter error, whether it's military or African American voters in Duval county.

R: Correct, I agree.

P: I talked to the Democratic lawyers and they thought that the military ballots was an issue they probably should have pursued.

R: If I had been their lawyer, and they'd asked me, I would have told them not even to pursue that one because I don't think they were going to win it, no matter what. There's just no way that a court is going to say that because somebody whose job it was to make sure that these things were properly dated and notarized didn't do it, even though there's no evidence that they don't reflect the voter, I don't think any court, conservative [or] liberal, is going to throw the ballot out. It may be that they should have waged an earlier, more vigorous campaign in Duval County.

P: How did this experience impact your life?

R: Well, it was the most fun I've ever had practicing law. It was, after 30 years of practice, certainly an invigorating experience. It was interesting to be recognized everywhere I went for a period of time. And it had a dramatic impact upon my practice. But it hasn't had a lot of impact on my personal life. I have a wife and four children, including two toddlers, who are the center of my life, and continue to be.

P: Did you ever get any specific letter or telephone call from Jim Baker or George W. Bush thanking you for your performance?

R: Yes. I actually have a framed handwritten note from Bush, thanking me. I don't recall getting a letter from Baker. I got invited to the party that he had in Washington, the Inauguration.

P: You didn't do this pro-bono.

R: I charged my standard hourly rate that we charge. I generally charge a discounted rate for government agencies and for candidates, but the same rate. As a matter of principle, I do that in all races because my firm is about evenly divided between Republicans and Democrats. If we're going to do this, we have to do it on a strictly nonpartisan basis.

# ➤ Acknowledgments ◄

In the completion of a manuscript, there are always many individuals who have contributed to the final product. In this instance, I am particularly grateful to the 43 participants in the recount who agreed to sit for a lengthy interview. Without their insights and recollections this book would not have been possible. Only two people were unwilling to be interviewed. Al Cardenas, Chairman of the Republican Party in 2000, refused outright. Katherine Harris, perhaps the most important player of all, never responded to two letters, contact with her chief of staff and appointments secretary, and overtures to her friends and supporters. Perhaps she thought she had said all she needed to say in her book, *Center of the Storm*. However, as a historian, I wonder why those involved in a highly controversial event would pass up the chance to tell their side of the story rather than leaving interpretations to the media and their opponents.

Dr. David Colburn, Provost of the University of Florida, originally suggested the topic and provided funding for the initial stage. Dr. Neil Sullivan, Dean of the College of Liberal Arts and Sciences, has been steadfast in his support of the Proctor Oral History Program and his assistance has been essential for its functioning. I am grateful to Pam Iorio, the current Mayor of Tampa and former Supervisor of Elections for Hillsborough County, for graciously allowing me to use her interview with Theresa LePore. Professor Elizabeth Dale did a superb job in advising me on the use of legal terms and correct citations for court cases. Jeri Merritt, an old and dear friend, suggested the title. Jack Mueller, a brilliant and innovative poet, made many valuable suggestions. I thank my editor, Brendan O'Malley, for his endorsement of the project, for his continued support, and for his flexibility in organizing the manuscript. Also kudos to Heather Van Dusen, Sonia Wilson, and the rest of the staff at Palgrave Macmillan for their outstanding work.

Within the Proctor Oral History Program at the University of Florida, there were many major contributors. As always, Roberta Peacock, the office manager, provided invaluable help by working on all aspects of the manuscript and keeping the office staff focused on the final product. Ben Houston read the introduction and the court cases, made some insightful suggestions, and caught several errors. Shane Runyon, Craig Dosher, Melissa Mayer, Kelly Crandall, Kristin Dodek, and Holly Fisher helped immeasurably with research, biographical sketches, and editing.

The transcribers, Melissa Roy, Emily Worfarth, Danielle Navarette, Elise Jacobus, and Kristi Shields, did their usual superb work. Matt Flower, an undergraduate volunteer, helped with some key research. Finally, I would be remiss if I did not recognize Dr. Sam Proctor, who founded this oral history program and who has made immeasurable contributions to this university and to the state.

In choosing which interviews to include in the book, I have tried to provide a broad perspective and different viewpoints. I included two members of the Palm Beach County Canvassing Board, since it was at the center of the dispute. I thought it advisable to have some input from the press, so I chose Lucy Morgan, a Pulitzer Prize–winning writer for the *St. Petersburg Times*. Craig Waters, the public information officer at the Florida Supreme Court, offered a unique perspective. Two key players from the political side of the recount, Mac Stipanovich and Tom Feeney, were essential to understanding the activities of the Republican Party. Verdicts by the judiciary, especially the Florida Supreme Court and Justice Major Harding as well as the Circuit Courts, with Judge Nikki Clark and Judge Terry Lewis, were critical in determining the outcome of the recount. The insights of these three jurists enable the reader to understand and appreciate the tough decisions they faced. Finally, the two top Florida lawyers, Dexter Douglass for Gore and Barry Richard for Bush, described the legal strategy on both sides. In selecting these eleven interviews, I had to omit several very significant participants due to space limitations. It was with great reluctance that I did not include interviews with David Cardwell, who knows more about Florida election law than anyone I know; Bob Butterworth, the attorney general; Tom Fiedler of the *Miami Herald*, and Mitch Berger, a close friend and supporter of Al Gore. Many other interviews were excellent in providing little-known facts and in contributing to the general knowledge of the 2000 election, but were also omitted due to space considerations.

In editing these interviews, I chose approximately 30 to 40 percent of the entire transcript, focusing on the most relevant and interesting parts of the document. Ellipses indicate where material was omitted from the original transcript. For space reasons and to avoid an excessive number of ellipses, I have omitted them at the beginning and end of sentences. Occasionally, sentences have been repositioned to make a passage more comprehensible and to make the transition smoother, but I changed nothing in the actual wording. Also, on occasion, I modified the question asked, both for space reasons and to clarify the question for the reader. Factual material supplied by the author was placed in brackets.

# ➤ INDEX ◄

324.973   Pleasants, Julian M.
P
          Hanging chads.

| DATE | | | |
|------|------|------|------|
| | | | |
| | | | |
| | | | |
| | | | |
| | | | |
| | | | |
| | | | |
| | | | |
| | | | |
| | | | |
| | | | |
| | | | |
| | | | |